The Heritage of Augustana

Essays on the Life and Legacy of the Augustana Lutheran Church

Edited by
Hartland H. Gifford
and
Arland J. Hultgren

Kirk House Publishers
Minneapolis, Minnesota

The Heritage of Augustana:
Essays on the Life and Legacy of the Augustana Lutheran Church
Hartland H. Gifford and Arland J. Hultgren, editors

Copyright 2004 Kirk House Publishers. All Rights reserved.

Library of Congress Cataloging-in-Publication data
The heritage of Augustana : essays on the life and legacy of the Augustana Lutheran Church / edited by Harland H. Gifford and Arland J. Hultgren.
     p. cm.
  Includes bibliographic references and index
   ISBN: 1-886513-73-2 (trade paper : alk. paper)
    1. Augustana Evangelical Lutheran Church—History I. Gifford, Hartland. II. Hultgren, Arland J.

BX8049.H47 2004
284.1'333—dc22

2004051595

Kirk House Publishers, PO Box 390759, Minneapolis, MN 55439
Manufactured inthe United States of America

Dedicated to the Memory of

Donald J. Palmquist

(July 14, 1928—May 13, 2004)

With Thanksgiving for His Life

Contents

Preface 7
Foreword by Donovan J. Palmquist 10
In Memoriam 12
Authors and Editors 14

Sweden and America
Norman A. Hjelm, "Augustana and the Church of Sweden" 19
Alf Brorson, "Augustana Roots in the Church of Sweden" 37
Karl-Johan Tyrberg, "The Background of the First Pioneers of the
    Augustana Synod and the Härnösand Diocese Today" 50
Nils Hasselmo, "Swedish America—and America—Forty-five
    Years Later" 59

Illinois
Myron J. Fogde, "Jenny Lind Chapel: An American Story" 67
Myron J. Fogde, "The 'New Church' at Andover: A Swedish Retreat" 77
Myron J. Fogde, "Moline: An Example of an Early
    Swedish-American Urban Parish" 86

Kansas
Thomas N. Holmquist, "The Swedish Immigration into Kansas" 97
Vance L. Eckstrom, "Lutherans in the Smoky Valley: A Rich History" . 110

The Church
Peter T. Beckman, "The Heart of Augustana" 131
Herbert E. Anderson, "Theological Foundations of the Augustana
    Lutheran Church" 143
Robert L. Anderson, "The Awakening Social Consciousness of the
    Augustana Lutheran Church" 153
Mark A. Granquist, "The Augustana Synod and the Evangelical
    Covenant Church" 161

The Seminary
John L. Kindschuh, "Augustana Seminary Remembered" 173
Allan O. Pfnister, "Augustana: A Teaching Church" 177

Harold R. Lohr, "The Liturgical Core: Augustana at Worship" 181
Constant R. Johnson, "The Shepherds" 187
LaVern K. Grosc, "Eric H. Wahlstrom (1892-1980): An Augustana
     Paradigm and G. Everett Arden (1905-1978):
     Passion and Perspective" 189
Marbury E. Anderson, "Three Years for Which I am Thankful" 196

Global Outreach
Vernon G. Swenson, "Augustana's First Ventures into Africa" 201
Allan J. Gottneid, "Augustana's African Presence in a Later Era" 206
Eleanor Danielson Anderson, "The Zamzam Story" 213
Lois Danielson Carlson, "Elmer Danielson: Vision, Joys, and Tears of a
     Missionary Dad" 227

Women of Augustana
Jane Telleen, "The Women's Missionary Society" 241
Alf Brorson, "Two Augustana Women: Wife Anna Olsson, Daughter
     Anna Olsson" 244
Doris L. Spong, "Alma Lind Swensson" 251
Kathleen S. Hurty, "Emmy Carlsson Evald: Passion, Power, and
     Persistence" 254

Two Notable Persons
Gretchen Revay Esping, "Gustav Andreen: Up Close and Personal" 265
Byron Swanson, "Conrad Bergendoff as Ecumenist" 280

Two Sermons
Dennis A. Anderson, "Our Awful God" 289
Reuben A. Swanson, "For Such a Time as This" 293

Preface

This book contains many of the presentations made at the 2000 Augustana Heritage Gathering at Augustana College in Rock Island, Illinois, and the 2002 Gathering at Bethany College in Lindsborg, Kansas. Due to a variety of circumstances, we have not able to compile a complete collection of all the presentations, but the ones contained in this book are a rather good overall representation.

Several problems present themselves in assembling a collection such as this. Some of the materials are much more formal than others. That is due, in part, to the fact that different presenters used different approaches in dealing with their subjects. A presentation made before a group is usually more informal than a printed piece. Speaking provides a different cadence from that of a written manuscript. We have tried to "formalize" the material, but there are points at which it seemed best for readers to "hear" the presentation. This is especially true in cases where we would do a disservice to the presenter if we tried to make his or her material too formal.

Some presentations used graphic and visual aids, which we have not been able to reproduce. The presentations by Myron Fogde were made on a "Tour of Sesquicentennial Congregations." The five presentations concerning Augustana Seminary were made at the outset of a panel discussion led by John Kindschuh, following opening remarks by him. There was a musical play by Ann Boaden and Joan Beaumont entitled "An Evening with Emmy Evald" staged at the Rock Island event. The libretto is not printed in this book, but anyone wishing a copy may obtain it from the Augustana Heritage Archives.

One decision that faced the editorial committee was whether we should section the book off into two parts (Rock Island and Lindsborg) or arrange it by subject matter. We have chosen the latter course. Thus, the book is divided into nine parts made up of presentations from both Gatherings.

We extend our thanks to all those who had a part in both Gatherings and especially to those who made this volume possible by allowing us to publish their presentations. We also thank the Augustana Heritage Association for authorizing, encouraging, and supporting this project.

During the days just prior to the publication of this book, we were informed of the untimely death of the Rev. Dr. Donovan J. Palmquist. The Augustana Heritage Association would never have come into existence, nor would it have been sustained, without the dedication and energy of a small core of committed pwrsons, and none was more committed to the organization or the cause than Donovan. He sought to further the goals of the organization as he led the Association as its ExecutiveDirector from its beginning. His friendship, organizational skills, natural charm, and dedication will be remembered by countless people far and wide. This book was originally to be dedicated to the memory of those whose names are listed in the "In Memorium" section. But now we must add Donovan's name, giving it a special place. Without his encouragement and support, this book might never have been.

The Presentations

Rock Island, June 23-25, 2000

Norman A. Hjelm, "Augustana and the Church of Sweden: Ties of History and Faith"

Karl-Johan Tyrberg, "The Background of the First Pioneers of the Augustana Synod and the Härnösand's Diocese Today"

Myron J. Fogde, "Jenny Lind Chapel: An American Story"

Myron J. Fogde, "The 'New Church' at Andover: A Swedish Retreat"

Myron J. Fogde, "Moline: An Example of an Early Swedish-American Urban Parish"

Peter T. Beckman, "The Heart of Augustana"

Herbert Anderson, "Theological Foundations of the Augustana Lutheran Church"

Robert L. Anderson, "The Awakening Social Consciousness of the Augustana Lutheran Church"

John L. Kindschuh, "Augustana Seminary Remembered"

Allan O. Pfinster, "Augustana: A Teaching Church"

Harold R. Lohr, "The Liturgical Core: Augustana at Worship"

Constant R. Johnson, "The Shepherds"

LaVern K. Grosc, "Eric H. Wahlstrom: An Augustana Paradigm and G. Everett Arden: Passion and Perspective"

Marbury E. Anderson, "Three Years for Which I am Thankful"

Jane Telleen, "The Women's Missionary Society"

Gretchen Revay Esping, "Gustav Andreen – Up Close and Personal"

Byron Swanson, "Conrad Bergendoff as Ecumenist"

Dennis A. Anderson, "Our Awful God"

Lindsborg, June 21-23, 2002

Alf Brorson, "Augustana Roots in the Church of Sweden"

Mark A. Granquist, "The Augustana Synod and the Evangelical Covenant Church"

Nils Hasselmo, "Swedish America—and America—Forty-five Years Later"

Thomas N. Holmquist, "The Swedish Immigration into Kansas"

Vance L. Eckstrom, "Lutherans in the Smoky Valley: A Rich History"

Vernon G. Swenson, "Augustana's First Ventures into Africa"

Allan J. Gottneid, "Augustana's African Presence in a Later Era"

Eleanor Danielson Anderson, "The Zamzam Story"

Lois Danielson Carlson, "Elmer Danielson: Vision, Joys and Tears of a Missionary Dad"

Alf Brorson, "Two Augustana Women: Wife Anna Olsson, Daughter Anna Olsson"

Doris L. Spong, "Alma Lind Swensson"

Kathleen S. Hurty, "Emmy Carlsson Evald: Passion, Power and Persistence"

Reuben T. Swanson, "For Such a Time as This"

Hartland H. Gifford and Arland J. Hultgren

Foreword

**The Heritage of Augustana:
Essays on the Life and Legacy of the
Augustana Lutheran Church**

This is the second volume on the Augustana Lutheran Church to be published by the Augustana Heritage Association. It contains the presentations which were given at the Augustana Heritage Gathering at Augustana College, Rock Island, Illinois, in June 2000, and at Bethany College, Lindsborg, Kansas, in June, 2002. The first volume, *The Augustana Heritage: Recollections, Perspectives and Prospects*, published in 1999, included the presentations given at the Augustana Heritage Sesquicentennial held at Chautauqua Institute, Chautauqua, New York, in September, 1998.

Since 1998 the meaning of "heritage" for the Augustana Heritage Association has evolved. Initially, many thought of "heritage" as the nostalgia which reminds us only of the moments in time which we treasure but which will never return again. As the Augustana Heritage Association has examined its purpose "to define, promote and perpetuate the heritage of the Augustana Evangelical Lutheran Church," however, the word "heritage" has come to mean those things we want to keep that give us a sense of the past and our faith identity, and that we want to protect and pass on to future generations. This does not mean that our "heritage" is all good, nor is it all bad. It does mean that when we reflect on the journey of faith as expressed in and through the Augustana Evangelical Lutheran Church, we discover that our "heritage" has meaning and purpose for the present and the future. That is the focus of this volume of *The Heritage of Augustana: Essays on the Life and Legacy of the Augustana Lutheran Church*.

The opening section of essays marks the link of Augustana, Sweden, and the Church of Sweden as it was and as it is experienced today. This is followed by reference to specific pioneer communities in Illinois and Kansas and how these places still represent the spirit and life of Augustana. These stories speak of the beginnings of the Augustana Lutheran Church in North America which in 1962 had over 1200 congregations. Today over 800 congregations in North America continue to live the heritage given to them from their beginnings in the Augustana Lutheran Church.

The essays in the sections called "The Church" and "The Seminary" reflect the fact that the seminary and the church were inseparable. In worship, in theological study, in social consciousness, and in relationship to other churches with Swedish roots, Augustana had an identity that was clear and focused. Dr. P. O. Bersell, former president of the Augustana Lutheran Church, once said: "As the seminary goes, so goes the church." Augustana Theological Seminary was a place of inquiry, nurture, and the workshop of the Holy Spirit that prepared pastors to preach, teach, lead, and minister in the name of Christ.

The presentations on "Global Outreach" reflect the priority of global missions in the life of Augustana. It is not coincidence that a year after the the Augustana Lutheran Church was organized in 1860, the Church voted to establish a Committee for Foreign Missions because "the extension of the Kingdom of God among the heathens is one of the chief concerns of the Church of Christ." The first report from the committee recommended "that a sermon on foreign missions be an established part of every synodical convention." This concern for global missions was one of the motivating factors in the establishment of the Augustana Heritage Professorship for Global Mission at the Lutheran School of Theology at Chicago in the 1990s.

Two sections of six essays focus on the heritage we revere which comes to us through men and women of faith and vision. The task of defining, promoting, and perpetuating the heritage of Augustana is from generation to generation through people whose lives are models of leadership in the church. Finally, this volume concludes with two sermons—signs and symbols of what was the center of the life of Augustana—the proclamation of the Gospel.

We express our thanks to all those who participated in these presentations at the Gatherings at Rock Island and Lindsborg. These essays are a significant contribution to a sense of the past which we want to protect and pass on to future generations who continue to search for the meaning of faith. We thank Hartland H. Gifford and Arland J. Hultgren who edited this book. We acknowledge with gratitude the gifts given in memory of servants of the Augustana Lutheran Church that have helped make possible the publishing of *The Heritage of Augustana: Essays on the Life and Legacy of the Augustana Lutheran Church*, and which is dedicated to the memory of those persons listed in the section called In Memoriam.

The Augustana Heritage Association's activities are underwritten by membership fees and gifts. Information about the Association and applications for membership can be obtained by contacting the office of the Augustana Heritage Association at 1100 East 55th Street, Chicago, IL 60615 - 5199. (phone: 800/635-1116, ext. 712) or on the web site www.augustanaheritage.org.

Donovan J. Palmquist
Executive Director
Augustana Heritage Association

In Memoriam

(Place and year of ordination in parentheses; years of service noted for presidents.)

In memory of the presidents of the Augustana Lutheran Church and their spouses:

The Rev. Tufve N. and Eva Helena Hasselquist
(Lund, Sweden, 1839), 1860-1870

The Rev. Jonas and Maria Swensson
(Växjö, Sweden, 1851), 1870-1873

The Rev. Erik and Inga Charlotta Norelius
(Dixon, IL, 1856), 1874-1881, 1899-1911

The Rev. Erland and Eva Charlotta Carlsson
(Växjö, Sweden, 1849), 1881-1888

The Rev. Sven P.A. and Hannah Lindahl
(Moline, IL, 1869), 1888-1891

The Rev. Per Johan and Selma Swärd
(Linköping, Sweden, 1869), 1891-1899

The Rev. Lawrence A. and Anna Sophia Johnston
(Lindsborg, KS, 1881), 1911-1918

The Rev. Gustaf A. and Lydia Brandelle
(Andover, IL, 1884), 1918-1935

The Rev. Petrus O. and Emelia Bersell
(Denver, CO, 1906), 1935-1951

The Rev. Oscar A. and Effie Benson
(Minneapolis, MN, 1915), 1951-1959

The Rev. Malvin H. and Lorrain Lundeen
(Omaha, NE, 1927), 1959-1962

In Memory of:

The Rev. S. Kenneth Arntsen (Los Angeles, CA, 1954)
 by Marian Arntsen

The Rev. Carl A. and Esther Bengston (Minneapolis, MN, 1918)
 by C. Luther Bengtson, Paul J.A. and Eileen Bengtson, and Ruth M. and Leland Jackson

The Rev. Austin H. and Helen Brodeen (Des Moines, IA, 1928)
 by Eugene and Elizabeth Brodeen

The Rev. A. Hilding and Mildred Brodeen (Rockford, IL, 1923)
    by Eugene and Elizabeth Brodeen
The Rev. J. S. and Tina Brodeen (St. Peter, MN, 1894)
    by Eugene and Elizabeth Brodeen
The Rev. Robert W. Carlson (St. Paul, MN, 1955)
    by Darlene and Reuben Swanson
The Rev. Elmer R. and Lillian Danielson (Des Moines, IA, 1928)
    by Eleanor and Carl Anderson, Evelyn and Ray Ternstrom, Luella and James Holwerda, Laurence and Jean Danielson, Wilfred and Marilyn Danielson, and David and Lois Carlson
The Rev. Arthur A. and Irene Christenson (Chicago, IL, 1921)
    by Helen and James Hanson
Wilbert and Carmen Forse
    by Barbara and Dennis Anderson and Carol and Terry Hudson
The Rev. Clarence P. and Mildred Hall (Omaha, NE, 1927)
    by Delores and John L. Kindschuh
The Rev. Leonard I. and Ethel Johnson (Des Moines, IA, 1928)
    by Dorothy and Donovan Palmquist
The Rev. Howard W. and Frances Lindstrom (Omaha, NE, 1937)
    by Carol and Luther Luedtke
The Rev. Edwin C. and Hannah Munson (Omaha, NE, 1927)
    by Elizabeth and Eugene Brodeen
The Rev. Carl W. Segerhammar (Fargo, ND, 1932)
    by Ruth Segerhammar, Kathleen and David Hurty, Kathryn and Byron Swanson, Karen Parker, and Kempton and Christine Segerhammar
The Rev. A. Leonard and Pearl Smith (Rockford, IL, 1929)
    by Carlyle and Sharon Smith and Leonard and Sharon Smith
The Rev. Bernard Spong (Lindsborg, KS, 1939)
    by Doris L Spong, David and Gloria Spong, and Louise and Ed Doucette
The Rev. William C. Stanton (Detroit, MI, 1962)
    by Enid Stanton
The Rev. C. A. and Edith Strandberg (Jamestown, NY, 1920)
    by Doris and Vernon Swenson
The Rev. Clarence W. and Julia A Thorwald (Jamestown, NY, 1931)
    by Clarice and Vance Eckstrom
The Rev. Walter A. and Bertha Tillberg (Galesburg, IL, 1916)
    by Nils Hassselmo
The Rev. Eric H. and Ruth V. Wahlstrom (De Kalb, IL, 1924)
    by former students: Arvid Anderson, Peter Beckman, Harold Bolm, Charles Bomgren, and Virgil Juliot

Authors and Editors

Dennis A. Anderson, Omaha, Nebraska, served as Bishop of the Nebraska Synod, Lutheran Church in America, Bishop of the Nebraska Synod, Evangelical Lutheran Church in America, and as President of Trinity Lutheran Seminary, Columbus, Ohio.

Eleanor Danielson Anderson, Rock Island, Illinois, daughter of Tanzania missionaries Elmer and Lillian Danielson, was on the ill-fated *ZamZam* in 1941 and has written about that experience in *Miracle at Sea* (Bolivar, Missouri: Quiet Waters Publications, 2001).

Herbert E. Anderson, Seattle, Washington, served as a parish pastor in California and New Jersey, and on the faculties of Princeton Theological Seminary, Princeton, New Jersey, and Wartburg Theological Seminary, Dubuque, Iowa.

Marbury E. Anderson, St. Paul, Minnesota, Visitation Pastor at Gustavus Adolphus Lutheran Church, St. Paul, Minnesota, served previously as a parish pastor in Wyoming, Texas, Minnesota, and Colorado.

Robert L. Anderson, Moline, Illinois, served as a parish pastor in Illinois, taught at Augustana College, and served in the Lutheran Office of Governmental Affairs, Washington, D.C.

Peter T. Beckman, Tucson, Arizona, was a parish pastor in Massachusetts and Montana and Professor of Religion at Augustana College.

Alf Brorson, Torsby, Sweden, teaches at the Stjerneskolan, a secondary school in Värmland. He is the author of several works about Lindsborg and its pioneer leaders and has interests in Swedish-American ties. He is on the editorial staff of *Bryggan/The Bridge* and on the Board of the Society for the Promotion of Emigration Research in Karlstad, Värmland, Sweden.

Lois Danielson Carlson, Russellville, Missouri, is the daughter of the late Tanzania missionaries Elmer and Lillian Danielson. She returned to Tanzania to serve two terms as a social worker in Dar es Salaam.

Vance L. Eckstrom, Lindsborg, Kansas, is Professor Emeritus of Religion at Bethany College, Lindsborg, Kansas, where he taught from 1982 to 1996 and served as Academic Dean from 1992 to 1996. With Arland J. Hultgren, he is co-editor of *The Augustana Heritage: Recollections, Perspectives, and Prospects* (Chicago: Augustana Heritage Association, 1999).

Gretchen Revay Esping, Manhattan, Kansas, is a doctoral student in educational administration and leadership at Kansas State University, Manhattan, Kansas, and a teaching assistant there at the Center for the Advancement of Teaching and Learning.

Myron J. Fogde, Moline, Illinois, is Professor Emeritus of Religion at Augustana College.

Hartland H. Gifford, Co-editor, Schnecksville, Pennsylvania, served as a parish pastor in Pennsylvania, Massachusetts, and Connecticut and then in editorial and field support positions with the Division for Parish Services, Lutheran Church in America, from 1973 to 1987.

Allan J. Gottneid, Lindsborg, Kansas, served as an education missionary to Tanzania from 1954 to 1984 and is editor of *Church and Education in Tanzania* (Nairobi: East African Publication House, 1976), an ecumenical study sponsored by the World Council of Churches and the Holy See.

Mark A. Granquist, Northfield, Minnesota, teaches American religious history in the Department of Religion, Gustavus Adolphus College, St. Peter, Minnesota.

LaVern K. Grosc, Lincoln, Nebraska, was a pastor in Iowa, Minnesota, and Pennsylvania, and served on the staff of the Lutheran World Federation, Geneva, Switzerland.

Nils Hasselmo, Washington, D. C., is President of the Association of American Universities, Washington, D. C. A native of Sweden, he came to Augustana College in 1956 on the Mauritzon Scholarship, taught at Augustana, the University of Wisconsin, and the University of Minnesota, where he also served as President.

Norman Hjelm, Wynnewood, Pennsylvania, was Director and Senior Editor of Fortress Press, Philadelphia, Pennsylvania, from 1973 to 1978 and 1980 to 1985; Director of Communication, Lutheran World Federation from 1985 to 1991; and Director of Faith and Order, National Council of the Churches of Christ in the USA from 1992 to 1996.

Thomas N. Holmquist, Smolan, Kansas, teaches history and music at Marquette Middle School, Marquette, Kansas. He is the author of two books and is a specialist on Swedish immigration into Kansas.

Arland J. Hultgren, Co-editor, St. Paul, Minnesota, is the Asher O. and Carrie Nasby Professor of New Testament at Luther Seminary, St. Paul, Minnesota, where he has taught since 1977. With Vance L. Eckstrom, he is co-editor of *The Augustana Heritage: Recollections, Perspectives, and Prospects* (Chicago: Augustana Heritage Association, 1999).

Kathleen Segerhammar Hurty, Oakland, California, is involved in research, writing, and fund development. A graduate of Bethany College, her work has included teaching, school principalship, and ecumenical administration. Her doctoral dissertation at the University of California, Berkeley, focused on leadership and power from the perspective of women.

Constant R. Johnson, Galesburg, Illinois, served as a parish pastor in California and Illinois and as a leader in social ministry organizations, including memberships on the Boards of the Knox County Housing Authority and Bethphage Mission, Axtell, Nebraska.

John L. Kindschuh, Rock Island, Illinois, served as a mission developer and campus pastor in Arizona, 1952-1956, a parish pastor in Iowa, 1956-1963; and thereafter in college administration, including Vice President for Administration at Augustana College, 1968-2001.

Harold R. Lohr, Berlin, Massachusetts, served as a parish pastor in Illinois, as an executive in various positions with the Lutheran Church in America, New York and Philadelphia, and as Bishop of the Red River Valley Synod, Lutheran Church in America, and Bishop of the Northwestern Minnesota Synod, Evangelical Lutheran Church in America.

Donovan J. Palmquist, Phelps, Wisconsin, and Sun City West, Arizona, was until his death in May of 2004, Executive Director of the Augustana Heritage Association. He was Vice President for Development at the Lutheran School of Theology at Chicago and President of the LSTC Foundation from 1979 to 1995.

Allan O. Pfnister, Denver, Colorado, a graduate of Augustana College and Augustana Theological Seminary, has been a professor and administrator at Wittenberg University, Springfield, Ohio, and the University of Denver.

Doris Hedeen Spong, Minneapolis, Minnesota, was President of the Women's Missionary Society and Augustana Lutheran Church Women, from 1956 to 1962 and Vice President and President of the Lutheran Church Women, Lutheran Church in America, from 1962 to 1971.

Byron Swanson, Fort Collins, Colorado, served as a parish pastor in Gladstone, Missouri, and in campus ministry at Arizona State University, Tempe, and he was Professor of Religion at Midland Lutheran College, Fremont, Nebraska from 1968 to 1979, and at California Lutheran University, Thousand Oaks, California, from 1979 to 2001.

Reuben T. Swanson, Omaha, Nebraska, served as a parish pastor in New York and Nebraska, President of the Nebraska Synod, Lutheran Church in America, and Secretary of the Lutheran Church in America.

Vernon G. Swenson, Lindsborg, Kansas, served as a missionary to Tanzania from 1954 to 1971 and to Liberia from 1973 to 1976.

Jane Telleen, Minnetonka, Minnesota, is Assistant Vice President of University Relations, Hamline University, St. Paul, Minnesota, and the descendent of pioneer pastors in the Augustana Lutheran Church.

Karl-Johan Tyrberg, Härnösand, Sweden, is Bishop of the Härnösand Diocese, Church of Sweden.

PART ONE

Sweden and America

Augustana and the Church of Sweden: Ties of History and Faith

Norman A. Hjelm

In 1965 the sixth revised edition of Gustaf Aulén's well-known dogmatics *Den allmänneliga kristna tron* was published in Sweden. I was then an editor at Fortress Press in Philadelphia and we had asked Eric Wahlstrom to prepare a translation of this new edition, an assignment that he completed in near record time. In 1948, a translation of the fourth edition of this work, which appeared in Swedish in 1943, had been published under the title, *The Faith of the Christian Church*,[1] a translation done jointly by Eric Wahlstrom and G. Everett Arden. And in 1960 a translation of the fifth edition of Aulén's book had been published under the same title, a translation done by Professor Wahlstrom alone. Since the sixth edition of 1965 was by Aulén's own testimony the most thorough revision since the book first appeared in 1923, it seemed appropriate to have a new translation for English language users. After all, *The Faith of the Christian Church* was then perhaps the most widely used one-volume dogmatics in the English language. The assignment to prepare Wahlstrom's new translation for publication was given to me.

In the course of my work I raised some editorial questions with Bishop Aulén himself. To my considerable surprise I learned from Aulén—whom I knew well personally—that he had never been informed of the intention of Fortress Press to have this sixth edition translated and published in English. Moreover, he made a strong personal appeal that we stop the project. This old man, who was then nearly ninety and still writing books, said that if he

---

[1] Gustaf Aulén, *The Faith of the Christian Church*, trans. from the fourth Swedish edition by Eric H. Wahlstrom and G. Everett Arden (Philadelphia: Muhlenberg Press, 1948). The fifth Swedish edition, translated by Eric H. Wahlstrom, was published by Fortress Press, formerly Muhlenberg Press, in 1960.

were then to write a dogmatics, he would have to write an entirely different book. "Times have changed," he wrote me, "and I now regard *Den allmänneliga kristna tron* as at most only an element in the history of Christian thought." I urged my superiors at Fortress Press to honor Aulén's request, and even though they were horrified at the potential loss of sales, they followed my lead. And Professor Wahlstrom did too; his English translation of the sixth edition never appeared.

I tell this story not as a commentary on either Bishop Aulén or Professor Wahlstrom, although it says a great deal about each of these fine persons. Rather, I recount it because for me it typifies the dynamic character of church history. To get stuck in the past—even with the sixth edition—is a misuse of our history. And to ossify that past in order to score current points is equally a misuse of our history. This has something to do with the well-known aphorism of Jaroslav Pelikan, "Tradition is the living faith of the dead, traditionalism is the dead faith of the living."[2] As children of Augustana, it is important that we ask ourselves about the *use* we make of our past, the use we make of our tradition. This is an extremely important point in the present life of the ELCA when the history of the Augustana Church in respect to the "historic episcopate" is being badly used, chiefly by those opposed to our church's entry into full communion with the Episcopal Church. But perhaps we will speak more about that later.

Now I regard myself as an extremely unlikely person to reflect on the history of the relationship between the Augustana Lutheran Church in North America and the Church of Sweden. I am surely not a professional historian and my use of important sources for our topic is virtually non-existent. (Those sources are best found, say, in Rock Island or Chicago rather than in Philadelphia, and yesterday I must admit was my first day in Rock Island since June 12, 1960, the day I was ordained at Rock Island High School.) I did, to be sure, live and study for a while in Sweden, and I even married a member of the Church of Sweden—but in this country she communes in an Episcopal parish. Personally, I have often been confused about, and not particularly interested in, our forbears in Augustana—Esbjörn, Hasselquist, and Norelius are not clearly profiled in my mind. I have never been mightily moved by what happened at Bishop's Hill or, for that matter, at Illinois State University or even Augustana College. Yet the story is important, I think, and worth commenting on. But it is worthy of far more careful research than I have been able to give to it. What you will now hear are basically impressions, even vignettes, rather than the result of comprehensive research. Bear with me.

For the structure of my presentation, I find myself again inspired by Gustaf Aulén. One of his many books covers roughly the same historical period as the life of the Augustana Church: *Hundra Års Svensk Kyrko Debatt* (*A Hundred Years' Swedish Church Debate*). Published in 1953, this book surveys both theological and political debates concerning the Swedish under-

---
[2] Jaroslav Pelikan, *The Vindication of Tradition* (New Haven: Yale University Press, 1984) 65.

standing of the church, ecclesiology, as they were carried on from the middle of the nineteenth to the middle of the twentieth century. We would do well to pay serious attention to Aulén's presentation since it illumines what was going on within the Church of Sweden during virtually the entire history of Augustana.[3] But my present use of this book is structural. It is subtitled, "Drama in Three Acts." Aulén surveys the century in three sets of movements: from the high ecclesiology of Lund in the mid-nineteenth century, which was in conflict with a low church movement at Uppsala, through the young church movement led by Einar Billing and the ecumenical orientation of Nathan Söderblom, to the liturgical revival associated largely with Gunnar Rosendahl and the biblical view of the church found in the volume partially translated into English as *This Is the Church*.[4] This structure has led me to view the ties between Augustana and the Church of Sweden also as "a drama in three acts." My suggestion is that up to about 1891 we have an act which I call "Uncertain Ties"; a second act which I call simply "Encounter" that lasted through World War II; and a third act which I call "Communion" that lasted to the end of Augustana's life; indeed it is an act which continues even today.

UNCERTAIN TIES

I had initially thought that at the beginning Augustana's relation to the Church of Sweden could be described in a very different way: my title for this first act was going to be either "Hostility" or "Abandonment." I had been taught that my grandparents and their predecessor immigrants came to the United States at least partially in order to escape the heavy hands of the Swedish state church. And what is more, I had been taught that the Church of Sweden had pretty much allowed those who migrated to North America to fend for themselves. And there is, of course, some truth to both of these views. After all, Professor Arden in his *Augustana Heritage* described the response in 1849 of leaders within the Church of Sweden to the decision of Lars Esbjörn to leave his pastorate in order to accompany some one hundred sixty immigrants to America like this:

> Though Esbjörn may have been something of a hero in the eyes of those who yearned for a broader freedom and more secure future, in the estimation of the ecclesiastical officials in particular he was more like an irresponsible fanatic. When he applied for a leave of absence from his Swedish charge, Archbishop Henrik Reuterdahl took occasion to administer a rebuke by warning him about "restless minds" which do not thrive within the church, and of "ambitions to power which subdue the consciences and wills of other people." Even some of Esbjörn's friends among the

---

[3] Gustaf Aulén, *Hundra års svensk kyrko debatt* (Stockholm: Svenska Kyrkans Diakonistyrelses Bokförlag, 1953).

[4] Anders Nygren, ed., *This Is the Church*, trans. Carl C. Rasmussen (Philadelphia: Muhlenberg Press, 1952).

clergy tried to dissuade him, as evidenced in a letter dated at Strömsbro, February 5, 1849, in which the writer concludes that "(1) Your journey is not of God; (2) your motives in going to America are not entirely pure, and that which is pure is not sufficiently valid and powerful for such an undertaking; (3) the journey, on the whole, will be unsuccessful."[5]

But really, the story is more complicated. Even a person so consistently critical of the Swedish Church as Erik Norelius could write in the first of his two volume work, *De Svenska Lutherska Församlingarnas och Svenskarnas Historia i Amerika* (1890, 1914; *The Swedish Lutheran Congregations and the History of the Swedes in America*), "With the exception of the Erik Janssonists, there were certainly very few who left their homeland to find more religious and political freedom." And the Swedish scholar of emigration, Sten Carlsson, could write:

> Whether religious motivations except in extreme cases, have been decisive for the great emigration during the 1860s is very questionable. As far as the research in this field has come, the onus of demonstration rests with those who contend that dissatisfaction with the religious situation played a noteworthy role in comparison with the poverty which was caused by several poor crops.[6]

Officially, of course, the Church of Sweden did not accompany its children to the new world. The situation with the nineteenth century immigrants was different from that of the immigrants to "New Sweden"—Pennsylvania, Delaware, and New Jersey—in the seventeenth century. Those parishes, which we now call "Old Swedes' churches," were officially sponsored and supported by the Swedish Church.

No, the Church of Sweden did not officially go with its children in the nineteenth century. But significantly, others did. A case can be made, for example, that while Augustana was not straightforwardly a daughter of the Church of Sweden it might well be described as a daughter of the Evangeliska Fosterlands-Stiftelsen, the EFS. This, of course, was the movement of C. O. Rosenius, and while its origins were associated with the work of George Scott, the British Methodist evangelist, it remains to this day a movement firmly *within* the Church of Sweden. Hugo Söderström has characterized the EFS like this:

> EFS was a branch of the great revival in Sweden and held firmly to the Lutheran Confession. Its members used to gather for their own services. They supported their own preachers, had a school for preacher-training, often built their prayer-houses and carried out their own mission work. But their children were baptized and confirmed in the Swedish Church, they attended the morn-

---

[5] G. Everett Arden, *Augustana Heritage: A History of the Augustana Lutheran Church* (Rock Island: Augustana Book Concern, 1963) 29.

[6] Both Norelius and Carlsson are quoted in Hugo Söderström, *Confession and Cooperation: The Policy of the Augustana Synod in Confessional Matters and the Synod's Relations with other Churches up to the Beginning of the Twentieth Century* (Lund: C.W.K. Gleerups Bokförlag, 1973) 166.

ing service in the parish church and the evening service in the prayer-house. They were very critical of high-church tendencies but they did not wish to leave the Church. The leaders of the Augustana Synod were products of [this] religious revival in Sweden.[7]

Now this is extremely important—that the primary revival movement from which Augustana was hewn has always remained within the Lutheran confession, the Church of Sweden. The founders of the Augustana Synod were under the greatest of pressures to give that confession up. The interconfessional Svenska Missionssällskap had given them considerable support, to Esbjörn especially. The Methodist preacher Olof Gustaf Hedström greeted countless immigrants from Sweden at the New York harbor. Magnus Håkanson in New Sweden, Iowa, was heavily influenced by the free Methodist Jonas Hedstrom and for a time even resigned his charge as leader of the New Sweden flock and considered leaving the Lutheran confession. The onslaughts of the Swedish Baptists Gustaf Palmquist and F. O. Nilsson followed to further confuse the New Sweden congregation. And the proselytizing efforts of Gustaf Unonius and his Episcopalian followers during this time are well known; indeed, the initial relations between Augustana and the Episcopal Church continue to provide a major subject for research, perhaps now more than ever as the two church bodies draw closer.

Arden draws the following lesson from the turmoil caused by denominational competition at New Sweden:

> Even Håkanson was momentarily carried away by the zeal of the Baptist missionaries, and is said to have made plans to be rebaptized. But through the help and encouragement of faithful friends and brethren, he recovered his equanimity, and was once more stabilized in the Lutheran faith.
>
> Neither Håkanson nor his congregations ever forgot the lessons they learned through these painful experiences. The American frontier with its free, pluralistic and competitive religious situation was no friendly place for theological obscurantism. Congregational survival depended upon confessional integrity, and such integrity necessitated *differentiation* at exactly those points which distinguished one denomination from another. The alternative was confusion, chaos, and eventual dissolution. This lesson was becoming clear not only to Håkanson and the New Sweden community, but also to all those who were endeavoring to establish a Swedish *Lutheran* church on the broad prairies of the Middle West a hundred years ago.[8]

About being a Lutheran body, the nineteenth century Swedish immigrants reached greater and greater certainty; soon there was absolutely no doubt. America required it. According to Hugo Söderström, the fathers of the Augustana Synod:

---

[7] Ibid, 170.
[8] G. E. Arden, *Augustana Heritage*, 26.

did not have any clear opinion about the particular doctrines of Lutheranism when they left Sweden. They were revivalists. They more or less opposed the conventional religious customs and the lack of personal involvement of the members of the Church of Sweden. They longed for a renewed Church. However, while they were working in the New World with its many churches, they were forced to study the Lutheran doctrines more closely. Having earlier stressed Christian life, they began to emphasize Christian doctrines. Pure Christian doctrines became more important than a true Christian life. From having been willing to cooperate with all Christians who *sincerely* believed in Christ, they wanted only to cooperate with those who *correctly* believed in Christ. And they were firmly convinced that the *Book of Concord* gave the correct interpretation of *the Holy Scriptures*.[9]

This growth towards a Lutheran confessional self-understanding within Augustana increasingly commended the body to the Church of Sweden. At the beginning, however, Augustana's friends in Sweden were almost exclusively within the revival movement: Peter Fjellstedt and Peter Wieselgren especially. These men took it upon themselves to look for pastors suited to travel to America to care for the immigrants, but their efforts were not outstanding. Only seven pastors, by one reckoning which has been challenged, who were ordained in Sweden, became ministers in the Augustana Synod during its first half-century. And of these seven, three—O. C. T. Andrén, Lars Esbjörn, and J. P. Swärd—returned to Sweden and finished their ministries there.[10]

Contacts between Augustana and the Church of Sweden continued to grow. At the turn of the year, 1860-61, T. N. Hasselquist, Erland Carlsson, and O. J. Hatlestad sent an appeal to Sweden: "From the Swedish Evangelical Lutheran congregations in North America to the mother Church in the old homeland." The appeal was for support of the new American body:

1. The immigrant Church expected help from those to whom it could say: "We are bone of your bones and flesh of your flesh."

2. Money had been given to the Gustaf Adolf Foundation to be used abroad. Money should also be given to the Swedish-American Church. Without the Augustana Synod many immigrants would join other denominations and some of those Swedes would be sent as missionaries to Sweden in order "to propogate alien confessions."

---

[9] H. Söderström, *Confession and Cooperation*, 20-21.

[10] Ibid., 174. Bernhard Erling, citing Conrad Bergendoff, *The Augustana Ministerium* (Rock Island: Augustana Historical Society, 1980) 14-34, has stated: "From 1849 to 1884 only ten pastors who had been educated and ordained in Sweden entered the Augustana Ministerium." Cf. his essay, "Augustana, Bishops, and the Church of Sweden, Part One," *Lutheran Forum* 26/1 (February 1992) 35. In a 1996 paper Erling uses yet a different figure: "From 1849 to 1896 a total of fifteen [pastors trained and ordained in Sweden] came, four of whom later returned to Sweden," "The Augustana Synod and the Church of Sweden: Changes and Influences," *American Religious Influences in Sweden*, ed. Scott E. Erickson (Tro och Tanke 1996:5; Uppsala: Svenska kyrkans forskningsråd, 1997) 52 with documentation.

3. Most immigrants never became familiar with the English language, but their children would speak English better than Swedish. A college, Augustana, of high standards was needed for coming generations.[11]

This appeal was not at all successful, and Augustana was disappointed that its "mother church" was seemingly so indifferent to the needs of the immigrants. But our fathers continued their appeals.

O. C. T. Andrén had traveled to Sweden, before his final return, in 1860 in an effort to raise money and secure books for the new Augustana College. He was successful: around 4,000 books were donated to the college from King Charles XV's library, and he collected $10,846 for the institution. In 1862, also before his final return, Lars Esbjörn made a similar journey to Sweden in the course of which he delivered a lecture at the annual convention of the Evangeliska Fosterlands-Stiftelsen in the course of which he described the situation and needs of the immigrants. And in 1870 Tufve Nilsson Hasselquist, the Augustana Synod's first president and the first pastor of the Church of Sweden who had come to the new world in support of the pioneering work of Lars Esbjörn, himself went to Sweden. Hugo Söderström has pointed out that this journey had a double effect: it made the Synod known in wider circles and it also made Hasselquist more aware than ever of the problems of the Church of Sweden, creating for him a more sympathetic attitude towards his former church. Even if Hasselquist was vigorously opposed to the state church system, "he considered the Church of Sweden as 'the most honorable and best governed State Church of all.' He went so far as to say that he would maintain that religious persecutions in America were worse than in Sweden."[12] And most of the Augustana leaders followed Hasselquist in developing a new and more positive view of the Church in Sweden. The ties were still uncertain, but they were becoming stronger.

Now at this point, let me simply score a point on behalf of the Church of Sweden. We are inclined to look at the whole relationship only through the eyes of our fathers and mothers in Augustana—an initial hostility and sense of abandonment moving with unsteady steps towards a relation of communion. It is important, though, to recall—and that is all we can do in this presentation—something of the actual situation in Sweden, a situation in which it was perhaps not so easy to give support to those who had emigrated to the United States. There were inner-church debates concerning the very nature of the church itself, including its relation to the state, and those debates had enormous political consequences throughout the country. Revival movements within the Church at times appeared out of control, and the movement towards "free churches" reached its apex with the establishment of the Mission Covenant Church in the late years of the century. In

---

[11] H. Söderström, *Confession and Cooperation*, 174.
[12] Ibid., 176.

society, currents which would result in the social democratic movement were already in full stream. What we would now call "secularism" was rife. It is worth remembering that although the Augustana Synod was by far the largest association of any kind of immigrant Swedes, it never claimed for the Lutheran church more than 20% of all Swedish immigrants to the United States. Of this period in the history of the Church of Sweden, Gustaf Aulén has written:

> As the 19th century came to a close, the Church of Sweden found itself in the midst of a critical crossfire the likes of which it had never before experienced. The critique had actually gone on since the 1850s when separatistic streams and religious liberalism dueled with each other to bombard the "state church." Sharpness and acrimony increased as forces radically opposed on materialistic grounds to Christianity gained strength during the century's final decades. No one can assert that the position of the Church of Sweden was strong at the end of the century.[13]

In such a beleaguered situation, it is perhaps no wonder that the Church of Sweden was uncertain in its ties to Augustana. There were other matters that occupied its attention.

Let this rapid and superficial description of what were initially these "uncertain ties" between Augustana and the Church of Sweden come to a close with an ambiguity, a description of ambivalent ties.

In 1909 Erik Norelius, then president of the Synod, submitted to the journal *Augustana*, a letter concerning the Church of Sweden, which the editor, L. G. Abrahamson, refused to publish. L. A. Johnston, who in 1911 was to succeed Norelius as president, wrote to Norelius like this: "I have consulted Dr. Abrahamson, Dr. Andreen and the Theological Faculty and found that all have the opinion that Uncle's (*Farbror*) letter about the Swedish state church should not be published in *Augustana*." In that letter, President Norelius had written: "We have many dear Christian brethren in Sweden of the sound Lutheran confession. We shall always welcome them as guests to our meetings but with the State Church as such, we cannot have any relations."[14] Strong words.

Yet in 1910 the Archbishop of Uppsala and the Primate of Sweden, J. A. Ekman, in discussions with Anglicans—two English bishops, an American bishop and two canons—when asked about the Church of Sweden and the Augustana Synod answered like this: "It [is] a self-evident and commonly recognized fact within the Church of Sweden that the Church in America, which [has] its confession in full conformity with the Church of Sweden and which [is] its daughter, is the Augustana Synod."[15]

An ambiguity. Uncertain ties. The first act comes to a close.

---

[13] G. Aulén, *Hundra års svensk kyrko debatt*, 75-76.
[14] H. Söderström, *Confession and Cooperation*, 177-78.
[15] Ibid., 177.

ENCOUNTER

The process by which Augustana first became a Swedish-American church and then an American church was played out over the course of a long time. Perhaps the best study of this process, both theoretical and historical, is the 1997 Uppsala dissertation of Dag Blanck, *Becoming Swedish-American: The Construction of an Ethnic Identity in the Augustana Synod, 1860-1917*.[16] For our purposes, the principle point is that as Augustana became "Swedish-American" and was no longer simply "Swedish," it became more and more possible to construct a healthy relationship with the Church of Sweden. This has to do with identity, self-awareness, and confidence. As Augustana became less preoccupied with proving that it was an American church body, it became more and more natural to look home, to the Church of Sweden. The well-known axiom about all immigrants—"What the first generation wants to forget, the second generation wants to remember"— an axiom which describes the experience of many of us, can well be applied to corporate bodies as well as to individuals. As the Augustana Church became authentically American, it also became able to remember its roots.

After 1890 there were new possibilities for encounter between the churches. We have already referred to the clear description of the Church of Sweden's relation to Augustana given by Archbishop Ekman to a meeting of Swedish and Anglican Church leaders. Similarly, in the early 1890s the faculty of Augustana Seminary wrote to the bishops of the Church of Sweden to ascertain how they viewed the Synod, and six wrote back saying that they saw the Synod as their "daughter church" in America.[17]

And the visits of Knut Henning Gezelius von Schéele, Bishop of Visby (Gotland), to America and the Augustana Synod in 1893, 1901, and 1910 were of signal importance. 1893 was the three hundredth anniversary of the "Uppsala Möte" when the Swedish Church officially adopted the Augsburg Confession as its own and this anniversary was marked by a major celebration in Rock Island. Erik Norelius and P. J. Swärd welcomed von Schéele as the official representative of the Church of Sweden and noted with great pleasure that his visit marked the first official recognition from the Church of Sweden that the Augustana Synod had received since its beginning in 1860. Norelius publicly noted, in welcoming von Schéele, that the Synod thought "it took very long" before "the mother church turned her eyes upon the daughter church."[18]

Interestingly, Bengt Sundkler reports that Bishop von Schéele's impression on the Augustana Synod was so deep that he was approached about a permanent episcopal position in the Synod:

---

[16] Dag Blanck, *Becoming Swedish-American: The Construction of an Ethnic Identity in the Augustana Synod, 1860-1917* (Uppsala: Acta Universitatis Upsaliensis, *Studia Historica Upsaliensia* 182, 1997).

[17] Cf. Maria Erling, "Hospitality and Influence: Encounters between Augustana and the Church of Sweden, 1893-1925," *American Religious Influences in Sweden*, ed. S. Erickson, 82.

[18] D. Blanck, *Becoming Swedish-American*, 52-53.

Episcopacy was a live if controversial issue in the Synod at that time, and had been for more than two decades. Bishop von Schéele of Visby had visited Augustana on three occasions… and the matter was raised then, in fact, the Bishop himself was approached in 1907 with a view to his exchanging Visby for Rock Island. He declined, and in terms which showed that it was probably a good thing that he did so: "I have always rejected any suggestion of this kind. I strive to give unto my life as uniform a character as possible, and I could not at [the age of] 63 accept this proposal."[19]

It is, of course, tempting now to ask, "What if…?" But it was in 1914, in my judgment, that a new chapter in Augustana's relations with the Church of Sweden began. This chapter—the second act of our story—centers largely around one figure, the theologian and ecumenical pioneer, Archbishop Nathan Söderblom. His role, controversial in many respects—as theologian, representative of the historic episcopacy, advocate of what was then a new kind of church unity, and as the provider of Swedish hospitality to its sons and daughters in North America—became pivotal for many aspects of Augustana's life. Jaroslav Pelikan has written of this man:

> It was said of Nathan Söderblom that he could be "a Catholic at the altar, an Evangelical in the pulpit, and a Modernist in the study"—and all of these with a sense of complementarity rather than of contradiction. For a historical-theological scholar who has preferred a method of both/and to one of either/or, this complementarity (which Söderblom termed "Evangelical Catholicity") has demonstrated that it is not necessary to choose between particularity and universality, nor in the name of the Cross as the once-and-for-all gift of God to humanity to say no to the reality of divine truth wherever it has appeared within the history of that humanity. Those qualities made themselves evident in each of the several vocations of Söderblom's lifework….Those who knew Nathan Söderblom personally have unanimously invoked words like "magical" and "unforgettable" to describe the effect that even one hour with him could have on an entire lifetime.[20]

While much has been written about each of Söderblom's "vocations," there remains a great deal of research to be done concerning this remarkable figure. Of particular importance in our present Lutheran ecclesial and ecumenical situation is his advocacy of "Evangelical Catholicity" which should be explored and, in my judgment, appropriated. (In this connection, the seminal work of Professor Sven-Erik Brodd clearly needs to be brought into the American discussion.[21])

---

[19] Bengt Sundkler, *Nathan Söderblom: His Life and Work* (Lund: C. W. K. Gleerups, 1968) 305.

[20] Jaroslav Pelikan, *The Melody of Theology: A Philosophical Dictionary* (Cambridge: Harvard University Press, 1988) 239, 241. The best available biography of Söderblom is Bengt Sundkler's *Nathan Söderblom: His Life and Work*; cf. also B. Sundkler, *Nathan Söderblom och hans möten* (Stockholm: Gummessons Bokförlag, 1975).

[21] Brodd, Sven-Erik. *Evangelisk Katolicitet: Ett studium av innehåll och funktion under 1800- och 1900-talen* (Lund: C. W. K. Gleerup, 1982).

Augustana's public encounter with Söderblom began in 1914 when he was consecrated Archbishop of Uppsala. L. G. Abrahamson, the editor of *Augustana*, was designated the Synod's official representative to the event. In addition to participating in the actual laying on of hands, the Consecration of the new Archbishop, he was invited by Söderblom to deliver a public address concerning the life and work of the Augustana Synod.

Now it has already been hinted at that there were movements within Augustana favoring the establishment of an episcopacy within the church; we have mentioned this in relation to Bishop von Schéele. And this issue was to mark much of the encounter between the Synod and the new Archbishop of Uppsala. Sundkler has described this in the following way:

> Soon after Söderblom's taking office, he was informed that his Augustana friends were pursuing the episcopacy issue. Dr. Gustav Andreen could tell him that the New England Conference of the Augustana [Synod] had decided to accept episcopacy, on their own if need be, or with the consent of the Synod as a whole. The idea, however, was fatally bound up with "Swedishness." The protagonists of episcopacy thought of it in terms of a uniting link between the "Swedish mother Church" and her "daughter" in America. Plans were sufficiently advanced for this party to hope that the first Bishop could be consecrated in Uppsala Cathedral at the Reformation Jubilee in 1917, and Söderblom was duly informed about these plans, but the enthusiasts found that they could not cajole the tougher brethren of the Mid-West and so the matter was postponed.[22]

We shall return to this matter.

When Nathan Söderblom made his visit to America and the Augustana Synod in 1923, he was fully aware of the controversies that swirled around his head. The year 1923 was itself significant for Augustana, for that was the year when the Minutes of the annual synodical meeting were published for the first time in English. For some, 1923 became the last "Swedish" year in the existence of the church body. Obviously, the Swedish Archbishop had to tread carefully. And he knew that within the Synod, and Lutheranism generally, he was a marked theologian. His work in the history of religion was seen by some as relativistic and syncretistic. Professor Adolf Hult at Augustana Seminary kept a list of notable "heretics" on the blackboard of his classroom, and Söderblom's name was often at the top right alongside that of Adolf von Harnack. In 1914, *The Lutheran*, the magazine of the General Council to which Augustana belonged, laid down a challenge to the Synod on the occasion of the Archbishop's consecration. Citing Professor Hult as its authority, the journal editorialized

> Dr. Söderblom has arrayed himself among the radical liberals in Sweden, already sadly afflicted with a most dangerous rationalism, and cannot be recognized as an advocate of the faith to

---

[22] B. Sundkler, *Nathan Söderblom*, 305.

which he pronounces loyalty ... by any Lutheran synod which means to hold fast to the Confessions. We regard [his invitation to participate in his consecration at Uppsala] as thrusting upon the Augustana Synod its first confessional test.[23]

And during the same year as his visit to the United States (1923), Söderblom had nearly been prevented from making a presentation at the crucially important convention of the Lutheran World Convention held in Eisenach, Germany—again being tainted as a "liberal." It was in part due to the intervention of one of his Augustana friends and supporters, the synodical president G. A. Brandelle, that he was given time on the platform of the world meeting of Lutheran churches.[24]

The visit of Söderblom and his wife, Anna, has taken on great importance in the history of the Augustana Lutheran Church and far more happened than can be recounted here. The Archbishop won many, many friends by his evident evangelical spirituality, his warmth and geniality, his enormous curiosity concerning the life of the Swedish-American community, and by his wholehearted support of Augustana on its journey towards becoming a genuinely American church. Not everyone was converted, to be sure; many of his critics both within and outside Augustana remained unconvinced. But more were won over, and the visit went far to cement relations with the Church of Sweden.

Two final words concerning Nathan Söderblom and his impact on Augustana. First, concerning his strategy in respect to the episcopacy issue. He was clearly known as a protagonist of episcopacy and the historic succession; in Europe he had himself brought that succession to the Lutheran churches in Latvia and Estonia. And he clearly wanted to bring it to Augustana. However, he knew the explosive character of the issue in Augustana, and he avoided pressing it. On occasion he attempted to disarm criticism by a somewhat roundabout interpretation of episcopacy which he hoped appeared reasonable. In his published reflections on his journey "From Uppsala to Rock Island," he wrote this:

> In the house of Lutheranism in America there are many mansions. They are solid, and the walls rise slowly but surely: but the Episcopalians have placed a flag-pole with a flag on their roof. Does it greatly matter if you live in a house with or without a flagpole? Would anybody consider moving on account of that flag? How do I know? But if it were so, that some people prefer to see a flag waving on their roof, it would be bad if because of this, he felt tempted to leave the great building of Lutheranism. If he ascribes unreasonable and almost magical importance to the flag, then the matter cannot be helped. But if it is a question of taste and style, of convenience and tradition, then nobody must accuse

---

[23] *The Lutheran* (July 23, 1914) 698.
[24] B. Sundkler, *Nathan Söderblom*, 294.

Lutheranism of callous stubbornness which abhors to place a flag on the house. Because to the essence of Lutheranism—if the name does not betray—belongs not to be afraid, not to be bound by forms, but to be free. The flag is Episcopacy![25]

As the ELCA moves into full communion with the Episcopal Church, and as vitriolic and misguided criticisms of that development persist, we would do well to turn toward the Church of Sweden for guidance. Yet it must be said that Augustana really did not devote much attention to questions of ecclesial polity since its attention was always directed towards the individual and his or her salvation, and, further, the ecclesial, theological, and ecumenical climate in which we now live is surely qualitatively different from that known by our fathers and mothers. I personally doubt that our history in Augustana—especially such incidents as the often discussed presentation of a gold pectoral cross by the Swedish bishops to the Augustana church in 1930, or even the short-lived dialogue which Augustana had with the Episcopal Church in 1935—I doubt that such incidents give us much guidance in regard to the episcopacy—one way or another. To think that it does is, I am quite convinced, to misuse our history.

And the other concluding word about Augustana's encounter with Nathan Söderblom has to do with his regional and ecumenical strategy for world Lutheranism. In an extremely important essay, "A Swedish Archbishop between American and German Lutheranism,"[26] Sven-Erik Brodd, Professor of Ecclesiology at Uppsala University, has described Söderblom's strategy after World War I as "the tripartition of Lutheranism." The font of Lutheranism was, of course, Germany, and the Nordic churches for long lived under that shadow. Moreover, the American Lutheran churches up to the time of the war (and in some cases beyond) were seen chiefly as extensions of the European churches. But Söderblom's concern, especially after experiencing the dynamism of the American Lutheran churches first hand, was increasingly to see global Lutheranism as made up of three discrete yet united blocks: the German churches, the Nordic churches, and the American churches. This strategy was especially evident in the life of the Lutheran World Convention and the early life of the Lutheran World Federation with, of course, the addition of at least a fourth block of Lutheran churches in the subsequent life of the LWF, the churches of the so-called Third World.[27]

---

[25] Nathan Söderblom, *Från Upsala till Rock Island: En Predikofärd i Nya Världen* (Stockholm: Svenska Kyrkans Diakonistyrelses Bokförlag, 1924) 367-68. (The translation above is by Bengt Sundkler.) The Archbishop's wife also published concerning the journey to the United States: Anna Söderblom, *En Amerikabok* (Stockholm: Svenska Kyrkans Diakonistyrelses Bokförlag, 1925). The Archbishop's book is dedicated "To the Swedish Congregations in the United States"; the book of his wife is dedicated "To Doctor L. G. Abrahamson."

[26] Sven-Erik Brodd, "A Swedish Archbishop between American and German Lutheranism: American Influences on the Ecumenical Strategies of Nathan Söderblom," *American Religious Influences in Sweden*, ed. S. Erickson, 94-108.

[27] This general view of twentieth century Lutheran history and Söderblom's strategies is shared by E. Clifford Nelson, *The Rise of World Lutheranism: An American Perspective* (Philadelphia: Fortress Press, 1982) passim.

Further research, I understand, is being done at Uppsala concerning the turn of the Church of Sweden, and perhaps all of the Nordic churches, away from Germany towards the English-speaking world. It was, after all, in 1922 during the Archbishopric of Nathan Söderblom, that full communion was established between the Church of England and the Church of Sweden. How this relationship subsequently nourished *The Porvoo Common Statement* of 1992, establishing a relationship of full communion between the Nordic Lutheran Churches (with the remarkable exception of the Church of Denmark), the Baltic Lutheran Churches, and the Anglican Churches of the British Isles,[28] is surely an important question. Moreover, the question as to whether the Northern European Lutheran Churches will increasingly, especially in light of the European Union, relate with the churches of the United Kingdom rather than with, say, the Evangelical Lutheran Church in America, is a most important issue for the future. It must candidly be acknowledged that many within the Church of Sweden, an evangelical Lutheran church, increasingly find themselves more at home with the Anglican tradition than with historic Lutheranism. What is the meaning of this? Confessionally? Ecumenically?

But let our second act—*Encounter*—come to a close. The Augustana Church, increasingly at home in America and by the end of its century of life a fully American church body, has been set free for mutual exchange and encounter with its mother church. The uncertain ties have been strengthened.

COMMUNION

In 1990, at its Eighth Assembly, the Lutheran World Federation adopted a new constitution. The first constitution, adopted at the First Assembly, which was held in Lund, Sweden, in 1947, had defined the Federation as "a free association of Lutheran churches," an extremely weak ecclesiological statement. The new constitution of 1990 strengthened this statement: "The Lutheran World Federation is a communion of churches which confess the triune God, agree in the proclamation of the Word of God and are united in pulpit and altar fellowship." *A communion of churches.*

Those familiar with current ecclesial and ecumenical conversations are fully aware that "communion," *communio, koinonia*, has become a key and sometimes controversial notion in the life of churches. (There were those, especially from Luther Seminary in St. Paul, who opposed the adoption of this language by the Lutheran World Federation. And they continue in that opposition in respect to "full communion" between the ELCA and the Episcopal Church. But this is not here our concern.) Our question, as you might expect, has to do with the character and quality of *communio* between the Augustana Church and the Church of Sweden. Let me point briefly to three areas in which *communio* has been a reality between the two bodies.

---

[28] Cf. *Together in Mission and Ministry: The Porvoo Common Statement with Essays on Church and Ministry in Northern Europe* (London: Church House Publishing, 1993).

First, the churches were united in liturgy and worship. The official *Handbok* and *Psalmbok* of the Church of Sweden were used by the Augustana Synod from the beginning. The liturgical order was that of 1811. By today's standards and practices this was really not much of an order. In fact, Gustaf Aulén, in a volume presented to the Augustana Church at its centennial in 1960, described the development of this order in a rather caustic way:

> The Liturgy which appeared in 1693...remained in use until 1811. But this does not necessarily mean that the directions of the Liturgy were conscientiously followed during the eighteenth century. The pietistic movements of the time had little appreciation of the liturgical aspects of the divine service, and the Enlightenment had still less. Actually, a progressive dissolution of the ritual was taking place, accelerating as the views of the Enlightenment gained acceptance. Consequently, a low point was gradually reached and became codified in the Liturgy of 1811.[29]

In 1894 the Church of Sweden published a new liturgical manual and this was adopted in 1895, with certain revisions, by the Augustana Church. The annual convention of Augustana in 1896 requested that an English translation of this manual be prepared, a task completed in 1905. From that year, the Augustana Church had liturgies in both Swedish and English, each following the 1894 rite of the Church of Sweden. How well we were nourished by that Service! It remained our principal order of worship until the publication in 1958 of the inter-Lutheran *Service Book and Hymnal*, in which the Second Setting of the Service was made notable by the music, largely based on melodies from the Church of Sweden, of Augustana's Regina Holmen Fryxell.

The story of our communion with the Church of Sweden in respect to our hymns is similar. I will not tell that story except to mention two things. Hymns are, in large part, the way in which faith is carried from generation to generation. The legacy of persons like John Olof Wallin, indeed the legacy of the whole Swedish *Psalmbok* tradition, has been one of Augustana's richest treasures. And in this connection, the new *Songs of Two Homelands*, edited by Glenn Stone, Ronald Englund, and John Swanson, published for this Gathering, is a fine gift to us all. *Hemlandssånger* lives.

A third area in which Augustana's communion with the Church of Sweden was expressed, especially in the time after World War II, was that of theological reflection. Let me comment at a bit more length. Largely through the work of Muhlenberg Press and, in the Lutheran Church of America after 1963, Fortress Press, a substantial body of theological work was translated from Swedish into English. The publication in 1949 of an English translation of Anders Nygren's theological *Commentary on Romans* which had been published in 1944 in Sweden shaped a generation. And at the beginning of this presentation we referred to Gustaf Aulén's remarkable volume, *The*

---

[29] Gustaf Aulén, "The Renaissance of Liturgy and Music in the Sunday Service," *The Church of Sweden: Past and Present*, ed. Robert Murray (Malmö: Allhem, 1960) 242.

Faith of the Christian Church and much, much more could be said about that good Bishop's incredible production. The names of the "fathers and doctors" of the Twentieth Century Church of Sweden are well known: Einar Billing, Nathan Söderblom, Gustaf Aulén, Anders Nygren, Ragnar Bring, Gustaf Wingren, and Olov Hartman. In this connection, let me single out three specific contributions from Augustana.

In 1947, the Augustana Book Concern published a translation by Conrad Bergendoff of *Vår kallelse* (*Our Calling*) by Einar Billing. Dr. Bergendoff himself wrote of this book:

> Nowhere have I found a simpler, more direct statement of the relationship of Christian faith and Christian living than in this little book by a keen thinker of the Church of Sweden a generation ago, Einar Billing. He goes to the heart of Christian faith and finds how the heart moves the hands of the disciple.[30]

Several generations of young American Lutherans, not least in the Lutheran Student Association, read this small book in their quest for a sense of "Christian vocation." Sadly, we don't talk so much these days of that kind of vocation, either among clergy or laity; and we and our church are the poorer for it.

About Anders Nygren, secondly, a great deal could be said, indeed books have been written about him. He is perhaps best known in the English-speaking world for *Agape and Eros*,[31] a translation of his work from 1930 and 1936, *Den kristna kärlekstanken genom tiderna* (*The Christian Understanding of Love Through the Ages*). This work has stimulated countless scholars and has been the source of considerable controversy. It has frequently been criticized, sometimes correctly but often, I think, out of ignorance. What has been missing in English has been Nygren's foundational works that provide an understanding of the method followed in *Agape and Eros*, the Lundensian method of "motif research." The best study of this methodology has surely been Bernhard Erling's dissertation, *Nature and History*,[32] but Nygren's own basic writings have never been translated. Happily, however, another of the sons of Augustana has made at least partial reparation for this lacuna. I speak of our late brother, Walter Capps. In 1997, when he was still at the University of California, Santa Barbara, and before he entered the halls of the U.S. Congress, Walter teamed up with Professor Kjell Lejon of the University of Linköping in Sweden to edit and translate Anders Nygren's important dissertation of 1921, *Religiöst Apriori* (*Religious Apriori*).[33] This book may well be appearing too late, but it is an important contribu-

---

[30] Conrad Bergendoff, "Introduction" to Einar Billing, *Our Calling*, trans. Conrad Bergendoff (Rock Island: Augustana Book Concern, 1947; Philadelphia: Fortress Press, 1964) 1.

[31] Anders Nygren, *Agape and Eros*, trans. Philip S. Watson (Philadelphia: Westminster Press, 1953).

[32] Bernhard Erling, *Nature and History: A Study in Theological Methodology with Special Attention to the Method of Motif Research* (Lund: C. W. K. Gleerup, 1960).

[33] *Anders Nygren's Religious Apriori*, ed. Walter H. Capps and Kjell O. Lejon (Linköping: Linköping University Electronic Press, 2000).

tion to theological reflection and we are in debt—as in many other instances—to Walter Capps.

And finally, let me single out the important work of Edgar Carlson. In 1948 his survey of twentieth century Swedish scholarship on Martin Luther appeared, *The Reinterpretation of Luther*.[34] This positive survey and estimate of distinctively Swedish Luther studies remains a most valuable source for understanding and appropriating the Reformer.

Now more could be said about Swedish theology, a subject dear to my heart.[35] It took too long for Swedish biblical scholarship to be known to English readers, not really until after the arrival of the Professor and Bishop Krister Stendahl in this country in the mid-1950s. And we could reflect on the doldrums into which Swedish theology fell after the age of the giants, Aulén, Nygren, and Bring. Happily, there are signs of new vitality within the Swedish theological community.

But we must bring this to a conclusion. We have attempted to trace—from uncertainty at the beginning to a sense of *communion*—we have attempted to trace Augustana's ties to the Church of Sweden, ties of history and faith. Much more work needs to be done accurately to trace this story. And what of the future? Augustana is gone, but the Church of Sweden, to which Augustana related first as daughter and then as a sister church, assuredly is not. Its situation is changed; since January 1, 2000, a form of disestablishment has taken place in Sweden, thrusting on the church new problems and new opportunities. Can the ties be maintained?

To cite one attempt to maintain and deepen these ties of *communio*: there is a new initiative being taken—by the Berkeley Divinity School (Episcopal) at Yale, the Philadelphia Lutheran Theological Seminary, and the Church of Sweden's Peter Fjellstedt Foundation in Uppsala—to create among the three traditions an ongoing program including the exchange of parish clergy and designed to contribute to renewal within the churches. Its first theme is to be "Sacramental Presence in a Changing World." We need more such initiatives.

CONCLUSION

After World War II, visits between the two churches increased. In 1948 Archbishop Erling Eidem of Uppsala and Bishop Arvid Runestam of Karlstad participated in Augustana's synodical convention. In 1960 Archbishop Gunnar Hultgren, Bishop Gert Borgenstierna of Karlstad, and Dean Robert Murray of Strängnäs participated in Augustana's Centennial Synod here in Rock Island. I can recall at one of these synod meetings the presentation of a doctorate *honoris causa* by Lund University to Eric Wahlstrom. In lieu of

---

[34] Edgar M. Carlson, *The Reinterpretation of Luther* (Philadelphia: Westminster Press, 1948).

[35] A somewhat helpful though dated survey of Swedish theology up to 1966 is Nels F. S. Ferré, *Swedish Contributions to Modern Theology: With Special Reference to Lundensian Thought* (New York: Harper & Row, 1967).

the traditional cannon shots, the Swedish presenters asked the audience robustly to shout "Boom! Boom! Boom!" in honor of the new doctors.

As I have already indicated, a special volume was presented at the Centennial Synod as the Church of Sweden's gift to its daughter church. Edited by Dean Murray and entitled simply, *The Church of Sweden: Past and Present, A Book Sponsored by the Swedish Bishops' Conference*, the volume, which was lavishly illustrated, included essays by the Bishops of each of Sweden's thirteen dioceses and a number of essays on other subjects.

As the curtain comes down on our drama, let me quote from the Dedication of the volume, prepared by Archbishop Hultgren:

> This book was written to mark the Centennial Celebration of the Augustana Church in the United States. Through the ties of faith, history, and ancestry Augustana and the Church of Sweden are closely related. Mindful of this, we tender our sister Church in America this modest but warm and grateful tribute. It is prompted by our wish to commend and congratulate Augustana upon the completion of her first century.
>
> Our Churches live and have their being in settings and circumstances of wide divergence. But the foundation on which they both were built is ultimately the same: the Word of God and the Lutheran Confession. A hundred years ago the pioneers brought this patrimony with them to the foreign shores as their rallying point. And Augustana, the Confession from the days of Martin Luther which our forefathers adopted at the Uppsala Council in 1593, became their symbol of unity.
>
> For us in Sweden it is a source of pride and joy that many of those who left our homeland were instrumental in building the Augustana Church. It is a never-finished labor of love, now passing gradually from the hands of those born in Sweden to their descendents. We are gratefully aware of all our kinsmen and friends beyond the great waters.
>
> Claiming neither perfection nor completeness, this volume tries to portray the Church of Sweden as it is today and her historical background. It is a greeting from friends to friends. It carries our gratitude for your faithful preservation of our common heritage and conveys to you our blessings for the days ahead.[36]

The curtain falls on our drama. *Communio.* Let it rise again.

---

[36] Gunnar Hultgren, "To the Augustana Church with Respects and Fraternal Greetings," *The Church of Sweden*, ed. R. Murray, 11.

Augustana Roots in the Church of Sweden

Alf Brorson

INTRODUCTION

On behalf of my family, I would like to give our most sincere thanks for your gracious invitation to be here with you to share this very special event, the Augustana Heritage Association Gathering of 2002.

As we all know, the original language of *Augustana Evangelisk Lutherska Kyrka*, the Augustana Evangelical Lutheran Church, was Swedish, and I have been told by Lindsborg people that an elderly Swedish lady here once said, "Us Swedes will have a lot of leisure time when we are in heaven, while everyone else is busy learning Swedish."

Be that as it may. I even like to think that God speaks with an American accent....

I was six years old, pushing seven, when I first learned about pioneer pastor Olof Olsson from my father who, on his return from Augustana College in 1951, wrote a biography entitled *He Gave God Glory* that was recently published in English by the Smoky Valley Historical Association. The translation, it should be noted, was made by the Rev. Martin Ringstrom, whose mother had the same schoolmaster in Sweden as Dr. Olof Olsson once had—the legendary Mr. Anders F. Sedström. But Pastor Ringstrom is not only the man who offered to translate my father's book; he has also become an important person to my family and a friend in Christ—gently reminding us about what seems to be so easily forgotten by twenty-first century Swedes: We live by the grace of God.

Over the years, and not least from historical documents, among them thousands of pages written in excellent, good old Swedish and printed in the United States, I've followed and tried to visualize what Augustana people accomplished in America. And so, my dear close friend, Mr. A. John Pearson, has given us another awesome challenge: The Swedish Roots of Augustana.

In the main, my presentation, or to put it like a Swede, my attempt at a presentation, will be based and focused on the life, work, and thoughts of Lindsborg's spiritual founder, and Augustana's third president, Dr. Olof Olsson.

GREETINGS

It is the very greatest honor for us, on behalf of the leader of our church, the Swedish Archbishop, Dr. Karl Gustaf Hammar, to convey to you all the greetings, well-wishes and commitment of the Church of Sweden!

Being here is, in so many ways, a Godsend, and it is a great joy for us, and such a privilege, also to bring to you personal greetings from our new Bishop of the Karlstad Diocese, Dr. Esbjörn Hagberg.

Bishop Hagberg wants us to say to you that his coming to Värmland as a Bishop also brings him back to his own roots. As a part of a greater whole it is for us to perpetuate our roots, and in doing so we will also find ourselves closely connected through our common church roots, in Sweden and America.

Our bishop prays for you and the Augustana Heritage Gathering, and he gives you his blessing, hoping to share and promote our heritage in days to come.

I would also like to dedicate my presentation today to Pastor and Mrs. Donald E. Trued. You see, after Dad's return from the United States, we had a visit from one of his new friends—a theology student now dressed in an American soldier's uniform. Some time later, Robert Ward Sutherland came to see us again, but time flies. Eight years ago, however, it so happened that the Trueds showed me *The Augustana Ministerium* by Conrad Bergendoff! From what I then found I immediately wrote a tentative letter, asking "Are you Bob?" and soon got an affirmative answer, and I think it was in Swedish, "Yes, I'm Bob!"

So, Bob, now that we have crossed paths again, almost fifty years later, what could I, once upon a time that little red-haired P. K. back in Sweden, say about Augustana roots in the Church of Sweden?

SWEDISH-AMERICAN HISTORY

The heavenly blue and gold Swedish flag carries a Christian cross on it—for a reason. Our church, *Svenska kyrkan*, the Church of Sweden, is an evangelical Lutheran church dating back to the ninth century *Anno Domini*—although Sweden was a Roman Catholic country for many centuries, in fact to the early 1520s.

No Swedish organisation or institution has such a long, cultural tradition as the Church of Sweden. Where we live, in Torsby, Värmland, that means a time span of more than 800 years (long before 1776), during which time the Word and the Sacraments have been administered. The community itself has grown up around the church—a monumental landmark to be seen for miles around, on the northern shore of a big lake in one of Sweden's most beautiful valleys.

We usually say that Christianity was first brought to us from the European continent by Ansgar, the Apostle of the North, although we may have reason to believe that there were Christian people out west, on Lake Vänern, even before he came. However, about one thousand years later, in 1882, as the Augustana faculty at Rock Island was to select themes for graduates, as part of their final examinations, and several theological subjects having been proposed and rejected, Dr. Olof Olsson is said to have suggested, with a twinkle in his eye, "Odin's address to Ansgar upon his arrival in Sweden."

As we also know, over four hundred years ago, in 1593, the Swedish Church finally adopted *Confessio Augustana*, the Augsburg Confession of Faith. From then on the established Church wished to maintain institutional religious unity, based on laws, decrees, rules and regulations for everyone to follow, until constraints gradually began to loosen in the nineteenth century. By that time, Swedes were also seeking American freedom—confronting new realities.

But they didn't do so for religious reasons only—as is often the case, the reasons were fundamentally economic.

LUTHERAN SWEDES IN AMERICA

Swedish-American history originally goes back to New Sweden, Delaware, where the first independent colony of Lutherans was founded at Fort Christina in 1638, and although no longer Lutheran, Holy Trinity Church in Wilmington, dedicated in 1699, is today said to be the oldest Protestant church in America.

But for an interval of 18 years, following the death in 1831 of one of the founders of the University of Philadelphia, the Rev. Dr. Nicholas Collin, until the arrival of pastor Lars Paul Esbjörn at Andover, Illinois, in 1849, there is an unbroken Swedish Lutheran pastors' tradition in America, dating back to 1638—a tradition including church buildings, schools and hospitals, or in the language of Dr. Conrad Bergendoff, "Gothic style church buildings, with altar, pulpit and organ; the Swedish liturgical service, baptismal and eucharistic practises; as well as parish schools and ministry to the sick and dying."

In fact, forty-one Swedish pastors were sent to America by the Swedish government, from 1638 through the late 1770s, the last minister being Nicholas Collin, who in 1820 also warned people from Sweden from coming, "as there were too many Swedes in the land already."

Still, there were many more to come, including a small group of Swedish Lutheran pastors. By then, however, Swedes in Delaware were something of the past, and Swedes were no longer colonizers, but immigrants to the United States of America.

THE SWEDISH ELEMENT

From the 1800s there was a breaking-up of Swedish Lutheran unity, which had so far been a fundamental feature of Swedish social structure—a religious dimension as well as a matter of common concern. Ninety per cent of our population back then lived in rural areas, and the state of affairs was religious, inasmuch as spiritual and temporal matters were united within each parish, each parish being the foundation-stone, with the emphasis on family as the smallest unit of a naturally composed society. What every household needed might be had within the parish: relief of the poor, public education, child welfare, to some extent even health care and medical treatment, in addition to ecclesiastical matters—church services, with liturgy and sermons, hymn singing, Bible reading and catechism, christenings, weddings and funerals. The frame of reference, we might say, was a churchly one with social functions and dimensions—even cultural offerings, like music, arts and crafts, as well as books.

What then happened in Sweden, from the 1850s, has been looked upon as "a constitutional revolution" as municipal boroughs and parishes emerged, in addition to other denominational churches. All things didn't change overnight, but officially, at least, the state-church relationship that goes back to medieval times came to an end on January 1, 2000.

Evangelical revivalism in nineteenth century Sweden, however, was not just one movement, and the maps sometimes used do not always correspond to Swedish reality—or at least not the way I would like to see it.

I feel it is important to bear in mind that among so-called Pietists in nineteenth century Sweden there were not only *Läsare* or *Nyläsare*, "New Readers," who were critical of both the Church and the clergy of the Church of Sweden, but also *Gammalläsare*, "Old Readers," who were strictly loyal to the Church.

People in Sweden, like my God-fearing ancestors, could therefore be part of a strong, churchly Revivalist movement called *Schartauanism*, a Swedish tongue-twister, emphasizing a pure doctrine, the clarity of thought, and the established order of the Church. It was a churchly Pietism, *en kyrklig väckelse*, which in comparison to the New Readers' movement, *väckelserörelsen*, was regarded as old, conservative Pietism.

Consequently, those who left for America must in most cases have been New Readers. In their opinion, religious matters in Sweden were "superseded by a juridical outlook." In daily labor, though, the doctrinal distinction among pastors of the two Revivalist groups could be hard to tell! Being a servant of the Lord is not exclusively a matter of church terminology, whether we label it "New Evangelism" or "a conservative theological stance." There are fourteen Lutheran pastors in my family background, and telling you, for instance, about my great-grandfather, the Rev. G. D. Sillén who was an Old Reader, and a very churchly Schartauan, might very well make you think that I am talking about Olof Olsson! Pastor Sillén's work, though, kept him in the Church of Sweden, and eventually he became a rural dean in Värmland, with a white beard and a heavenly look in his eyes.

Eternal truths are found in the gospel. Our own worded truths might be called "qualified truths." Opinions are based on a diversity of facts and impressions, and in order to understand we sometimes have to simplify complicated matters. But to me, hearing, like I did just a few years ago, a white American Baptist preacher say things from the pulpit like religious tolerance was not practised in nineteenth century Sweden, and that anyone who opposed the Lutheran Church was severely prosecuted, and so had to leave their homeland, is (at best) a qualified truth! The same thing goes for what could be found in books and articles on Swedish religious matters at that time.

It is difficult to categorize, because categories often overlap. My objection is that one might get the impression that Sweden was not only a poor country torn apart by religious strife, but a totalitarian country as well, ruled by dictators known as abominable Lutheran pastors. Therefore, although it might be wrong to call this pure myth, it is not true to life either! Life is always more complicated than that. The clergy of the Church of Sweden, as part of the administrative machinery of the Swedish society, was an integral part of the power structure. They were well-educated, two-fold office holders—preachers but also civil servants. A vicar, like a county sheriff or a schoolmaster, commanded respect in local communities, as they were responsible not only for *mantalslängder*, the census, but also for the upkeep of important public functions, as well as Christian values.

Maybe I am partial now, but as a Lutheran Swede I think it is not only fair but also vital to point out the historical as well as contemporary importance of Lutheran pastors in Sweden. To a large number of Swedes, like members of the Olof Olsson party, emigrating to the Smoky Valley of Kansas, religious freedom meant emigration to America—it only makes sense that strong personalities with equally strong religious convictions were opposed to any kind of church body governed by the state! No church should be governed by a secular government, but that does not mean that we should disregard how much the Church of Sweden and her servants in fact have meant to people both at home and abroad. Whatever the world may say about the Church of Sweden, her pastors represent a very long and rich, churchly tradition—and Olof Olsson, for one, was an ordained, Swedish Lutheran pastor, and so were pastors like Lars Paul Esbjörn, Tufve Nilsson Hasselquist, Erland Carlsson, Jonas Swensson, and Olof Christian Telemaque Andrén—all of them Augustana founding fathers.

THE AUGUSTANA HERITAGE

In 1853 there were in all, three ordained Swedish Lutheran pastors in America, Esbjörn, Hasselquist, and Carlsson, and three years later, in 1856, Eric Norelius was the first Swedish-born American to become an ordained Lutheran pastor. But the number of pastors was still very low when the register was signed at the historic Wisconsin meeting at Jefferson Prairie on June 5, 1860, and when Olof Olsson came in 1869, being the first Lutheran pastor from the province of Värmland. His Swedish colleagues were 17 Augustana pastors, serving 36 congregations and 3,000 communicants across the American continent.

As history tells us, even if these men, some of whom had served in subordinate positions of the Swedish state church, were "like a drop in the Atlantic ocean," *Augustanasynoden* nevertheless became not only the largest church body among Swedes in North America, but also a unifying center for them. Many things made Augustana what it was, not least thanks to great leaders and the work done by a large variety of devoted, noted or anonymous, people all over the United States. From a distance, even the kings of Sweden made various contributions. But, as Professor Ulf Beijbom, at the Swedish Emigrant Institute in Växjö, has written in one of his books, the Augustana membership in itself was not as large as we might think, considering its great importance. In 1910 every fifth Swedish immigrant was a member of our Augustana sister in America.

Dr. Conrad Bergendoff once wrote to me, "I hope you share my feeling that the Augustana story is a part of the Lutheran church in Sweden." It is, and I do share his feeling.

The history of Augustana pioneers is a remarkable historical process of about fifty years. From small beginnings there was expansion, and finally, integration with the American society. In a sense, what happened in Lutheran Swedish America mirrors in many ways what had slowly happened in Lutheran Sweden for hundreds of years. The big and most decisive difference, apart from literally breaking ground, was that the Augustana Synod was not a state institution! Given America's religious and cultural diversity, Swedes had to adapt themselves to American religious freedom, democracy, and benevolent organizations—and, in the language of George M. Stephenson, "the frontier was not fruitful soil for planting still, formal, liturgical churches."

What I have seen for myself in the United States, and in American churches of several denominations, is another tradition of personal responsibility and participation that is hard to find with us. Although our one and only Lutheran church is rich in tradition, and has a solid financial position, she also carries a heavy burden, the load of an institutionalized public institution.

OLOF OLSSON

What a pioneer like Olof Olsson was able to achieve for the Kingdom of God can be seen by taking a look at Swedish America in the second half of the nineteenth century. I'm not a man of great eloquence, just a plain-spoken native from Out West, and English words fail me here, but in the words of Dr. Emory Lindquist, this is what happened close to where we now live, and where almost 9,000 years ago the oldest site in the province of Värmland was a Stone Age settlement, three miles from the present church: "In a small study at Sunnemo, following consultations with his wife and friends and after serious prayer, the decision was made. Lindsborg came into being that hour."

Olof Olsson was the founder of Bethany Church in Lindsborg in 1869. Before becoming a professor at Augustana College and Theological seminary from 1876 through 1888, he was pastor in Woodhull, Illinois (1890-1891). He was President of Augustana College and Theological Seminary from 1891 through 1900.

Olsson was born on March 31, 1841, on a modest farm property in eastern Värmland, and we can still see the home where he was born, where his family lived in meagre circumstances. He died on a Saturday afternoon, May 12, 1900, at the age of 59. His grave marker stands in Riverside Cemetery in Moline, Illinois.

I have been fascinated with this man for quite some time, in actuality since my father went to America in 1951. Before Dad left, he told me that the reason for his journey was not to play cowboys and Indians among herds of buffalo, although he did in fact buy me an American cowboy outfit. His reason was to learn more about a man whose name was Olle—Olof Olsson.

Olof Olsson had a vision for a valley—a vision of a pure congregation. He wanted to help create an ideal, Christian society. After some years, though, of hard testings under the wide arch of heaven in Kansas, he was to experience the impossibility of a Christian paradise on earth—even in the United States of America.

God has made life a learning process for all of us, no matter who we are or where we live. No one escapes criticism in this world of ours, either, and Olof certainly did not! But he remained true to his conviction of religious freedom, and he was prophetic. What he foresaw in 1866 happened in Sweden in the year 2000.

In retrospect, serving Värmland prepared him for Kansas, and his pioneer work on the Great Plains finally resulted in urgent calls to be third president of the Augustana College and Theological Seminary. He thanked them for their confidence, but not for the election, saying, "Why should a sensitive person as I bear the burdens of this office?" I won't speculate whether that remark was another example of a Swedish attitude, or a deep and personal insight. Perhaps it had to do with "behind-the-scene maneuvering."

Still, Olof Olsson was cut out for a higher calling. Truly supported by his wife Anna and their four children, he went all the way. He started out as a herdsboy, a young shepherd guarding his family's cattle, and in a truest sense of the word, he remained a shepherd all his life. He was ordained at the age of 22, and when he was 28, he was the leader of a Värmland group of emigrants to America, where he became an American citizen in 1876.

On leaving Sweden, Olof Olsson was a young idealistic pastor. He was deeply concerned about the spiritual care and education of young people.

He loved music; he had a burning desire to deepen spiritual life; and, not least, he disapproved of any distinction of rank.

To him, Christianity was both teaching and living, and as a newly ordained pastor, and a Lutheran at heart, he endeavored to keep the evangelical revival within the Swedish state church. But this also meant that he, from the very outset of his ministry, was at odds with the official attitudes of Swedish church leaders. He was a troublemaker in regard to the status quo. People loved him, but he was a thorn in the side of the bishop of Karlstad, later the Archbishop of Sweden, Anton Niklas Sundberg—the bishop that many people still remember as the one who during the great fire of Karlstad, while cursing and swearing, energetically tried to extinguish the flames, in contrast to the mayor who reportedly stayed where he was, weeping and praying.

Olof Olsson had a brilliant mind, and as an Augustana professor and president, he was one of the most influential and most learned theologians of his time. In Sweden he learned how to engage in polemics, and in the United States he soon learned how to raise funds, to mention just two things. I wouldn't call him a saint, but in less than a decade in Kansas he had accomplished more than most of us can do in a lifetime.

In Sweden, Olsson couldn't reconcile himself to official state church formality, but conditions in the Land of the Free were different. Consequently, he wouldn't, as he expressed it, "yield one iota of Lutheran doctrine," which also explains why as an Augustana pastor he defended his belief to such a degree that he was looked upon as a conservative Lutheran—and he remained as true to his democratic conviction of religious freedom. Maybe I tend to romanticize when it comes to pioneer times in the United States, but hopefully I stay with the facts when it comes to nineteenth century Swedish church history.

In Sweden, Olsson had labored to revitalize the church; in his struggle for religious freedom in America he wished to maintain his churchly pietism in a religious chaos of innumerable and competing denominations of faith, and the support he needed was to be found among the pastors of the Augustana Synod.

Under the circumstances, the will to maintain Lutheran church order was only reasonable, and in my opinion there are no more "dead dogs" to be found in the history of our church than in the history of any other religious denomination. God in His mercy lets his Adams and Eves turn to Christ as their Lord in different ways, or as Olof Olsson phrased it, "If we have the Gospel we can be saved in the state church or in the free church, under this or that type of church organization, yes, even if we have bishops."

Likewise, he had his own clear idea of Roman Catholicism. As was often the case, he was outspoken, and at times provocative, and in his extensive travelogue *Till Rom och hem igen* (*To Rome and Home Again*) he says, "an apostolic inheritance has been preserved by the ancient mother even though it is deeply buried under a stack of human traditions, papal bulls and a large amount of old rubbish."

From his pulpit, Olof Olsson proclaimed God's grace, earned through Christ's sacrificial death. As my father pointed out, the structure of Olsson's sermons, both in Sweden and in the United States, were quite uniform—the central theme always being the Lutheran doctrine of atonement and justification. The sermons also presented points of contact with different religious movements which he had encountered, but the main theme always related to grace and the order of grace—similar, in fact, to Schartau's in form as well as content.

There are so many things to say about this man, and what he did, whether church-wise, education-wise, or law-wise, but as the time-saving syndrome is part of our lives today, I'll focus on one aspect only. It has to do with music.

One of Olof Olsson's musical contributions to America had to do with the Messiah, and it also had to do with violins.

THE SONG OF MESSIAH PEALS FORTH FROM THE PRAIRIE

Throughout his life, Olof Olsson loved music. He always saw to it that his church, or his school, had an organ. Already as a school teacher in the small mining town of Persberg, Värmland, he taught his young students, the children of poor and hard-working miners, to sing in parts, using the numerical scale in numbers as a teaching method. It has been said that the first thing he wrote on the blackboard of that local school was the numerical scale.

Olof's mother Britta was deeply influenced by the preaching of pastors who bore the stamp of Schartauanism, and Olof met with zealous pietism at an early age. She made him destroy a violin which he had acquired, as the "wicked violin" was a sinful instrument. No doubt this caused pain to music-loving Olle. He had to give in to his mother's decision, but he was not able to forget his violin.

Why "the wicked violin"? One explanation, apart from what it had to do with dancing and drinking, has to do with witchcraft in Swedish folklore. You had to keep in with supernatural beings in nature like fairies and elves. They could be dangerous.

Swedes have a strong love for nature, and we have a deeply rooted reverence for it, as reflected in our literature, visual arts, and music. It's close to religion, without actually being so! But in the old days, country people were also threatened by nature, that is, they were easily frightened as nature itself was believed to be charged with magic and populated with supernatural creatures, not only fairies and elves, but also gnomes, ghosts, goblins, and trolls, and on top of it all there was a siren of the woods, *skogsrået*, or in Värmland *skogsråa*, and *Näcken*, "the Neck," a water-sprite and the evil spirit of the water. The fear of these creatures was still there in the peasant society of the early nineteenth century. *Skogsrået*, who could be seen in the forest, was most dangerous to men, as she was a beautiful erotic temptation, although not when seen from behind, and similarly *Näcken*, who could be seen in streams and rivers where he sat on a stone in the falls, playing the violin, was an erotic danger to women. In other words, as some people might say, there was an aphrodisiac character to the violin.

Looking back on this, at the age of 38, Olof wrote: "Listen, you do not really understand what it is like to be a herdsboy in the untamed forest. In addition to other troubles, one had to face the constant terror of mountain trolls and woodland spirits. At least that is how it was for me. And now, old as I am, I still feel the same fear of forest nymphs. If one could place them in a confessional booth, that would help, but to see them is unbearable. So these forest deities still spook and terrorize."

Also, in his daughter Anna's book, *A Child of the Prairie*, there is a story about how her Grandpa met the Gnome when he was charcoaling in the forest, and also one story about how her Grandma frightened away the devil with her Bible.

We will come back to violins shortly.

As for music, Olle didn't really get started until he was thirteen, when he enrolled as a student in a public school in Västergötland, fifty miles from his home. His slumbering musical talent was awakened once and for all by Anders Fredrik Sedström, a respected schoolmaster who was also the cantor and organist in the Fredsberg congregation. Before that school year was over, Olle had learned to play a church organ and how to master the most frequently used church music. So, we should not be surprised to know that when the first service was held in the sod-and-stone pioneer church in Lindsborg, on New Year's Day, 1870, Pastor Olsson also presented a choir—his only instrument at the time being a tuning fork. Soon there was even an organ in the Lindsborg parsonage. Olof Olsson was Lindsborg's first organist.

Pioneer pastors worked themselves to exhaustion, and at times Olof Olsson was weak from overexertion. In Värmland he was never taken ill and never had to ask for leave of absence, which he had to do on several occasions in America. On one such occasion, in 1879, he went to Europe (although not back to Sweden) to recuperate and on his return he brought Handel's Messiah to his new homeland—and the song of Messiah is still pealing forth from the prairie!

In his own words, Olof was moved to the depths of his being by what he had heard in London's Exeter Hall on April 4, 1879, and back home in Rock Island he wished to recreate his European experience in an American setting. He rejoiced, in his own words, at "the pure words of the Bible, all of them a song with scriptural words about Christ." He appreciated the violins playing, but he was also wondering about what *Mor Britta* would say.

There is many a violin in the Messiah, and after he had heard the rendition in London, he put his own thoughts into writing. "I may well wonder what my old mother will say when she sees me enjoying the music of violins." He was convinced that the arts, be it music or fine arts, "could be used in the service of God, and the church," and he was convinced that "the Christians who have good singing voices can be powerful missionaries with this talent if they use it in the right way."

To Olof, therefore, this was a solution. God, the creator of all things, has given us things to be used to the benefit of mankind. Violins could be used in sinful ways, but also to the glory of God. We should use what we have been given wisely!

But now there was a problem to be solved, which not only had to do with his mother. As Dr. Ernst William Olson has pointed out in his *opus magnum*, Augustana church members in America also had "conscientious scruples about the use of certain stringed instruments." This fact caused Olof Olsson to make a lengthy argumentation in defence of their use, saying, "it so happens that in Handel's and other oratorios the singing is to be accompanied by various instruments." He then went on to say that "certain stringed instruments in particular are dangerous and detestable while used in the service of the devil, but become most delightful when employed by skilled hands to produce sacred music," and he finished it all by saying, "But, alas, how frightfully even the human voice has been misused in the service of sin and Satan! If, then, we were to discard everything that has been or may be misused, what would there be left of ourselves or of all that God has made?"

Beat that for Swedish-American argumentation!

In the spring of 1880, a small orchestra was organized in Rock Island, and in January the following year, the Augustana Oratorio Society—for the promotion of singing and music. The first rendition of the Messiah took place in Moline on April 11, 1881. It was Holy Week. At a later rendition in 1881, at commencement time in Rock Island, Lindsborg's Carl and Alma Swensson were in the audience, and they then went back home to bring the Messiah to the Smoky Valley—where, four years earlier, in 1877, and accompanied by Olof Olsson, Carl Swensson had come on his first visit to Kansas with the Augustana Silver Cornet Band.

The very thought of a Messiah festival among people whose living conditions were still those of an early pioneer world might even today seem impossibly close to the ridiculous, but as it turned out, the outcome was to be sublime

Thirteen members of the orchestra from Rock Island came, with Olof Olsson and Joseph Osborn, to Bethany Lutheran Church in Lindsborg on Easter Sunday, March 28, 1882, and it could not have been "a result of chance" that a number of historically well-known Swedish-American people were united in their efforts on this occasion, with Olof Olsson seated at the organ.

John Osborn, the director, who as a schoolboy had been looked after by Eric Norelius, was an Augustana professor and a son of L. P. Esbjörn—the first Swedish Lutheran pastor in nineteenth century America at Andover,

Illinois, and later professor and first President of the Augustana institution of learning in Rock Island; Carl Swensson, Olof Olsson's former student in Rock Island and his successor at Bethany Church, was the founder of Bethany College and the son of Jonas Swensson—once the President of the Augustana Synod and also Esbjörn's successor at Andover, where Carl Swensson at the age of 13 had first met Eric Norelius; Mrs. Alma Swensson, finally, who had been in charge of choir rehearsals in Lindsborg, was the soprano soloist—and also the first conductor of the Bethany College Oratorio Society.

Many such connecting links can be found in Augustana history, telling us the story of the possibilities of the impossible. Today, in all 302 renditions later, the Lindsborg Messiah is the longest running, continuous live rendition of the Messiah in the United States.

For that we may very well sing *Te Deum Laudamus*!

IN CONCLUSION

Swedish contributions to the Augustana heritage, in the final analysis, were all part of something bigger. Consider Jesus' words in the Gospel according to John: "Abide in me as I abide in you. Just as the branch cannot bear fruit by itself unless it abides in the vine, neither can you unless you abide in me" (John 15:4).

Now we are in for something new, although we will still be resting on a most solid rock until the end of time, but within both the Evangelical Lutheran Church in America and the Church of Sweden we see that our numbers are decreasing. I was told by Pastor Jerry Leaf two years ago how many congregations and pastors that the ELCA has lost in ten years, and likewise I have learned that the Church of Sweden will need 1,200 new pastors until the year 2010.

It no longer seems to be a matter of expansion, but a question of keeping what we have—a question of holding fast to what we have.

In the Revelation to John (3:11) it says, "I am coming soon; hold fast to what you have so that no one may seize your crown." Above the front door of Lindsborg's original church, Bethany Lutheran Church, words are written in old Swedish, among them the first part of this verse. In 1900, the year of his death, there was a devotional by Dr. Olsson, signed O. O. in Augustana's *Korsbaneret* (*The Banner of the Cross*). When, over a hundred years ago, he wrote his last devotional, *Varnings- och uppmuntringsord* (*Words of Warning and Encouragement*) he based it on these words, still to be seen on the sanctuary he founded here in Kansas. The last paragraph reads:

> Yes, dear Savior, you are still alive, and now I bring these words of warning and encouragement back to You in prayer.
>
> Oh, Jesus, because You possess me, I pray that You will hold fast to what You have. Hold me firmly, not because of my service but because of your great love for me. Keep me with you. I am the crown, the crown of Your bitter pain and death, just as the helpless criminal on the cross became your triumphal crown, when

You entered into the Holy of Holies and won eternal salvation for him and for us and for all. I am unable to hold firmly to what I have in these days of materialism, doubt, pride and scornful opposition. Oh Lord, hold me tightly in Your pastoral hands! Then I shall be saved; then I shall receive my crown.

Future prospects, and visions for the future, call for a thorough knowledge of the past, and as our ancestors once joined in the struggle for a better future, we now join in the effort to preserve history for future generations by bringing the old into new uses—in the turmoil of our world. In doing so, we also must hold fast to what we have.

That is our God-given legacy, in the continuum of time.

The Background of the First Pioneers of the Augustana Synod and the Härnösand Diocese Today

Karl-Johan Tyrberg

I. BACKGROUND

Thank you for inviting me to participate in the Augustana Heritage Gathering. It is the first time my wife Ingrid and I have visited the United States, and naturally it is with great anticipation that we have come here. I am very pleased to represent the Church of Sweden, and I have the warmest summer greetings to extend to you from the Archbishop and from the rest of the Bishop's Conference.

First, I have been asked to talk about the situation in the Church of Sweden during the period of the first emigration from Sweden to North America. This might cast a light on how and why the Augustana Synod was formed. Second, I will also talk about the present situation and church life in the Härnösand diocese which is one of the two northern dioceses in Sweden and where I have been bishop since 1991.

It is, naturally, not possible for me to give an account of the total situation in Sweden during the 1850s. It is over 30 years since I did research on the development in southern Sweden in the area where Tufve Nilsson Hasselquist came from. He was one of the pioneers of the Augustana Synod, and he came from southern Sweden—the Lund diocese—where I have had my main ministry.

During the 1850s all conventional and recognized standards and functions in Swedish church life were reconsidered. Among others, there was a demand to allow increased responsibility for laity in the church. Important impulses came from Germany along with a program for home mission in order to meet social and spiritual needs that were important for the church to meet with. It was a matter of intensifying the preaching as well as offering diaconal charity work. This combination of evangelizing and doing Christian social work did not become a principal line in the evangelical revival to come. But, these thoughts from Germany of diaconal home mission did linger on and became important for the development of the Swedish diaconal work. This resulted in a number of schools for the education of deaconesses. But not until now these deacons have been taken up in our new Church Order as part of the ordained ministry.

Hasselquist was part of the faction where home mission was considered important. One of the most inspiring men when it came to home mission was the Rev. Dr. Peter Fjellstedt. He had earlier been a missionary mainly in South India and became vitally important in Sweden through his magazines and Bible commentaries. According to Fjellstedt, home mission should be complementary to ministry through lay preaching and through voluntary diaconal and evangelical work in the parish. School teachers in particular were considered an important group to count on. But in the more conservative circles this was seen as a threat to the family and the family tradition. According to Fjellstedt, laymen's initiative did not have to be limited to the family circle. Laypeople could either form associations or be part of the ordinary activities led by the minister in the local parish.

The second faction representing free laymen engagement went in another direction wanting to concentrate on church politics. Strong impressions emerged from the Presbyterian tradition in Scotland and from political liberalism. In this reform work, it was considered important to strengthen a democratic structure which would engage the large group of church members. An important spokesman for this was the Rev. H. B. Hammar, who was a very good friend of Hasselquist's. To Hammar, laymen's engagement became a reform movement, having as a model the New Testament build-up of a congregation.

The spiritual priesthood is the foundation for the right to preach—for laymen as well as for ministers. It is vital to any church that everybody gets the opportunity to practice the gift given to him. With this, Hammar did not mean that laity had an unconditional right to preach, but rather that the simple testimony—the call for revival—is easier received by people through laymen. Hammar and his friend Carl Abraham Bergman also propagated for the separation of the church from the state. To these two men it was important to make organizational changes for the progress of the gospel. Large meetings were arranged with talks about ecclesiastical reforms. The Presbyterian tradition had quite a large impact on how the associations were formed.

There was also a third group of people involved with the development of the free laymen's engagement which was characterized by pure evangelical intentions. In this group there was less interest in social work and in church organization; the one and only interest they had was to preach the gospel for the conversion of souls. Here it became important to focus on the believers and protecting their right to have gatherings without interference of authorities neither from the church nor the state. The home mission had a double program that is social as well as evangelical engagements. This faction had one only which was to preach. A unanimous view of how the church should be organized did not exist here. As time went on, no ministers were involved in these associations; they were led by laymen. The meetings were not about reform programs, but were talks about doctrine and faith and how to become a believer. What characterized this faction was that the preaching of the gospel was the only important thing; everything else was unnecessary.

Around 1860 the laity revival had developed into two different forms of free associations; one with the interest in making a political reform program for the church and separating it from the state. The other group wanted a church with lay preachers. The original home mission program with social and evangelical engagements did not become the mainline of the revival to come.

Another issue connected to free laity is about the role of lay persons in ordinary church life. One way of giving authorization to the preaching by laymen was to establish a ministry for deacons or another form of authorized lay workers. Dr. Fjellstedt was one of those who energetically brought forth a ministry for deacons for evangelical and charity tasks basing it on the examples in the New Testament. Some of the more conservative were thinking in ways of a church authorization for free lay preaching, while others wanted to keep the tasks of the ministry together. The thought of a ministry for deacons was to come back but was rejected at the Church Assembly in 1868.

Another model for solving the question of laymen's engagement in the church was to approve of an association model. In conservative circles, any kind of lay preaching was disapproved of and the association model was considered as a threat. The associations might become another church authority apart from the parish and the diocese. The association was considered justified only for diaconal purposes and should be limited to the parish and be led by the minister. In this debate several attempts were made to connect the ordinary church leadership to the formation of different associations.

Most of the attempts made to range laymen's engagement under ordinary church life went back to the local parish. Some referred to the head of the family, which was the father of the house, who—according to the Lutheran view—was responsible for the spiritual life in the family. Outside the family, no layman was allowed to preach. Others thought that the minister sometimes could delegate the task to preach, but that he would be ultimately responsible just the same. An important renewal of the increased responsibility of laity in the parish is among those who wanted to activate the members of the parish council according to the Presbyterian model. Then—with reference to the spiritual priesthood—some were of the opinion that the minister could engage laymen with specific gifts in the social work of the church. A layman, who had an inner call to preach, was to receive an outer call from his congregation, i.e., to receive a confirmation from the believers—who were to judge the gifts the layman had received. If this was fulfilled, it was considered as biblical lay preaching. The minister was responsible for a more profound teaching. There was no reason to think that there would be a conflict between the two.

This was one part of the debate in the Church of Sweden 150 years ago. Some of these issues were brought to North America by the immigrants from Sweden. In the new country there was freedom to create new organizations and the bonds to ecclesiastical authority have had no impact on the development of the Augustana Synod.

For the past 150 years there have, naturally, been mutual influences between the Church of Sweden and the Augustana Synod. The emigration from Sweden took place gradually, and each group brought their own traditions and had their spiritual background. Some were not able to go along with the conformism in Swedish church life and left the compulsion of the old country for the freedom in the new country. The Lutheran Church with roots in Sweden became a uniting power for the Swedish immigrants in the US, but the mission became different from that in the old country. I have not studied the developments thoroughly here, but I have understood that the mission of the Augustana Synod was to elucidate a Lutheran identity in an environment of many other confessions.

II. THE CHURCH OF SWEDEN, DIOCESE OF HÄRNÖSAND, IN THE YEAR 2000

The Church of Sweden has changed a lot in 150 years. Our churches have a common Lutheran foundation, and we have developed this heritage in different ways. Naturally, it still is a matter of how we see our responsibility in the church and how our church relates to society in general. Here in the US, the Augustana Synod—with its Swedish and Lutheran heritage—had its mission in a society with different cultures and denominations. In Sweden it has not been until recent years that our church of the majority has had to seek our identity in a multicultural context. Now it is our turn to receive many immigrants, and we are eager to find our ecumenical mission today and our responsibility when it comes to the many new Swedes of different faiths and cultural backgrounds. During the past 150 years many important impulses have reached Sweden from the United States, through relatives here, and also through emigrants who have returned to Sweden. I strongly believe that experiences from the U.S. can be of help for us in the Church of Sweden in our new situation.

Church and State

In order to describe the present situation in the Church of Sweden and the Diocese of Härnösand, I have to introduce to you the big change which took place in January 1, 2000, when the ties between the state and the church were loosened. The Church of Sweden became free from the state in most respects. However, there is still a special law for the Church of Sweden, which includes some important paragraphs about the identity and organization of the church: that it should have nation-wide coverage. Some other denominations in Sweden have protested against this specific law for the Church of Sweden. It was mainly passed to ensure continuity, that is, to guarantee that the Church of Sweden will continue to be a church for all, open for those of implicit faith as well as for the doubtful. When thinking about it, it might not be so remarkable that the state wanted a general law for the Church of Sweden since it holds the majority—almost 90 %—of the people. The church tax has earlier been collected through the income tax, and the present procedure is still the same. It is not called tax any more. Instead there is a membership fee that is still proportional to one's income. Gifts to the church are not deductible. Other denominations are also free to have their church fees collected through the state income tax.

The Church and the People

Even if the Church of Sweden in most respects has become free from the state, that does not mean that the relationship between the church and the people has changed. The state church has had a character of authority which has been changed into a more offering and serving attitude. Naturally, there is a risk that the church comes less in focus as secularization keeps proceeding. There is of course also the risk that people might leave the church, which might lead to quite an impairment of its economy. So far nothing dramatically has happened. Eighty to ninety percent of the Swedish people are still members of the Church of Sweden. However, the number decreases by one to two percent a year, and the decrease might speed up after the separation from the state. Many Swedes have had double memberships—belonging to the Church of Sweden as well as to another denomination. The non-conformist churches openly recommend their members to leave the Church of Sweden in order to realize higher financial contributions for the denomination to which they belong.

We know that approximately seventy-five percent of the Swedish people consider it natural to belong to the Church of Sweden. Only five to ten percent of the people regularly attend church services. But the membership in the Church of Sweden has a lot to do with being a Swede; the Swedes count on their church when they need it, just as naturally as they count on the hospital or the police force. The parish church in the center of town is a sign of belonging. Even if people do not go to church often, or at all, they consider the church building as theirs. There is also a demand among people to be able to go into the church for a private worship. Personal piety is increasing and is sometimes finding its place in the Church of Sweden.

The ceremonies of the church—i.e., baptism, confirmation, marriages, and funerals—still reach the majority of the people. Unfortunately, baptisms and the number of confirmands are noticeably decreasing. But we establish contacts with many families, since a majority of the people prefer to have their funeral services in the Church of Sweden. This, I believe, is the most evident sign of our church as the church for all.

People continue to ask for the services and help of the church on those occasions when life needs to be explained, whether happiness or sorrow. It has also become quite obvious for us that the church is indispensable for society at times of crises or catastrophes. Then the representatives of the church are there to talk to, as well as for symbolic ceremonies, thus helping people cope with difficult situations.

The Meeting Places of the Church

As I have said, the majority of Swedish people still consider it natural to belong to the Church of Sweden. People need holiness and therefore go to church especially at Christmas when there is a longing for solemnity and an expression for life beyond work and every day difficulties. The church can also meet with people on other important occasions, above all at the ceremonies of the church. At the baptism of a child, the parents express their gratitude for the birth of their child, and the baptism gives security in God's hands for the future. At confirmation, the church meets the confirmand on the verge of becoming an adult together with his or her family. Confirmation sends the young person out as a Christian and as an instrument for God's love in the world. Similarly, people need the care and devotion of the church at deaths. Ninety-five percent of all funeral services take place in the order of the Church of Sweden. The church helps people to express their sorrow at these difficult times in life.

Another meeting place is at times of crisis when the church offers diaconal charity and care. We have suffered severe catastrophes, and the church has proven very important on those occasions, in spite of the secularization in our country. Also at crises on a more local level, ministers and deacons have been asked for, and people have expressed a wish to keep the church open for quiet prayers and private worship. Ecumenical cooperation with other denominations sometimes takes place, but since the Church of Sweden has a nation-wide coverage, it becomes quite natural that the authorities turn to the church for assistance.

Openness: Our Identity

The openness of our church means that we do not exclude anyone. We would like to maintain a church known for an attitude where everyone is welcome regardless of class, race, or religious and political convictions. The non-conformist churches want us to express the importance of belonging to one church only. But to try people's confession and urge them to leave our church goes against the idea of the Church of Sweden. Openness goes together with the very core of the Gospel. The essence of the Gospel is not to demand, but to offer. Gospel and grace are unconditional, always welcoming. To me it is vital that we meet with people's needs and confirm their way of expressing their belonging to our church. When we talk to people about their contacts with the church, they talk about how important it is to them that they are baptized, even though they have not been confirmed or taken part in the church life later on in life.

Increased Responsibility

The openness of our church can be combined with increased responsibility of those who represent the church. We want to maintain an including and permissive openness but want to also emphasize responsibility more than before. The elected representatives in the church councils and in other elected organs must be baptized, and the responsibility of all God's people is emphasized in our new Church Order. It is mutual responsibility, founded on the spiritual priesthood, which is important in order to bring the gospel to the people of our time. In baptism, all Christians are ordained to take responsibility for the faith of the church. During some decades, the church councils have obtained a more profound responsibility for the church services. Previously the church council was to give the minister the necessary resources, whereas now it is pointed out that everybody has to share the responsibility. This, of course, means that the responsibility of laymen is clearly stressed. In Härnösand's diocese, fewer church services are being held due to lack of ministers. This offers the possibility of church services led by laymen. This means that we have to prepare the laymen in their task to preach from their perspective, that their experience is expressed in the church service, and thus the experiences of people's everyday life is brought forward in their preaching.

Even if the responsibility of everyone is emphasized, the ordained ministry is important. The church needs ordained people for a life-long ministry who are sent out to the congregations by the bishop and the diocese. With the promises given by ordained deacons and ministers goes a special responsibility towards the bishop and the cathedral chapter. Those who have been elected for different functions by the congregations do not have the same personal responsibility. Not until now, with the new Church Order coming into force, has the ministry of deacons been regulated in the Church of Sweden. Before this, the deacons related to their education institution according to the German model, but today the deacons are connected to their bishop and the cathedral chapter.

The co-operation between ministers and elected representatives is presently an important issue in the Church of Sweden. Ministers are sent out by the bishop and the diocese, but the elected representatives are elected by the local parish. Both parties must cooperate in order to bring the gospel forward in the local parish. In this respect they have a common mission. Sometimes there are conflicts regarding power or influence. In my capacity as bishop, I am to supervise the congregations and urge collaboration instead of pulling in different directions.

Participation and Collaboration

In August (2000) we will have a conference in Härnösand for different co-workers in our parishes. The first day is for the elected representatives and the volunteers; the days to follow are for all other employees. Previously, the bishop summoned ministers to a conference every sixth year. But now I want to emphasize everybody's responsibility for the work of our church. The diocese is to promote the development of the congregation when it comes to form and content along with forms for collaboration—between all employees, between employees and elected representatives and ways of integrating volunteers. In the diaconal area volunteers play an important part, such as visiting groups for the sick and lonely, or in groups responsible for worship programs. Another important area for the employees and volunteers is the work with the confirmand groups. The teenagers need to learn how different people express their experience of their Christian faith.

Worship is our main mission, and in this we need to get more people involved. If people feel that they are asked for, they do want to take part. There is a renewal program for worship in order to stimulate the participation of many. Presently there is an on-going work in the parishes for pastoral programs concerning the different parts of congregational life. A program for baptism has been made by all congregations in our diocese; for example an invitation to baptism, to talks about baptism and the preparations for it, the worship with baptism where many participate, and different kinds of follow-ups involving parents and children.

In a similar way there will be programs for worship and other church ceremonies as well as the teaching, mission, and diaconal work. In our diocese we devote a special interest for the minority languages: the language of our original population in the north, the Lapps (or the same population) as well as the sign language for the deaf. We are supporting the education in theology for a deaf student who will be the first deaf minister in Sweden. We also support church work in the Finnish language, since the Finns are our largest immigrant group. We want to be a church for all, which means that everybody should be able to hear the gospel in his or her own language.

Collaboration in Society

The Church of Sweden is now disconnected from the state, which means that it is not part of society as it used to be. However, the Church of Sweden is now the responsible authority for funerals inclusive of those who do not belong to the church. It was a natural consequence that we kept this duty, which always has been ours. As I have already mentioned, the funeral services are important contacts with the majority of the Swedish people.

The church is also asked for by the schools. The school is the largest working place in Sweden. It therefore comes quite natural that each congregation has a program for school contacts in indifferent age groups. During my visitations in the parishes I always visit some schools to talk to the students in a class. The teachers are also eager to receive the representatives of the church, and the students regularly visit their local church. The congregation is also important for the hospitals, home care, the care for senior citizens, and the police. The church supports activities for the unemployed and takes part in crises groups. With more personnel and other resources we could meet a lot more needs in society.

The congregations cooperate with different non-profit associations in order to support people's goodwill. The Church of Sweden is not an association among others. Non-profit associations for different purposes started to be formed in Sweden about 150 years ago. The church was there before them, but was willing to collaborate with them. This creates confidence in the mission of the church. The members of the different associations and organizations are invited to share the church services where they have the freedom to express their thoughts, sorrows, or gratitude in prayer and intercession. It is important that the church stands for the whole, the entirety: body, soul, and spirit. People also ask for a common value-system for church and society. It is not only a matter of good standards but also of love as the ultimate power of life. It is a matter of hope as a Christian experience emergent from hopelessness in the imitation of Christ. It is a matter of faith and trust as a foundation for the meaning of life. It is a gift of grace. Also, in a secularized society like ours, people listen to this testimony—not as a word from above, but as a message gently offered to men and women in need.

The church has another mission, to give criticism and to be a prophetic voice in society. At the beginning of this month, the Swedish bishops made a contribution to the debate, appealing to our government to fight the poverty in the world together with other European countries. Sometimes it is the mission of the church to point out that the market forces are not always representing the common good. We are called to be the voices of those to whom others do not listen.

Pilgrim Time

The year 2000 is the Pilgrim Year in Europe. To celebrate a new millennium means to review the meaning of time and life. To many Swedes, the pilgrim motive fills a general human need to break away from something intolerable and to look for meaning. In our diocese, the medieval pilgrimages went from the Baltic Sea coast to Trondheim in Norway and the Nidaros Cathedral with St Olof. Today those same old routes are being prepared, and people go together on pilgrimages to confess their longing. The churches are important places of rest. This summer I will celebrate mass in different places by the Norwegian border and meet people, not only regular tourists wanting another experience, but meeting pilgrims looking for God. And the Lord meets them as their fellow wanderer in the word and in the sacraments.

I believe that our church can meet with the people of our time by connecting to an historical interest and to confirm that which people long for.

We meet here today to confirm the common heritage in which the Church of Sweden is one part. Here you have developed your heritage for the needs you find most important to meet. Now we meet as pilgrims and may remind one another about the way and the goal. And just like the medieval pilgrims, let us return home with a new understanding and a new experience helping us in our vocation as Christian individuals and as a church!

Swedish America—and America—Forty-five Years Later

Nils Hasselmo

Today I live on Connecticut Avenue in Washington, D. C., only a few blocks from Augustana Lutheran Church where I slept in the basement forty-five years ago! In 1957, I attended a seminar for foreign students in the capital together with friends from Augustana College. We were introduced to American government and actually met with members of Congress. Little did I think that forty-five years later, I would be visiting with their successors to help argue the case for federal support for research and financial aid for American universities as part of my role with the Association of American Universities!

I want to share with you a few reminiscences—and a few speculations—from the past forty-five plus years. These years began at Augustana College, and have been shaped in many ways by my fortunate association with "Augie" and her people. It's a story about events and people, and about my interpretation of America.

"Augie" opened the door for me to many interesting experiences. It incorporated me into a network of friendships that has enriched my life in numerous ways. It gave me the opportunity—miraculously—to find a most wonderful wife and become part of a family of warm and dedicated people. I have always cherished being "the son-in-law of 'Twenty-Minute Tillberg'"—something that, I feel, gives me a certain standing in the Augustana family. (It's a sign of the times that, when I mention his nickname to my grandchildren, they wonder why he preached "so long"!) I'll even give "Augie" some credit for my three children and six grandchildren, although the college's contribution was only circumstantial!

I arrived in Rock Island by Greyhound bus, quite bedraggled after eight days at sea, a couple of days in New York in 90-degree weather, and the long trek through endless cornfields. I staggered into the house of Dr. Arthur

Wald, the legendary teacher of Swedish and former Dean of the College, and he turned me over to "Ma" Domeij, the housemother at Andreen Hall.

During the next few days, as a 25-year old budding intellectual from Uppsala (the world's greatest university), I was introduced to freshman life in an American college. It was culture shock of the highest order! What on earth had I gotten myself into?

Fortunately, I was soon sitting in classes with Dr. Theodore Celms, Dr. Henriette Naeseth, and Stanley Erickson. (I assume that Dr. Erickson was never referred to by that title, but only by his first name, because he was the only Democrat—at least overt—on campus?) I became engrossed in "objective and subjective culture" under the tutelage of one of Europe's fine philosophical minds, the displaced person, Dr. Celms of Latvia. (The first few weeks, he was the only one whose English I really understood, with its fine Central-European flavor.) I could indulge my already considerable appetite for the authors who caused the "rise of American realism" with the formidable and inspiring Dr. Naeseth over in South Hall. And I was fascinated, and puzzled, by all the intricacies and strange folkways of American government that Stanley Erickson introduced me to. I got to know Dr. Conrad Bergendoff. I had some interesting conversations with him as he addressed me in his stately and precise nineteenth century Swedish. I sat in chapel and marveled at the gems of wisdom and well-crafted English that seemed to just spring from his erudite mind.

In other words, I discovered the real Augustana behind, well, what I regarded as all that "freshman foolishness."

My acculturation to America did not really take off, however, until I met the first two students to sign up for my Swedish evening class. Dr. Wald called me into his office to meet my first two students. Students? Who were these beautiful young women that he introduced me to? I'm sure that my always embarrassingly ruddy Swedish cheeks became even redder. The two were Betsey Brodahl, professor of history, and Pat Tillberg, alumni director. Little did I know that Betsey would—a couple of years later—be revealed as my Dad's second cousin, descended from Magnus, one of my great grandfather Olof's two brothers, who had emigrated to Nebraska in 1869. And little did I know that Pat would become my wife a couple of years later. Don't say that life at Augustana can't be exciting!

Within a few weeks, I made a discovery that also became life-determining. Under the guidance of Dr. Fritiof Ander, professor of history, I had begun to look into what had happened to the Swedish language in America. I had encountered one kind of Swedish in Dr. Bergendoff, a very highly educated, albeit somewhat old-fashioned, Swedish. I encountered similar kinds of Swedish in "Nytta och Nöje," the society on campus that was devoted to "utility and pleasure," and where lectures and discussions were conducted in the immigrant language. Dr. Schersten kept meticulous minutes—in Swedish.

The real revelation came, however, when one day I climbed the stairs to the hot attic of Denkman Library and discovered another remarkable aspect of what had happened to the Swedish language in America. Here were rows of metal cabinets, filled with stacks of Swedish-American newspapers—*Nordstjernan*, *Svenska-Amerikanska Posten*, *Svenska Amerikanaren-Tribunen*, *Vestkusten*, and many others. Here were book cases filled with novels, short stories, collections of essays, reams of poetry, even plays–all in Swedish. It was in the midst of this incredible evidence of the work of Swedish-American pens that I decided what my linguistic studies were really going to be about. I was going to study what were clearly the wonderful adventures of the Swedish language in America, from seventeenth century New Sweden to nineteenth and twentieth century Chicago. Augustana was providing me not only with a wife (eventually children and grandchildren) and new relatives, but also with a scholarly vocation that eventually produced a book about *Amerikasvenska*!

One book in particular struck my fancy, G. N. Malm's *Charli Johnson, svenskamerikan* (*Charlie Johnson, Swedish-American*, 1909). Malm, a successful businessman in Lindsborg, Kansas, and also a successful painter of altar paintings, described the reactions of a young Swedish student who had just arrived in America. "Charli" was a "student" in the Swedish sense, that is, someone who had passed the "studentexamen," which until the last few decades was *the* class marker in Swedish society. "Charli" could disdain immigrant culture with the full fury of the sophisticated holder of the "studentexamen," including the adapted Swedish-American language that the immigrants and their descendants spoke. (Malm actually wrote the dialogue in his novel, and in a five-act play he also wrote, in that language, which made his work even more interesting to me!) "Charli" did show his disdain—until he met "Änni," the daughter of a local farmer—and fell in love. He also went through an epiphany in Lindsborg. It happened when he attended the Messiah performance at Bethany College. It finally dawned on him that Swedish America actually had "culture," although in many ways it was a new culture that had developed from Swedish roots, but with adaptation to American land and society, and to the English language.

I will not go into whether there were possibly some similarities between good old "Charli" and another young man who had just arrived in America!

Now, I did have some knowledge of America when I arrived at Augustana. America was a very strong presence in Europe after World War II. I met American GIs on the train going to and from Uppsala all the time. I listened to American jazz—my favorite music—mostly from American armed forces stations in Germany. I read Mark Twain. Every spring my friends and I would build rafts on the little river by our homes (which we called the Mississippi) from the timber that was being floated down to the saw mills, expecting to make a run for freedom down the river as soon as the ice broke. I read James Fennimore Cooper—for fun! The woods were populated with Indian braves. Later, I read Steinbeck, Caldwell, and Saroyan, and other more contemporary writers. In the 1950s Sweden was also experiencing the beginning of an enormous interest in the Swedish emigration that was inspired, at least partly, by Vilhelm Moberg's novels about Karl Oskar and Kristina. My father was one of the contributors (one of his books) to the so-called "Värmlandsgåvan," the gift from Värmland, which was given to the American Swedish Institute in Minneapolis in 1952 as a sign of friendship across the ocean. (Its fiftieth anniversary was just celebrated). In many ways, there were many cultural bridges from my Sweden to what was going to become my America.

There was one theme in Malm's writings that was especially important. It was the theme of the "kulturbärare," the carrier of culture. Malm and many of his contemporaries among the Swedish-American intellectuals were quite insistent that the Swedes must contribute important traits of *their* culture to the emerging new American culture. Swedish America was not only a cherished heritage, and a comfortable haven for the immigrants while they adjusted to the new land; it was a contribution to American culture!

The remarkable thing about all this is that, in spite of some discouraging signs in the 1950s, when interest in "ethnicity" was not very high, perhaps as a reaction to the national challenge of World War II (as happened dramatically after World War I), the remarkable thing is that Swedish-American cultural life has continued to flourish, and is still flourishing as we enter the twenty-first century. The Swedish language is mostly only a distant memory, except among Swedes who have come to this country in recent decades. But a number of organizations continue to prosper and renew themselves. Among them are the American Swedish Institute in Minneapolis, The American Swedish Foundation and Museum in Philadelphia, the Swedish American Museum Center in Chicago, the Nordic Heritage Museum in Seattle, and the Swedish American Historical Society. Newer organizations, such as SWEA and the Swedish American Chamber of Commerce, have added new vigor to the organizational life of Swedes in America. The Swedish Council of America supports many activities on a national level through its publications, its grants program, and a variety of events, and its affiliates number about 300.

I now want to turn to three aspects of my experience of America that I consider especially important. They are, in a way, paradoxes, but I regard them rather as tensions that are part and parcel of American society, and that we have to deal with in many different contexts.

First, I was struck from the very beginning of my stay in America by the mixture of "the old" and "the new" in American society. When I arrived, I had expected an America that looked like the most modern parts of Europe. I encountered, of course, an America that in many ways looked "old" to me. I had expected only shining wonders of modern construction, such as the skyscrapers in New York. I found sections of cities that looked, well, like "old" European cities. But, more importantly, I found a mixture of "old" and "new" attitudes, or even values. I was struck when I arrived at Augustana by the fact that in this college of "modern" American freshman, with all that 1950s pop culture had to offer, I also encountered the world of my grandparents. What gave me this impression was not only Dr. Bergendoff's stately Swedish; it was the very ethos of the place, of the people I met. Here were modern people who voiced a piety that was that of my grandparents, and in some ways actually behaved that way too. Underneath what one might consider expressions of the "worldliness" of modern society, that would certainly have been frowned upon by both my grandparents and those of the "Augieites," you found among the "Augustana people" a willingness to express their Christian faith and an adherence to rules of personal behavior that seemed—to me—somehow quite "old-fashioned." The basic values of my grandparents had been carried over to my sister and me in Sweden, but with much less overt piety than I felt I encountered in America. At the same time, our lives were much less "modern" in the sense of fashions, including not least cosmetics, and in terms of other aspects of "modern" consumption, than what I encountered in America.

Second, I was struck by the fact that America could at the same time seem to be so open to the rest of the world, so generous and compassionate (this was in the aftermath of, for example, the Marshall Plan), and so isolationistic, even imperialistic (this was also in the aftermath of the McCarthy hearings).

I was treated with a personal generosity and hospitality by Americans that was overwhelming. The foreign students were supported, and welcomed with open arms. (This is important to remember, because those attitudes are being challenged now.) At the same time, to many Americans what was going on in the rest of the world seemed far away and of little significance to their lives. When I spoke about Sweden, as I was often called upon to do, I had the feeling sometimes that I was there to open some kind of curiosity cabinet. Some Americans seemed to me to live in a very self-contained, even self-satisfied world. I was offended by the fact that so many people kept asking me if I was going to stay in America! Why on earth would I want to do that? (Little did I know!)

Third, I was struck by the fact that Americans were so patriotic, so devoted to their "Americanism," while at the same time many of them were quite devoted to their ethnicity—and ethnicity of every conceivable kind seemed to flourish in their midst. The American Constitution, in contrast to all other constitutions, including the Swedish one, seemed to me to be a living document. People actually quoted the Constitution, and the Declaration of Independence. I knew no Swede who could quote anything from the Swedish Constitution of 1809. At the same time, so many people I met referred to themselves as "Swedes" or "Norwegians" or "Germans," not even necessarily "Swedish Americans," etc. It turned out to be one of the fascinating aspects of my study of the Swedish language in America to observe how Swedish-American writers, and cultural leaders in general, dealt with this paradox—being a full-blooded American while at the same time being "a Swede." It may well be only in America that such double identity is possible—and perhaps because America is both a country, land and people, and a philosophical concept (embodied in the two documents I mentioned)!

I have come to develop an enormous respect for America over the past forty-five years, even love. I continue to see the tension among the elements of the three paradoxes I have tried to describe. I have come to appreciate that you can be both "an American" and "a Swede," because that is what I am now. I continue to admire the openness that is still exhibited by Americans, while fearing for the consequences of strong expressions of isolationism, or unilateralism. I have come to cherish the fact that it is possible to live a "modern" life, and still believe in, and try to live by, some "old-fashioned" values.

It has been an exciting forty-five years!

PART TWO

Illinois

Jenny Lind Chapel: An American Story

Myron J. Fogde

Lars Paul Esbjörn arrived in Andover, Illinois, in the fall of 1849, and from remnants of his immigrant group he organized the Swedish Evangelical Lutheran congregation on March 18, 1850. It was during his pastorate, which lasted until the summer of 1856, that this edifice was built. Our purpose is not simply to retell the history of this building, but also to seek to interpret what we see around us and what happened here.

I. A THESIS PROPOSED

I am suggesting that this building, particularly as seen from the outside, was constructed to look like an American public building of the 1850s, built in the popular Greek-revival style being used at the time. It is uncanny how the exterior of this building looks so very similar to the exterior of the Norwegian-American Lutheran Church at Jefferson Prairie, Wisconsin, where in 1860 the Augustana Synod was formed. What I am suggesting is that this structure is a physical embodiment of the spirit of the newly arrived Esbjörn.

At that point in time he was determined to become an American. Unlike other early immigrant pastors from Sweden, Esbjörn was competent in English, though hesitant to preach in the language. In a report to the American Home Missionary Society, dated September 13, 1851, he wrote: "I am sometimes invited by Americans to preach to them in English, which I also a few times have endeavored to do." On the afternoon of the dedication of this church at a conference of Swedish immigrant pastors and before a Swedish immigrant congregation, a sermon was delivered in English by a Presbyterian, Mr. Doing. Also showing Esbjörn's commitment to American ways was his *Day Book*, in which he noted his financial activity in English.

Esbjörn was financially supported in his ministry by funds provided through the aforementioned Congregational-Presbyterian missionary society based, in part, upon his friendship with Jonathan Blanchard, the President of Knox College. In another report to the AHMS, dated February 21, 1850, he acknowledged following the Society's rule in not allowing anyone to become a member of the congregation without having been, in the language of today, born again. No simple letter from a Swedish pastor or a baptismal certificate would suffice. As will be noted, already in Sweden he was inclined toward this position. He had been greatly influenced by what he expected to find on the American religious scene by another Presbyterian, Robert Baird, the author of a *View of the Valley of the Mississippi or the Emigrants' and Travelers' Guide to the West*, whom he had met in Sweden. Esbjörn came to America with high expectations of what religious life could be like in this land.

Also his interests were not just limited to the Swedish immigrant, as he was a strong supporter of the Synod of Northern Illinois, a synod of German, Swedish, Norwegian, and English-speaking Lutherans, and in which the English language was to be used at synodical meetings.

Esbjörn is not unique among the earliest immigrant religious leaders from non-English speaking homelands, for it did indeed occur that among such individuals there were those dedicated to making the transition to English and the American way as soon as possible.

May I repeat: this is what I think we see represented in this prairie church—an American, not a Swedish building.

II. THE STORY OF THE CONSTRUCTION

From April to July of 1851, Esbjörn traveled throughout the eastern United States soliciting funds to build pioneer churches. He returned home with some $2200. $1500 of this was a gift from the "Swedish Nightingale," Jenny Lind. After Esbjörn returned to Andover, an additional $800 came in response to his visit, bringing the total amount gathered to $3000. Of the $1500 from Jenny Lind, $340 was given to the Swedish Lutheran Church in Moline, $300 to build a church at New Sweden, Iowa, and the rest to help build this structure. In fact, one half of the money Esbjörn raised was dedicated to this project.

Concerning this endeavor, Esbjörn wrote in the *Lutheran Standard* (the Ohio Synod paper) on March 24, 1852:

> During my absence our people had begun to make bricks for the church in this place. But the heavy rainfall, which had continued for some time throughout the area, had again and again ruined thousands of unburned bricks, so that the poor people were very discouraged. But now they took hold again with renewed strength, battled with rain and storm beyond words. When at last the bricks were baked, which incidentally cost the life of one of our most valued members who had caught a serious cold one stormy night while he watched the kiln [remember this person, Mr. Alexander Anderson], the floods swept our sawmill away so

that we were compelled to haul the timbers thirty-four miles over very bad roads through the unusually deep swamp. Stone, lime, sand, and other materials must be brought from distant places. But in spite of it all, we began building a brick structure with a basement, measuring 30 by 45 feet. A choice village plot of about 10 acres was donated by the real-estate company, half of which will be for the church and half for the parsonage. We had hoped to have the basement ready for services by Christmas, but a severe cold spell set in, making it necessary to postpone operations until spring. On account of these difficulties, we have already spent most of our funds, since all of our supplies are bought at high prices, and the Swedes themselves have been able to contribute very little, because the rain has ruined fields, fences, and crops on many places and the farmers, consequently, have experienced real difficulties. In one way or another, most of the material for continuing the construction has been purchased, even though it will cost a great deal to complete the work. Not much help can be expected from the immigrants whose only capital is their time.

Indeed Esbjörn was fortunate to have the $1500 from his trip and $200 from the Andover Land Company to underwrite the project.

In that same March 24, 1852, issue of the *Standard* he also reported the project had become more complicated:

> I am sorry to have to say that we cannot complete the building without further help. Our people consist of new settlers in a strange, uncultivated land. . . . Death has also robbed us of many valuable members and, even worse, a swarm of sectarian tradesman, farmers, etc., commissioned as preachers by other denominations, do their utmost to undermine the Lutheran congregations, draw their members away or at least chill their enthusiasm and make them discouraged.

This was in reference to the former blacksmith turned Methodist circuit rider, now Methodist presiding elder and financier, Jonas Hedstrom, who had organized the Andover Methodist Church in 1849 just before Esbjörn arrived. (That congregation disbanded in 1999, and one can see their most recent building from the road in front of the chapel by looking to the right, i.e., south. The structure is now owned by the Andover Historical Society.)

Also included in this scathing attack were the Swedish Baptists, led by Gustaf Palmquist, who as a Lutheran came to Andover to assist Esbjörn. Instead Esbjörn sent him to Galesburg to minister to the Lutherans there, but Palmquist soon became a Baptist and started organizing Baptist churches. And do not forget the menacing presence of the nearby Bishop Hill Colony. Esbjörn's account in the *Standard* (March 24, 1852) continued:

> It is therefore imperative that our church buildings are made ready as soon as possible, otherwise the enemies of our church will mock us, saying, "This man began to build but was not able

to finish," and moreover, our friends will perhaps be led to say, "Why did you not first count the cost?"

But progress was slow. In the July 14, 1852, issue of the *Standard* he wrote:

> Our churches in Moline and Iowa have progressed so far that they have been in use several Sundays, although not yet completely boarded up or furnished with benches, pulpit, etc. We continue every day to work on our brick church in Andover, but little more than the basement is finished. I hope that within a few weeks we can gather in the basement. It will be a beautiful and substantial building, if we only can obtain more money.

On August 16, 1852, Esbjörn reported in this same periodical the receipt of $55 for the church building, which still lacked "a steeple and bell, floor and roof in the sanctuary and sacristy, plastering, pulpit, benches, etc."

III. A TURN OF EVENTS

Esbjörn's greatest concern was no longer the building project or competing preachers; it was the cholera epidemic, which was sweeping through the neighborhood. From a quarterly report he made to his patron, the AHMS, on September 20, 1852, it was evident the dark shadow of death hovered over church, home, and village:

> The cholera has raged among us during this quarter. Large parties of emigrants have arrived from time to time, with practically every one of them poverty stricken and a large number sick with diarrhea and cholera. It is impossible to describe the difficulties which arise under such circumstances in a rural colony: what difficulties in obtaining shelter, food, medicine, nursing care, etc., for all of them. They have been accommodated in the church, in barns, in cottages, etc., and in the midst of my own afflictions, I have had four of these immigrant families in my own home, every one of them, except three sick; at least three of them dying of the cholera. All in all, we have buried at least forty persons. Finally, I succumbed to an attack of the illness, which left me in a weakened condition for a long time.

He noted that during the epidemic a large part of the lumber purchased for the church had to be used to make coffins for the poor, newly arrived immigrants, and his own wife, who, however, did not die of cholera. His obituary for her, which he submitted to the AHMS on September 9,1852, read:

> On July 11, my dearly beloved wife, my faithful companion in joys and sorrows, departed from this life, after suffering most grievously in giving birth to the ninth child, a little daughter who still lives. I need not relate how she gave up the comforts of her home, her friends and relatives and accompanied me to the distant wilderness of the West for the purpose of helping me build up the Kingdom of Christ among our countrymen; how she al-

ways remained faithful to me under every adversity, and often had faith and courage sufficient to strengthen me when I felt downcast by labor and difficulty; how she took an active part in all the activities of the missionary work which could and should be done by a woman. I need not speak, either, of that bitter grief which has pierced the hearts of my five motherless children.

On the headstone the epitaph which Esbjörn, the sorrowing husband, inscribed reads:

Here rests the wife of the first Swedish Lutheran Pastor in Andover,
L. P. Esbjörn;
Amalia Maria Lovisa Gyllenböga,
Born 17/10, 1810
Died 11/7,1852

The newborn daughter survived her mother only three months and was buried beside her. In a little over a year, Esbjörn's second wife died, and the two women and four of Esbjörn's children are buried to the immediate right of the exit to this building in the southwest corner of the cemetery. Moreover, what appears to be the church's front lawn is in fact an area containing the unmarked gravesites of those for whom tombstones were never erected. Even on the stones that are present today, a good number of them give the death date as the early 1850s.

IV. A DUAL PURPOSE

On January 24, 1853, Esbjörn reported to the AHMS:

> We have not been able to finish our church building. There is a roof on the church, but an opening in it of 10 feet square in the end intended for a steeple and no floor except in the basement where we have our meeting without a stove. . . . We have worshipped all winter under an open sky.

It must be noted that the steeple was never built, the opening finally being closed over. And this in a congregation that now numbered 210 communicants, up dramatically from the 10 original members only three years earlier.

In one respect the Andover church became a pattern for daughter churches; it was constructed with two stories. This was an American accommodation. The lower story, or basement, was completed first, and for several years its chief significance was as a hospital and immigrant home. Indeed, the entire church was made to serve this purpose. An immigrant, Helson Gustus, recalled an episode which was typical. The setting was the year 1854, and this building was not quite completed. He had arrived with a party of twelve people, after having walked all the way from Geneseo while a hired driver hauled their goods by wagon. They arrived in Andover about dusk. In the words of Gustus, as reported in the January 20, 1896, issue of *Augustana*:

The driver pulled up beside the Swedish church where we were to stop over night. The afternoon had been very hot and humid and a threatening thunder cloud hung on the western horizon. We stopped at the church because its basement quarters were used as sort of a poorhouse, or perhaps more correctly as a temporary shelter for poor settlers. We entertained the hope of spending the night in the church basement, but when we arrived we found it already full of people on account of which we were compelled to lie down on the grass outside the church. Just outside the church entrance there was a huge mound of clay which had been dug from the church basement. Leading to the entrance of the sanctuary was a large plank sawed from a big log, reaching from the church wall to the clay mound. Since the end of the plank on the church wall was much higher than that which rested on the clay heap, the angle was rather steep, and to give sure footing, cross pieces had been nailed to the plank. We were very tired after the long afternoon march, and we soon fell asleep. Meanwhile, an even larger party of immigrants arrived on the scene, and they too stopped at the church for rest. I was awakened about midnight by a sharp clap of thunder, and as I regained my senses enough to realize where I was, I suddenly discovered that I was almost submerged in water and floating clay. But where was my party? I found their footprints in the clay and followed them into the sanctuary—that is, I followed them, but with some difficulty. The cross pieces on the tilted plank were now so full of wet clay that I could find no footing. Finally, I got down on all fours and crawled up the plank and into the sanctuary. And after having crept into the church, I found that the place was absolutely crowded with sleeping immigrants. I crawled along up to the front section and succeeded in finding a place to lie down. I have never had the courage to inquire who it was that cleaned up the church after our visit. At daybreak we continued our journey to Berlin [Swedona], which we imagined would be something like Chicago.

The caretaker once declared that nearly every family coming to Andover lived for some time in the basement of this church.

V. EARLY ASSESSMENTS

It was not until Advent Sunday, December 3, 1854, that this building was dedicated in conjunction with a conference meeting. The minutes of this gathering record the following:

The members, who, after more than three years of work and struggle, now assembled in their completed church, joyously raised their songs of thanksgiving to the throne of God, and it was very apparent that they felt themselves greatly edified and strengthened to continue the Lord's work without wavering.

But an unidentified observer described the dedication service in another vein:

I recall when the church was dedicated. I felt that it was not sufficiently festive; none of the pastors (or few) wore the priestly altar-robes. Shortly before I emigrated to America, the church in Näslanda, Kalmar district, was dedicated. I was present and saw the bishop dressed in his festive vestments and the pastors garbed in their chasubles and heard fine organ music by the director of music.[1]

This was not a Swedish setting, but the American frontier. The building did not replicate the Swedish scene, but presented an American view—more a rustic chapel than a "real" church.

But it was not a Swedish building; this was not Esbjörn's objective. It was an American public building on the 1850s Illinois prairie. The pain of this reality was cogently expressed by Eric Norelius, one of the earliest commentators on the Swedish immigrant church:

> The pulpit, surrounded by a half-circular altar rail in the middle of one gable, looked like one of those cupboards for pots and pans which were commonly found in Swedish homes years ago. The pulpit had the size and appearance of a salt barrel with a side portion removed and it was placed right up against the wall.[2]

VI. A LITURGICAL LEGACY?

This points to one of the most interesting features of this building: the architectural style of the altar and pulpit with a small altar table topped by a pulpit. It is my understanding that this style is rare in Sweden, but this style was the arrangement of the altar and pulpit at the chapel in the factory community at Oslättfors, where Esbjörn served as a chaplain just before he emigrated to America.

While the exterior of this building does not look like a Swedish church, neither does the chancel, except in rare instances. This style was carried over to the "new church" in 1870, and also became the chancel design in Moline until 1918. The example introduced by Esbjörn here became very common in the Swedish American churches in this area of west central Illinois. To list them all (insofar as I have been able to determine chancel styles in this area) produces a list including Swedona, New Windsor, Altona, Henderson Grove, and Galesburg along "Swedish Alley," i.e., Highway 150 between Moline and Knoxville. Also included would be Geneseo and Princeton. However, I have not located pictures of the interiors of other churches in the original area of the Andover parish to learn how complete this pulpit-altar style was in the latter half of the nineteenth century.

And the style was common in churches outside the area as well—at least in the pictures I have been able to view. Among these were the oldest congregation in New England at Brockton, Massachusetts; Bristol, Connecticut; Jamestown, New York; La Porte and Chesterton, Indiana; Ishpeming

---

[1] Sam Rönnegård, *Prairie Shepherd: Lars Paul Esbjörn and the Beginning of the Augustana Lutheran Church*, trans. G. Everett Arden (Rock Island: Augustana Book Concern, 1952) 232.

[2] Ibid.

and Grand Rapids, Michigan; First in St Paul, Augustana in Minneapolis, First in Duluth, Cambridge, and Parkers Prairie, Minnesota; First and Zion, Rockford, and Sycamore, Illinois; Swedesburg, Chariton, and First in Des Moines, Iowa; Salinas and Andover Lutheran, Windom, Kansas, Vermilion, South Dakota, and Portland, Oregon.

I saw the most practical reason for this arrangement in a picture of the 1879 sod church built at Funk, Nebraska. It seemed just right in that situation. Moreover, this style is also found in very early Norwegian-American churches as, for example, the oldest Norwegian-American church, Muskego, now preserved on the campus of Luther Seminary, St. Paul, Minnesota, and the Jefferson Prairie, Wisconsin, "West" church where the Augustana Synod was organized.

VII. THE BUILDING IS PRESERVED

According to the historical narrative of Andover resident A. E. Anderson, written in the 1920s, a decade after construction began on the "new church," the trustees determined to sell or tear down the old church and build a frame school house near the "new church" to which "ladies with infants and small children could retire when needed during the long services on Sunday, as it was noted it was general for wives and children to come to church in those days." Thus the proposition had merit, but Mrs. Anna M. Anderson, widow of Alexander Anderson, who perished in the making of the brick for the old church, and Mrs. Jonas Anderson appeared in person at the annual business meeting of the congregation and said, "No, it shall stand as long as we live at least." And it was reported that no one dared oppose. In fact, it was decided not only to preserve the old church, but also to restore it and make it more attractive than ever. Thus, it was again put to use and served the congregation for many years as a schoolhouse and a congregational hospice.

This was the first in a series of refurbishing endeavors. In 1948, at the centennial of the organization of a congregation in New Sweden, Iowa, the Augustana Synod began work once again to restore the chapel. Then in 1973 the Illinois Synod of the Lutheran Church in America assumed ownership of the building, and a Jenny Lind Chapel Committee took charge of the preservation attempts. On June 13, 1976, in the Bicentennial Year, the building was rededicated after a $30,000 effort funded by the Illinois Bicentennial Commission, Lutheran Brotherhood, and more than 200 friends. Now the Chapel is in the care of a committee of the Northern Illinois Synod of the Evangelical Lutheran Church in America.

But it is more than a monument and museum to the extraordinarily difficult first years the Swedish immigrants experienced here on the American prairie. Sunday evening vespers are conducted by pastors of area ELCA churches in the summer months, and the Office of Chaplain at Augustana College and the Andover congregation arrange a celebration of Holy Communion here just before the Christmas break. Also the Jenny Lind Committee of the Northern Illinois Synod conducts a Founders Day Service on a Sunday afternoon in April with a Swedish high mass in the fall.

But what I want you to consider is that while this building was constructed for the Swedish immigrant, it was the initial intention of the pastor that these immigrants be quickly brought into the American mainstream and, in spite of those exceedingly difficult years, this building still bears testimony to that mission.

The "New Church" at Andover: A Swedish Retreat

Myron J. Fogde

At this point in our tour we are at a place of transition: the transition between the early Lars Paul Esbjörn of Americanization and the subsequent Jonas Swensson of strong Swedish attachment. These first two pastors in Andover represented two contrasting views: the original religious leader hoped for a better religious milieu in an American environment, whereas the second leader feared the immigrants would lose their cultural and religious underpinnings if they Americanized too quickly. I have made suggestions as to how Jenny Lind Chapel of the Esbjörn era represents the first accent, and now I will suggest how this "new church" built during the pastorate of Swensson represents the counter thesis.

What is initially important is to seek to get a handle on how this transition occurs theologically, which will give us a deeper understanding not only of the architecture we are seeing today, but also the early history of the Swedish immigrant that sets the stage for the origin and early development of the Augustana Synod.

I. A THEOLOGICAL TURN

When Esbjörn arrived in Andover to begin his ministry of putting down the roots of the Swedish Lutheran Church, he labored in the midst of fellow Swedish immigrant religious leaders, the Methodist Jonas Hedstrom in Andover, the "prophet" Eric Jansson at Bishop Hill, and the Baptist Gustaf Palmquist in Rock Island. Whereas Esbjörn and Palmquist disagreed strongly over baptism from the moment Palmquist left Lutheranism to become a Baptist, a slower split developed between Esbjörn and the ardent perfectionists Hedstrom and Jansson. Jansson preached a misunderstanding of Luther in which he accepted only one-half of the Reformer's insight that we are at the same time a saint and a sinner; teaching instead that by faith a person could leave sin behind and become a perfect saint and even pass this character on to the children. Jansson, however, died in May of 1850, just months after Esbjörn arrival, but the theological warfare continued with Jansson's successors at Bishop Hill. Hedstrom taught a corrupted Wesleyanism in which he refused to acknowledge the presence of evil in a mature Christian. Both men saw west central Illinois as an Eden where the human race could start over and not experience sin, but dwell in the perfection of God's children.

In contemplating a move to America, Esbjörn had been in contact with Hedstrom. The latter had been somewhat hesitant about having a competitor in the area, but then thought if Esbjörn could be converted to Methodism, they could be co-workers. Soon after his arrival, Esbjörn realized the two could not work together. This was not initially because of theological differences; rather, it consisted of a clash of personalities. Actually Esbjörn imbibed some of the same pietistic spirit as Hedstrom at the time of his arrival. Though formally but not thoroughly trained in the Lutheran tradition in preparation for ordination, Esbjörn had also been personally influenced by classic Lutheran pietism and by the Methodism that had been brought to Sweden. Even his pastoral methods conformed to Methodist patterns. He took many liberties in his use of the liturgical handbook; he packed his ministerial vestments away in a chest; and he arranged for "Methodistic" prayer and testimonial meetings.

Like frontier Methodism, Esbjörn also acknowledged the lasting effect in his own life of a "new birth" moment experienced at a religious rally. The effect of this had not left him when he organized the Swedish Evangelical Lutheran Church in Andover in 1850 as evidenced in a letter written to Peter Wieselgren on May 23:

> I have adopted the practice of the best denominations here, not to admit anyone into the congregation before his heart is changed so that he knows his evil deeds and has a real hunger for the righteousness of Jesus Christ. Because of that, my congregation here in Andover consists of only twenty-eight persons, but more are attending services.[1]

This view was also reflected in his patron, the Congregational-Presbyterian American Home Missionary Society that, in fact, insisted upon it as a condition for financial support. Just imagine what a society would emerge in this new land peopled by the reborn, and as already promoted by these denominations at work in the American West.

However, there was also strong attachment to the Swedish national church. In spite of its character in the mid-nineteenth century, and Esbjörn's experience with it, he stated in a greeting to Scandinavian immigrants shortly after his arrival in Andover:

> You are born and raised in the Lutheran faith. . . . Don't leave it. . . . Retain the teaching, but change your life. Seek association

---

[1] Lars Esbjörn, "Greetings to the Swedish, Norwegian and Danish Emigrants," trans. John Norton (typescript, 1997).

with such Lutheran congregations in this country which recognize the Augsburg Confession and use Luther's Small Catechism.

But this was not enough:

> Don't ever believe that a human, who by knowingly sinning, breaking their baptismal compact, can be saved without conversion. . . . No, if you've not been converted before, you have never experienced any anguish in your heart for your sins, and have no fear of damnation, as well as a new, blessed life in your heart; so hasten to turn yourself to Jesus Christ, like the Lost Son, to Him (Luke 15), confess your sins and pray for grace and forgiveness in His name, that you may be given grace to become God's child, so that your soul dies in grace, when you are called home.[2]

Fellow Lutheran, Eric Norelius, in critiquing Esbjörn's early preaching in Andover, made this claim: "It seemed that he placed too much emphasis upon the work of grace within man, and not enough upon Christ and his work for us. And he stressed the doctrine of sanctification at the expense of justification through faith."[3]

This was also evidence of a tension between popular Lutheran piety and Methodist piety that Esbjörn did acknowledge, but at the moment had little trouble with. Before he left Andover after a six year pastorate, Esbjörn acknowledged: "I came here with great confidence in Methodism, and it is only through the bitterest kind of experience that my eyes have finally been opened to the wretchedness and sectarianism of this system."[4]

Esbjörn had quickly modified his thinking from his original position, which included his briefly considering becoming a Methodist in order to secure financial assistance. This was before he received support from the AHMS. The story is that his wife helped him make this particular decision, asserting: "I will rather work as a washwoman, than forsake my faith."[5]

He admitted in the spring of 1852 that he had "seen, read, and experienced much"[6] since leaving Sweden. His pietistic/perfectionist underpinning was not providing the results he had expected, and by 1853 he was maturing into a distinctly Lutheran theologian. On May 13 he wrote to Eric Norelius, whom he sponsored at the Lutheran Seminary in Ohio: "I have found it necessary once again to read through the symbolical books, with special reference to the various interpretations and contentions which we meet here."

Esbjörn was now making a distinction between "born-again" pietism leading to perfection and the classical teachings of Luther and Wesley. This was a theological perspective he would continue to develop after 1856, first

---

[2] Ibid.
[3] Sam Rönnegård, *Prairie Shepherd; Lars Paul Esbjörn and the Beginning of the Augustana Lutheran Church* (Rock Island: Augustana Book Concern, 1952) 232.
[4] Ibid.
[5] Oscar Olson, *The Augustana Lutheran Church in American: Pioneer Period 1846-1860* (Rock Island: Augustana Book Concern, 1950) 119.
[6] S. Rönnegård, *Prairie Shepherd*, 224.

at Princeton, then as a professor in Springfield, and finally, before his return to Sweden, in Chicago at the newly established Augustana College and Theological Seminary. Gustaf Unonius commented that this shift was to be found frequently in the earliest Swedish Lutheran leaders. He bemoaned that such persons had been led to a practice whereby: "regardless of the meaning of child baptism, the ministers' sharp eye made sure that a person was 'born-again' before he could become a church member or take part in the privileges of the congregation."[7]

As Esbjörn turned on Hedstrom and the Methodists, he also continued to fight the Janssonists. And the Bishop Hill colonists responded in like kind; as observed in the comment of Janssonist Eric Olsson: "He [Esbjörn] is held for nothing here among those who rightly understand the Scriptures."[8] How delightful and challenging it would have been to have gathered these three religious leaders around the pot bellied stove in the colony store in Bishop Hill in the winter of 1849. It never happened, but it might have. Hedstrom and Jansson did meet for a scheduled three-day debate, but the proceedings were cut short in less than a day when "some uncouth language was used."[9] Hedstrom fared no better with Esbjörn. The Lutheran pastor wrote that in his first year at Andover:

> He [Hedstrom] continually sought to destroy the Lutheran Church. He wanted to have a public discussion with me which I declined, but I did not get rid of him before I told him straight out that the Bible forbade me, saying: "Avoid disputings of one corrupted in mind and bereft of the truth." (I. Tim. 6:5).[10]

It was in this tumultuous, entrepreneurial religious setting that Esbjörn lost the optimistic vision of humankind and society he brought with him to America. The more perfectionist Jansson and Hedstrom never did lose their optimism. Esbjörn developed a greater and greater appreciation of the Sacraments, especially Baptism, as a result of a series of articles in the *Lutheran Standard*. He wrote to Eric Norelius on January 30, 1856: "I have received clearer light concerning the gospel and know that in Christianity the new birth occurs in baptism and not specifically in the conversion of the sinner in later life." He also developed an increased appreciation of the Lord's Supper. One wonders if he had built a second church in Andover if he would have continued the altar-pulpit arrangement of the Jenny Lind Chapel.

He even renounced revivalism, as he saw it as alien to the spirit of Lutheran Christianity. His return to classical Lutheranism raises the question of how far he had roamed both in Sweden and in America. A point to remember is that he appeared a day late at the gathering that produced the

---

[7] Gustaf Unonius, *A Pioneer in Northwest America*, trans. J. O. Backlund, 2 vols. (Minneapolis: University of Minnesota Press, 1960) 2, 204.
[8] Lilly Setterdahl, "Emigrant Letters by Bishop Hill Colonists from Nora Parish," *Western Illinois Regional Studies* (Fall, 1979) 144.
[9] Sigrid Stoneberg, Interview with Philip Stoneberg, 1915, Stoneberg Collection, Bishop Hill Heritage Association Archives, Steeple Building (Bishop Hill, IL) 3.
[10] O. Olson, *The Augustana Lutheran Church in America*, 119.

Synod of Northern Illinois in 1851. He missed the adoption of a constitution that declared the Augsburg Confession "mainly correct." He protested and brought in his three congregations—Andover, Moline, and Galesburg—under this protest and worked to have this subscription changed, and in 1853 was successful in his endeavors.

Today we can appreciate Esbjörn's vision of the potential of the human and society, and the struggle which ensued as he came to another understanding, theologically more Lutheran. The transition from the early Esbjörn slant on perfectionism as appropriate to the American religious scene has taken place, and the "new church" embodies this shift.

II. THE NEED FOR A "NEW CHURCH"

Esbjörn resigned his pastorate at Andover and moved to Princeton, Illinois, in the summer of 1856. After a troubled interim Jonas Swensson, coming from Jamestown, New York, assumed the pastorate in 1858; five years later in 1863 the need for a larger building was noted.

This expression occurred in the midst of the American Civil War; yet here in Andover this was a time of exploding growth in the congregation. Within five months of Swensson's arrival the congregation had increased by a third. In 1860, at the time of the organization of the Augustana Synod, this was the largest congregation represented, and in 1865 this rural parish was second only to Immanuel in Chicago in terms of size.

This was true even though the geographic extent of the parish, that is, the area served first by Esbjörn and then by Swensson, was constantly getting smaller. The original parish, from Moline in the north to Galesburg in the south and from Princeton in the east to at least Berlin (Swedona) in the west, was seeing independent congregations being organized with regularity. With the decline in the size of the territory there was such a growth in the immigrant population that the congregation was actually rapidly increasing in numbers. From the minutes of synod meetings these statistics document the story. Between 1850 and 1856 six congregations were organized within the area originally visited by Esbjörn; between 1858 and 1873, the era of Swensson's pastorate, eleven more congregations were organized within this territory. Yet the communicant membership of the Andover church continued to rise from 210 in 1854 to 339 in 1860, to 943 when the new church was put into use in 1868, and peaking just before Swensson's death in 1873 at 1082. This was the communicant membership, not the baptized membership.

At the 1863 annual meeting discussions were held on whether to enlarge the existing church or build a new structure. The decision was to take interim action: to put a hole in the floor so that those forced to be seated in the basement, and watched over by deacons to assure quietness, could hear the service from above.

At a special meeting of the congregation on September 28, 1864, it was decided a building project should be undertaken the following spring. A building committee was selected with one of the five members being Pastor Swensson. The men were to obtain building plans and cost estimates. The committee was instructed to plan "a church large enough to accommodate one thousand persons."[11] What a building—in a town that did not exceed 200 inhabitants. Yes, this was to be a large building as the congregation recommended the dimensions at the first meeting: 100 feet in length, 60 feet in width and 75 feet in height. The tower was to measure 16 x 16 and rise to a height of 118 feet.[12]

At a special meeting of the congregation almost exactly two months later, November 23, 1864, it was decided the structure should be built of brick. Mr. Charles Ulricson of Peoria was contracted to draw up the plans. Solicitation for funds from parish members was also begun. By May 12, 1865, $5,978.84 had been collected (the month the Civil War ended) and eventually parish members gave the entire cost of the building ($38,927). Some of the pledges were difficult to collect, but at the annual meeting of 1873, five years after the building had been put into use, the indebtedness stood at only $1,658.40.

At a meeting in January 1865, five people asked the congregation to reconsider building with brick and suggested wood instead. On February 19, the congregation overwhelmingly reaffirmed the decision to build with brick. In October of that year, Pastor Swensson reported that "about 550,000 bricks had been made." A native of Andover writing the history of his hometown said of this endeavor, "It could not have been built, but for the fact that the members of the congregation donated work to make the brick on the Charles Charlson place just ½ mile south of the church, and all the stone, lime and sand and wood material was hauled by donated teams and men."[13] Records indicate that "one day of labor at the kilns was required from every male member."

However, these bricks were stacked, and at a June 19, 1865, meeting it was decided to postpone building for one year to allow more time for raising funds.

III. THE "NEW CHURCH" EMBODIES A RETURN TO SWEDEN

Let's interrupt this narrative to seek to provide an interpretive format. I have tried to make the case that the early Esbjörn was committed to becoming an American, and I have suggested that the look of Jenny Lind Chapel represents this; moreover, we have considered how theologically he rather quickly denounced this idea and became increasingly a Swedish Lutheran. But Esbjörn is gone—he returned to Sweden in 1863—and Jonas

---

[11] Sources for the information and quotes pertaining to the building of the "new church" in Andover come from Emmet E. Eklund, *His Name Was Jonas; A Biography of Jonas Swensson* (Rock Island: Augustana Historical Society, 1980) and Carl P. Edblom, *Memorial Album: The Sixty Year Celebration, 1910*. Trans. Margaret Nelson, 1982.

[12] Actual measurements are: 125 feet long, 60 feet wide, 35 feet to top of ceiling from center aisle, and 136 feet to top of spire.

[13] "Andover History Revised by A. E. A." (typescript, 31).

Swensson is now the pastor. A son, Carl, makes this comment about his father: "My father could feel nothing other than an alien in the new world. He was and remained a Swede."[14]

Compare Swensson's thought with the description of the immigrant father drawn by Marcus Lee Hansen in his famous address "The Problem of the Third Generation Immigrant" given before the Augustana Historical Society in 1937. Hansen declared:

> Even the immigrant father who compromised most willingly in adjusting his outside affairs to the realities that surrounded him insisted that family life, at least, should retain the pattern that he had known as a boy. Language, religion, customs and parental authority were not to be modified simply because the home had been moved four or five thousand miles to the westward.[15]

I suggest that we put this analysis in the broader picture of what I have come to conclude became dominant in many European churches that came to America. The thesis is this: In the face of increased immigration, the immigrant churches came to assume a burden that they had not necessarily expected, that of becoming the pillow to cushion the shock the non-English speaking immigrant experienced upon arrival in America. A development of this was that the immigrant church turned its back on Americanization and became more and more ethnic, or in the case of the Augustana Synod in the American West, increasingly Swedish in character. I posit the interpretation that the "new church" at Andover (still standing) represents this tone of the 1860s after the career of the "Americanist" Esbjörn is past.

Helpful in defending this interpretation was an incident in 1975 when I hosted a number of Swedish pastors coming to Rock Island to learn how the church in Sweden could survive without tax money as the Swedish government was contemplating the separation of church and state. (This is now being implemented in stages.) I took these gentlemen on tours to Bishop Hill, Andover, and First Lutheran Church, Moline. One of the pastors, Dr. Åke Haglund, a member of the clerical staff of Brännkyrka in Stockholm, was asked if a Swede were to enter the building we are now in would he or she feel at home. With almost no hesitation this Swedish pastor responded: "If a Swede would enter this building, and look around, sit down, and hear the familiar Swedish liturgy and hymns, he or she would be perfectly at home." In fact, he went on to assert, "for the time that person spent in this building the individual would not be in America, but at home in Sweden." His primary point was that the architectural style of this building was nearly an exact copy of that seen in parts of rural Sweden.

The pastor made one more assessment when he attested that nowhere outside of Sweden had he seen the Swedish yellow so faithfully reproduced.

---

[14] E. Eklund, *His Name was Jonas*, 49.

[15] Marcus Lee Hansen, *The Problem of the Third Generation Immigrant* (Rock Island: Swenson Swedish Immigrant Research Center and Augustana College Library, 1987) 13.

I do not know how much fluctuation is tolerable in Swedish yellow, but I do know that the Swedish blue in the flag comes in widely different shades—sometimes determined, I suspect, by fading in the sunlight. But it may well have been the windows to which he was referring, not the walls. As I do not know the paint color of the 1870s, and the windows, of course, have been constant since they were installed in 1891, almost a quarter century and certainly a full generation after the first services were held in this sanctuary.

Now back to Swensson. Of the early immigrant pastors, he was the one least affected by the revival movement in Sweden, and he had a more positive relationship with the national church. Having said this, it must be recognized that there yet was a strong current of the accent on sanctification in his preaching, but within a strong churchly tradition—remember that in 1870, less than two years after worship began in this building, he was elected the second president of the Augustana Synod—at the time it became exclusively a Swedish body, the Norwegians having just withdrawn. It was also at that meeting the synod formally declared the work among the immigrants a very high priority. Do indeed this building and Swensson presage the future of the Augustana Synod?

However, there was a bit of Esbjörn in Erland Carlsson, Pastor of Immanuel, Chicago. He asserted that the Swedish language would be dead by the mid 1890s, and encouraged a more rapid transition than Swensson was willing to accommodate. This tension was evident in the periodical *Augustana* and later between *Augustana* and *The Lutheran Companion*. It was ultimately not a question of using English, but when English would be used. Swensson supervised the building of the "new church," but two years after his death in 1873, Erland Carlsson became the pastor here in Andover. What might the building have looked like if Carlsson had supervised its construction?

IV. DISTINCTIVE SWEDISH FEATURES

Now returning to our narrative, but within this interpretive framework. At the special congregational meeting on November 22, 1864, when the decision was made to build with brick, and a Peoria architect was contracted, it was stated that the ceilings and windows should be rounded at the top. This was indeed carried out and also, as requested, there was a barrel ceiling—in this church constructed of wood. We shall note a more perfect plaster barrel ceiling in the Moline church. Is this Swedish? I posit that, in fact, it is. This is common in Romanesque Italy, but not in the more Gothic style of Germany. Pastor Lynn Bergren, current incumbent, has told me that last year when a group of Swedes were visiting the building, they did comment on the windows and ceiling as a feature they immediately recognized as familiar Swedish ecclesiastical architecture. Let us make a distinction between straight rectangular windows like those in Jenny Lind Chapel, the more pointed Gothic window tops we will see later in Moline, and the rounded tops we see here and evident in Augustana Synod churches more insistent upon being particularly Swedish in character. Then also consider the barrel ceilings, not the flat ceilings that come to a point or achieve this in steps, but rather the rounded vault as significant in church buildings designed to be emphatically Swedish.

Also in the initial stage of planning it was suggested that there be a tower at the south gable and that this provide an entrance. While this is common in Sweden, so is it general in the Germanic world at large. But another, also European feature, is the placing of two entrances, one on either nave wall. I have seen this also in Sweden and have found it quite common in larger English parish churches as well. I do not think it is inherent in American design. And in looking at a goodly number of pictures of Augustana Synod churches built in the nineteenth century, I have found very few buildings with these European, and definitely Swedish, nave entrances. The closest parallels to this building I have found were in the nineteenth century designs at Center City (Chisago Lake) Minnesota, Vasa, Minnesota, and Stanton, Iowa.

In the spring of 1868 the bricklaying was completed and the interior finishing begun. Benches were put in place and Swensson himself fashioned a temporary altar. The first service was held in the church on November 15, 1868. At that time the congregation numbered 943 communicants and a baptized membership of over 1900. No wonder the original proposal was for a church to seat a thousand people.

The permanent pews were rushed to completion and the altar-pulpit arrangement completed just in time for the tenth anniversary synod meeting held here in June, 1870. Note that the altar-pulpit is a more elegant version of that at the Jenny Lind Chapel and similar to a significant number of Augustana Synod churches in the nineteenth century.

A pipe organ was installed in 1875 and a bell weighing 2,471 pounds was hung in the tower in 1881. In 1891 an altar painting, depicting Jesus being taken down from the cross, was finished and hung—and then removed in 1956. There was a twin to this painting in the 1887 church at New Scandia, Minnesota, also a product of the B. Lundahl Studio in Moline. Recall that the stained glass windows were also installed in 1891.

One of the most interesting stories, and one typical of Protestantism in the nation at that time, concerns the symbol at the top of the tower. The architect planned for an urn at this location. Swensson was strongly opposed, and since there was no time for a congregational meeting, he and the building committee had a golden gilded cross placed at the highest point of the church. Five members objected to the symbol and declared—some indication of being in a less than sober state—that this symbol would indicate the church was Roman Catholic. The number five required the calling of a special congregational meeting, which was held on October 15, 1867. For the sake of peace it was decided to take the cross down, but by whom? The building foreman refused to do so, and the enemies of the cross did not dare to remove the cross because it was so near to heaven. Another congregational meeting was held on November 6, and it was voted to rescind the motion to take it down, but a compromise was reached in placing a copper globe under the cross. The meaning of the globe symbol was not explained. The whole episode demoralized Swensson for a time. He even seriously considered submitting his resignation as a result of the controversy. A globe and cross are still in place—but not copper or gold.

Documentation in the Andover records suggests that Jonas Swensson was adamant about stylistic considerations. He was going to replicate a rural Swedish church in rural Henry Country, Illinois. Yet in Andover, Swensson—from within a Lutheran confessional and churchly stance—made a strong emphasis on sanctification, and left intact the altar-pulpit design that Esbjörn had known in his last chapel in Sweden and incorporated into Jenny Lind Chapel. We must return to this altar-pulpit arrangement when we visit First, Moline, and note how that congregation handled this issue.

As noted earlier, I have almost no other example of such extensive Swedish church architecture as seen in Andover. I think Swensson and that building are a very strong example of the immigrant church turning inward in the face of a huge, continuing immigration so that the church became a place of familiarity, a comfort zone as it were, for those finding themselves in an alien land and culture.

Moline: An Example of an Early Swedish-American Urban Parish

Myron J. Fogde

On a Scandinavian tour in the summer of 1992, my wife and I visited Lillehammer, Norway, in the months preceding the Olympic games scheduled in that area. As we entered the city we soon came to the brow of a hill that allowed us to look down on the central city. The dominating structure that rose up from that lower level was the Lillehammer parish church. The building stood out because of its size and the tall tower with a clock facing in each direction. Some months later, watching the Olympic games on TV, the logo chosen to open the nightly coverage was that church tower with the large clock faces.

I invite you at this moment to transplant yourself back to the early 1880s. While standing at the brow of the hill overlooking downtown Moline from the south, the sight before you will be this large church building and its somewhat stunted tower (because of financial reasons the spire was never built) and the large clock with a face in each direction. You will note this dominating building anchors the west end of Moline's downtown and towers over the John Deere factories and allied industrial plants just to the north along the Mississippi River.

I. A SWEDISH PARISH

Ecclesiastically, the scene before you is very European. The new church does not house a congregation so much as it identifies a parish, a parish originally including Rock Island as well as Moline. A congregation is the typical American ecclesial organization, a voluntary group of people who have come together to pursue religious and other goals. A parish, however, is a geographical area in which a church building is located, a pastor in residence, and the two have a spiritual responsibility for all living in that defined area.

As Swedes in significant numbers were coming to this developing industrial center, many worked in the factories, while others engaged in endeavors supporting the lives of those who did. And part of the cultural and religious baggage that these Swedes brought with them was the concept that there be one Lutheran parish in Moline-Rock Island no matter how large the community. Therefore, a church was to be built to serve all these Lutherans, and to be a place where they could all gather at one time.

It is easier to call the Moline church a parish church than it is to identify the "new church" in Andover this way. In Andover the large rural territory, initially included in the spiritual oversight of the Andover pastor, was quickly and repeatedly broken into smaller congregational units. In Moline there was only one reduction in the size of the parish for sixty years, that coming in 1870 when the residents of Rock Island organized their own parish and took some forty percent of the membership of the mother church with them. The parish concept continued in Moline uninterrupted for forty years, at which time two chapels were built "in the country," that is, "on the hill" away from the river valley. This was the English "chapel of ease" tradition in which, when distance or topography became too difficult for easy access, chapels would be built nearer to the people.

Finally, nearly twenty years after these chapels were built, a new congregation, Salem, was formed from these endeavors. Once this happened, the Moline parish idea was weakened, but not dissolved, and in time other neighborhood congregations arose. Yet First Church, as it became known after 1919, retained the parish idea, serving people from a wide distance including Augustana College. But in the 1880s we are in the midst of Moline as a single parish with a parish church built for the expanding city.

II. THE BEGINNING OF THIS PARISH ENDEAVOR

Swedish immigrants began to arrive in this area in the 1840s, and in 1849 they organized the first Swedish religious institution, which was a Methodist Church. This had been organized by Jonas Hedstrom the same year he established the Andover Methodist Church. The Moline congregation continues today at Bethel-Wesley United Methodist Church located near the brow of the hill overlooking downtown Moline from the south.

The national church of Sweden, with its Lutheran confession, was soon to be here as well. On December 1, 1850, Lars Paul Esbjörn organized the Swedish Evangelical Lutheran Church in Moline less than nine months after the establishment of the Andover Church. It should be noted that in 1852 Gustaf Palmquist organized the first Swedish Baptist Church in Rock Island. Thus, from the beginning the Swedes were religiously fractured.

Construction of their own church building was begun by the Swedish Lutherans in 1851. This undertaking was abetted by the funds collected by Esbjörn on his eastern trip that year, including the sizeable gift from Jenny Lind. Writing in the *Lutheran Standard* on March 24, 1852, Esbjörn noted:

It was the desire of Miss Lind and many other contributors that we begin building first in the most important places. Accordingly a wooden church, 24 x 36 feet has been erected in the city of Moline, a town on the Mississippi. This building which has a roof but is not yet boarded up or furnished will be used for the first time next Sunday.

Of the money given by Jenny Lind, $340 was allocated to this project, and this building became the first Lutheran church to be built by Swedish immigrants in the American West. This church was not actually dedicated until January 11, 1857, but unlike Andover, did have a small bell tower housing a bell from a Mississippi River steamboat.

This simple wooden building soon became too small for the congregation and in 1858, one year after dedication, an addition of 14 feet was constructed, and again in 1866 a second enlargement, this time 12 feet in length and 14 feet in width.

A decade later on January 1, 1876, Pastor A. G. Setterdahl noted in his annual report that during the preceding year there had been 114 baptisms, 40 youth were confirmed, 10 weddings celebrated, and 36 funerals held (26 being for children). The congregation numbered 919 communicants with a total of 1,550 members.[1] In addition to the Sunday school, a parish school was operated for eight months of the year at the church and one month "in the country." Because of limited space, the older youth attended two months of the fall semester and two months of the spring semester, permitting the younger children to attend the other four months. Much of the concern at the annual meetings had to do with this school. It was abundantly clear that the small wooden church was no longer capable of housing the congregation and its activities.

When the present church was built, the earlier church was then moved so that it could continue to be used until the new church was ready. Eventually the building was sold to John Deere for use as a plow warehouse. Thus, there is no Moline version of Jenny Lind Chapel.

On the previous November 3, at a special meeting of the congregation, there was a unanimous vote to build a new church, and a committee of five (including Pastor Setterdahl) was identified "to work out a plan as to the size of the proposed building, and even make a plan for the structure, as well as the approximate cost of such a building." (This sounds just like what had been done in Andover a decade earlier.)

III. CONSTRUCTION OF THIS PARISH CHURCH

Now to interpret what was happening in the construction of the building according to the parish thesis which has been proposed.

---

[1] Elsie Hagberg has prepared an English translation of the Annual and Special Congregational Meetings, including pastors' annual reports that are the source for the content and quotations for these documents used in this essay.

Helpful here, as in Andover, have been the comments of the Stockholm pastor, the Rev. Dr. Åke Haglund. For as we toured this building, I again asked whether a Swede coming inside would feel at home. Without hesitation he turned to me and said: "Not if the individual were a Lutheran. There is very little here that would remind one of a Swedish Lutheran church." (Remember the chancel originally appeared like that at Andover.) I was a bit stunned, but he explained himself by noting: "The architecture here is that of a Swedish Baptist Church." Is there American support for this European observation?

Well, yes, indeed. Worship was first held in the sanctuary in October, 1878. Some six years earlier the first service was held in the new Immanuel Lutheran Church in Chicago, which had been built to replace the two-year-old structure destroyed in the Chicago Fire. When a church was built in Rockford, Illinois, in 1883, the historian of that congregation noted the building was heavily influenced by the style of Immanuel. He then commented:

> Although the overall design has Gothic lines, it is obvious that non-Lutheran influences were very strong. The location of the pulpit in the central position above the altar betrays the non-liturgical influence. This was the day of the pulpit-centered service led by Dwight Moody, Billy Sunday, and Charles Spurgeon.[2]

Gustav Peters, pastor of the Rockford church, stated: "It is not what one might describe as churchly appearing, but it is comfortable and easy to preach in."[3] Again we are left with the perplexing issue of this altar-pulpit arrangement so common in Augustana churches in the 1850s to the 1880s and occasionally still being built at the turn of the century.

According to the minutes of this congregation, the matter of altar-pulpit design was put in the hands of a committee and sub-committee. The tentative conclusion I have reached is that this style was not Swedish in particular, but represented a strain of piety in Lutheranism in the middle to the late nineteenth century. While teaching in Strasbourg in the "German" area of eastern France, I observed the same phenomenon of the "Word" taking precedence over the "sacrament" in what is called the "new church" built for the Lutherans in the 1870s. Rather than an ethnic style, I propose it was the expression of a pietistic perspective found among European Lutherans, brought to America, and frequently reproduced in the latter half of the nineteenth century. What makes Andover unique is that it has retained the arrangement. I repeat, it is not so much an American influence as it is a Lutheran pietistic influence, but it does occur at a time on the American scene when indeed there were well known "pulpit princes" who encouraged a pulpit centered style of church architecture even at the expense of sacramental observance or liturgical settings. In 1918 the altar-pulpit con-

---

[2] *Centennial: The First Evangelical Lutheran Church, Rockford* (Rockford: Creative Printed Crafts, 1954) 91.

[3] Ibid.

figuration we see today came into being and subsequently well served the more liturgical style of worship that came to characterize this congregation.

In the Andover church we noted the particularly Swedish style of the rounded windows and the barrel vault, much different from the straight rectangular windows and flat ceiling of the "American" Jenny Lind Chapel. Here we still have a Swedish barrel ceiling and rounded archways, but the more Gothic pointed windows, and as we will note, this was done intentionally. I am suggesting that while not entirely Swedish, this building was built to look like what Americans thought a church should look like—it should embody some Gothic characteristics.

But now we come to a distinctive feature of the building, the U-shaped balcony that originally was complete and connected to stairways where we now see organ chambers. This was what, more than anything else, led the Stockholm pastor to identify the building as non-Lutheran. Was the issue a building program by a group of people who did not have access to tax money, were dependent on voluntary contributions, and thus of necessity had to crowd people in pews in every available inch of space, including stacking them in a U-shaped balcony? (When I first visited this building in the mid-sixties, pews occupied nearly every inch of space and there was no narthex as the pews extended to the north wall.) The phenomenon of the U-shaped balcony is not totally absent in Sweden. The Great Cathedral Church in Stockholm, for example, has a partial U-shaped balcony added in the eighteenth century, and the style was well represented in urban Augustana churches. It began at Immanuel in Chicago and in the Immanuel daughter churches such as Salem, Trinity, and Bethlehem, but was continued in other churches such as First, St. Paul; First, Rockford; First, Jamestown; Augustana, Minneapolis (complete circular balcony); Immanuel, Omaha; Augustana, Sioux City; etc. This design was not an Andover replication of a rural Swedish Church, but was rather strongly influenced by American political and economic realities as well as European–American pietistic accents.

IV. THE MIND OF THE CONGREGATION

Now how is this documented in the actions of this congregation? At that initial meeting of the congregation on November 3, 1875, before a building committee was organized or an architect engaged, guidance came from the floor of the congregation. As a start it was suggested that the building should be made of brick and have a basement and a gallery on three sides of the sanctuary. Five weeks later on December 8, 1975, at another special meeting the five-person committee reported:

> 1. That the church building shall be built of stone and brick and be Gothic in style, 116 feet long, 62 feet wide, with five six foot spires approximately 120-130 feet high; 12 foot high basement of stone, the side walls of brick 27 feet high, and the gable shall also be brick 55 feet from the basement to the edge of the roof.

2. The basement shall be furnished according to the needs of the school [definitely an American consideration], but shall also allow room for smaller meetings and gatherings, and a study for the pastor, etc. The interior of the church shall be divided into four sections of benches, with a large aisle in the middle, and narrower aisles on each side of the "chancel arch" for the pulpit, etc.

3. The ceiling shall be supported by rows of pillars which will also support the gallery which will be built across the entrance and along both sides all the way forward; there will be an arched ceiling between the pillar sides and a flat ceiling out to the side walls.

4. The total cost of the building should not exceed $25,000.00.

5. The architecture will, on a whole, be simple and tasteful with good proportions without unnecessary costs and gaudiness, yet not lacking the necessary adornment for proper style and strength so that it gives a definite impression of being a church and have a worshipful atmosphere.

The report was accepted with the provision: "As soon as $15,000 has been subscribed, and $5,000 of that amount has been collected, the building project shall then be started."

On March 22, 1876, it was noted that $10,615 has been subscribed "from Swedes in the community." It was a parish idea—that all Swedes in the community were being solicited, not just members of the congregation. It was also noted: "Several persons, both within and outside of the congregation have promised to contribute a monetary gift as soon as the building project has actually begun." Again the parish idea, and then this was reinforced by this comment: "No subscriptions have as yet been collected among the Americans, but many of the business men have been contacted and several have promised to contribute." Some thought it best to approach the "Americans" once the building was actually under construction. At this March meeting it was recommended that there be no further delay in waiting for $15,000 to be subscribed and $5,000 collected, but that construction begin immediately so that the building might be enclosed by winter. Thus the corner stone was laid on June 15. Also for the first time there was mention of an architectural competition and the plan of J. N. Holms of Rock Island being accepted.

V. FINANCIAL STRUGGLES

On July 17 an enclosure date of December 1 was urged, with the notable exception of the tower which was an issue for years until the decision was made on June 22, 1881, to eliminate the spire, thus producing the rather "stunted" look the building has until this day. Also at this meeting was the first authorization to take out a loan. The issue of loans along with collecting the subscriptions made became a dominating problem for years—in fact, until the debt was paid off on June 9, 1889. We must recall that this project was being carried out in the wake of a national depression that began in 1873. Pastor H. O. Lindeblad noted in 1879: "The church was now enclosed, but not nearly finished, and a shrewd business man was needed to straighten out the tangled affairs." Lindeblad succeeded A. G. Setterdahl, who was pastor of the congregation during the planning and building of the basic structure. In the midst of the project Setterdahl read the following to the congregation (March 25, 1877):

> Because my health has been so wavering this winter, and the rest of the time I have been so broken down, I have in our Father's name, decided that I shall take a trip to the fatherland around the first of May this spring. I am hoping that through baths and rest during the summer that I might regain my health.

He was absent when the first service was held in the partially completed upper floor on October 13, 1878. Among those in attendance that day was John Fryxell. He noted in his memoir: "The basement was finished, but the upstairs was still unplastered. However, the upstairs was opened for service that Sunday for the first time, all previous services having been held in the basement. We sat on planks put out for the occasion."[4]

One month earlier, a supply pastor had presided over a special meeting to take out another loan. It is interesting that the resolution to take out this loan (one of numerous taken out, sometimes a loan with a lower rate of interest to pay the existing loan which was at a higher rate) was in English, not Swedish.

The strain on the pastor continued. After eight years in the pastorate, H. O. Lindeblad announced to the congregation on September 15, 1887, "I feel that the congregation feels that the lowering of the church debt, and the collection of the communicant's fees all depend on the congregation's pastor, and the responsibility rests upon his shoulders." Then, after announcing he had performed over 100 baptisms that year, he resigned, saying a man with better health and more talent was needed for the job. The congregation asked him to withdraw his resignation, and he did, and remained until 1892, three years after the debt had been retired.

As to the cost of the building, the basic structure came to about $19,000, and the furnishing and decorations raised the cost to slightly more than the $25,000 estimated by the building committee that made the original plans for the structure.

Even though the congregation was growing, the debt issue was not the only serious problem. There was a membership drain, as people who did not want to support the building of the large structure left the congregation to form Gustaf Adolph Lutheran Church, which in turn became the present First Covenant Church in Moline. It was noted in the pastor's annual report on January 1, 1877:

---

[4] Quoted in *A Century of Stewardship: First Lutheran Church, Moline, 1950.*

> Because of the dissatisfaction of some of our members in the beginning of the year [1876 just after the unanimous vote taken to build], and because of encouragement from people outside of the congregation, a new congregation has arisen beside this congregation and tried their utmost to draw other members away from this congregation. Even though our congregation has not suffered any great loss, it certainly caused many problems.

VI. THE BUILDING IS COMPLETED

The congregation continued to grow and shortly after his arrival H. O. Lindeblad told the congregation (June 17, 1879): "We are overjoyed in seeing so many people come regularly to the worship service, as we can hardly fit everyone in the sanctuary to listen quietly and reverently to God's word in the sermon."

Plans to finalize the upstairs sanctuary moved along. On February 25, 1880, the following resolution was adopted:

> That the pews be arranged in such a manner that there will be 5 aisles; one in the middle of the church, which will be 6 feet wide; one on each side of this section, they shall be 4 feet wide; finally one on each side along the wall which shall be 2 1/2 feet wide. The room will then be adorned with four sections of pews each of the pews will have a length of about 10 feet.

The pipe organ was dedicated on December 16, 1881. Also in that year the frescos were completed, and a year before the altar painting had been executed on the chancel wall.

In the pastor's report on January 2, 1882, he commented: "Our beautiful sanctuary has proven to be slightly small rather than too large." He reported the number of communicants as 1082 with 1800 baptized members. A year later it was noted that the benches were now in the balcony, and the shortened church tower was soon to be completed. And in 1884 the clock was placed in the tower.

Then at the annual meeting on January 1, 1887, a request was received to organize a Swedish and English Lutheran congregation at Augustana College and Theological Seminary. In evaluating the congregation's response, recall that Augustana moved to Rock Island just months before the decision was made to build a new church, and note how a new interpretation for the large building was presented in the response to this request:

> 1. Since the congregation agreed to build the new, costly church building, it was done largely with consideration of Augustana College, and the needs we have in common, and since the indebtedness is still very large, the congregation cannot approve this petition because of monetary reasons.
>
> 2. Many of the teachers, students, and other persons outside of the college confines, belong to this congregation; therefore it

would cause a great moral as well as a monetary loss for the congregation.

  3. Furthermore, the signers of the petition do not seem to be a sufficient number to organize a new congregation, inasmuch as the distance between the school and the two organized churches [the churches in Moline and Rock Island] seems to be insignificant.

  4. Furthermore, it is clear that, with the exception of the administering of the sacraments, the school can handle all that the average congregation can offer such as God's word in services, as well as personal care, discipline, etc. and it is even clear to this congregation that the college has more of these things than any congregation within the synod, and would not have any better results by organizing its own congregation.

So as the church building was completed, the parish idea was reaffirmed, and the college continued to be a part of it.

Eventually more congregations were organized; some Swedish-speaking and some English-speaking, yet the parish did not become a neighborhood church, but continued to draw members from a wide area.

It is hard today to visualize the Sunday school of 928 as reported in the 1894 annual report, or to visualize a men's Sunday evening Swedish Bible study drawing 150 participants begun in 1912, the year the English speaking Trinity Lutheran Church was organized out of this congregation.

Jenny Lind Chapel was designed as an American building, the Andover "new church" was to replicate rural Swedish churches, and this building was to be churchly, but strongly in an American context. Thus, in these buildings of the two oldest congregations in the Augustana Synod, celebrating their one hundred fiftieth anniversary this year, we see evidences of the immigrant Swedes' determination to transplant and invigorate their faith here in the Valley of the Mississippi.

PART THREE

Kansas

The Swedish Immigration into Kansas

Thomas N. Holmquist

There is a valley resting upon the Great Plains and in the central part of Kansas that is a special place to the people who live there and also special to those of us who call ourselves Scandinavians. Wheat fields in which giant tractors and combines till the earth and harvest the grain, and tall native grass pastures where thousands of cattle graze, cover the land. The towns and hamlets such as Falun, Smolan, New Gotland, Salemsborg, and Lindsborg bear names reminiscent of the forests and rocky soils of Sweden. And above them all tower the Smoky Hills, rising above the gently rolling landscape and peaking out amid the smoky haze that gives the valley its name.

High on the northernmost of these hills is a cross of whitewashed sandstone. Set into the side of the hill, the cross is visible in the morning sun for many miles. To those who live in the valley, the cross is a constant reminder of those early pioneers who came so many years ago to the great plains of Kansas from Sweden.

What brought so many Swedes to this Smoky Valley of Kansas? Why does Swedish culture still flourish here to the fifth and sixth generations, well beyond the time when most Americans have replaced their cultural roots and identity?

Sweden of the mid-1800s was a country in religious, social, and economic turmoil. The onset of the nineteenth century brought about great changes in the social and economic conditions of Sweden. The old traditions of strip farming changed as well as the village community. Dating from the middle ages, the village communities functioned with small stable populations of villagers sharing fields and pastures equitably, conducive to the good of the community.

The appearance of new agricultural practices changed the economic structure of the Swedish rural communities. Small plots of farm ground, cultivated by each family, were combined to form large farms. As a result, large acreages controlled by a few owners who hired cheap labor quickly eroded and soon replaced the traditional village community. Experimentation with new agricultural practices, new implements, and alternative crops offered fresh opportunities to those with financial backing and enterprising minds. What emerged was a new class of agricultural laborers who were dependent on working on the newly established farms.

At the same time, the population of Sweden also continued growing. The absence of recent wars, vaccination of the populace for disease, and the rise of the potato as a food source brought a rise in population just as the number of jobs available began a steep decline. This increase in the country's population quickly overwhelmed the government's economic policy and its ability to provide better health care. In regions of Sweden where farmland was still held in small family units, the village communities were incapable of absorbing large gains in population. A further reason for the population growth was the traditional inheritance practices. These dictated that landholdings would be passed down to a single inheritor, usually the oldest son. So many children died at an early age that parents produced large families to insure that they would have a future generation to inherit the land. Large families also provided the farmer with a ready source of labor. Some families were blessed, and the majority of the children reached adulthood. Few opportunities existed for the non-inheriting children. They were often hired out to the other farmers and ended up among the landless peasant classes.

For many of these landless non-inheriting children, emigration offered the only real hope of economic survival or upward social mobility. The economic demands that brought about emigration were usually rooted in a yearning to earn more than a meager subsistence, build a savings, have amusement, and achieve economic and social security. Love of home was strong and most emigrants stated that they would have stayed in Sweden if there were a chance to have their own home. In America a settler may live in a sod hut, but he could hope to build a two-story palace soon. In Sweden, however, he who began life in a sod hut had every expectation of ending his life there. Hunger for land and home enticed thousands of Swedes to the Great Plains of North America. One said it was a question of "bread and meat in America, or skin and bones in Sweden."

The Lutheran Church in Sweden became steeped in the bureaucratic morass of a state-run organization and lost sight of its spiritual duties. It was more concerned with its own self-perpetuating institutionalization than the spiritual well being of the Swedish people. Political considerations and state policy often determined the church's ecclesiastical attitudes and actions. State-supported clergy became totally involved in the paperwork and governmental forms needed to keep state money coming into the church coffers. Unfortunately, this attitude allowed the clergy to lose contact with the church's most important work, the people. Parishes in the rural areas were also so large that it became exceedingly difficult for pastors to visit parishioners and for the rural people to attend worship services regularly.

As a result, the church became so rigid and steeped in formality that it lost sight of the needs of the people, especially those in the more isolated rural areas of the Swedish countryside. To fill the unmet spiritual needs of Sweden's rural population, there arose in the most isolated areas a movement whose premise was a return to a more fundamentalist Bible-reading form of private worship called the *Läsare* Movement. Followers of this movement would gather together in private homes and read the Bible and the devotional writings of Martin Luther. They would then read prayers and confessionals of the church, ask for a benediction and return to their homes. The *Läsare* Movement began very quietly but eventually grew to impact all of Sweden.

This underground spiritual movement was illegal. In Sweden, the policy of state control of the church brought about laws that prohibited the reading of the Bible without the presence of a clergyman. Even though it meant breaking the law, these secret meetings were held and Bible reading flourished despite the efforts of the church and state to retain control.

Before the first quarter of the nineteenth century had passed, revivalism had taken hold in Sweden. Revivalism was in fact the spiritual manifestation of the political, cultural, and economic upheavals that pushed Sweden into the modern world. Spiritual revivalism swept the country and soon developed into a more formalized form known as the Pietistic Movement. Pietism centered on the "emotional and subjective aspects of the Christian experience and the ethical and moral demands of sanctification."

During this same period in Sweden, the most pressing social problem was alcoholism. The lack of a spiritual emphasis in the church, extreme poverty among the rural population, and a lack of hope, were among the reasons for the problem. Temperance, or the abstinence of drinking alcoholic beverages, became closely associated with the Pietistic movement. Among the leaders of these movements was a Methodist missionary from England by the name of George Scott. Also leading the Pietists was Carl Olaf Rosenius, who later published an exceedingly influential newspaper, *Pietisten*, which was widely read both in Sweden and the United States, and Peter Fjellstedt, the renowned preacher, educator, writer, and linguist. He has been called the "Passavant of Sweden" because of his work on behalf of social and foreign missions. These religious and social leaders came to the forefront in the debates over philosophical thought and fundamental change in the religious and social fabric of Sweden. They were trying out new ideas and attitudes. Their teachings influenced others to change and become intolerant of the old ways, and to look toward new freedoms of thought and religion. For many Swedes, no longer able to accept the limitations placed upon them by the church and the state, the search for freedom meant emigration.

TO AMERICA

The first attempt by a significantly large group to leave Sweden came in 1846. The religious zealot, Eric Jansson, a man of eccentric character and violent temperament, led this assemblage. Seeking the freedom to practice his religion safely away from prosecution, Jansson gathered his followers and left Sweden in 1846. These "Janssonites" came to America and settled at Bishop Hill, the so-called "New Jerusalem" on the plains of western Illinois. During the course of the next two years, approximately fifteen hundred of Jansson's followers joined him there.

Not long after, in the spring of 1850, Jansson was killed in a dispute with the husband of his cousin, a man by the name of John Root. After that time the Bishop Hill Colony began a slow decline. Most importantly, though, Bishop Hill had become a beacon by which other Swedish groups took their bearings. Many of the Swedes who followed these early Janssonite pioneers came to western Illinois. Large numbers of Swedes built homes, farms, and businesses in neighboring communities. Illinois became the jumping off point for subsequent migrations into Iowa, Minnesota, and the Great Plains, including Kansas.

The second major wave of colonization was lead by Pastor Lars Paul Esbjörn. He lobbied and was finally given permission by the Swedish Lutheran Church to continue his ministerial work in America but refused any financial support. Most of his fellow clergymen considered him an irresponsible fanatic. In America, Esbjörn and his flock would be on their own.

In June of 1849, Esbjörn and one hundred and forty-six of his followers departed from Gävle, Sweden, on a voyage to the New World. The ocean voyage proved extremely difficult as cholera plagued them throughout the entire journey. Many of the Swedish immigrants died from the dreadful disease, including both of Esbjörn's infant twin sons.

Finally arriving in Chicago, Esbjörn procured land near the Bishop Hill Colony in western Illinois. He was promised beautiful land, already developed, next to a navigable river. Arriving at their town site, they found not the beautiful community of their dreams, but a few miserable shacks on the banks of the Edwards River, which was actually a small muddy creek. Undaunted, Esbjörn and his followers settled the town of Andover, Illinois. The first few months in Illinois were difficult, and the Andover Colony persisted largely through the courage and personal will of Pastor Esbjörn. Despite terrible hardships, devastating sickness, and numerous deaths, the colony survived.

Before long, after stories of the marginal successes of Bishop Hill and Andover reached Sweden, many hopeful Swedish immigrants flooded into the existing towns and cities of western Illinois and some even founded new communities. In Iowa, such towns as Swede Bend and Bergholm were established. Moline, Dekalb, Rock Island, Galesburg, Rockford, Swedona, Andover, and Chicago counted a large percentage of Swedish-born residents among their populations. Other states including Pennsylvania, Indiana, and especially Minnesota, also became the destinations for hundreds of Swedish immigrants.

As the ranks of Swedish immigrants swelled, Pastor Esbjörn sent the call to some of his former colleagues in Sweden encouraging them to join him on this new spiritual front in America. One of the most important of the early congregations founded by Esbjörn was First Lutheran Church in Galesburg, Illinois. With Esbjörn's influence, First Lutheran called Tufve Nilsson Hasselquist from Sweden. Pastor Hasselquist arrived in Galesburg in 1852 and worked to make First Lutheran one of the finest Lutheran spiritual centers in the Midwest. Hasselquist traveled widely and worked to found numerous Swedish congregations in the ever-expanding Swedish communities.

Hasselquist also found the time and energy to establish the first Swedish-American newspaper in the United States, *Det Rätta Hemlandet*, which translated means, appropriately, *The Correct Homeland*. It was an extremely important link for all of the Swedish immigrant pioneers in America. Written in the Swedish language, it contained American news, reports from the various Swedish communities in America, news from the homeland, and always-spiritual guidance from the pen of Hasselquist himself. The *Hemlandet* was widely read and in many cases was one of the only links a Swede had with the old country.

The second man to answer the call to minister to the needs of Swedish Lutherans in America was Pastor Erland Carlsson. Carlsson accepted the call of the newly formed Immanuel Lutheran Church in Chicago. He served his parish with great distinction for twenty-two years, all the while giving aid to the masses of new Swedish immigrants that arrived in Chicago each year. A tireless worker, Carlsson ministered extensively to the countless cholera sufferers in Chicago. Meeting every new trainload of Swedish immigrants, he assisted each one to establish a steady foothold in the new land.

Jonas Swensson and O. T. C. Andrén also accepted calls to parishes in America. Swensson served congregations in Sugar Grove and Jamestown, New York, and later replaced Pastor Esbjörn at First Lutheran in Andover, Illinois. Andrén answered the call to minister to the Swedes in Moline, Illinois.

The first of many outstanding pastors who were ordained in America was Eric Norelius. He worked mainly among the Swedish pioneers in Minnesota. His papers and writings concerning the history of the Swedish people and Lutheranism in America are of profound importance to church history and the development of Lutheran Church doctrine.

As immigration expanded, a need for more Lutheran ministers to meet the growing spiritual demands of America's Swedish population became apparent. During the year 1859 an exceptional young man, only seventeen years old, and not yet finished with his schooling, answered the call to the Lutheran ministry in America. His name was Anders Wilhelm Dahlsten.

Young Anders Dahlsten was a man of average height and slight build, but in his eyes there shone the quiet intensity of his faith and the strength of determination that was the essence of his character. He was born on November 7, 1836, in the parish of Nåshult, Småland, Sweden, the fourth of eight children. His father was a poor farm laborer who died while Anders was still quite young. A gifted student, Dahlsten attended the parish school at Nåshult and later gained admission to the Fjellstedt Mission School in Stockholm. While at the mission school, he studied intensely with Dr. Fjellstedt and there gained the passion for the missionary field like so many before him.

While a student at the Fjellstedt School, Dahlsten was a classmate of Lindsborg, Kansas, founder, Olaf Olsson. Olsson was five years younger than Dahlsten, but the two young men were close friends during their school days. Both Dahlsten and Olsson left the Fjellstedt School in 1859. Dahlsten sailed for America, and Olsson continued his studies in Sweden. The two schoolmates lost contact with each other for a number of years. When their friendship resumed a decade later, it was on the plains of Kansas.

As one of Fjellstedt's finest students, Dahlsten was recommended to Pastor Erland Carlsson in Chicago, and so Dahlsten sailed for America to assist Pastor Carlsson in his work there. After nearly a year with Pastor Carlsson in Chicago, Dahlsten enrolled at Illinois State University to study with Pastor Esbjörn. While in the seminary, Dahlsten proved to be a brilliant scholar and a leader among his peers. Through his outstanding accomplishments, he was soon considered one of the best young pastors who would soon join the work of the church in Illinois.

The leaders of the Swedish Lutherans soon came into conflict with their Norwegian peers over control of the Synod of Northern Illinois. When it became apparent that a split would occur, the Swedish Lutherans broke away and formed the Augustana Synod with Pastor Lars Paul Esbjörn as president. However, before many months passed, the long years of toil and strain of leading the Swedish church in America forced Esbjörn to retire. The loss of his son, killed at the Battle of Lexington, Missouri, seemed to be the last straw. He returned to Sweden to spend his final years in retirement.

The Augustana Synod met to choose new leaders to succeed the retiring Esbjörn. The synod chose Erland Carlsson to be the new synod president. T. N. Hasselquist was chosen as the temporary President of the Augustana Seminary until a new theologian could be found in Sweden to take the position. Hasselquist remained in this "temporary" position until his death in 1891.

When called to serve as seminary president, Hasselquist resigned from his position at First Lutheran Church in Galesburg. This church was one of the most prominent in the synod. The pastor chosen to occupy this pulpit would also inherit great prestige and power. Many applied for this coveted position, but instead of choosing one of the senior pastors of great reputation, the congregation chose one of the most promising of the young pastors serving the synod. The name of the successful candidate: A. W. Dahlsten.

DAHLSTEN'S MINISTRY IN ILLINOIS

The mid-1860s brought a huge increase in the number of immigrants arriving from Sweden. This great influx of immigration was largely due to famine conditions in Sweden. The failed potato crops of 1865, 1866, and 1867 left no choice for the poor but to move to a new place in order to survive. Most of the Scandinavian immigrants who came to America in the 1860s made their way to either Minnesota or to Illinois. Those who arrived in Galesburg, Illinois, were directed to Pastor Dahlsten and First Lutheran Church.

Pastor Dahlsten worked very hard to help the newly arrived immigrants. He had learned well from working with Pastor Erland Carlsson at Immanuel Lutheran Church in Chicago, and all who came to Galesburg soon learned that Dahlsten was there to help them. At the church, they could receive a meal, perhaps locate an acquaintance from Sweden, or enroll their children in the *församlingens skol* (congregation school). They could also receive help in finding a place to stay or even a tip about a job. Most importantly, these immigrants could find a sympathetic ear, spiritual guidance, and relief from the grief that accompanied them on their long arduous journey from Sweden.

THE GALESBURG COLONIZATION COMPANY

The most severe problem that Dahlsten and the newly arrived Swedes faced in Illinois was unemployment. The return of thousands of soldiers, both Swede and non-Swede, from the American Civil War, created severe economic problems. The economy was ill prepared to accept a huge workforce in the post-war economy. Land was tightly held and was nearly impossible to acquire. The Swedes of Galesburg began discussing the possibility of moving out to the western lands. Dahlsten, writing in the third person, explained the situation himself:

> Pastor Dahlsten, who was pastor in Galesburg, as well as many of the older Swedes in the locality, had long realized the necessity of moving out. Many said that they wished to go out in the west to take land, but would not go there if they should be left without church or pastor. Pastor Dahsten granted that if many of them should go to the same place, that they could have both (land and church).

In early August of 1868 a meeting was called for the First Lutheran Church Congregation School in Galesburg. Between two and three hundred hopeful men attended this meeting. After much discussion about the seriousness of the intentions of the prospective pioneers, it was decided to hold a second meeting and make formal agreements about what to do.

News of this meeting spread fast among the Swedes of western Illinois, and the second meeting was attended by between three and four hundred people. Most of those who attended were originally from Sweden's Småland province while many others were from Dalarna, Östergötland, and Kalmar.

After much discussion, a plan was adopted to form the Galesburg Colonization Company. John P. Stromquist was elected secretary and Olaf Thorstenburg was made president. The meeting then focused on what they should actually do. It was decided to appoint a committee that would look for land in Missouri, Kansas, or Nebraska.

Olaf Thorstenburg, as President of the Galesburg Colonization Company, was elected to lead the expedition to search for land. He was a long-time Swedish citizen of Galesburg, a leader in community affairs, and a member of the church council at First Lutheran Church. He was to be accompanied by Gustaf Johnson, another member of the church council. John Rodell and William Johnson, both members of the church council of the Andover Lutheran Church, were also elected to the committee. Pastor Dahlsten also promised to go if the congregation gave its approval of his absence.

Preparations were then made by the search committee to leave as soon as possible. They decided to first explore Missouri for a possible destination. Each week the *Hemlandet* carried an article on the successes of the Missouri Land Company. The reports were so glowing that they thought that Missouri should be considered first.

The Galesburg Company committee also made plans to search the river valleys of Kansas if their search proved fruitless in Missouri. The weekly issues of *Hemlandet* carried advertisements for the National Land Company of St. Louis. The company's purpose was to sell the land grants of the Kansas Pacific Railroad. They were promoting land in the Republican, Saline, Solomon, and Smoky Hill River valleys in Kansas. One site in Kansas that the committee was anxious to scout was the Smoky (Hill) Valley. They knew that this valley was already the home of several Swedish homesteaders.

Dahlsten also knew that a Swedish company was forming in Chicago and had just a few days previously purchased lands in northern McPherson County, Kansas. This Chicago based group eventually became the First Swedish Agricultural Company of McPherson County. This group, composed mostly of Värmlanders, arrived in the summer of 1869 and founded the Bethany Lutheran Church and the city of Lindsborg, Kansas. Since the Swedes were of a mind to settle near their countrymen, the search committee decided to explore the Smoky Valley for the Galesburg group as well.

The Galesburg search committee arrived in Salina in late August of 1868. The next morning, just as the first rays of the sun were glimmering in the eastern sky, the men walked south from Salina. Before them lay the land, misty in the morning light, with a constant haze that gave the valley its name. The grass stood as high as a man's shoulder and teemed with the creatures of the prairie, a sign of good land. The Swedes passed numerous creeks and streams, marked only by cottonwoods, the only trees to be seen. From their vantage point they could follow the path of a great river, the Smoky Hill River, as it snaked its way across the length of the valley heading in its unending flow toward the ocean.

Every so often, the men would bend down and scratch into the earth to touch the rich black soil. They were so amazed as they pressed the earth in their hands and smelled the thick rich aroma. These men of Sweden, used to the thin rocky soil of their homeland, could not believe that the earth could be as rich and fertile as in this valley.

As they gazed through the mist, the men could see in the distance the blue-green bluffs rising above the valley floor. Once the lookout of the Spanish explorer Coronado, searching for a treasure that he never found, the bluffs stood above the true treasure, the land itself. Little could they know that eventually a cross of stones would lie on the crest of the northernmost hill to commemorate the day they entered the valley and found themselves a home—home not only to a few, but for the many whose children still reap the riches these five men discovered in the Smoky Valley of Kansas.

On September 1, 1868, the National Land Company transferred to the Galesburg committee some 14,800 acres of land in southern Saline and northwestern McPherson Counties of Kansas. This land was to be held in escrow for the members of the Galesburg Colonization Company to purchase.

The committee hurried back to Galesburg where another meeting was held. It was decided that the land would be distributed by lottery. A section (640 acres) was designated as a unit. "Relatives and friends who wished to live on adjoining farms banded together in groups of four to eight, depending on their desire for an 80 or 160 acre farm. The section was then parceled out by agreement or by lot among the individuals." A delegate for each section then lined up and drew from a glass container the legal coordinates for their new homes in the Smoky Valley. The cost for the land ranged from $1.50 for upland to $5.00 for the best bottomland. In many cases the land, selected purely by chance so long ago, remains in the hands of the descendants of those original pioneers to this day.

The Swedes quickly started making preparations to relocate to Kansas. A few men, such as Gust and John Holmkvist and Mons Peterson and Bengt Hessler came to Kansas in the fall, but the vast majority traveled to Kansas in late February of 1869. At that time, Pastor Dahlsten chartered several rail cars and bid farewell to so many members of his congregation. After several days' journey the train carrying the Galesburg Company pioneers arrived in Salina, Kansas. The Swedes immediately started walking south from Salina and searched for their claims.

BUILDING A PARISH

By the late spring of 1869 houses were built, wells dug, and the thoughts of the people turned to establishing a church. The man who emerged as community and spiritual leader in Kansas was C. J. Brodine. He was a devout man and a staunch churchman as well. He was considered a lay deacon preacher and often led the worship services and worked whenever needed in the church. When the opportunity came to migrate to Kansas, he assumed the role of leader of the Galesburg Company and, until Pastor Dahlsten arrived later, served as the spiritual guide to the Swedish pioneers of the northern Smoky Valley.

John Rodell performed the same duties in the western reaches of where the Galesburg lands were located, near where the town of Marquette, Kansas, is located today. He was a sincere Christian and eager to begin a church in the community. Rodell walked from homestead to homestead inviting everyone to attend worship. It was said of him: "He was a noble man, very enterprising, maybe more enterprising than cautious."

Both groups met in the middle of June 1869 with the intention of forming congregations. The northern group met at the home of C. J. Brodine. They agreed to form a congregation and then discussed what to name the new congregation. Brodine asked that they take their copies of *Den Svensk Psalm-Boken* and open it to hymn #500, titled *Slutpsalm* (Endpsalm). Verse four of this poignant hymn, Brodine thought, explained so well his choice for the name of the new church:

O min själ! du skall dig svinga
Till det Salems berg en gång,
Där keruberrs harpor klinga
Bland de sällas segersång:
Låt ditt lof, ditt böneljud
Gå i föväg hem till Gud,
Medan än du, följd af sorgen,
Irrar utom fadersborgen.

The English translation of this beautiful passage is:

O my soul you shall soar
To the peaceful mountain one time,
their cherub's harps ring
among the blessed victory song.
Sound thy praise, thine prayer sounds
go ahead, home to God.
While even you, in consequence of sorrow,
Wander beyond the father's security.

"*Salems berg*" or the "peaceful mountain" in this hymn refers to the end of life's journey, that ending place where peace, joy, and contentment may finally be reached.

These settlers certainly hoped that they were finally at the end of their journey and could settle in this valley. Many of these Swedish people had been on the journey for years. They believed the hard bleak years in Sweden were far behind. Their emigration to America and settling in Illinois provided the life of freedom and contentment they had yearned for so long. But when these dreams faded among the strife, hardships, and difficulties they encountered in Illinois, they made another journey seeking a peaceful conclusion to this phase of their unsettled lives. They hoped that calm and peace could be found on the plains of Kansas.

Before many days had passed a dugout sod church was built, and a call was extended to Pastor Dahlsten to join his former parishioners in Kansas.

At nearly the same time similar meetings were held in the western reaches of the Galesburg Company lands. John Rodell encouraged his neighbors to meet and form a church near their home. A meeting was held and it was decided to form a joint parish with Salemsberg. "William Johnson proposed the name Fremont; as a motive he said that as John C. Fremont was the forerunner of civilization in the Southwest, so we hoped that this church organization would be the forerunner of the Swedish Evangelical Lutheran churches in the southwest." Before long the newly organized congregation began to build a sandstone church. It was completed in May of 1870 and stands as the oldest building in McPherson County, Kansas, to this day.

In September of 1869, Pastor Dahlsten and his family came to Kansas to serve the Salemsberg and Freemont (later spelling) congregations. He served Freemont for several years and then ministered solely to the Salemsberg congregation for eighteen more years. All the while he established nearly a dozen Lutheran congregations on the plains of Kansas.

And so they came, these Swedish immigrants, pioneers to the frontier. They searched for a place where they could live freely, own farms, and prosper. They searched for a place where they could worship as they chose, and where Swedish culture could flourish. They found all of those things in the Smoky Valley of Kansas.

As one travels down the country roads to visit the farms and hamlets of the Smoky Valley, one can still feel the influence of those Swedish pioneers. They were the best of that country, dispossessed by economic, social, and religious customs well beyond their control. They were artists, and musicians, businessmen and farmers, educators, and laborers. When they came to the Smoky Valley they found a fertile field lying fallow and ready for the plow. Soon the farms flourished and the towns prospered. In Lindsborg, Bethany College was founded as a center for Swedish culture, the arts, and music. The children of those pioneers worked hard to become successful Americans.

Today the descendants of those pioneers still farm the land, first homesteaded by their great grandparents. They send their children to Bethany College to sing *The Messiah*, the great oratorio by George Frideric Handel, first sung in the Smoky Valley 120 years ago. They continue the traditions and heritage of their ancestors in their foods, celebrations, and worship.

There is a poignant statue that stands in the harbor in Karlsham in Blekinge, Sweden. The statue is of Karl Oscar and Kristina, fictional characters made famous by Wilhelm Moberg in his novel *The Emigrants*. Karl Oscar stands facing the west ready for the challenge of the sea and the New World that lies over the horizon. Kristina stands next to him ready to face the dangers of the unknown, but she turns her head and looks back toward mother Sweden, back toward home. Those of us who live in the Smoky Valley are similar. We stand as Americans ready to face the future, the unknown, but always, we are a bit like Kristina, remembering the old country, looking back and remembering who we are, where we came from, and what those early Swedish pioneers did for us to enable us to be here.

We celebrate Saint Lucia and attend *Julotta* on Christmas morning. We serve *lutfisk* and *ostkaka* at holiday meals, and we dance around the Maypole on Midsummer's Day. Our children are taught Swedish prayers to recite before meals and they sing *Tryggare kan ingen vara* at church and at the local schools. At Hyllningsfest in October, we don our traditional Swedish folk costumes, adults and children alike, and celebrate the pride in our Swedish heritage.

When we wander into the cemetery at Salemsborg (modern spelling), we see the massive stones with names such as Carlson, Johnson, Danielson, Holmquist, Krig, and Brodine, and we stop and remember with silent thanks those who brought us to this place. Near the church, among the stones, there appears a small gray obelisk. On that stone, weathered by time, is inscribed the name, A. W. Dahlsten. He was a man too busy doing God's work to worry about himself.

To the southwest of the cemetery the bluffs rise above the valley floor and the white cross of stones is always visible. It has been fifty-six years since Carl Lindholm, with the labor of his own hands, built this cross to honor and remember the Swedish pioneers. Over 135 years have passed since the Galesburg Land Company search committee visited the Smoky Valley for the first time and found this prairie treasure, a home for themselves and their people.

Those first pioneers are gone now, and their descendants have scattered to various parts of the country, but to most of them the Smoky Valley will always be called home. They come back to visit now and then, attending church, greeting old friends on Memorial Day, placing flowers in the cemetery. The pioneers are not forgotten. Their hardships and privations, which was their cross to bear, are remembered in a family story, a glance at old picture albums, or a walk among the headstones in the cemeteries.

And always, a lift of the head will bring the Smoky Bluffs into view; the same now as 135 years ago with their lofty presence rising through the haziness of the valley floor. The cross, white and glorious, greets the eye, and we know that we are home—with a sense of peace and pride in the Smoky Valley of Kansas.

SOURCES

Books:

Arden, G. Everett. *Augustana Heritage: A History of the Augustana Lutheran Church*. Rock Island: Augustana Book Concern, 1963.

Holmquist, Thomas N. *Pioneer Cross, Swedish Settlements Along the Smoky Hill Bluffs*. Hillsboro, Kansas: Hearth Publishing, 1994.

Lindfors, Alan, and Elinor Burnison. *Elim Our Heritage.* Marquette, Kansas: Elim Lutheran Church, 1980.

Lindquist, Emory. *Vision for a Valley.* Rock Island: Augustana Historical Society, 1970.

Minnes Album, Svenska Lutherska Församlingen, Salemsborg, Kansas 1869-1909. Rock Island: Augustana Book Concern, 1909.

Minneskrift Album, Diamond Jubilee Anniversary, First Lutheran Church, Galesburg, Illinois. Rock Island: Augustana Book Concern, 1914.

Nelson, E. Clifford, ed. *The Lutherans in North America.* Philadelphia: Fortress Press, 1975.

Nyquist, Edna. *Pioneer Life and Lore of McPherson County, Kansas.* McPherson, Kansas: The Democrat-Opinion Press, 1932.

Olson, Ernst Wilhelm. *History of the Swedes of Illinois.* Chicago: Engberg-Holmberg Publishing Company, 1908.

Stephenson, George M. *The Religious Aspects of Swedish Immigration.* Minneapolis: University of Minnesota Press, 1932.

Wheeler, Wayne. *An Analysis of Social Change in a Swedish Immigrant Community: The Case of Lindsborg, Kansas.* New York: AMS Press, 1986.

Newspapers:

Salina Journal, Salina, Kansas.

Saline County Republican Journal, Salina, Kansas.

Det Rätta Hemlandet, Chicago, Illinois.

Numerous interviews and unpublished sources.

Lutherans in the Smoky Valley: A Rich History

Vance L. Eckstrom

I. INTRODUCTION

When Europeans first began to come to the Smoky Valley of Kansas, they found it occupied by various tribes of Indians. The first European to visit the Smoky Valley was Álvar Núñez Cabeza de Vaca, who traveled through this area in the 1530s, exploring for Spain. Another Spaniard, Francisco Vasquez de Coronado, working from Mexico, reached this far toward the northeast about 1541. A low butte of about 300 feet elevation, three miles northwest of Lindsborg, is named Coronado Heights, after this sixteenth-century explorer.

From Spanish exploration in the 1500s, we next jump ahead in time by some two and a half centuries. The presence of white men in this area really began to pick up in the early 1800s. The Lewis and Clark expedition passed through in 1804. Lieutenant Zebulon Pike, for whom Pike's Peak is named, was here in 1806. In 1822, covered wagons began to travel the Santa Fe Trail, passing just nineteen miles south of the present site of Lindsborg. Colonel John C. Fremont, for whom the community of Fremont would later be named, traveled through here in 1845. And then the Swedes began to come.

On the accompanying map, where congregations came to be located in towns, only the name of the town is given. For open-country congregations, the name of the congregation is given. There were of course no roads at all in those earliest days, but on this map a few present-day highways are included, to help in identifying the location of the various towns and churches. I thank my daughter Sharon Eckstrom for creating this map.

Augustana Congregations of the Smoky Valley

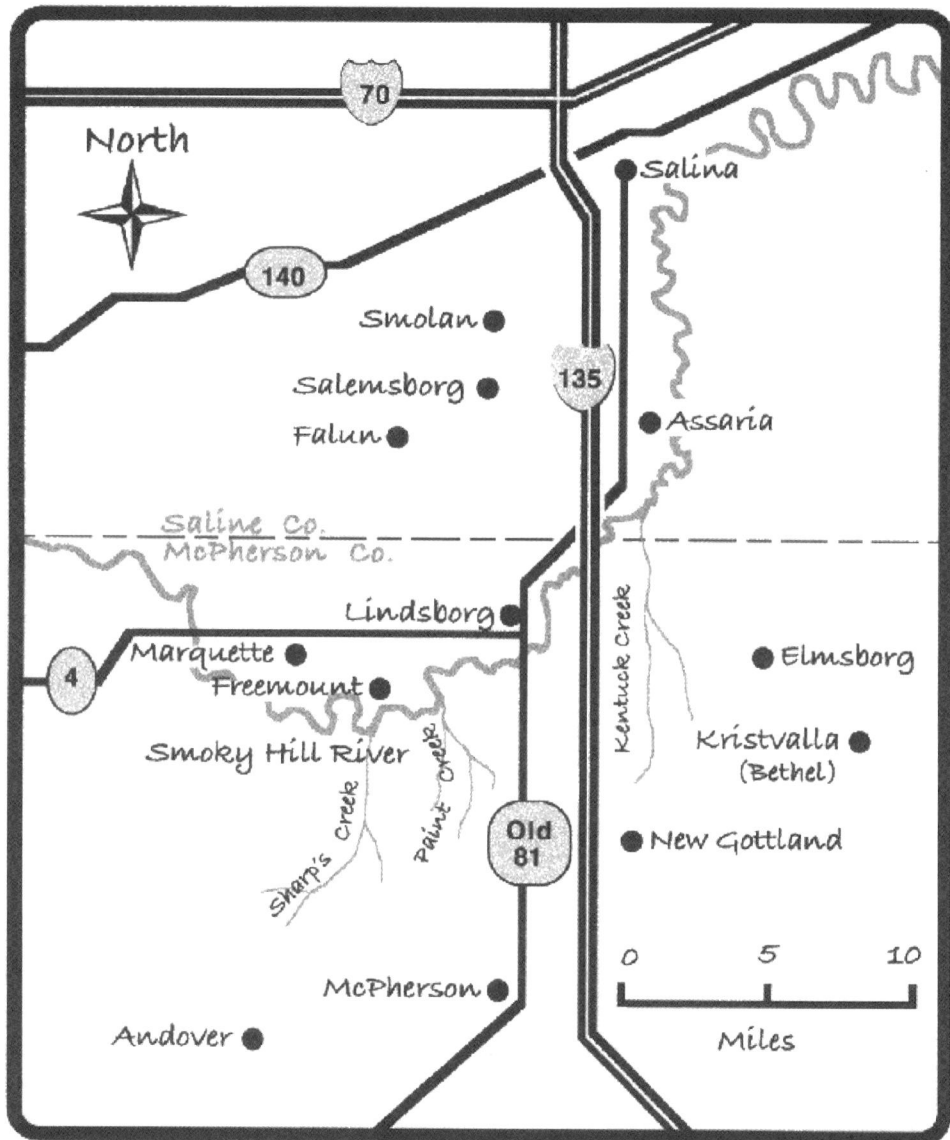

Map by Sharon Eckstrom

II. SWEDISH SETTTLEMENT

In Kansas, as in many other places, Swedish immigration was a gradual movement from the east toward the west. By 1848 there were Swedes living in the eastern part of the state. By 1858 they were within forty miles of this area. Then in 1859 came the very first Swede to settle in the Smoky Valley itself. In that year, Isaac Sharp settled on a creek southwest of today's Lindsborg, the creek which is appropriately known today as Sharp's Creek. He built a log cabin, which he used as his house and as a trading post.

However, reports soon began to circulate that there might be Indian attacks, so Sharp abandoned his log cabin and moved back further east.

Five years later, on February 15, 1864, a certain Anders Bengtson Carlgren settled in southern Saline County, thirteen miles north-northeast of today's Lindsborg. He was the first Swede to come to the Smoky Valley and stay. But his only importance for this story is that he was the first long-term Swedish settler in this Valley. He was an eccentric loner who played no part in the development of either the church or the community.

Incidentally, it should be noted that very many of the earliest Swedish immigrants to the United States were not churchgoing people. In fact, in the mid-1800s, well over half of the Swedish immigrants in the United States had no involvement with any church. Even here in the Smoky Valley, some of the early settlers were non-believers.

In any case, after the end of the Civil War in 1865, settlement in the Smoky Valley really began to pick up. In 1866 eight men plus one wife came from Junction City, and filed for homesteads near the present-day Freemount church. In that same year, Sam and George Shields set up a small trading post a few miles northeast of present-day Lindsborg. By 1867 there were 17 homesteads claimed in the Smoky Valley. The next year, 1868, more than 25 families or individual men settled in the Smoky Valley area. And so it went. The Swedes were coming in.

Though not all of these pioneers were religious people, many families did read their Bibles and Christian books, and sent up their prayers toward heaven. And a Lutheran circuit rider, a Pastor S. G. Larson, led a worship service one day in the spring of 1868 in the log house home of a family named Nordlund. That was the first worship service led by a pastor in the Smoky Valley.

In those early days it was a major challenge for people to come to the Smoky Valley, to homestead, or to buy land from the railroad. It helped if they had advance connections. Sometimes people who were already here would arrange for land for relatives or friends. This individualized arrangement worked relatively well when dealing with one or two families at a time. But it was much different if you were bringing thirty or forty families in one group. To deal with these logistical problems of large groups, land companies were developed, to help handle these arrangements. Some of the land companies sent agents back to Sweden, soliciting settlers to come to the United States. In their posters, these land companies, and the various ship lines, really exaggerated what it was like here. For example, one poster for this area pictured large sailing ships meeting and passing each other on the Smoky Hill River. It was these wild exaggerations that led one older woman immigrant to excessive expectations. As the classic story goes, when she arrived from Sweden, she surveyed the New York skyline with its tall buildings, and then commented, "If this is New York, what then must Lindsborg be?"

III. PASTOR A. W. DAHLSTEN AND THE GALESBURG LAND COMPANY

There were two land companies that were primary players in the settlement of the Smoky Valley. One was organized in 1868 in Galesburg, Illinois, under the leadership of Pastor A. W. Dahlsten.

Mentioning the Dahlsten name leads me to digress for a moment. Descendents of this pastor, and of many of the other pioneers, are still living in this area, and other descendents have come from a distance to be here for this Gathering. To mention just a couple of specific examples, two granddaughters of Doctor Alfred Bergin, long-time early pastor in Lindsborg, are here this weekend. And a man and his wife are here who bear the name Udden. J. A. Udden was the first professor at Bethany Academy, back in 1881, and this man's grandfather was a brother of J. A. Udden. In all cases, we hope that you who are descendants of the pioneers will feel some sense of reflected glory, as we honor your forebears, who were the early settlers in this Smoky Valley.

Also, it should be mentioned that Pastor Olof Olsson has become so well known as the great pioneer pastor in this Valley that it is easy to forget that Pastor A. W. Dahlsten was here first.

And how did Pastor Dahlsten come to be here? In 1868 he was serving a congregation in Galesburg, Illinois. There was a serious shortage of jobs there, so Pastor Dahlsten called a meeting for the purpose of organizing a land company to find land further west. More than three hundred Swedes came to this meeting. Obviously the need was great, and the decision was quickly made to send a scouting party to look for good land. The three scouts reached the Smoky Valley that fall. Here Pastor Dahlsten preached the second Lutheran sermon ever given in this Valley. The service was held in open country, near what is now Lindsborg, under a large tree. It is recorded that a wild turkey sat in the top of the tree through the entire service, joining its voice with that of the congregation. When the last song had been sung, the turkey rose up and flew away.

When Pastor Dahlsten and his colleagues got back home to Illinois, the Galesburg Land Company moved ahead with plans to establish a colony in central Kansas. Working with the Kansas Pacific Railway, the Galesburg Land Company bought twenty-two sections of land in Saline and McPherson Counties. This land ran in a broad arc, beginning about five miles south of Salina, and extending to the southwest, to three miles west of Marquette. The new landowners began arriving in December 1868, with the largest group, an entire trainload, coming in February, 1869. These newcomers settled in the areas around what are now the communities of Smolan, Salemsborg, Freemount, and Marquette.

This group of settlers was made up of Lutheran believers; in fact, contrary to the usual land company arrangements, to be a believer was one of the requirements for membership in this Land Company. And on March 2,

1869, the first service of what would become Freemount Lutheran Church was led by laymen in a home near the future location of the Freemount church. A second service was held in May. And then, on Saturday afternoon, June 12, 1869, a church business meeting was held, and it was voted unanimously to organize a Lutheran congregation. A letter was sent to the Augustana Synod, and the congregation was received into the Synod on June 23, 1869, along with fourteen other congregations from around the country.

Other members of the Galesburg Land Company, who lived up in the Salemsborg area, were moving on a similar timeline. On June 16, 1869, the Salemsborg group voted to organize a congregation, just four days after Freemount had voted to organize.

Pastor Dahlsten moved from Galesburg to the Smoky Valley in September of that year, 1869. Since no clergyman had been present at Freemount's June 12th organization meeting, Pastor Dahlsten held another organization meeting on September 25, 1869. He then went to Salemsborg and, apparently on the same day, September 25th, he held a second organization meeting for the congregation there. He was called to be the pastor of both congregations. For many years, Pastor Dahlsten regularly walked between his two churches, a distance of some ten miles. Money was, of course, very tight in those days, so Pastor Dahlsten usually walked barefoot between the two locations to save on his shoes.

There soon developed a town at the Freemount location, complete with railroad station, post office, and many business buildings. The town name was spelled the same as the name of that early explorer, F-r-e-m-o-n-t. But there were some black marks on Colonel Fremont's reputation, so the decision was made to call the congregation Free Mount, sometimes spelled as two words, but today written as one word, Freemount. A special distinction for the Freemount congregation is that their first church, a stone building erected in 1870, has been preserved, and has recently been nicely restored. It is the oldest public building in McPherson County still in its original location. The town of Fremont is now gone, leaving hardly a trace, but the church remains, its witness shining as brightly as ever.

Soon other congregations began to be organized. Bethany Lutheran Church in Lindsborg will be passed over for now, because it is the subject of a later section. But, apart from Bethany, the next Augustana congregation to be organized was in Salina. Salina was the commercial center for the Smoky Valley, because the first railroad line was there. Immigrants would come to Salina by train, and then move out from there to their intended location. But some of the incoming Swedes stayed in Salina to work. So from 1869 onward, pastors from Salemsborg and Lindsborg would come to conduct services for these Salina Swedes. On May 11, 1870, the decision was made to organize what we know today as Immanuel Lutheran Church. And it is recorded that that congregation was probably the first Swedish church anywhere in the world to have electric lights in its sanctuary.

As more and more Swedes poured into this area in search of good land, it soon became necessary to go further out to find suitable locations. In 1870 Pastor Dahlsten once again led a search party. They found more good land about seventeen miles south-southwest of Freemount. Swedes began to settle there, and this became a preaching point for the Freemount pastor. In 1879 New Andover was established as a separate congregation. It was called New Andover, because many of the members had come here from Andover, Illinois, but today it is known simply as Andover Lutheran Church. Andover lies outside the Smoky Valley, strictly speaking, but it is included in this account anyway, because its origins were so closely intertwined with the work of Pastor Dahlsten at Freemount.

At first the Swedes living in the Marquette area were members of the Freemount congregation. But, again because of distances, and also because of some controversy about where the Freemount church was built, the Marquette group organized its own congregation, Elim Lutheran, in 1878. The Freemount people weren't happy about this, and there were some rather sharp exchanges between the two groups, as often happened among these pioneer congregations when a group would separate to form its own new church. By 1880 Elim Lutheran in Marquette had its own pastor, Mauritz Stolpe. But when the congregation applied to join the Kansas Conference, it was refused. The president of the Kansas Conference at that time just happened to be A. W. Dahlsten, pastor of the Freemount congregation, and that might have had something to do with the Conference's decision to deny membership to Elim, Marquette. But in time, peace was restored. Elim Lutheran was admitted into the Conference in 1885, and that same year Pastor Johan Seleen accepted a call to serve both Freemount and Marquette congregations. So New Andover and Elim in Marquette were daughter congregations from Freemount.

Next came expansion from the Salemsborg church. The people in Assaria at first belonged to Salemsborg, but because of distance they organized their own congregation, Assaria Lutheran, on February 6, 1875. A quarter century later, in 1902, another group separated from Salemsborg, and formed a congregation in Smolan. The Smolan congregation merged back into Salemsborg in 1961, after a separate existence of 59 years.

Swedes had begun to settle in and around Falun around 1870. However, the first settlers there were not members of the Galesburg Company. A certain Major Erick Forsse (or Fors) and a group of about forty had left from the Eric Jansson colony at Bishop Hill, Illinois, and from the neighboring community of Galva, to settle at Falun. Forsse, unhappy with his experience at Jansson's communistic colony, was not eager to have a church at Falun, or at least not one affiliated with any specific denomination. In time, a community church was formed, but it was only on December 21, 1887, that Falun Lutheran Church was formally organized, and bought the other congregation's building. Many members of this new congregation had formerly held membership at Salemsborg; thus, the Falun congregation was considered to be a daughter church of the Salemsborg congregation. So from Salemsborg came Assaria, Smolan, and (in a certain sense) Falun.

Turning further to the southeast. By 1871 a good-sized group of Swedes had settled some ten miles south-southeast of Lindsborg, in an area they called Big Prairie. In time, they decided that their community needed a better name, so they called it New Gottland, "New Good Land." A congregation was organized there July 7, 1872, with the pastor from Bethany Church in Lindsborg in charge of the meeting.

The New Gottland congregation gave birth to two daughter congregations. The Evangelical Lutheran Church in McPherson (now Trinity Lutheran Church), organized in 1881, and the open-country Kristvalla Lutheran Church, organized in 1887. Kristvalla was later renamed Bethel Lutheran Church. Its building was destroyed by a tornado in 1925, and this rural congregation disbanded after an existence of thirty-eight years. Better roads and more reliable automobiles made it easier for people to travel greater distances to attend church. So by 1925, if a congregation lost its building, it wasn't too difficult for the members to decide to transfer to another nearby congregation. Thus, from New Gottland, Trinity in McPherson, and Kristvalla.

Even before getting into the story of Bethany Lutheran Church in Lindsborg, it can be mentioned that there was, in 1882, an offshoot, sort of, from Bethany Lutheran. A man named Asp moved from Wisconsin to a farm east-southeast of Lindsborg. He applied to become a member of Bethany Church, but that church, desiring to be as much as possible a pure church, refused him because of what were called "family troubles." So Mr. Asp began to work toward getting a new congregation started, out in his area, where he could be accepted as a member. He, and members of Bethany Church who lived in that area, formed Elmsborg Lutheran Church in 1882, and called a Pastor Nordling to be their minister. They held services in the Mount Hope schoolhouse. Though they did not build a church, they did build a parsonage for their pastor. However, the very next year the new parsonage was destroyed by fire. The congregation decided to disband, after only a single year of existence, and the members, en masse, returned to Bethany Lutheran Church, except for Mr. Asp. Bethany Church records make no mention of his becoming a member.

In summary, it can be said that, beginning with the organization of Freemount, Salemsborg, and Bethany congregations—all three of them organized in the year 1869—there was a rapid immigration of Swedish Lutherans into the Smoky Valley, which led to the organization of eight more Augustana congregations in this immediate area in the next eighteen years, and a few more new congregations yet after that.

IV. THE FIRST SWEDISH AGRICULTURAL COMPANY OF MCPHERSON COUNTY, KANSAS, AND PASTOR OLOF OLSSON

The beginnings of Bethany Lutheran Church and of the town of Lindsborg receive separate treatment because they were, in several ways, a special case. In his 1953 book *Smoky Valley People*, historian Dr. Emory Lindquist, in describing the situation about 1868, just before that pivotal year of 1869, has written these words:

> The Smoky Valley was being peopled by Swedes in scattered homesteads. The future was still uncertain. Nothing pointed to a large Swedish settlement until a young Lutheran pastor, the Rev. Olof Olsson, made the decision in December 1868, that he and his friends would emigrate to Kansas. *Lindsborg was born in that hour* (p. 4, emphasis added).

It must be clarified that Dr. Lindquist did not mean that there would never have been a Lindsborg if Olof Olsson had not decided to come here. The plans to have a town here were already laid in Chicago in 1866, under the leadership of S. A. Lindell and a group of other devout Swedish Lutherans, some forty in number. This was two years before Olof Olsson made the decision to come to Kansas. On April 17, 1868, in Chicago, the formal organization of the First Swedish Agricultural Company of McPherson County, Kansas, took place. The second article of its charter read, "Whoever joins this company must be a Christian, hold to the Evangelical Lutheran doctrine, must be industrious and diligent, and interested in the welfare and development of the company." Operations around the future site of Lindsborg began in August 1868. The Company bought 13,160 acres, about half of the land out of a block some six by nine miles in size, in southern Saline and northern McPherson Counties. They took possession of the land in October of 1868, and a large *bolagshus*, or "company house," was completed in December of that year, several miles north of the present-day location of Lindsborg.

Now, to be sure, the organizers of this Land Company knew Pastor Olof Olsson, and his close layman friend and advisor C. R. Carlson back in Sweden. And in fact, the organizers did write to Olsson and Carlson urging them to come and become part of their land company project. But the point, for the moment, is that Lindsborg would have gone ahead, even if Olof Olsson had not decided to come to the Smoky Valley.

But then, on the other side, it must also be said that the character of Lindsborg would surely have been quite different, if Olof Olsson and his group had not come. It wouldn't be the Lindsborg that has been known down through the years, and it wouldn't be the Lindsborg that we know today. Olof Olsson was such a strong leader, and he was supported by such a dedicated group of followers, that once he arrived here, he immediately became the primary leader in the community. He placed his stamp very strongly on Lindsborg in a way that is still felt today, some one hundred-thirty years later. In that sense, it is indeed true that "Lindsborg was born" in the hour when Olof Olsson decided to come to Kansas.

The Olof Olsson group came by boat to New York and by train to Chicago. Pastor and Mrs. Olsson stayed in Chicago for a few weeks while most of their party traveled on ahead. And Olof Olsson's staying behind turned out to have unintended negative consequences. To be sure, by staying behind in Illinois, Pastor Olsson was able to attend the national convention of the Augustana Synod. He and the leaders of the Synod got to meet each other. But in Olsson's absence, over half of his immigrant group were lured away from their Lindsborg destination by offers of good land and of employment in railroad construction in Missouri. Those Missouri land agents also frightened these people by false reports of danger from Indian attacks in Kansas. So a large part of Olsson's party ended up in Bucklin, Missouri, rather than in Lindsborg. Pastor Olsson felt this loss deeply, and in later years he went several times to visit these members of his flock, now living in Missouri.

Pastor and Mrs. Olsson arrived in Lindsborg on June 25, 1869. Their friends greeted them with great joy. The total number of the Olsson group that actually ended up in Lindsborg was about thirty-five families, or about 105-110 persons, including 39 children. The actual organization of Bethany Church took place on August 19, 1869, six weeks after Olsson's arrival.

Bethany Lutheran was not a conventional Swedish Lutheran congregation, and not a typical pietist congregation. These immigrants were committed to an even more intense form of pietism than were most of their countrymen in this valley. They wanted a church made up of people who practiced a certain kind of piety, and held to a certain kind of strict morality. Bethany Lutheran Church was conceived of by Pastor Olsson and his group in a relatively utopian way. It was to be a free Lutheran congregation. The original plan was that the congregation would not be a part of any larger church organization. And this new congregation was to be a pure congregation. That is, a conversion experience was assumed, and those who were not true Christians, as understood in the most stringent pietist sense, would not be permitted to join. In fact, as in the example already mentioned, there were applicants who were refused membership. Even Anna Olsson, Pastor Olsson's wife, had to submit to an extensive examination by the deacons before she could become a member of Bethany Church.

However, Pastor Olsson soon came to a major change of heart regarding affiliation with the larger church structure. And why did he have such a momentous change of heart? In Sweden he and the other Lutheran pietists had not needed to emphasize Lutheran doctrine; Lutheran teachings were so much a part of the religious atmosphere of that nation that those doctrines could be taken for granted, without further emphasis. Pietist leaders could assume Lutheran doctrine as a given. But in America, Pastor Olsson found himself in a much more pluralistic situation, where Swedish immigrants were being actively sought after by Methodists, Baptists, Congregationalists, traveling revivalists, and even by such groups as the Mormons. Pastor Olsson quickly sensed a need to emphasize Lutheran teaching, along with a vigorous version of the traditional pietist virtues. And Pastor Olsson concluded that part of what this meant was for Bethany Church to join the Augustana Synod.

So on April 15, 1870, less than a year after its organization, Bethany Lutheran Church dropped its original independent constitution, and changed over to the standard Augustana congregational constitution. Not every member of Bethany Church approved of this change; some members were still intensely committed to the free church concept, and were deeply uneasy about this move to affiliate with the Augustana Synod. But Pastor Olsson was a strong leader, and the majority of the congregation supported him in this change.

However, when Bethany Lutheran Church and Pastor Olsson applied for membership in the Augustana Synod, the Synod was not entirely sure that it wanted them. Synod leaders were apprehensive whether Olsson and his followers might be too pietistic, or even fanatical, to fit in with the Augustana Synod. Many Augustana leaders were committed to a less strict or less intense form of pietism than that of Pastor Olsson. So the Synod leaders asked Pastor A. W. Dahlsten of Freemount, a pastor in whose judgment they had confidence, to check out the situation at Bethany Church, and to take a look at the congregation's constitution, to verify that it really did conform to Synod standards. Now, Pastor Dahlsten and Pastor Olsson had known each other back in Sweden. They had been in school together, and had long had a fine respect for each other. Pastor Dahlsten's visit to the Bethany congregation was an entirely happy occasion, and the new congregational constitution was found to be quite in order. So in due course Bethany Church and Pastor Olsson were accepted into the Augustana Synod. And, in fact, not very many years later, in 1881, the Augustana Synod held its national convention in Lindsborg, at Bethany Church, the first of five occasions on which the Synod met there.

The first building for Bethany Church was built on a hill about two miles northwest of the present location. The site is now in the middle of a field. In 1993 a large monument was placed to mark the site, and one can see that tall monument from the roads at the edges of that section of land. (A smaller version of the same monument stands outside the present location of Bethany Church on North Main Street in Lindsborg.) However, that first building had been hastily constructed, and it was soon clear that a new building was needed. By this time, the Lindsborg town site had been laid out in its present location, on lower ground, near the river, where it was more likely that the railroad would in due time come through. Some members wanted to build a second church on the original hilltop site. But after much debate, it was voted by a narrow margin to build the second church in town, in the location where it now stands.

The tension between different views on the nature of the church—between the free church view, on the one hand, and, on the other hand, Pastor Olsson's decision that the right thing for the Bethany congregation was to affiliate with the Augustana Synod—this tension came to a head very early in the life of Bethany Church, in the notorious atonement controversy. The controversy began in Sweden when a Lutheran pietist pastor named Paul Peter Waldenström published a sermon in which he put forth a non-traditional interpretation of the atonement.

On the surface, it was a theological disagreement. In traditional theological jargon, it was a disagreement between the traditional vicarious atonement theory and Waldenström's moral influence theory.

The issue could be more accessibly expressed in these terms: Who is it who was most changed by the death of Jesus Christ on the cross? The traditional view was that it was God the Father who was most changed. That is, human beings had fallen into sin, and had thus drawn down on themselves the wrath of God. But Jesus, by dying on the cross, bore the punishment for all human sin. This satisfied God's requirement for justice, and turned away his wrath. This is the vicarious satisfaction theory or doctrine of the atonement. Jesus died in our place, thus satisfying God's judgment. And on this view it was God who was most changed by Jesus' death on the cross.

Paul Peter Waldenström, on the other hand, said that it was not God who was most changed by Jesus' death on the cross, but human beings. Waldenström was not the first to suggest such a concept. Others, most notably Peter Abelard (1079-1142), had put forth similar proposals. In any case, as Waldenström saw it, God never stopped loving human beings, even after the fall into sin. Rather, it was that sinful human beings were now antagonistic toward God. Jesus' death on the cross, bearing the blows of all the forces of evil, was a demonstration of how great is God's love for us. And the goal of that demonstration of love was to win sinful human beings to become, not hostile toward God, but loving and obedient to him. So it was human beings, not God, who were most changed by what Christ did. Not all human beings, of course, but only those who have responded to what Jesus did. They were changed, so that now they loved God and loved their neighbor. This was a form of the moral influence theory of the atonement.

Waldenström's interest in such an interpretation of the atonement is more understandable if one is aware that some preachers and theologians in Sweden in the mid-1800s were placing heavy emphasis on God's severe anger and judgment against sinners. Many of the pietists, on the other hand, wanted to stress the character of God as loving, gracious, and merciful. To Waldenström, it seemed that the moral influence theory of the atonement could help believers to understand God as loving rather than angry and punitive. However, to more traditional-thinking pietists Waldenström's interpretation seemed to make Christ's death on the cross less central to the atonement than it is in the more familiar view, and this depreciation of the cross was to them totally unacceptable.

In any case, the focus in this study is not on the fine points of theology involved in the atonement controversy, but on how the controversy played itself out in Lindsborg and in the Smoky Valley. People here quickly took sides and were very serious about which side they were on. Pastor Olof Olsson held firmly, even rigidly, to the traditional doctrine, and many congregants supported their pastor in his stand. But Waldenström's ideas received a sympathetic hearing from many people in Bethany Church, and elsewhere in the Smoky Valley. It was primarily the free church people, the ones who had opposed Bethany's joining the Augustana Synod, who were most sympathetic to Waldenström's ideas. And it was not just a doctrinal or theological issue. The dissenters' sympathy for the ideas of Waldenström was intertwined with their preference for a freer church structure and a less liturgically-oriented form of worship. One of the leaders in this free church faction was C. R. Carlson, Pastor Olsson's advisor and dearest friend from way back in Sweden.

A particular flash point in the controversy occurred when C. R. Carlson and others hosted traveling ministers in their homes. Pastor Olsson suspected many of these itinerant preachers of being doctrinally unsound. So far as he was concerned, the very truth of the gospel was at stake in the atonement controversy, so he insisted that no Bethany member could be allowed to provide hospitality for any of these travelers. But so far as C. R. Carlson and others were concerned, it was the very freedom of the Gospel that was at stake, and they would not submit to Pastor Olsson, whom they felt was now becoming excessively authoritarian. They had come to America, they said, not to be oppressed, but to be free. Clearly the young Bethany congregation was facing a crisis over this issue.

A major part of the lore of the Smoky Valley is how people "got into it" about this controversy. Two farmers would meet at a crossroads, each with his Bible under the seat of his wagon. Hours later they would still be there, arguing and quoting Bible verses at each other. At kitchen tables, late at night, men would raise their voices and pound their fists, as these earnest Christians struggled with each other over this issue.

The issue came to a head on April 12, 1874, when, during Good Friday services, Pastor Olof Olsson, from the pulpit, excommunicated sixteen members from Bethany Lutheran Church. It was a tense and tragic moment. Several of those whom Pastor Olsson expelled that day were his close personal friends from Sweden days, including C. R. Carlson. But, old friendships notwithstanding, Pastor Olsson excommunicated them, for what he called their "Waldenströmian sympathies." He did what he was convinced he had to do.

To be sure, by his own later judgment, Olsson over-reacted to the atonement controversy, and he later went to considerable lengths to try to re-establish good relationships with those he had alienated during that controversy. He and C. R. Carlson never agreed about this doctrine, but they did eventually resume their friendship. And once, in later years, when Pastor Olsson was on a visit back to Lindsborg, he was the invited preacher for an evening service at the Covenant Church.

But all of that came later. Returning now to that crisis year of 1874: Some of those who were excommunicated from Bethany Lutheran Church, or who left voluntarily, 42 in all, formed a congregation and built a church at Rose Hill, five miles north-northwest of Lindsborg. A year later, another

Covenant congregation was formed in Lindsborg, and in time the country congregation was merged into the town church.

The various Smoky Valley Augustana congregations fared differently, so far as the atonement controversy was concerned. In quite a few cases, members broke away and formed new congregations. Covenant congregations exist today in close proximity to the Lutheran congregations of Lindsborg, Salina, McPherson, New Gottland, and Marquette. A Covenant congregation was companion to the Augustana congregation in Smolan and continued for some years after Smolan Lutheran rejoined Salemsborg, until the Covenant congregation too was closed. But there is no Covenant congregation linked to either the Freemount or Assaria congregations. For a number of years, a little later on, Pastor Olsson for some time served both Bethany and Freemount congregations, and he once made the comment that the people at Freemount were not as "talkative" as the people in Lindsborg—meaning, it seems, not so inclined to argue about things. Olof Olsson thought that this might be because they had come from a different province in Sweden where, supposedly, people tended to be less disputatious.

In any case, it is surely of interest to know that the issue which was so divisive in the 1870s and 1880s is simply no longer an issue today. Today's Covenant church does not emphasize Waldenström's teachings, and the traditional doctrine of the atonement is entirely acceptable today in Covenant circles.

But back now to Pastor Olsson himself. Though Olof Olsson had at first been viewed with suspicion, he quickly gained the respect of the leaders of the Augustana Synod. He achieved this primarily through his writings. (Hold that thought; we will return to it.) In any case, it was this respect that took Olof Olsson away from Lindsborg after only seven years of service here. Augustana Theological Seminary at Rock Island needed a new professor of theology, and Olof Olsson—the man church leaders hadn't quite trusted to join the ministerium just a few years earlier—was the man they wanted to teach theology to future members of the Augustana ministerium! However, Olof Olsson, to sort of "make it up" to Bethany Church for leaving them, promised that he would send to them as their next pastor the very strongest student he could find at the Seminary.

V. PASTOR CARL AARON SWENSSON

That best student turned out to be a brilliant young seminarian named Carl Aaron Swensson. The caliber of this man may be suggested by the fact that, during the quarter century he served Bethany Church, he received four honorary degrees, was decorated by the King of Sweden with the prestigious Order of the North Star, and held numerous national-level and conference-level elected church offices, as well as many offices in non-church organizations.

These early Swedes in the Smoky Valley did not distinguish particularly between being a Lutheran Christian and being a Republican. Pastor Swensson, like Pastor Olsson before him, was quite active in Republican politics. On one occasion, when Carl Aaron Swensson was speaking at a Republican rally in Moline, Illinois, he received shattering applause when he declared, "A Swede is the best thing in Europe, an American is the best thing in the United States, and a Swedish American Republican is the best thing in the world!" On another occasion Swensson said, "Every Swede is born a Republican and will remain such if no unforeseen accidents overtake him."

The Smoky Valley had long been a Republican stronghold. In the first election ever held in McPherson County, in 1870, the vote was 197 to 1 in favor of the Republican candidate for governor. On the other hand, in 1882 there was one election in Lindsborg in which, wonder of wonders, for the first time a Democrat candidate won! The next day the town barber commented that he ought to charge double for giving a shave to any Republican in town, because their faces were so long.

Pastor Swensson was a faithful and effective pastor for the Bethany congregation. He was deeply involved in community life. But beyond all of the things that one might expect a pastor to do, Carl Aaron Swensson made two enormous additional contributions to the life of this area which are still very much with us today. In 1881 he started Bethany Academy, soon to become Bethany College. And in that same year he arranged for the beginning of rehearsals for the Oratorio Society, which gave its first performance of Handel's Messiah the next year, 1882, and which has since gone on to become nationally and internationally known for the longest, continuous annual presentation of the Messiah anywhere in the nation. Both the College and the Oratorio Society were bold, daring endeavors, which have had an incalculable positive influence on the life of this community and this area. Space does not permit telling in detail the story of these two utterly awesome endeavors; it must be trusted that readers will have some sense of what a major contribution has been made over the years by each of these two very ambitious projects.

But yet, on top of all this, Dr. Swensson was a very prolific writer. He authored eight books during his Lindsborg years, and he wrote extensively, both for church publications and for a wide variety of secular newspapers and periodicals. (Hold that thought; we'll come back to it.)

In addition to being Pastor of Bethany Church, as of 1888, Carl Aaron Swensson also took on the office of President of Bethany College. In that role he traveled constantly. It was on one of his trips for the college that, in Los Angeles, California, Swensson was hospitalized with pneumonia, and on February 16, 1904, he died. His pastor father had been President of the Augustana Synod when he had died at the early age of 45, and son Carl Aaron lived only to the age of 46.

Swensson's tragic and premature death marked the end of an era. The congregation, the college, and the community at large were dumbfounded. What was going to happen now? The Rev. Dr. Ernst F. Pihlblad, faculty member and vice-president of the college, assumed the presidential duties. He also took over as interim pastor of Bethany Church. Dr. Pihlblad served

Bethany College for forty-six years, thirty-seven of those years as head of the institution. He made great contributions to the life of the college, the church, and the community. However, the present account focuses next on the man who became the third pastor of Bethany Lutheran Church.

VI. DOCTOR ALFRED BERGIN

In 1904, the year of Pastor Swensson's death, Alfred Bergin was a young pastor serving a congregation in Cambridge, Minnesota, about sixty miles north of the Twin Cities. He was a man of great ability and enormous drive. During his seven years at Cambridge he had served that large congregation, but he had also commuted by train to the University of Minnesota at Minneapolis, and had completed both a Master's degree and a Ph.D. in Linguistics, complete with a dissertation. He had also, during these seven years, written two books. He was called to Lindsborg at age 38 to begin a ministry which continued for almost four decades.

Doctor Bergin—he was always Doctor Bergin—was a worthy successor to Pastors Olsson and Swensson. He was respected for his integrity, his dignity, and his pastoral manner. He carried an enormous workload for his entire thirty-eight years at Bethany Church. He had numerous opportunities to move elsewhere, but his dedication to being a parish pastor, and his love for Lindsborg, kept him at Bethany.

The first major problem that confronted Dr. Bergin in Lindsborg was the language issue. Many people at Bethany Church preferred to keep everything in Swedish, the language they knew and with which they were comfortable. This was especially true of the leaders of the Bethany congregation. But many college faculty and students didn't know Swedish. They, and some others in the community, needed to be able to worship in English. Bethany Church had offered some English-language services over the years, but somehow they were not seen as meeting the need. So in 1908 Doctor Bergin and the Bethany Church Council gave a reluctant, but honest, blessing for the beginning of Messiah Lutheran Church, which would be an all-English-language congregation. Between thirty and forty people left Bethany to join Messiah, and they were joined by about the same number of other people, who had never belonged to Bethany. Messiah continues today on the edge of the Bethany College campus, a block and a half away from its mother congregation.

Dr. Bergin was known in Lindsborg for the amusing things he said, things which no doubt sounded fine in Swedish, but which came out wrong in English. But it is the present author's thesis that most of these funny sayings were not really accidents at all. It may well be that Dr. Bergin often said these things on purpose, because (1) he had a good sense of humor; (2) he had enough self-confidence that he didn't mind letting people laugh, even when the laugh seemed to be at his expense; and (3) he thoroughly enjoyed being able to get people to laugh. There are hints that pastors at conventions would swap jokes based on these quirks of language, and that some of them would then use these bits of humor back home. The stock of humorous Bergin stories is legion, but here just one story is given, a story that helps to support the thesis that the humor was intentional. One afternoon Dr. Bergin was walking from the parsonage to the church to conduct a funeral. This was in the era when cars were becoming common. Dr. Bergin looked at all the cars parked by the church, and no buggies. And he said, "I wonder how old Mrs. Johnson would feel, if she knew that not a single horse came to her funeral." Now, this was not a language thing at all, but simply a perceptive observation about the changing times, and the comment was surely intended by Dr. Bergin to give bystanders a chuckle—as in fact it did.

Like his two predecessors at Bethany Church, Dr. Bergin was a writer. He edited two large books of congregational and area history, in both cases doing well over half of the research and writing. For years he edited a semi-monthly magazine titled *The Kansas Young Lutheran*. And in his thirty-eight years here, his total number of articles for secular and church publications totaled well over a thousand, and may well have been close to twice that number. Even though he had a full-time position as pastor of Bethany Church, he also served for many years as assistant editor of the Lindsborg newspaper. He was "into everything." The limitations of space preclude listing all the things he did, in the church, in the Lindsborg community, and in the larger world.

Dr. Bergin served Bethany Church far beyond what we would consider normal retirement age. It was only in 1942, when he was 76 years old, that he finally did retire. Two years after his retirement, he went on to his eternal reward, and his bones now rest in Lindsborg's Elmwood Cemetery next to those of his wife Anna.

VII. CONCLUSION

In thinking about the Smoky Valley, a person might well wonder how little Lindsborg, and the Smoky Valley around it, come to have such a large influence in the life of the Augustana Lutheran Church. Why is it that, when the King of Sweden visits the United States, he typically stops at major cities with large Swedish-background populations—places like Chicago, Denver, and San Francisco—and then he also stops at little Lindsborg? The influence of this small community in the center of rural Kansas—how is this phenomenon to be accounted for?

The key is this: The late 1860s and early 1870s were a pivotal time, both for the nation, just emerging from the Civil War, and for the Augustana Synod, that young church body just beginning to find its way and to determine its character. In this very fluid and formative period, Bethany Church in Lindsborg was a special situation, for two reasons. First, it was, more than any other congregation in the Augustana Synod, dedicated, from the very beginning, and with utmost seriousness, to being a pure church in the deepest pietist sense. And second, it was the place where the atonement controversy was fought out as intensely as anywhere, in a manner which had repercussions far beyond this one community. Clearly Lindsborg had significance far beyond its modest size. To be sure, in later times the Swedish connection has been enhanced by the adoption of the town motto "Little Sweden U.S.A.," the every-other-year Hyllningsfest (pioneer honoring festival), the Dala horse theme seen everywhere, the tourist-attracting Swedish import stores, and the like. But the groundwork for little Lindsborg's importance in Swedish-American circles was first laid, and well laid, in the pioneer period.

In that pioneer era, Bethany Lutheran Church was blessed with three successive pastors of extraordinary ability. Other most excellent pastors followed, but they did not face quite the same challenges as the first three pastors. The first three pastors of Bethany Church had the impact they had because they wrote so extensively, especially in periodicals, both religious and secular, which were read by mulitudes of people, both the leaders and the hoi polloi. These three men were also excellent orators, especially Carl Aaron Swensson. But their public speaking had mostly a more local effect. Writing and being published—that was the key to their influence on a wider scale. Other pastors wrote too, but no other pastor in the area wrote nearly as much as these three pastors wrote, nor to so great an effect. So it was the printed word, coming from the mind and heart of Pastors Olsson, Swensson, and Bergin, and then being read by people all over the country, and even back in the Old Country—it was this printed word which put Lindsborg and Bethany Church on the map, and in the minds of leaders elsewhere.

More specifically, it was Olof Olsson's writings that led the leaders of the Augustana Synod to find him trustworthy and knowledgeable, and thus they called him to come to the Seminary to teach future pastors. It was Olof Olsson's being at the Seminary that enabled him to handpick a brilliant successor to take his place at Bethany Church—Carl Aaron Swensson. And it was the bright aura with which Swensson surrounded this community, with its college, and its Oratorio Society, and with his own outpouring of writing—it was all this which influenced Doctor Bergin, who could have gone almost anywhere, to accept the call to Lindsborg, and to stay, and to write, and to influence the mind of the church, and the mind of the nation.

But let's not make Bethany Church stand out too individualistically. Bethany Church and its early pastors were never a solo performance. What happened at Bethany Church was simply one expression of the deep spirituality that permeated this valley, starting with those two unusual land companies which required that all their members be believing Lutherans. All of the pioneer pastors in this valley in those early years, and the strong lay leaders who worked with them, and who continued working even when they were without a pastor—all of them were deeply dedicated, working hard, serving faithfully. Things like the college, the Oratorio Society, Bethany Home, and the many larger-scale works of the church—they would just not have succeeded without the support of the pastors and the congregations in this valley and beyond.

As a way of paying tribute to these eleven present-day congregations, and to their 4,579 baptized members, and to their leaders down through the years, it seems good to conclude this "rich history" by naming the congregations and their pastors as they stand today. Moving from north to south, they are:

Immanuel, Salina, served until recently by Pastor Loren Mai, now in the process of searching for a new pastor

Assaria Lutheran, Pastor William Buschbom

Salemsborg, Pastor Ethan Feistner

Falun Lutheran, also served by Pastor Ethan Feistner

Bethany Lutheran, Lindsborg, Pastor Charles Humphrey

Messiah Lutheran, Lindsborg, presently served by Interim Pastor Rolland Christenson, and to be served by Pastor Stephen Pera beginning August 2002

Freemount, Pastor Jim Harrison

Elim, Marquette, Pastor Larry Cross

New Gottland, served by Associate in Ministry Ramona Carlin

Andover, Pastor Kris Bjerke-Ulliman

Trinity Lutheran, McPherson, Pastor Michael Fibranz

May the legacy of these churches in this valley be joined to the heritage of all the other Augustana congregations which graced the church universal for those 102 years, 1860 to 1962. And may this legacy be passed on through the Augustana Heritage Association, and through the people who knew Augustana—may it be passed on, to the enrichment of the church universal in our day, and until Jesus comes again.

MAJOR SOURCES

Alfred Bergin, *Pioneer Swedish-American Culture in Central Kansas*, translated from the 1909 original Swedish by Ruth Bergin Billdt. Lindsborg, Kansas: Bethany Lutheran Church, 1965.

Alfred Bergin, *The Smoky Valley in the After Years*, translated from the 1919 original Swedish and edited, with additional material, by Ruth Bergin Billdt and Elizabeth Jaderborg. Lindsborg, Kansas: Lindsborg News-Record, 1969.

Emory Kempton Lindquist, *Smoky Valley People: A History of Lindsborg, Kansas*. Lindsborg, Kansas: Bethany College, 1953.

PART FOUR

The Church

The Heart of Augustana

Peter T. Beckman

Several months ago the Grand Canyon Synod, to which I now belong, hosted a luncheon for the retired pastors and wives in the Tucson area. As part of the program, each of us was asked to tell the most personally significant change in the life of the church since we were ordained, which covered fifty years, give or take a few. As you might imagine, many of the persons remarked about the changed and enhanced roles for women in the church. I agreed with that, but I said that the most significant change for me had been the loss of the Augustana liturgy with its thoroughgoing emphasis on the merciful and loving character of God, unlike the more ideological character of more recent liturgies. I was somewhat surprised when four other persons in the group echoed my feelings.

After the luncheon, Pastor Harold Wennes, our bishop, came over to me to say that he had been impressed by the warm piety of the Augustana folks he had known. He suggested that the spirit of their piety seemed a reflection of the warmth and depth of the love of God to which the Augustana liturgy bore such faithful witness. I do not know to whom Pastor Wennes was referring; it may have been some of you.

The heart of Augustana, in my experience, was its liturgy, was its particular proclamation of the gospel.

In one sense, I am an unlikely choice to speak about the heart of Augustana. After all, I come from a mixed marriage. My father was the grandson of a pioneer Augustana pastor, but my mother was raised in Baptist churches. Besides, our family lived in Portland, Oregon, far from the Midwest centers of the Synod. I had little sense for the Augustana Synod as a coherent group of sister churches until I came to Augustana College after the war.

I do not remember much about my parents' religious involvement during my earliest years. I was baptized shortly after birth, but my four younger sisters were baptized all together much later in our living room one afternoon out of the cut glass bowl in which my mother made fruit salad every Sunday night.

When I was four years old, my parents decided that it was time for me to begin some religious training. I have the distinct impression that, even at that young age, it was intended to be remedial. I remember very well the Sunday morning when my parents brought me to a large Baptist church to begin Sunday school. After I had been left in the care of the superintendent, it was discovered that I did not know how to read. Since they had no classes for young illiterates, they puzzled over what to do with me. It happened that the church had a day nursery and in that room there was a large sand box. So they plunked me down in the sand box with a set of Lincoln Logs. I thought to myself, "This Sunday school stuff isn't half bad," and I looked forward to coming back the next Sunday. When I got home, my mother asked me what I had learned in Sunday school. When she heard about the Lincoln Logs, my mother was disgusted. The next Sunday I was enrolled in the Sunday School at Augustana Lutheran church at the corner of Rodney and Stanton. No more sand box, no more Lincoln Logs. From then on my parents belonged there, becoming pillars in the congregation and attending faithfully every Sunday in the third pew from the front on the right side.

Our Sunday school worship session was a great experience for me. We used the green *Junior Hymnal*, from which I learned to sing and love all those great old hymns which move me still. But what I loved most, growing up in the church, was the liturgy; I mean the regular Sunday liturgy, not the short form for Holy Communion. Our pastor had a pleasant and trained baritone voice, and he sang the opening Sentence, not as a vocal performance, but as heightened language naturally accompanied by music.

> Holy, Holy, Holy is the Lord of Hosts!
> The whole earth is full of His glory.

And you remember the following announcement and invitation:

> The Lord is in His holy temple; His throne is in heaven. The Lord is nigh unto them that are of an humble and contrite spirit. He heareth the supplications of the penitent and inclineth to their prayers. Let us therefore draw near with boldness unto His throne of grace and confess our sins.

The Confession which follows addresses God in the following terms:

> Holy and righteous God, merciful Father...heavenly Father....Thy Fatherly compassion.

By the time I got to confirmation age, I had heard those solemn words almost every Sunday for ten years, and more than anything else, they had shaped my image of God. As far as I can remember, no one ever explained them to me or pointed out their biblical basis. I knew all about what God thinks of naughty little boys, for my mother had been raised as a very conservative Baptist. She often warned me that it is a fearful thing to fall into the hands of the living God. Fortunately, Jesus had suffered and died to save us from God and his wrath.

During the years of my childhood, as I thought about the words of the liturgy, I formed a picture of God, not as an enemy or danger to be feared, but not as someone to be trifled with or taken lightly, either. Rather, God seemed more anxious to forgive than we were to repent. The phrases in the Confession of Sins, "tender mercy…merciful and gracious…infinite mercy," seemed to me to speak of caring, restoring love. The confession in the Sunday school liturgy, drawn from the 51st Psalm, used almost identical adjectives in describing the character of God.

The essence of sin, as it is defined in the Confession, seemed to me to be lovelessness: "we confess unto Thee that we have not loved Thee above all things, nor our neighbor as our selves." I could not believe that my gentle and kindly uncle was going to Hell because he drank beer—a sin, I had been led to believe, that was almost as bad as dancing.

Sin, for me, was loving my parents so little that I made them unhappy with what I did or said. Sin was loving one or another of my pesty younger sisters so poorly that I slugged her. I often felt guilty and wished that I could be a better person, but I always felt that though God was grieved over my sinfulness, we both felt better after he had forgiven me, even though he knew that I would do the same thing the next day. And that's how it went all through my childhood and early adolescence. I looked forward to the liturgy every Sunday because it was so reassuring to hear again, and to participate in, the good news of God's tender mercy and Fatherly compassion.

Finally I reached confirmation age, and that is when disaster struck. As part of our confirmation studies we were assigned to read the whole Bible, beginning with the New Testament. I didn't yet know that you are not supposed to take that sort of assignment very seriously, so I set out to do it over the course of the year, reporting every Saturday on the chapters I had read.

This assignment was a disturbing thing to do to an adolescent who has enough problems already. Like most people, I had never read the Bible in any connected way, a parable here and a story there, and the weekly texts, of course, but that was about it. In the beginning, as I started reading the gospels, I came across many familiar stories, as well as others I had not known before. In general, my vision of God, derived from the liturgy, resonated with the Sermon on the Mount, and many of the parables, especially the parable of the Prodigal Son. But there were also passages that troubled me because they seemed so contrary to what I had been taught about God by the liturgy.

And I was disillusioned to discover that the disciples, eleven of whom I had considered to be the greatest Christians of all time, admitted that they often didn't understand what Jesus was talking about. They tried to keep children away from Jesus; they wanted Jesus to call down fire from heaven and to burn up an inhospitable village; they thought God pushed towers over on people or blinded people for their own or their parents' sins. Two of the best disciples went sneaking behind the backs of the others and tried to get the best places in God's Kingdom. Long after Jesus' death and Resurrection, God had to hit Peter over the head with a dream on a rooftop in Joppa to get him to see that God had not called the Gentiles "unclean," and that the good news of God's love was a message for them too. How come Peter didn't learn that when he was with Jesus? What was happening, of course, was the loss of my naive and simple Sunday school mis-apprehensions.

Most of the other kids in my confirmation class read hardly anything in the Bible; some of them never even finished the gospels. As we talked among ourselves, I found that they really didn't expect to make any sense out of what they read, because only pastors can understand the Bible. They knew that I was trying to read the whole thing so sometimes they asked me to tell them where the "good parts" were. I directed them to some of the early stories in the Old Testament; there weren't any "good parts" in the New Testament!

But my fellow students didn't really need the Bible. They had already learned all you need to know about religion before they came to confirmation (probably in kindergarten). "If you are good you go to Heaven: if you are bad you go to Hell. It's a lot easier to be bad than it is to be good, so being religious helps you to be good." Some of my fellow students, in the full bloom of adolescence, weren't sure it was worth the trouble.

My real problems began with the Old Testament. I was fascinated by the historical parts—Genesis and Exodus, Judges, the Samuel and Kings books, but bored by the ritual sections and all the "begats." It was then that I began to see a God described who was very different from the God I had come to know from the Augustana liturgy. This new picture was not of a God full of kindness and tender mercy; rather, he was vicious and cruel, jerking Pharaoh around like a puppet so he could cause yet more disasters for the people of Egypt. He was dishonest, telling the Israelite women to borrow jewelry from their Egyptian neighbors and then skip off in the night with it. He ordered the Israelites to invade the land of the Canaanites and murder every man, woman, and child, an early example of ethnic cleansing.

All of this cruelty and killing was justified by the idea of the covenant. The Hebrews said that God had made a contract with them; he had chosen them to be his special people; and if they obeyed his commandments, they would receive special favors. All the other people of the world were not chosen and so were deserving only of contempt, punishment, and ultimately, death.

When Elijah had the 400 prophets of Baal lynched, that was okay because they were enemies of God. But when Elijah was piqued because he didn't get the respect he felt he deserved, he called down fire from heaven to burn up 102 relatively innocent Israelite men. How do you think God's name was honored in 102 homes that night when the little children asked, "Momma, when is Daddy coming home?" And their mother replied, "Daddy isn't coming home ever again because God burned him up today." What did they say? "Praise God from whom all blessings flow?"

When I got to the book of Job I was appalled all over again. God let the children of Job be destroyed by a tornado because of a sort of bet he had made with Satan, who seemed to be a kind of quality control officer. The children were simply killed and removed like checkers from a board as if they meant nothing to God at all. And then, Job and his friends, who didn't know about the bet, spent the rest of the book arguing about why this had happened. Job was right; his disasters were not punishment for his sins. But he did not realize that God was treating him and his dead children in a way that would be considered unspeakably despicable if it were done by a human.

Of course, years later I realized what the purpose of the author was and that one ought not to take the details of the frame seriously or literally. But in those adolescent years, when my concept of God was of one who invites us to approach his throne of grace with boldness, what I was reading was shocking and disturbing. It was not only the contrast between the God defined by love and mercy, and the God defined by ego and power, that disturbed me. What bothered me very much was that no one else seemed to be disturbed. I tried to talk to our pastor about my confusion, but he was clearly uncomfortable about the very same things and had no satisfying answer for me, so I never mentioned it to him again for fear I might not get confirmed. I had already earned his unfavorable attention for suggesting that the "fear" part of "We should so fear and love God" in the catechism was inappropriate (actually, I think I brashly said "wrong") because 1 John said that perfect love casts out fear. I knew that the perfect love had to be God's love, because mine was so chancy. I was not afraid of a God of perfect love. I must say that our pastor, Paul Randolph, became my lifelong friend, and in spite of everything, was my ordination sponsor. (Of course, this might have been a frightful lapse of judgment on his part.)

But I had learned where my mother had gotten her understanding of the gospel. She believed that the Holy and wrathful God was always lurking to punish us for our sins, which were many and incessant, but Jesus, who was gentle and loving, had come to earth and stands between us and God. God killed Jesus instead of us. Jesus saves us from God, from suffering the just penalty of our sins. For thirty years I listened to a parade of students tell me that that scenario is the gospel. I always replied that not only is it not the gospel, it isn't even monotheism. And it isn't what I learned every week from the Augustana liturgy. The liturgy was witness to the Fatherly heart of God, not to some brutal transaction between God and Jesus. The words of the liturgy were engraved on my heart, partly, I suppose, because I repeated the phrases every Sunday: "Holy and Righteous God," "merciful Father," "O heavenly Father," "thy Fatherly compassion."

It is true that the confession also mentions "the merits of the Savior, Jesus Christ." I had never heard of Anselm or of substitutionary atonement (which may or may not be implied here), and I supposed that the phrase meant that Jesus had been a merciful and loving person just like God. He knew God better than anybody, and he had come to tell us and show us what God is really like. And it was years later that I first connected the phrase "Agnus Dei," Lamb of God, with the Passover story where the blood of a lamb, smeared on the door post, marked a home to be passed over by the death angel. Dare I confess that in my childish ignorance, I thought that "Lamb of God" meant that, like Mary's little lamb, Jesus was God's pet and favorite. (I've never told anyone that before, so don't spread it around.)

I also began to understand the disciples much more sympathetically and to see where they were coming from. In fact, it is amazing that they did as well as they did, having been raised with all the stories that I found so contrary to the spirit of Jesus. Elijah, who specialized in calling down fire from heaven, was the great national hero of their day, along with Moses. The story of the Transfiguration seems to project the relative religious authority of Moses, Elijah, and Jesus: it is Jesus' words that are attested to by God. This is not to say that Moses and Elijah did not speak the Word of God, but the Word they spoke was so wrapped up in the mores, concepts, and culture of an earlier day that it is easy to miss the gospel in their words. It is sad to see how persons accept all those cultural wrappings as if they were the Word of God.

In a sense, the disciples' confusion was the opposite of mine. We began at opposite ends of the Bible, as it were. They began with Moses and Elijah and had trouble with Jesus. I began with Jesus and had trouble with Moses and Elijah. This is not to say that everything in the Old Testament was strange and disturbing. In the Psalms, for instance, in spite of a general air of self-righteousness, there was much that spoke of an humble dependence on the mercy and goodness of God, much like the Augustana liturgy. And in the Prophets, especially Hosea and the latter parts of Isaiah, there began to emerge a picture of God, grieved over the rebellion and sinfulness of the people he loved, but anxious to win them back and to rebuild their shattered lives, a picture Jesus must have cherished. He clearly continued in that strand of the Hebrew tradition. But he just as clearly rejected the picture of a God of tender ego, ferocious retribution, and arbitrary power.

The baptism of Jesus was his call to his ministry, his ordination, as it were, much like the calls of Moses, Isaiah, Jeremiah, and Peter too. The succeeding story of Jesus thinking through and deciding what form his ministry should take is quite properly called "The Temptations." In the wilderness, Jesus considered and rejected three forms of power as ways to gain control of people's lives and faith. These were ecclesiastical power, social welfare power, and finally, political power. In order that his ministry should reflect and reveal the character of God, Jesus chose, not power at all, but the vitality of love. In the end, in the face of the opposition to Jesus by ecclesiastical power, social power, and political power, the vitality of love led him inevitably to the cross. Power always wins the battles with love before it loses the war.

People often mistake Jesus' ministry as one of divine power because of the miracle stories. But these are stories of the love of God sharing in the suffering of the world, not stories of power. The very essence of power is domination and control; there was no attempt by Jesus to use power, divine or any other sort, to gain control, to gain advantage, or even for self-protection. In fact, Jesus tried to hush folks who mistook the vitality of love for power.

This is where Jesus has differed from most of the prophets of every other time in his understanding of God. God is almost always interpreted in terms of the dominant authority figure of that time, the alpha male of the culture. In ancient times, God was described like one of the petty despots of the age, male, of course, autocratic, arbitrary, and ego-driven. A notable exception was Hosea, as I have mentioned. For Augustine, in the early Christian era, the model for God was the Roman Emperor, chief of a great military presence, administrator of a vast network of authority to order and control the Empire. For Anselm, God was a feudal king, chief figure in an intricate network of rights and responsibilities binding society tightly together. Neither the Old Testament writers, Augustine, nor Anselm were evil or ignorant. They were simply children of their times, as are we.

There is a great divide in the Bible between a view of God as Power, Law, and Wrath, and a view of God as Love, Grace, and Mercy. This tension has persisted in the history of the domination and control of the church and still persists in the lives of individual Christians. In the early church, Marcion was so appalled at many of the stories told of God in the Old Testament that he said that that God could not possibly be the Father that Jesus talked about and prayed to. Therefore, there must be two Gods, a Jewish monster god who had killed Jesus, and the loving Father of Jesus. Of course the early church could not buy that and rejected Marcion's attempted solution to the tension.

The Jews dealt with this tension between the two understandings of the character of God with the notion of the covenant. They said that God had chosen them for his own people and showed them steadfast love; all the other people of the earth are Gentiles, outside the love of God. The apostolic church took over the "chosen people" notion from the Jews and made it their own. They said that the church was now the new chosen people, inheritors of all the promises which the Jews had forfeited by killing Jesus. The Jews had now become cursed, the objects of God's wrath—which the newly chosen people of God got to administer.

During the history of the church, new "chosen people" have continued to appear and set themselves over against the rest of the church. Until recently, one such group who call themselves the Latter Day Saints, called all other people "Gentiles."

I suspect that the Jews were right. I agree with Karl Barth who asserts in his famous essay, *The Humanity of God* (Richmond: John Knox Press, 1960) that God chooses to be with and to be for humankind. That by his election of humankind in steadfast love, his vitality is constantly at work in us and among us for redemption and rehabilitation. But I also suspect that the Jews were wrong in thinking that God's choice and election applied exclusively to them, and not to Gentiles, Samaritans, Romans, and all people. And the church has been just as wrong in continuing that error, thinking that it is the only recipient of God's grace, mercy, and steadfast love, that only church Christians are God's people.

The "chosen people syndrome" appears in many forms. In the course of human history, it has probably cost more human deaths and suffering than any other ideology. Religion seems to have generated at least as much hate as love among people.

One summer Sunday, not so long ago, I went to supply preach in a small rural congregation. I came into the church basement just as Sunday school was over and met a young man with a baby in his arms. He pointed a finger at me and said with a grin, "Rehabilitation, not Retribution, right?" It turned out that he had been in one of my classes some years before and he still remembered a catch phrase I frequently used to describe the will and purpose of God.

It is Sovereign Power that must demand retribution or be diminished; it is Sovereign Love which, by it very nature, seeks the rehabilitation of its object. Sovereign Power which is disobeyed generates wrath. Sovereign Love that is disappointed generates pain and sorrow in the Lover. Truly he has borne our grief and carried our sorrow.

Some religious people think that it should be just the opposite; the sovereignty of God must create pain and suffering in the disobedient. God must unfailingly punish people for their sins. In fact, they tend to see every unfortunate event as a punishment from God. Remember the disciples and the man born blind, or the friends of Job. If God didn't punish sinners by making them suffer, they would get off scot-free, the argument goes. That was the complaint, you remember, of the elder brother in the Parable of the Prodigal Son, the parable more properly called the Waiting Father. When the younger son came back and got a welcome home party, his older brother protested to his father: "You mean to tell me that your son can go off and waste your property in riotous living and then come home and get rewarded with a big party? At least he should be made to pay back all that money and be put on probation. All this time I have been a straight arrow, and what has it gotten me? It's just not fair."

The elder brother had a point. He was a good pious man, no doubt, who believed that if you spare the rod, you spoil the child. He had heard that whom the Lord loves, he chastens. He thought that his father should follow the example of his God and reward the faithful, himself, and punish the wicked, his brother.

In my classes, whenever we read the Parable of the Workers in the Vineyard in Matthew 20, plenty of elder brothers would speak up saying, "That's just not fair." You remember the parable—workers were hired at various hours during the day, but at the end, each was paid a day's wage, no matter how long they had worked. Naturally, those who had worked all day complained, but the owner simply said, "Get used to it. That is how I choose to do things." It was not fair, or just, from the perspective of power, but it is God's way, who gives people what they need, not what they deserve.

There is a great gulf between the justice of the God of Power and the justice of the God of Love. The God of Power is fair and just, giving you what you deserve, retribution. But when you have failed the God of Love, in his sorrow, he seeks to give you what you need, rehabilitation.

Of course, the prodigal son did not get off scot-free. His father suffered during the absence of his son, especially every time he got another report on what his son was doing, but he was overjoyed at his son's repentant return. The son at first knew the pleasure of rebellion, of doing his own thing, of not having to answer to anyone, of an undisciplined and wastrel lifestyle. But then he knew the pain of discovering the emptiness of his life, of losing his fair weather friends, the pain of coming to his senses, of realizing what he had done to his father, the pain and humiliation of having to acknowledge his self-centered and loveless behavior. No, the prodigal son did not escape pain and shame, but it emerged in his own heart out of his own lovelessness, especially in the presence of his father's waiting love. The aim of his father's love was rehabilitation, not retribution. For me, that is the will of the God whom I learned to know in the liturgy.

It is only rehabilitative, restoring love that makes confession possible. The prodigal son only dared to come home when he recalled the gracious kindness of his father toward the hired hands. He came home hoping to share in that kindness, not daring to expect what he did receive, full restoration—with a party!

In our liturgical confession we began with the announcement of God's loving kindness and were encouraged to approach his throne of grace with boldness. We acknowledged that we deserved to be cast away from God's presence because of our failure to love, but we asked for, not what we deserved, but what we needed, forgiveness.

God's forgiveness simply means that he does not cast us away in rightful disgust and rejection, but he accepts the pain our lovelessness causes him, as he also rejoices when we turn to him. Forgiveness has nothing to do with forensic or legal transactions or law courts. Forgiveness, for God, means participation in the suffering of the world, even to the injustice of the cross. Forgiveness means that God keeps unbroken, on his side, a rehabilitating, restoring love even at the cost of pain and suffering. The love of God is a vitality always present among us to restore and to redeem.

God does not punish us for our sins; he does not send floods or droughts, illness or disasters, Jesus said. Rather, God seeks by the vitality of his love to save us from our sins, from the kind of life and acts which alienate us from one another, which diminish our lives, which enslave and overpower us. God seeks to save us from what we do to each other, to ourselves and to our world through our lack of love. Christ, weeping over Jerusalem, was sorrowing over the future the people were creating for themselves and their children through their self-righteousness and blindness, not for what a wrathful God might do. God in Christ was trying to save them from their headlong plunge into that terrible future, but they would not listen.

This is not sentimentality; God is realistic, not sentimental. The love of God is love for his enemies. Everyone loves their friends, Jesus said, but God loves his enemies. Sentimentality is easy love; we love the good, the beautiful, the true because they are so lovely. We love whatever makes us feel good, feel pious, feel righteous. All this is self-love in disguise, of course.

The love of God is not sentimentality; it heals us as it judges our failure to love as we have been loved. In the presence of God's love in Jesus Christ, we are found wanting. "We confess that we have not loved Thee above all things, nor our neighbor as ourselves." The measure of God's love is the measure and judge of our own lack of love and self-righteousness. We are judged for our lovelessness, but we are not condemned. God sent his Son into the world, not to condemn the world, but that the world might be rehabilitated through him. Even if our hearts condemn us, God's love does not condemn us; it judges us, it offers us rehabilitation. To refuse judgment is to refuse rehabilitation.

At the conclusion of the Parable of the Talents in Matthew 25, the master says to the two servants who have been faithful, who have shared and invested the love which they themselves had received, and thus expanded and increased the store of love in the world, "Enter into the joy of your Lord." But on the other hand, perhaps, just perhaps, the Master may say to those whose lovelessness, whose self-righteousness, whose pursuit of power have been a cause for God's sorrow, "Enter into the suffering and sorrow of your Lord." Thus the weeping and wailing and gnashing of teeth.

I have spoken of my confusion over the contrast between the picture of God given me by our liturgy and various images of God in the Bible. The person who helped me come to terms with my confusion more than anyone else was Eric Wahlstrom, who taught New Testament at the seminary. For me, he was typical of the best of the Augustana church in his quiet, gentle, and irenic spirit. We had many conversations during my seminary years and especially later while he was writing his book, *God Who Redeems* (Philadelphia: Muhlenburg Press, 1962). He helped me to see that the various theories of the Atonement, for example, are simply mythic ways of trying to express the suffering that God's love entails for him, that forgiveness is not simply God saying, "Well, that's alright" and passing over our sin. Like much else in the Bible and in historical theology, these theories are expressed in terms drawn from their times and cultures.

One of the good things Wahlstrom did for me was to point me to a book that was written by a Swedish bishop just at the time I was going through confirmation. I felt almost that the book had been written for me. The book is *The Suffering God*, by Erling Eidem (Rock Island: Augustana Book Concern, 1938). He helped me come to some of the understandings which I have expressed today.

Nothing I have said today should be taken to imply that the Augustana church was a paragon of angelic Christians. As you well remember, and perhaps know better than I, there was a variety of streams of faith in the church: persons with a variety of special interests and orientations, differing backgrounds, as well as lots of just plain folks—and some pretty big and aggressive egos, too, if the truth be told. How could all this be held together in one church?

I believe that the identity of the Augustana Synod was shaped by its liturgy. Of course, the distinctive liturgy was a tag by which Augustana could be identified. If you visited in an unfamiliar Lutheran church, the liturgy told you immediately whether it was Augustana. But more significantly, the liturgy was the thing we all shared every Sunday. It was truly the heart of Augustana. If our Christian love for one another is, at its most basic, simply the recognition and acknowledgement of our shared humanity before God, with all our limitations, our particularities, not to say our peculiarities, then the weekly liturgy continued to announce the gospel, to instruct us, to shape our faith, and to bind together our varied ways of trying to be God's faithful people.

To be sure, there always seemed to be some issue or other simmering along upon which people took opposite sides, but nevertheless, there seemed to be a kind of irenic spirit in the church. I know there were outsiders who said that Augustana was not really confessional enough; if it were, they would fight like the rest of the Lutherans. But I believe that the more irenic spirit of Augustana was based upon a confidence and trust in God's love at work in each person, however idiosyncratic he or she might seem. Over the years, the gospel of Jesus Christ, the good news about the Fatherly love of God which Jesus preached and demonstrated, expressed every Sunday in the liturgy, seeped into our corporate life and faith. The yeast of the gospel worked slowly but surely, leavening the whole lump.

Back when the American Lutheran Conference was beginning to talk about a wider association, it was Augustana that pressed to make any merger as inclusive as possible over against the pressure to be as ideologically correct as possible. Some in Augustana spoke of Augustana as a "bridge church." At first I thought that concept was rather self-serving, but later I came to see it as a function for which Augustana was well suited. It was clear that in any merger, Augustana would give up both its life and whatever corporate influence it may have had in religious circles. I heard people say, "Watch out for the Norwegians; they are aggressive and power hungry" or "Watch out for the ULCA, they are full of church politics, and besides, they will just submerge us." In spite of fears like these (which turned out to be generally ill-founded), Augustana was willing to give up its corporate life in order to share its vitality more widely.

For some Lutheran churches, the heart of their life was a carefully defended and preserved ideology. But Augustana's focus on faith in the loving character of God rather than on ideology, or on religious experience, for that matter, made it easier for the Augustana Church to find fellowship with others. More than most streams of American Lutheranism, Augustana was supportive of ecumenical work like the National and World Councils of Churches and the Lutheran World Federation. Augustana supplied leadership in these enterprises disproportionate to its small size.

As a boy growing up in an Augustana congregation, the only Augustana activities I was aware of beyond my local congregation were the Bethphage institution, the local Emanuel Hospital, and most important, foreign missions. The first I knew of because we collected our nickels and dimes for Bethphage in Sunday school. Emanuel Hospital I knew because it was only a few blocks from our church, and its superintendent was my Sunday school teacher one year. Missionaries home on leave visited our congregation at least once a year. I remember two things about this. They preached long sermons, and on Sunday afternoons, or sometimes weekday evenings, they presented programs and displayed interesting objects from their fields.

Like most of the kids in Sunday school, my sisters and I belonged to the Junior Mission Band. We met on Saturday afternoons once a month; we worked on projects like cutting out squares for patchwork quilts; we had Kool-Aid and cookies; and we heard stories about our missionaries in China, Africa, and India. Yes, we joked about Miss Minnie Tack's name. The Mission Bands were a wonderful program. I grew up knowing that a fundamental purpose of the church, fundamental, not optional, was mission work, sharing the gospel of God's love and responding to the needs, especially the health needs, of all people. In the context of the gospel expressed in our liturgy, all this seemed very natural to me.

The heart of Augustana was its liturgy. As a sometime supply preacher, I was glad that the liturgy began with a clear expression of the gospel. Then whatever else came after, even if the sermon were 18 minutes of law and 2 minutes of gospel, as the old accusation had it, nevertheless, the gospel shaped the worship experience.

Well, I'm afraid that this discourse has been more personal witness than anything. It may resonate with your experience, or there may have been something else from our corporate life which was most meaningful to you. But for me, in this day of near liturgical anarchy, what I miss most from my Augustana experience is its liturgy. I thank God that it was the definitive element of my religious life and experience.

Theological Foundations of the Augustana Lutheran Church

Herbert E. Anderson

Although I lived there for only seven years, I usually say that I grew up in Scandia, Minnesota. My father, Ernest G. Anderson, was pastor of Elim Lutheran Church from 1947 to 1954, during which time Scandia celebrated its centennial (in 1950) as the first Swedish settlement in Minnesota and Elim Church turned 100 years old (in 1954). When we moved to Scandia in 1947, Swedish was regularly spoken at the mercantile store, worship was sometimes in Swedish, and there were no paved roads into this community of 95 people. By the time we left Scandia in 1954, there was a paved road through the village, but the population had not yet grown. Today Scandia is part of the suburban sprawl of Minneapolis and St. Paul, and Elim Lutheran Church is a thriving congregation with over 1700 baptized members and three pastors.

In the summer and fall of 1850 three young men—Carl Fernstrom, Oscar Roos, and August Sandahl—staked out a claim for forty acres and built a substantial log house on land near the town of Marine. By the next year, 1851, they had sold the land to Daniel Nilson. It was Nilson who helped Pastor Erland Carlsson from Chicago organize the Swedish Lutheran Congregation on May 19, 1854. Carlsson stopped at the Scandia settlement on his way back home to Chicago, having already founded congregations in St. Paul and Chisago Lake. There were 80 adults and children present for this first meeting. The following words are ascribed to Pastor Erland Carlsson's sermon at that occasion in a play written to celebrate the 95th Anniversary of founding Elim Evangelical Lutheran Church:

> Some of you may ask, or you have heard others say it, "Why should we establish a Lutheran Church in this new land? Since we are renouncing the citizenship of our mother country and seeking one in this land, would it not be better if we did likewise with our religion?" Yes, and some are going even further than that. They

urge you to renounce your God and your church altogether and live as unbelievers in America. Let us not be foolish, but let us consider how great a spiritual heritage we have received, and which is ours as members of the Evangelical Lutheran Church. We have the pure gospel of Jesus Christ....We have an open Bible. We have a free and evangelical worship. We have the sacraments which Christ instituted. We have a glorious treasure of hymns, sacred songs, devotional writings....This is the heritage of three hundred years in our great church. Is it not worth preserving among us, for our own and our children's blessing?

The history of the founding of Scandia and Elim Lutheran Church suggests some themes we will explore under the topic "Theological Foundations of Augustana." In the founding years and still 100 years later when I lived there, worship was traditional and austere, simple but not too formal, and, in my remembrance, slightly anti-Catholic. So, for example, the shift from electric candle lights to wax candles lit by acolytes caused quite a stir in the early 1950s. From the beginning of this congregation, the influence of pietistic movements in Scandinavia in the mid-nineteenth century was not only reflected in the patterns of worship but also in the puritan nature of daily life. I remember the custodian Emil Arkman scolding me for playing ping-pong in the church on Sunday, even though, in fact, we were playing in the parish hall. It was, however, Sunday. When the parish hall was used for community events like the annual cooperative creamery meeting and a polka band played, the painting of Jesus in the Garden of Gethsemane was turned to face the wall. Such fun and frivolity did not fit easily with the somberness and piety of church life in Scandia. The close connection between the pietism and the temperance movement in Sweden no doubt influenced the policy that the person who owned the establishment that sold liquor in the village could not belong to this congregation. My intent with these brief reminiscences of Scandia is to stir your own memories in order to locate our reflections of the theological foundations of Augustana in the experiences of concrete communities like Elim Lutheran Church in Scandia or places in your memory.

In reflecting on the transformations that had occurred in Augustana in its first 100 years, G. Everett Arden made an observation we know to be generally true. "The outcome of any development [is] to a large extent determined by the elements which were present at the beginning."[1] My understanding of our task is to explore the beliefs and values and traditions from Sweden that were the "theological foundations" the founding fathers and mothers of Elim Lutheran Church and other faith communities begun during the second wave of Swedish immigration. Before we look for theological foundations, however, we need to identify the distinctive characteristics of Augustana. Each of us has our own list. G. Everett Arden once

---

[1] G. Everett Arden, *Augustana Heritage: A History of the Augustana Lutheran Church* (Rock Island: Augustana Book Concern, 1963) 3.

described the *Augustana Ethos* as "the steady faith of Old Lutheranism with the activism and spontaneity of right-wing Swedish dissent."[2] At the last Heritage Gathering, Herbert Chilstrom listed personal piety, dignified worship, social consciousness, and global awareness as marks of the "Augustana Spirit."[3] When I think about the theological characteristics of this heritage, I have regularly identified five things: theological openness, solid or sensible ecclesiology (i.e., view of the church), missionary zeal, an evangelical (albeit sometimes limiting) piety, and a rigorous social ethic. Once we establish the enduring qualifies of Augustana, we can ask how or in what way these elements were "present at the beginning."

What I have learned through the process of research for this workshop reinforces what I believe is the core of the spirit of Augustana. Over and over again, in the historical accounts of our beginnings, two things will be linked together that seem to be in contradiction. So, for example, G. Everett Arden suggests that the evangelical revival in Sweden was critical of the established Church but not antichurch. It promoted a subjective, personal, pietistic approach to the practice of faith while at the same time holding to the basic principles and truths of confessional Lutheran thought. In an article for *Christian Century* prior to the forming of the Evangelical Lutheran Church in America, Richard Koenig suggested in a similar way that Augustana embodied firm Lutheran confessionalism and a warm, evangelical piety.[4] I am proposing that the Augustana spirit is paradoxical at its core.

In his presentation, LaVern Grosc suggested that Eric Wahlstrom embodied this spirit with his warm heart and brilliant mind. While I agree, I would add another dimension from my experience of Wahlstrom that is near to the essence of Augustana. He embodied the spirit of paradox. Wahlstrom would often say: "Well, boys, it could be this way, and then it could be that way. It really doesn't make any difference. It could be one or the other. Both are true." These contradictions are part of the mystery of life rather than a problem to solve. I would encourage us to keep Wahlstrom's embrace of contradiction in mind as we explore the theological foundations of the Augustana heritage. The principle of paradox is, I would submit, one of the theological foundations of Augustana and an important contribution to the future of Lutheranism in this society. In his discussion of "piety and polity in Augustana" at Chautauqua, Lyman Lundeen made a similar point. One cannot simply pick one thing out of the Christian faith or Christian life and exploit it at the expense of the rest, or even make a list of things isolated from one another, "for there is an organic unity in which the pieces fit

---

[2] Ibid., 16.
[3] Herbert W. Chilstrom, "What Is/Was Augustana?," *The Augustana Heritage: Recollections, Perspectives, and Prospects*, ed. Arland J. Hultgren and Vance L. Eckstrom (Chicago: Augustana Heritage Association, 1999) 3.
[4] Richard E. Koenig, "The New Lutheran Church: The Gift of Augustana," *Christian Century* 104/19 (1987) 555-58.

together."⁵ In a moment we will explore the origins in Sweden of this spirit of paradox,

Keeping alive this principle of paradox has a particular relevance for our time. In a speech at the second Mahtomedi free conference on "Upholding Lutheran Confessions" in May of 1999, Mark Granquist argued against using the Church of Sweden to support the historic episcopate and Called to Common Mission. In the Church of Sweden, the historic episcopate was important, but not regarded as the essence of the Church, useful but not necessary. Augustana, Granquist argues, did not continue the historic episcopate in America. "It had no bishops, and was organized along a Presbyterian, synodical model of organization instead (as did most other American Lutheran groups)." Granquist's conclusion is that "the history and practice of the Church of Sweden and the Augustana Synod is a consistent argument against the adoption of the proposed Called to Common Mission."⁶ Perhaps and perhaps not. One might propose that at the core of our heritage from the Church of Sweden was the freedom and willingness to allow two traditions regarding the historic episcopate to exist side by side in a spirit of love and gentleness. On the matter of changes in liturgical practice in the 1940s, Conrad Bergendoff made the following comment that has some application today: "We are much more apt to succeed if we do not become violent on either side. In order to decide what to lay aside there must be experimentation. My belief is that in the course of time we give our consent to some changes and refuse to accept others."⁷ While I grant you that whether black preaching gowns should give way to cassock and surplice or alb and chasuble is less weighty than the historic episcopate, the spirit of gentleness and openness is the same.

In order to understand the spirit of Sweden from which the Augustana heritage was fashioned, in order to determine elements from Sweden "present at the beginning," I want to propose a number of dialectical statements in which two themes or ideas that are both true seem in contradiction, may in fact be in contradiction but cannot be understood in isolation from one another. This principle makes the Augustana heritage distinctive and remarkable among Lutherans in its capacity to keep paradox alive without rancor and in a spirit of gentleness. In his *Augustana Heritage* G. Everett Arden connects *differentiation* and *accommodation* as parallel processes that shaped our history. This is an instance of keeping paradox alive. Both are necessary. "Differentiation exposes and underlines that which makes the group, at least in its own mind, distinctive, and which must, therefore, be preserved in order to be transmitted ....[whereas] accommodation is the process by which the Church had adjusted to its environment, adapting its

---

⁵ Lyman T. Lundeen, "The Piety and Polity of Augustana," *The Augustana Heritage*, ed. A. Hultgren and V. Eckstrom, 16.

⁶ The text is available at www.wordalone.org/archives/speeches/granquist.htm.

⁷ Conrad Bergendoff, *Our Attitude toward Liturgical Innovations* (Rock Island: Augustana Liturgy Commission, 1946) 6.

own life and tradition to the content in which it must live and have its being."[8] While some of the following statements overlap considerably, it is important to read them all to see "the organic unity in which the pieces fit together."

ONE. Although the Lutheran church AND the culture in mid-nineteenth century Sweden were influenced by the French Revolution principles of liberty, equality, and fraternity, tradition was transformed rather than rejected. As a result, challenging the status quo was not understood as unfaithfulness to God's will.

In *The Augustana Lutheran Church in America*, Oscar Olson offers this quotation from a book on the history of Sweden. "In no country, perhaps, outside of France herself, did the ideals of the French Revolution, in the abstract at least, find more enthusiastic reception than in Sweden."[9] Ideals like liberty, equality, and fraternity affected all classes to produce a liberal climate in Sweden that no longer considered the *status quo* God's will but looked to the future as the bearer of real promise for new and better life. G. Everett Arden even more explicitly locates the origin of the Augustana spirit in revolutionary France. From about 1810 on, Swedish liberals looked with suspicion on the *status quo* and wrote *Reform* on their programs of action. "They [Swedish liberals] questioned the nature and character of all existing authority, whether of wealth, class, position or dogma, and were certain that if the principles of freedom and equality were only permitted to operate, Swedish life would quickly enough be lifted to a new era of enlightenment, progress, and well-being."[10] The Swedish immigrants who founded Augustana would have brought this revolutionary spirit with them to the new land. The early founders would have been critical of some practices of the Church of Sweden even though they had drunk deeply of its life for centuries. Although no area of human life was free from critique, tradition is reformed but not rejected. Because it is our heritage to understand the gospel and the church that remembers the Gospel as earthen vessels subject to change, challenging the *status quo* is a mark of faithfulness, part of a forward looking spirit and a willingness to be open to the new thing that God is doing in our midst. Locating the origins of Augustana in that way has helped me understand the spirit of theological openness in our heritage.

TWO. While revivalism and the evangelical spirit challenged the status quo in the church, it did so within the institutional norms and without promoting separatism.

Many strands were woven together to shape the evangelical movement in Sweden in the nineteenth century. One strand came from German pietism. Henric Schartau, who lived until 1825, developed a Swedish version of German pietism that was at once personal and orthodox. Here is

---
[8] G. E. Arden, *Augustana Heritage*, 17-18.
[9] Oscar N. Olson, *The Augustana Lutheran Church in America: Pioneer Period 1846-1860* (Rock Island: Augustana Book Concern, 1950) 1.
[10] G. Everett Arden, *The School of the Prophets: The Background and History of Augustana Theological Seminary 1860-1960* (Rock Island: Agustana Book Concern, 1960) 5.

how "Schartauism" is described in a handbook on Swedish church history: "A personally experienced and doctrinally Lutheran Christianity, concentrating on the conversion and sanctification of the individual and with clarity of thought, ethical earnestness and deep insight into the religious life, its care and growth."[11] Another source of Swedish pietism originated in the English Methodist Church which promoted Bible reading and preached the gospel of Jesus, repentance, and faith without respect to outward forms. Carl Olaf Rosenius was influenced by pietism from England but still sought a balance between doctrinal orthodoxy and evangelical spirit.

Spiritual unrest was one mark of the climate of Sweden in the mid-nineteenth century when the immigration began that formed the Augustana Lutheran Church. Here is how Oscar Olson describes it. The evangelical ferment was "born out of evangelical preaching, nurtured by Bible reading, postils, hymnbook and prayer book….It was a protest against the dead formalism, hierarchical intolerance, and worldly spirit that characterized a large portion of the official church and its leaders….It was subjective and individualistic, and often bore the stamp of some outstanding leader."[12] It did not, however, tend toward separatism or sectarianism. Separatism would not only hinder and delay the renewal of Swedish religious life that must be achieved within the established church; it would give too much power to human activity in the practice of faith. The church that constantly needs to be reformed is Christ's church. The church is a creation of God to unite us with Christ and with one another.

THREE. *The Christian message does not exist outside the context of concrete history and yet the church, as the carrier of Gospel, is an act of God that continually transcends the insights of a particular culture.*

In an essay on "The Theology of the Augustana Lutheran Church," Karl E. Mattson argued that the life of the church "must always be understood as a creation of God" and that "the divine character of the life of the church does not deny its own peculiar and concrete set of historical circumstances."[13] Mattson begins with an assumption not shared by all scholars of our heritage: "that the founders of Augustana were loyal sons and daughters of the Church of Sweden, who had drunk deeply of its life and tradition."[14] Other movements we have noted like revivalism and pietism also had shaped our founders but "the liturgy, the church order, the devotional literature and the Psalm Book which they carried were all inheritances from the Swedish Church."[15] That was the message of Pastor Erland Carlsson to the folk who gathered in Scandia to found Elim Evangelical Lutheran Church.

---

[11] O. Olson, *The Augustana Lutheran Church*, 17.

[12] Ibid., 26-27.

[13] Karl E. Mattson, "The Theology of the Augustana Lutheran Church," *Centennial Essays: Augustana Lutheran Church 1860-1960*, ed. Emmer Engberg et al. (Rock Island: Augustana Book Concern, 1960) 30.

[14] Ibid., 33.

[15] Ibid.

The form of church government that was embodied in the first constitution of Scandia was, however, an inheritance from other Lutheran groups on American soil influenced by the Reformed tradition and not an inheritance from Sweden or a rejection of episcopal order. A new context called for a new form.

The story of the Evangelical Synod of Northern Illinois illustrates how the new context required a new and sharper focus on the importance of the Lutheran confessions that transcended the culture. Being Lutheran was not simply part of the culture as it had been in Sweden. The Evangelical Lutheran Synod of Northern Illinois was formed of representatives of American, German, and Swedish churches. It adopted a constitution in 1851 which regarded the Augsburg Confession as "mainly correct." Lars Paul Esbjörn, however, regarded the phrase "mainly correct" as too ambiguous and vague. The symbolical books of the Lutheran Church, he insisted, "contain a correct summary and exposition of the divine word, wherefore we declare and adopt them as the foundation of our faith and doctrine, next to the Holy Scriptures."[16] The Swedish congregations finally separated from the Synod of Northern Illinois and established completely independent existence partly on confessional grounds. The question of adapting to American life would continue to be a dynamic process. Being Lutheran in response to the emerging Protestant culture in America was primary. Differentiation prevailed over accommodation. Twenty-five years later, Eric Norelius summarized the experience in this way:

> Through this union we learned a great deal about the organization and government of a free church; furthermore, we began to be aware of the significance of the change in language and Americanization which we would inevitably meet....More important than these other matters was the fact that we had reason to place a higher evaluation on, and to be even more faithful to, our Evangelical Lutheran Confession than we had ever been before. In the Northern Illinois Synod we saw and experienced the sad results of looseness in doctrine and practice....Our eyes were opened to the danger, we awakened, as if from a bad dream, and this, God be praised, happened before our congregations had been ruined and developed a taste for this poor diet.[17]

From the beginning, Augustana has been aware that differentiation without accommodation could lead to insulation from the connections that would foster a growing connection with the American environment.

FOUR. The connection between the Augustana Lutheran Church and its environment continued an alternation between identification and separation that had begun in Sweden.

Because of their state church origins, understanding the relationship between the church and culture was a particularly difficult question for the

---

[16] G. E. Arden, *School of the Prophets*, 74.
[17] Quoted from K. Mattson, "The Theology of the Augustana Lutheran Church," 42.

Swedish immigrants who founded Augustana. At one level, there was an equation between Swedish and being Lutheran that was difficult to change. There were many people on the membership roll of Elim Lutheran Church in Scandia who would send in their $10 dues each year from all over the United States. I suppose I conducted at least 10 funerals while on internship at Angelica in Los Angeles under the tutelage of Oscar Benson for old Swedes who had not been in the church since they had been baptized in the old country. Having a Lutheran funeral was an entitlement left over from a time when the State Church performed those functions for its citizens whether they were practicing Christians or not. Furthermore, the liberalism of nineteenth century Sweden had cultural as well as political and economic dimensions. Cultural liberalism was reflected most clearly in the secularization of education, including theological education. By 1831, all pastors were educated in the university by a theological faculty. As a result, Arden observes, men like Esbjörn, Hasselquist and Erland Carlsson, and their successors "understood that religious values cannot endure in isolation, but must be dynamically related to the total life of the individual and that such relationships are predicated upon an intelligent awareness of the whole culture."[18]

There was, however, an impulse of isolation from the culture that was part of the pietism that had begun in Sweden and continued in this country. University trained pastors would not have been as open to the personal experience of faith that the revival movements in Sweden sought to effect among the believers. The encounter with American Lutherans, as Eric Norelius had reported it, had been distressing. Esbjörn gave this report in support of plans for separation from the school in Springfield and the Evangelical Synod of Northern Illinois: "Worst of all is the deplorable influence being exerted here upon the piety and morals of our own youth. For that reason alone, it is impossible to keep our ministerial candidates in a 'mixed institution' among American youth who have all kinds of faiths or no faith at all." One student said that if the Scandinavian students are not taken from Springfield, "they will become more like the Americans than anything else."[19] Differentiation was more important than accommodation.

Ten years after leaving Scandia, my father made the following observation in an article in the *Elim Messenger*, a monthly church newsletter: "For nearly a century the parish existed in social and cultural isolation from the larger community. This was dramatically shattered when the broad new highway cut through the center of our peaceful village. Perhaps it was my imagination, but it seemed to me from that moment, for better or for worse, all the forces, influences, striving, goals and means of our changing world poured into our remote little community. We were suddenly caught up with the sweep of our modern age." My father's comment has the same over-

---

[18] G. E. Arden, *School of the Prophets*, 33.
[19] Quoted from G. E. Arden, *Augustana Heritage*, 66.

tones of isolationism as Esbjörn's observations 100 years earlier. Building a highway through Scandia meant that all the forces of the modern life invaded this little, isolated community and it was caught up with the "sweep of the modem age."

Two themes dominated the Swedish citizens who emigrated to America in the 19th century. They came from a society dominated by Christian principles in which the church played a crucial role in the care of the sick and the needy. They were also influenced by the spiritual upheaval of Sweden in the mid-nineteenth century that was not only critical of the Swedish church but promoted a kind of isolationism for the sake of personal salvation and sanctified living. In his Chautauqua presentation on "The Augustana Heritage Vis-à-Vis the Role of the Church in Society," Louis Almén outlined fundamental changes that occurred in Augustana in the 1930s, including change to greater social activism without at the same time neglecting the evangelical principles that undergirded its founding. "Liberal churches were socially active but had departed from classic Christian theology. On the other hand, most theologically conservative churches did not get involved in social action. Augustana stood out because it was evangelical, confessional, liturgical *and* socially active."[20]

When Sydney Ahlstrom wrote in 1960 about Augustana and the American Challenge, neither the LCA nor the ELCA had been formed. His concern was that we must "strive with constant diligence and concern lest ours become a mere 'culture Christianity', so adapted and conformed to the world that it has nothing to say or do but provide tea parties for young adults, recreational facilities for their children, and old peoples' homes for their parents….We must claim and use the resources which are ours if the Lutheran Church is to be a countervailing force."[21] Keeping balance between differentiation and accommodation in relation to the church and culture has been an ongoing agenda for Lutherans in America. Until recently, I would submit that we have erred on the side of differentiation. Decisions by the ELCA to be in fellowship with both the Anglican and Reformed traditions are a major step toward accommodation and what I would call the "Americanization of Lutheranism." The distinctive contribution of Augustana to this pivotal moment in the history of Lutheranism in America is best expressed in a statement from 1935 by Conrad Bergendoff quoted in the Heritage *Newsletter* in1997. The statement was made about a proposed reunion between Augustana and the Church of Sweden. It is, I would submit, the contribution of the Augustana Spirit to this present moment of American Lutheranism:

---

[20] Louis T. Almén, "The Augustana Heritage Vis-à-Vis the Role of the Church in Society," *The Augustana Heritage*, ed. A. Hultgren and V. Eckstrom, 150.

[21] Sydney E. Ahlstrom, "Facing the New World: Augustana and the American Challenge," *Centennial Essays*, ed. E. Engberg, 23.

Reunion is not a question of subtraction but of contribution, not an effort to discover the least common denominator which would he harmless, but a willingness to incorporate and harmonize the fruits of Christian experience from all sides.[22]

There is probably no better place to stand as we look to the future than on the shoulders of such a spirit from such a giant man of faith.

---

[22] The quotation appears in the *Augustana Heritage Newsletter* 3/1 (August 1997) 6.

The Awakening Social Consciousness of the Augustana Lutheran Church

Robert L. Anderson

This essay is an abbreviated transcription of the notes used for an oral presentation at the Gathering of the Augustana Heritage Association in June of 2000. Its primary intent is to explore the development of the social consciousness of the Augustana Lutheran Church in the post World War I and II periods. The basis for the presentation is the author's S.T.M. thesis written in 1958-59 at Union Theological Seminary in New York City under the guidance of Professors John Bennett and Robert Lee, with the special encouragement of and comments by Professor Reinhold Niebuhr. It is difficult to go back to a study now more than forty-five years old and imagine how we thought and looked at the confluence of our theology and social action then as compared with where we are now. But hopefully the effort will yield something of value as to how some of us got to where we are today.

INTRODUCTION

When the author mentioned to a friend his selected topic—that of social consciousness in the Augustana Lutheran Church—the friend commented, "That should be a short and easy job. There wasn't any." The quick response was, "I can be equally short. You're wrong!"

A perusal of the literature dealing with the application of Christianity to social problems, or the relationship of religion to society, reveals much that has been written, and that Christians have long been active in this field of endeavor, sensing a social responsibility. But one may be surprised to find that the Lutheran Church, the largest Protestant denomination in the world, is rarely mentioned in this literature either with respect to significant contributions in the way of social action or with respect to theory and works published in this field, at least at the time of this study. As this was true of the Lutheran Church in the world generally, it was no less true of the Lutheran Church in the United States.

When the Lutheran Church is mentioned, it is often done in a rather negative frame of reference to show the quietism, or inactivity, of the Lutherans in the field of social action. Reinhold Niebuhr well illustrates this as he writes in his book, *Does Civilization Need Religion?*: "Lutheranism is the Protestant way of despairing of the world and of claiming victory for the religious ideal without engaging the world in combat."[1] Elsewhere he has said, "Unfortunately, Lutheran piety, at its best, is too pure to affect the world."[2] Although he chided this author a bit for using two quotations so dated even in the 1950s, his comments were in part a reason for the choice of topic.

Niebuhr's statements are nevertheless consistent with a majority of theologians and religious observers for whom the record of Lutheran social consciousness had not been particularly significant or impressive. Yet in *A Basic History of Lutheranism in America*, Abdel Ross Wentz wrote:

> Since World War II, Lutheran social activities and pronouncements have entered new areas that would have seemed unapproachable a generation earlier. Lutherans have concerned themselves with Christian citizenship, international affairs, social security for old age, universal military training, the atomic and hydrogen bombs. The influence of church groups is now regularly exerted upon lawmaking bodies....At mid-century Lutherans are prepared to bear corporate witness to the power of the gospel as a leaven in social life.[3]

Concerning these two sets of viewpoints several questions arose at the time of this study. If the earlier comments were correct, did they still hold true, or was there a significant change? If they were true at one time, why were they so? And if they were no longer true, as Wentz argued, why had there been a change, and what proportions had this change assumed?

This writer believed that there definitely had been a shift to an observable trend toward increased social responsibility. The task of the study, then, was to investigate this thesis—to see to what extent there had been a shift in social concern; to determine if there were any significant countervailing trends, and if there were, their causes; to find reasons for the earlier quietism; and to determine the factors that brought whatever shift that could be substantiated to obtain by the date of the study.

Because it was literally impossible to study all eighteen of the Lutheran Church bodies existing in the l950s, and because the author had access to

---

[1] Reinhold Niebuhr, *Does Civilization Need Religion?* (New York: The Macmillan Company, 1928) 110.
[2] Reinhold Niebuhr, "English and German Mentalities," *Christendom* 1 (Spring, 1936) 474.
[3] Abdel Ross Wentz, *A Basic History of Lutheranism in America* (Philadelphia: Muhlenberg Press, 1955) 335-36.

special materials of the Augustana Lutheran Church, particularly in the library of Upsala College in New Jersey, this church body was the only one investigated in detail. Some comparisons were made with the United Lutheran Church in America, the proposed major partner in a pending merger of Lutheran Church bodies at the time, to give added depth to the study and to identify some of the problems that might arise in the new merged Lutheran body after the proposal was finalized. Because of the participation of the Augustana Lutheran Church in the National Lutheran Council and the American Lutheran Conference, the study of developments in those bodies was used to further legitimize the conclusion of the new trend in American Lutheranism. Although many interviews with Lutheran Church leaders were conducted, the primary evidence investigated was that of written documents of the Augustana Lutheran Church as is shown by the outline of the thesis provided below.

SUMMARY OF FINDINGS

The primary finding of the study is that the data reveals a very strong beginning on the part of the Augustana Church of a recognition of the fact that the Church must bear a corporate witness to the problems of society and must use its corporate influence to see that insofar as it is possible, the will of God done in all of life, including the political and social aspects of our common life.

This was a change from an earlier emphasis almost solely on the Word and Sacraments and the individual, a totally evangelistic approach to society, and an aloofness as a church from the majority of social problems except for the important, but *ex post facto*, work of the missions of mercy. The fact that the Augustana Church became increasingly willing to take definite stands on less superficial and more basic and controversial issues led to the expression of social concern playing an increasingly significant part in the program and reports of the presidents of the church. The church in turn made continued and intensified use of its Commission on Social Action; and the pages of its journals, papers, and other literature became more and more open to a social message. These among other manifestations of the trend showed that the church had rethought and reinterpreted its position concerning its relation to society. It is safe to say that social action became a permanent, integral, and vital part of the program of the Augustana Lutheran Church.

The foundations upon which the new social attitude was based can be summarized as follows:

a. The primary task of the church is still to work with individuals, to produce changed hearts. The primary tools of the church in this task are the Word and Sacraments.

b. Sin lies behind social problems. The task of the church, therefore, is still focused on the redemption of people from their situations and to the new life lived by the grace of God in fellowship with him.

c. But life in fellowship with Christ and in obedience to him must issue in love to one's neighbor. As the welfare of the neighbor is bound up in the structures of society, so the Christian who ministers to that neighbor must concern him or herself with the structures of society.

d. Furthermore, it is also understood more deeply that the evils of society are in a very real way a hindrance to effective proclamation of the gospel and to the life of faith in obedience to Christ.

e. Social action, therefore, is a logical extension of the Christian faith as well as the particular theological position of Luther and the church which bears his name. Social interest is not a new theology, but a correction of a misconception and a new emphasis corresponding to modern needs and problems.

f. Social action must also be theologically grounded and in keeping with fundamental Lutheran confessional principles. It does not mean a sacrifice of these principles, but is rather a modern reinterpretation of the spirit and meaning lying behind them.

g. The church continues to shy away from a conception of the church as a political body, or any inference that the gospel be used as a means of compulsion for social reform.

h. To implement this social attitude there is a need for the church to make a corporate witness to society in the form of definite stands taken and submitted to the public and to appropriate government authorities.

i. There is also a corresponding need to emphasize social education within the church so that church members will fully perform their obligations as Christian citizens wherever they are and in whatever stations they may find themselves. Christianity is not a Sunday morning affair. Christian politicians, persons active in business, laborers, and homemakers must live out all of their lives as specially responsible servants of Christ. This is a chief way to reform society and bring it into harmony with the will of God.

j. At the same time, the church must not neglect nor minimize its institutions of mercy which minister to the unfortunate and needy of society and fellowship of faith. This is an important way to abide by St. Paul's admonition to do good to all, and especially to those who are of the household of faith (Galatians 6:10). Social action and social service, preventive and remedial concern, go hand in hand.

k. The church also sees the need to cooperate with other bodies, church and non-church, to achieve these ends of social justice and Christian service.

It would be wrong to assume that this list of presuppositions is a general manifesto of social policy that was accepted by all Augustana Lutherans in the same manner. To the end of the synod's separate existence, there were widely varying degrees of social consciousness in the church. That this may be seen more clearly, the following typological summary is presented. This is, of course, an over-simplified typology and should not be taken in an absolute sense. The actual situation is much more confused and more fluid that such a division would indicate. But nevertheless, the different types are real and to a degree distinguishable.

1. The first type is one that is based on sound Lutheran doctrine, but is largely motivated by an emphasis stemming from the social gospel literature and interests. There is no capitulation to social gospel theology, but there is an indebtedness to this movement for impetus and literature. As far as social attitudes are concerned, while both Lutheran theology and social concern are present, they often appear tangentially rather than integrally related. This attitude is also typified by a very liberal political outlook. The positions of Professor A. D. Mattson, especially his emphasis on the concept of the Kingdom of God as opposed to that of the church itself, illustrate quite well this type of social position.

2. The second group of Augustana Lutherans is characterized by a more conservative political outlook. Adherents of this position felt that the old quietism was outdated, but they were also more conservative doctrinally, and did not go as far as the fourth group listed later in interpreting Lutheran theology. While neither the first nor second group interpreted the Lutheran theological position very thoroughly, the second group was held back somewhat by theological and political conservatism and the lack of reinterpretation efforts; while the first group was not so hindered because its adherents felt that primary importance was in getting something done. For this purpose they adopted new presuppositions which, while not in conflict with Lutheran principles, were not directly derived from them. The second type was socially concerned, but not as enthusiastically so and in the same way as the first type. Its proponents cautioned that the church must not forget to be the church as it becomes the conscience of society. The function of the church is more to protest evils and set limits to government than to positively participate in political programs. The editorial policies of the *Lutheran Companion*, especially under the direction of Dr. E. E. Ryden, illustrate this second group.

3. The third group is made up of what may be called the theologically uninformed activists. This group saw that something must be done to help society. But the presuppositions underlying this belief came from a melange of sources. Some of the enthusiasm was caught from ecumenical influences. They were sensitive to the criticism of others. Another influence was a twentieth century form of "Enlightenment" liberalism that was rooted in and propagated by the public school system. A third influence was that of the secular world and especially contemporary liberal politics. There was no departure from general Lutheran theological principles, but neither was there any consciously perceptible impetus from it. These Lutherans felt that God loves all people, and that somehow this is related to the message of the church, and that Christians should be concerned to alleviate bad social situations. This group was typified by the pastor who cryptically remarked in a discussion of social consciousness in the Augustana Church, "What the Lutheran Church needs is more Democrats!" This group likely included a

majority of those Augustana people who felt a social concern. It was, therefore, a very important group; for without this base, the appeals of Church leaders for more social responsibility would have gone unheeded much longer and been much less effective.

4. The fourth type is one represented by those who share much of the enthusiasm of the first group along with an appreciation of the Lutheran theological heritage espoused by the second type. The chief difference is that they rely for social motivation on a serious reinterpretation of the Lutheran theological position and a new study into the spirit of Luther and the Reformation. They see a dynamic relationship between Luther, his theology, and the current social situation. Typical of this fourth group would be many individuals in the ULCA. One of them who was a professor at Augustana's Gustavus Adolphus College is Dr. George Forrell, well known for his doctoral dissertation (later published as a book) on Luther's concept of "faith active in love."[4] Others might well include Dr. Edgar M. Carlson, former President of Gustavus Adolphus, and to a certain degree, Dr. Conrad Bergendoff, former President of both Augustana College and the Augustana Theological Seminary. The influence of these latter two individuals, however, was largely confined to their writings, rather than actual social leadership. There is a good reason to believe that the following quotation from a 1942 article in the *Lutheran Companion* was from someone prominent in this fourth group:

> The Church must seek the individual soul, but the church must be the salt of the earth. The Church must call men to repent, but to repent of very personal and social sins. The Church must preach the gospel to every creature, but it is a gospel that calls men from sin's power and death's grip to walk in newness of life. The Church must not be a third political party, but it must be a conscience and challenge to every political party. It may yet be in the minority, but it must witness even to a world that doesn't want to hear, of the saving gospel and righteousness of God. It calls men to a citizenship in heaven, but the man whose citizenship is in heaven must be and will be the best citizen on earth. The Church must sincerely and continually pray, "Thy will be done *on earth* as it is in heaven."[5]

5. There was, however, a fifth type within the Augustana Church. This was a probably large, but unmeasurable, residual group which maintained the old attitude. It was characterized for some by social lethargy, lack of concern, or conservative political bias. For others it was a belief that the church should not be "conformed to this world." These people typify the perfectionist tendency in Christianity as opposed to the tendency for social responsibility (in the terms of Dr. Reinhold Niebuhr's ethico-historical analysis). For still others it is a continuation of the belief that the church has no

---

[4] George Forell, *Faith Active in Love: An Investigation of the Principles Underlying Luther's Social Ethics* (Minneapolis: Augsburg Publishing House, 1959).

[5] *The Lutheran Companion* 50 (May 28, 1942) 683.

business in social affairs other than social missions, except perhaps on the liquor question and threat of war issue. This group was not vocal; no articles appeared to represent its position in official literature in the final years of the Augustana Church. Yet it was very real and very present. Its impeding influence was felt in many quarters and on many occasions. This group operated not so much by opposition as by foot-dragging. Whatever were its causes, and whatever were its manifestations, the group had to be recognized and had to be approached with the message of the social obligations of the church, if the church was to advance in its course of a more enlightened social consciousness and greater social responsibility.

PERSONAL CONCLUSION

My study began with the observation that at the time of the study there was little mention of any significant Lutheran contribution to the social responsibility of the church in general literature. It was also noted, however, that many observers began to notice a change in the traditional Lutheran attitude to social problems. As was true of the Lutheran Church in this country generally, so it was with the Augustana Lutheran Church. Historically, the stoical Augustana Lutherans exhibited a quietiestic attitude typical of the Lutheran Church generally. Some of the reasons for this were explored. But the bulk of the study was devoted to an examination of the evidence that there was a change after World War I, particularly after 1935, and most significantly after World War II.

My conclusion was not that social action became a dominant motif, nor did the Augustana church in general move as fast as many of the leaders had hoped. But some real beginnings were made in this period, beginnings that Augustana brought with it through its clergy and lay members into the Lutheran Church in America and continuing into the successor Evangelical Lutheran Church in America.

The theological basis for this awakening social consciousness found its roots for the development in the theology of Luther and the Lutheran confessions. While Luther and his early followers can be interpreted in a variety of ways, his theology does not necessarily lead to quietiestic social attitude, separation from the world in which people live, or a concern only with individual piety and an approach, where present, to the ills of society through remedial, or an inner mission approach.

The theology of Luther and the Lutheran confessions can, and did, lead to a viable and dynamic social responsibility. This new attitude has not been possible without some serious reinterpretation and contemporalizing of traditional Lutheran positions. Yet this has been done without a sacrifice of what Lutherans hold to be essential in the Christian faith and the task of the church.

In fact, it is believed now by Lutherans that this social responsibility in our day and age is an imperative of the vision of the church, and that a quietiestic or strictly private ethic is a corruption of the Christian faith as well as the spirit of the Reformation.

The conclusion to my 1959 study was, therefore, that one may expect not only a continuation of the social programs now begun in the Lutheran churches, but also that there would be an enlargement of social concern as more and more Lutherans became convinced of the importance of the social task of the church and see its integral relationship to the Christian faith and the mission given Christians by our Lord.

As final evidence of this, I must be quite personal. I consider myself to be a rather typical Augustana Lutheran, and I became Director of a very active Lutheran Office of Governmental Affairs in Washington, D. C., where I was succeeded by another Augustana Lutheran pastor, Charles Bergstrom, who had been a pioneer in our church in seeing community needs and what concerned church members can do about it.

I also think of two former Augustana congregations with which I have had a long association. In the month of June, 2000, as this presentation was being prepared, I participated in the initial meeting at my home congregation, Trinity Lutheran Church of Moline, as a parish committee planned its participation in the just inaugurated Lutheran Advocacy Network, a project sponsored by Lutheran Social Services of Illinois in the 3 ELCA Illinois synods. The purpose was to expand the advocacy role of the Lutheran congregations in the State of Illinois.

Earlier in the same month I also had the opportunity to worship at Augustana Lutheran Church in Washington, D. C. This is the place where as a student in the nation's capital I felt the call to the ministry, and where I learned so much about social action from the Pastor, Clarence T. Nelson, his wife, Ruth Youngdahl Nelson, and their children, Elizabeth, David, Jon, and Mary—names almost synonymous with Lutheran social action. There I also met and came to revere Ruth's brother, former Minnesota governor and then Federal Judge Luther Youngdahl, his wife, and son Bill, another pioneer in Lutheran action in race relations.

This congregation continues to change its ministry from Lutherans transplanted to the nation's capital, to people of different racial backgrounds in the church neighborhood, and now to people of different sexual orientations who also have moved into the neighborhood. As the buttons distributed for members to wear on that Pentecost Sunday, and which were also distributed at the congregation's booth that day at the D.C. Gay Pride festival said, "GOD LOVES US ALL."

This is and was the Augustana Lutheran Church and its heritage. We might differ on some of the ways we come down on given issues in a given year. But that we have the duty to witness to God in whatever conditions his people live and work, I believe, is without dispute. There is a social conscience and a social justice dimension to our faith that will not leave us.

As Sven said to his wife, when she wondered why they still walked to church, when so many neighbors rode in new autos: "We may be a little slow, Lena, but we get there." Lutherans, and no less Augustana, may have been a little slow in moving, but in the terms of our topic, we're getting there.

The Augustana Synod and the Evangelical Covenant Church

Mark A. Granquist

The old cliché is probably very true—family fights are often the most intense! When you fight with those who are nearest to you, the conflict is often more nasty and more pointed than when you fight with total strangers. This can be true for organizations as well, as it most certainly was for the relationship between the Augustana Synod and the Evangelical Covenant Church. Founded by Swedish immigrants in the United States, both denominations came out of the same tradition in Sweden, that of the evangelical wing of the Church of Sweden, and both shared many personal and organizational bonds throughout the nineteenth century. But growing divergence between the two provoked a bitter fight at the end of the nineteenth century, and the two groups went their separate organizational ways. In the twentieth century, they shared moments of contact, but eventually found themselves in different wings of American Protestantism. Perhaps there are ties that remain strong within the local expressions of these churches, but merger and differences of affiliation have weakened the bonds that once held the two groups together.

Both the Augustana Synod and the Evangelical Covenant Church were formed mainly by Swedish immigrant religious leaders who had come out of the evangelical religious awakenings in eighteenth and nineteenth century Sweden. These awakenings were deeply influenced first by Moravians and Lutheran pietists in the eighteenth century, and then by Anglo-American evangelicals in the nineteenth century, all of whom brought to Sweden a stress of what has been termed a "Religion of the Heart." The hallmarks of this during the Swedish awakening were numerous: a strong emphasis on the need for an intense internal awakening or conversion, stress on prayer and study of Scriptures by the lay believers, a central concern for strict personal morality, a renewed appreciation of Luther's idea of the priesthood of all believers, and a common concern with the "dead formalism" that they perceived as characterizing many of the priests and congregations of the Lutheran Church of Sweden.

The Church of Sweden, as a state church, saw itself as the church for all Swedes. By law, being a Swedish citizen meant that one was a member of the Swedish Lutheran Church, and one's baptism was equivalent to citizenship. This model of the church, of being a folk-church for all Swedish citizens, was strongly ingrained in Swedish society, and yet it caused no end of problems. If all Swedes were to be members of the Church of Sweden, then the standards of Christian faith and conduct within the church had almost inevitably to be of a fairly modest nature, as enforcement of church discipline was difficult at best. The Church of Sweden as a whole was often characterized by a certain sense of religious formalism, in which emphasis was placed on external acts of religiosity—being baptized and confirmed, attending the worship of the church and receiving the sacraments, obeying the priests and the bishops, and adhering to minimal standards of Christian ethics. Many of the leaders of the Church of Sweden thought that this was a good model for a Christian society in Sweden and sought to maintain this model and their power in it through a close partnership between the church and the Swedish government.

Yet there were some within Sweden who were not satisfied. They sought what they saw as an "awakened" evangelically and pietistically oriented Christian community that would demand stronger participation of the lay people in the Church of Sweden and stronger standards of Christian belief and conduct. Sometimes their sharp critiques of the Church of Sweden almost reached the point of caricature, but there is no doubt that they represented a strong portion of Swedish lay society, and a significant segment of Swedish priests. Their initial push was for change within the system of the Church of Sweden by means of education, preaching, and tightening of church discipline. Eventually some of these "awakened" Swedes would begin to form religious organizations and networks outside of the Church of Sweden itself, finding that the state church structure was generally hostile to their vision of reform.

The first outside influences toward awakening came early in the eighteenth century, when soldiers returning from foreign wars brought home Moravian ideas and piety. These reforms, as well as the related ideas from German Lutheran pietism, were often inwardly directed, with "awakened" believers gathering in small groups, called conventicles, for prayer and Bible study. If there was no sympathetic pastor in the local congregation, then these groups could meet by themselves, using printed sermons and Bible study materials for guidance. Although these groups were not meant as a substitute for worship in the local congregations, their existence was a threat to the control of the local state church clergy, and the Swedish Church and government reacted strongly to such conventicles, which were made illegal in the Conventicle Act of 1726. Under this act it was illegal in Protestant Sweden for people to gather for Bible study and prayer without the presence of the local pastor, although enforcement of the law was subject to much variation. Nevertheless the awakening movement grew and spread across Sweden.

In the nineteenth century the awakenings were further enhanced in Sweden by new ideas from British, and later American, evangelicals such as the Methodist George Scott, and the Presbyterian Robert Baird. A new generation of Swedish pietist leaders, such as C. O. Rosenius, P. P. Waldenström, Oscar Ahnfeldt, Lina Sandell Berg, and many others, were deeply influenced by these new ideas and began to build structures of reform within Swedish society. The journal *Pietisten* and many new publications were distributed around the country by wandering lay colporteurs, who not only handed out materials, but also sang the new revival hymns and preached to large gatherings of Swedes. Awakenings swept many parts of Sweden during the 1840s and 1850s, and the growth of the movement was further strengthened by the formation in 1856 of the "Evangeliska Fosterlandsstiftelsen" (Evangelical National Foundation), known popularly in Sweden to this day as the "EFS," a national organization to foster the growth of religious awakening and temperance.

The revival movement in Sweden, however, had its own internal tensions and debates as to the directions, goals, and methods of this reform. Rosenius and the leaders of the EFS sought to maintain the revival movement within the Church of Sweden as a reform movement, but there were others who were pushing for a break with the doctrinal Lutheranism of the established Church. Awakened "prophets" such as Eric Jansson and others formed separate religious communities outside of the Church of Sweden, and Methodists, Baptists, Mormons, and others also made inroads into Sweden, especially after 1858, when the Conventicle Act was repealed. Separatists argued that the Church of Sweden was not capable of reform, and that converted individuals should not have fellowship or receive communion with unconverted individuals at the altars of the state church. Although Rosenius and others sought to maintain the unity of the movement, tensions were building through the period from the 1850s to the 1870s.

Rosenius led the EFS and the revival movement until his death in 1868. Control of the movement then passed to P. P. Waldenström, who moved further from doctrinal Lutheranism as the year went along. Waldenström broke with Lutheranism in 1872 when he published a sermon criticizing the Lutheran understanding of the doctrine of Atonement, and incited a firestorm of theological debate among Swedes (and Swedish-Americans). After several years the debate split the EFS, and the "free" (that is, non-Lutheran) branch formed the Swedish Mission Covenant, although traditionally many of those within the Mission Covenant retained a nominal membership within the Church of Sweden, which as a state church operated as a religious "umbrella" for many in Sweden.

When Swedes began to emigrate to the United States in the 1850s and 1860s, they found that religious conditions in their new country were vastly different from those in Sweden. There was a wider array of religious options available to the immigrants but, more importantly, there was no state church, nor any form of governmental support for religion at all. If the immigrant Swedes wanted to form their own congregations, they had to do so as private, voluntary organizations, imagined and directed by themselves. Here in this free land of no established religion, the immigrants would have to take on the enormous task of structuring their own religious traditions in a very foreign land.

Most of the religious leaders who emigrated to the United States from Sweden during the nineteenth century were from the evangelical wing of Swedish Christianity. Very few of the early leaders or pastors of the Swedish immigrant denominations were state church Lutheran pastors; indeed many priests and bishops of the Church of Sweden initially maintained quite a hostile attitude toward the whole process of emigration and had deep suspicion of the new Swedish-American denominations. Most of the Swedish-American pastors were not trained in Swedish universities, but were trained in American institutions or in the various mission schools in Sweden. They in turn had little regard for the state church form of religion, which they could not have replicated in the United States, even had they wanted to do so.

The early leaders of Swedish-American immigrant religion thus shared a number of common characteristics, including an evangelical outlook and a suspicion of the old state church structures of Sweden. Most of the Swedish-American pastors held that one needed an awakened faith and piety to be truly religious, and they looked to a common heritage from the Swedish evangelical leaders, especially Rosenius and those in the EFS. Yet the divisions that were manifest within the evangelical movement in Sweden during the mid-nineteenth century were also painfully apparent within the Swedish-American denominations, and without the "umbrella" of the state Church of Sweden, these divisions eventually broke out into full-scale splintering. These splits within the immigrant congregations and denominations were all the more painful because many, on all sides of these issues, were nurtured by similar forms of piety and many deep bonds of personal affection.

The key issues which affected the Swedish-American religious world were the same ones that affected evangelicals in Sweden: conversion as a requirement for membership in the religious community, whether to practice open or closed communion, the validity of Lutheran forms of worship and ritual, and the nature of adherence to and understanding of Lutheran doctrinal and confessional theology. The more "free" wing of Swedish-American religion desired congregations or societies strictly limited to "true" believers and sought minimal formal ties to Lutheran theology and practice. Other, more "Lutheran" evangelicals envisioned a reformed version of Lutheranism along awakened lines.

When the Lutheran Augustana Synod was formed in 1860, it was composed of local Swedish-American congregations containing many sorts of piety and outlook. The course of development within the synod reflected many of these tensions, as Swedish-Americans sought an appropriate structure in the United States for their own understandings of religion. The Augustana congregation in Chicago, Immanuel Lutheran congregation, was typical of many of these early congregations and their struggles. Immanuel was formed in 1853 and soon was being led by Pastor Erland Carlsson, who was very open to the evangelical awakening in Sweden. But others within the congregation desired the formation of a Mission Society within the congregation that would be open only to those who were "truly spiritually minded people," and such a society was formed in 1868, under the leadership of a Swedish immigrant colporteur, J. M. Sanngren. The Mission Society and Immanuel congregation maintained ties for several years, but when the Mission Society built its own chapel in 1869 and formally incorporated as a separate entity in 1870, the break between the two was complete.

Developments like this were taking place throughout Swedish-America. In Galesburg, St. Paul, and Lindsborg (among many other places) separate mission societies were being formed out of Lutheran congregations or independently by Swedish immigrants. There were also the beginnings of national organizations for such independent mission congregations, especially with the founding of the Swedish Evangelical Lutheran Mission Synod in 1873 and the Swedish Evangelical Lutheran Ansgarius Synod in 1874. In addition, there was a more radically "free" element, composed of persons suspicious of any sort of organization outside of the local congregation.

For the mission and free congregations, the Augustana Synod seemed too much like the Church of Sweden for their comfort. The Augustana Synod saw itself as *the* church for all Swedish immigrants. It wasn't as inclusive as the Church of Sweden, but sought the form of a modified Lutheran folk church, with the intent of applying education and church discipline to raising the moral and spiritual level of the Swedish-American community. It did not practice closed communion, nor did it require evidence of a conversion experience for congregational membership; in short, it most closely resembled the position of the "Lutheran" wing of the EFS. For the mission people among the Swedish Americans, this position was not good enough, representing a fatal compromise with the Lutheranism of the state church in Sweden.

In 1872, when Waldenström ignited the Atonement Controversy in Sweden, the battle soon raged also within the Swedish-American religious community. Predictably, the Lutherans in the Augustana Synod opposed Waldenström's rejection of traditional Lutheran doctrine on this issue and cast him as a heretic. Among the mission and free church people, the reaction was more varied; some sided with Waldenström's new position on the atonement, while others did not. Yet the Atonement Controversy was masking a deeper division between the Lutheran evangelicals and the mission and free church elements, this time over the role of the Bible and the Lutheran Confessions as normative theological documents. Waldenström's rejection of the Lutheran doctrine of the atonement was predicated on the idea that he could not find such a doctrine in the Bible, and therefore it had to be rejected as unscriptural, no matter how important it was in the Lutheran Confessions. Whatever they thought of his ideas about the atonement, the mission and free church leaders defended Waldenström's theological method of strict biblicism against the claims of Lutheran confessionalism; for them, the only authority could be Scripture.

This was a direct challenge to the Lutherans, both in Sweden and in the Augustana Synod, and they attacked Waldenström and his supporters with zeal, the battle raging throughout much of the 1870s. As the underlying issues became clearer, many of the mission and free church people followed Waldenström's lead and dropped any formal adherence to the Lutheran Confessions, and any identity as Lutherans whatsoever. The Mission Synod and the Ansgarius Synod, both originally founded as Lutheran bodies (in a fairly loose sense), soon moved away from any formal or explicit Lutheran identity whatsoever. The late 1870s and early 1880s were a time of great fluidity within the mission and free church community in Swedish-America, and many within were searching for some new form of organization to bring them together.

The Atonement Controversy also resulted in a great deal of conflict within the congregations of the Augustana Synod, as opponents and proponents of Waldenström fought over the issues of theology, biblical authority, and confessional loyalty. These disputes were often deeply painful and divided many in the Swedish-American community who shared the heritage of the evangelical awakenings in Sweden. During the 1870s and 1880s, synodical records show that Augustana pastors exercised church discipline and excommunication against 1000-2000 members per year (on the average), most of whom were supporters of Waldenström. Many times congregations and communities were split deeply by these actions, nowhere more so than in Lindsborg, where Synod pastor Olof Olsson battled against the mission element in his congregation, which included his good and long-time friend, C. J. Nyvall, who became an early leader in the Evangelical Covenant Church. Friends were turned into opponents, and long-standing divisions were etched into the fabric of the immigrant community.

Augustana Synod pastors enforced the Lutheran nature of the Synod, even if it meant division. Sometimes this necessitated the expulsion of pastors as well as parishioners, including the high profile case of Pastor J. G. Princell, leader of one of the large Augustana congregations in New York, who was expelled from the synod in 1876. Princell went on to become the leader of the free church element within the Swedish-American community, so radically free church that they long opposed *any* type of formal religious organization beyond that of the local community. It is understandable why Princell often referred to synods as "organized sin."

It was in this context, then, that the mission people in Swedish-America began the long, slow process of moving together to form some sort of national organization. On the one hand, they were moving away from the explicit Lutheran confessional identity of their past; they would retain many elements of Swedish Lutheran piety, but would not consider themselves as formally Lutheran. On the other hand, they did not go as far as the Free Church in a strict congregationalism, but sought some form of positive national organization that would bind them and their congregations to each other.

In 1885 the mission people established the Swedish Evangelical Mission Covenant, with 48 pastors and 38 congregations, the greater part of which had come originally from the Augustana Synod. The use of the term "Covenant" (*Förbund*) in their organizational title is important; it suggests that they sought a positive, almost organic entity, with themselves and their congregations as a part of a society or living body of biblical believers. This was a positive union of congregations in which the central biblicism was expressed through the often asked question, "Where is it written?" The sticky question of baptism was sidestepped by leaving the issue of infant or adult baptism to the individual parents to decide; no pastor or congregation could insist solely on one or the other option.

The results of the split between the Augustana Synod and the Mission Covenant were traumatic for both communities, especially during the latter half of the nineteenth century. In the long run, however, it is clear that any number of positive developments occurred for both denominations, which strengthened them as they moved out of the nineteenth century, and into the twentieth. For the Augustana Synod, the Atonement Controversy and defection of the mission factions solidified the Lutheran identity and polity of the new denomination and gave a renewed focus to a more centralized authority for the national denominational organization. The formation of the Mission Covenant gave a positive national expression to the evangelical pastors and congregations scattered around the Swedish-American community, and helped them clarify their ideas on theological and scriptural authority. Both groups solidified and focused their identity through the heat of this painful controversy, even though they would both face important issues in the future.

For the Augustana Synod, future issues would grow out of the heat of the Atonement Controversy. One organizational question involved the balance of power between the three expressions of denominational organization: congregations, the conferences, and the national synodical authority. Augustana also faced the issue of church discipline and how to deal with members who did not live up to the strict moral code of the Swedish evangelical awakenings, as well as the question of how to balance the spirit of awakened Swedish Pietism with the Lutheran confessional identity. For the Mission Covenant, the key questions centered around how to "jell" its nascent organic identity within formal organizational boundaries—in a sense, how to become a "living" covenant. Here the continuing attacks from the free church people were both difficult and clarifying; the Covenant and the Free Church had intermittent discussions toward merger for many years, until such negotiations were abandoned in the 1920s. Also, the Covenant faced long controversies over the nature of the biblicism that the denomination espoused, including such questions as how biblical authority operated, how authority is to be vested in the Scriptures, and the legitimate means of biblical interpretation. On one side, the Covenant saw the Free Church, which increasingly adopted the premillennial dispensationalism of American evangelicalism, and on the other side, they saw the higher biblical criticism of the friends and sponsors in the American Congregational Church. The Covenant often sought a position somewhere between these two options.

In the twentieth century, despite scattered attempts at cooperation, the Augustana Synod and the Evangelical Covenant Church would go their own separate directions, although they faced many similar situations down the road, including language transitions and adapting their congregations and denominations to the reality of American Christianity. The role of ethnicity was a key concept in the Covenant much longer than in the Augustana Synod; the Covenant maintained their Swedish language and roots longer than the Augustana Synod did, especially because of their close relationship with the Covenant in Sweden. The Lutheran confessional identity of the Augustana Synod allowed it, ironically, to go "out of business" when the transition to English and American denominationalism took place. The key here was Augustana's Lutheran identity; the end of the Synod as an organization, though painful, was not the end of its Lutheran identity (although "bigger is better" has been shown to have serious drawbacks).

For both the Augustana Synod and the Evangelical Covenant Church, the role of confessional partners has been key to the shaping of their modern identities. The long-term ecumenical relations that the Augustana Synod had with other American Lutheran groups played a vital role in the development of the Synod's identity, and gave it a natural group with which to relate after it made its transition to English and to American religious culture. The Covenant's choice of ecumenical partners, especially the congregational and free church groups in the United States and around the world, have had an important impact, as has the world of American evangelicalism in the second part of the twentieth century. Both denominations were greatly affected by a set of ecumenical relationships that helped shape and determine their identities in the twentieth century.

The Augustana Synod is no more; it ceased to exist after the 1962 merger that formed the Lutheran Church in America. The Evangelical Covenant Church still exists, but it is a very different denomination than it was a century ago, then a small band of struggling Swedish-American congregations. But in many ways, there were continuing bonds between Augustana and Covenant people and congregations, some of which continue to this day. In local, regional, and national arenas, people from both denominations cooperated on many different projects and endeavors, and contacts exist even today, mainly on the local level. One would like to think that the Swedish immigrants of 150 years ago would be amazed (and perhaps proud) of the institutions that grew out of their initial efforts at planting their religious vision on American soil, institutions both Covenant and Lutheran.

Bibliography

Arden, G. Everett. *Augustana Heritage: A History of the Augustana Lutheran Church*. Rock Island: Augustana Press, 1963.

Hale, Frederick. *Trans-Atlantic Conservative Protestantism in the Evangelical Free and Mission Covenant Traditions*. New York: Arno Press, 1979.

Olsson, Karl A. *By One Spirit*. Chicago: Covenant Press, 1962.

Olsson, Karl A. *Into One Body—by the Cross*. 2 vols. Chicago: Covenant Press, 1985.

Söderström, Hugo. *Confession and Cooperation: The Policy of the Augustana Synod in Confessional Matters and the Synod's Relationions with Other Churches to the Beginning of the Twentieth Century*. Lund: C. W. K. Gleerup Bokförlag, 1973.

Stephenson, George. *The Religious Aspects of Swedish Immigration*. Minneapolis: University of Minnesota Press, 1932.

PART FIVE

The Seminary

Augustana Seminary Remembered

John L. Kindschuh

It is the task and delight of the panel this evening to guide our recollection of Augustana Seminary and its impact on the Augustana Lutheran Church. The panel agreed that what has been prepared with care is likely to be more constructive than casual repartee. So we consider ourselves a panel of participants—more than a panel in the sense of seminar or interactive discussion. Each of us will take something in the range of ten minutes, and along the way we will share some personal recollections of seminary faculty. We shall think primarily of those who taught during the World War II years. One notable exception—Dr. Conrad Bergendoff's role—will receive singular attention in a separate presentation by Byron Swanson.

In the wider sense, virtually no one who participated in the Augustana Church family and tradition could go untouched by the Seminary and its leaders. The justification for tonight's program is the fact that whether we are clergy members within the former Augustana ministerium or lay members within congregations who called seminarians into service, Augustana Seminary was at the heart of the life of the Augustana Church.

Remembering the work of the Seminary is supported with the help of a panel representing former students. Each panelist is a Seminary graduate who followed a rather distinctive career path.

- Allan Pfnister finished Seminary at the top of his class, to continue thereafter as a full-time academician and educator.
- Harold Lohr was a dual-career pioneer in the church: initially a scientist, then parish pastor and church executive, and eventually bishop.
- Connie Johnson: As Swedish, as Lutheran, as pastoral as the church ever could have hoped. Connie is Exhibit A of a life that began in a parsonage and was expended wholly in parish ministry.

- A fellow Nebraskan, Deke Grosc, combined Seminary studies and subsequent theological study and editorial responsibilities in Europe, with parish ministry in the U.S., all in context of enduring ecumenical interests.
- Marbury Anderson was to be the fifth panelist; is unable to be present because of imminent, major surgery. He sends his greetings and we have agreed that I should read core items from his paper, which will comprise the final component in the series of presentations.

The broad theme tonight is the seminary in its institutional role. As previously noted, panelists will add informal comments as they wish regarding individual faculty. Regrettably not all can be included as one might wish.

A few additional introductory comments regarding each presenter will be made at the time of his appearance.

The panel might be aided to some degree by thinking of themselves in the light of a pair of aphorisms from Dr. Hjalmar Johnson. He frequently proffered this not so subtle perspective to seminarians: "Some pastors want to be so heavenly minded that they are no earthly good." As the record indicates, these men took Dr. Johnson's implications to heart.

Hjalmar Johnson also had a perspective on those overly ambitious in matters of theology: "There's not much good to be gained from the effort to unscrew the inscrutable." None of that tonight either!

Many of us who grew up within the environment of the Augustana Lutheran Church have been inclined to impute piety and religious dedication to virtually all Swedish immigrants. The reality is just the opposite. Dr. G. Everett Arden treats this matter specifically in an early chapter of his book *The School of the Prophets*: "The unfortunate fact…is that the greater part of Swedish immigrants preferred to join some other church or remain outside all church connections," adding this footnote supported by two different sources: "Of the 97,000 Swedes in the United States in 1870, only 17,000 were members of the Augustana Church, and this was far more than were associated with any other group, religious or secular in this country at the time."[1]

Dr. Arden earlier had emphasized a reality we too want to keep in mind:

> Any consideration of the history of the Augustana Lutheran Church or of its chief institutions must take into account *the Swedish background* [emphasis mine] which made the founding fathers what they were.
>
> The period which marked the coming of the Swedish founders of the Augustana Lutheran Church….was an era of change, ten-

---

[1] G. Everett Arden, *The School of the Prophets: The Background and History of Augustana Theological Seminary 1860-1960* (Rock Island: Augustana Book Concern, 1960) 66.

sion and unrest in the old country, a time when old traditions and former ways of life were being questioned and abandoned, while new proposals and new experiments were being tested, tried, revised and adopted....

> [The] Swedish immigrant who came to the new world...would likely have been unable to analyze or delineate this new spirit of his age, he was, nevertheless, one of its very real products.[2]

It is intriguing to find that before his text deals with the history of the seminary proper, Arden proceeds through some four or five chapters in pursuing the following contentions:[3]

1. That the matrix of the new Swedish spirit was revolutionary France.

2. That French concepts of liberty, equality, and fraternity were found in the most potent and dynamic concepts influential in Sweden because they expressed a compelling program of reform in the body of society.

3. That this profound change in Sweden occurred when three forces—cultural liberalism, political liberalism, and economic liberalism—combined with religious individualism and revivalism to produce a wholly new social climate.

Such change conveyed numerous ramifications for the church, especially two sides of the educational coin:

> As [on the one hand] efforts were being made to "emancipate" public education from Church control, pressure was also being exerted to tie theological training more closely to the universities, and to require ministerial candidates to meet the same exacting academic standards which were required in other areas of learning.[4]

In due course steps were taken by the universities to raise the standards for theological studies. In 1806 at Uppsala, and in 1809 at Lund, followed some twenty years later by an act of the Swedish Parliament (1831), a comprehensive statute required that:

> ...every theological student, prior to presenting himself for ministerial examination before the diocese in which he will serve, must furnish to that diocese an affidavit certifying that he has been matriculated in the university by the theological faculty and has there been examined in all the required courses and has been approved as possessing such competence in dogmatics, moral theology, introduction, symbolics, exegesis, church history and pastoral theology, that he can be admitted to candidacy for the ministerial examinations by the diocese.[5]

What was the significance of these changes for the future of the Augustana Seminary? Arden's synopsis of the pivotal reality is as follows:

---

[2] Ibid., 3-4.
[3] Ibid., 4-5; cf. also pp. 11-57.
[4] Ibid., 31.
[5] Ibid., 32.

> When these people [the immigrants] were ready to organize a church in the new world, it was natural for them to choose a polity that would accord with their instinctive notions of a democratic society. Therefore, they repudiated the Episcopal in favor of a more democratic form of government, and vested authority not in ecclesiastical office but in the congregation. But when they established a central educational institution, they endeavored to pattern their school along lines they had known in the homeland.[6]

(Meaning, university education in the pattern of Uppsala and Lund.)

This unique and complex mix of competing loyalties and values shaped the climate in which the Augustana Theological Seminary came into being, destined not only subsequently to grow and make a contribution which impacted the Augustana Synod but the entire Lutheran Church in this country. Linking some bits and pieces of that story we remember Augustana Seminary with gratitude and affection.

The time has expired, perhaps also your patience. If so, the situation is not dissimilar to the experience of an elementary-grade Nebraska boy in the mid-1930s on Sunday morning at Elim Lutheran Church, Swaburg, who recognized that the end of the hour was at hand when he heard from Pastor Arnold V. Thoren the words of a prayer familiar to all of us:

> Let the light of Thy Word ever shine within our homes. Keep the children of the Church in the covenant which Thou hast made with them in Holy Baptism, and give all parents and teachers grace to nurture them in Thy truth and fear. Bless, we pray Thee, the institutions of the Church: its colleges, its seminaries, and all of its schools; that they may send forth men and women to serve Thee, in the Ministry of the Word, the Ministry of Mercy, and all the walks of life.[7]

Augustana Seminary was an answer to that prayer.

---

[6] Ibid., 65.
[7] *The Hymnal and Order of Service* (Rock Island: Augustana Book Concern, 1925) 577.

Augustana: A Teaching Church

Allan O. Pfnister

No institution begins entirely anew. Its roots are deep and entangled with the history of the time and with other institutions. Conrad Bergendoff, in 1993, wrote that the higher institutions of Sweden, such as the University of Uppsala, sent highly trained clergymen to churches founded by Swedish colonists in America.[1] While most returned to influential positions in the Swedish church after a period of service, they left a heritage of respect for education in the institutions that followed. A. R. Cervin completed the Ph.D. at Lund, then completed theological education and was ordained. He taught mathematics at Augustana. Another Ph.D. from Lund, Joshua Lindahl, founded the science department at Augustana. Anders Bersell came to Augustana in 1880 and served until 1903. Others were Lars Paul Esbjörn, T. N. Hasselquist, and J. G. U. Mauritzon.

Lars Paul Esbjörn, who was instrumental in creating the first resident theological education in Swedish America, was a pastor of a small parish in northern Sweden. Converted during a temperance rally in 1840, he began to gain some renown as a temperance speaker and evangelist. Then leaving Sweden in 1849, he was directed by a land agent to Andover, Illinois. Because of illness he remained in Chicago, while the group that accompanied him to America continued west. Esbjörn received some help from the American Home Mission Society, and in March, 1850, organized his first congregation in Andover. With the urging of William Passavant of Pittsburgh, he and others formed the Synod of Northern Illinois in September, 1851. Tufve Nilsson Hasselquist became pastor of the Galesburg congregation in 1842 and encouraged Esbjörn to establish a Scandinavian professorship in the

---
[1] Conrad Bergendoff, "A Swedish University Tradition in America," *The Swedish-American Historical Quarterly* 44 (January, 1993) 4-20.

newly-founded Illinois State University, a short-lived institution prior to the federal land-grant funds that made possible the creation of what is now the University of Illinois.

Esbjörn was able to bring together enough funds to establish the professorship. He was elected to fill the position in 1858, but it was not long before he found that the lot of the Swedish students was difficult. They were not permitted to join the literary societies, nor were they allowed to form their own. Esbjörn resigned in 1860. In June of the same year, the Scandinavian group left the Illinois Synod, and 36 Swedish and 23 Norwegian congregations met at Jefferson Prairie, Wisconsin, and created the Scandinavian Evangelical Lutheran Augustana Synod in North America. The constitution of the new synod provided for a school of theology with two departments: theological and preparatory.

The new institution began in a schoolhouse of the Swedish Immanuel Lutheran Church in Chicago in September, 1860. The school received its charter in 1863 as Augustana College and Seminary. In the preparatory department, the new institution stressed classical languages and included the subjects common to the European gymnasium (upper secondary school) such as history and geography, mathematics and natural science. To keep the school afloat, O. C. T. Andrén went to Sweden, raised some $10,000, and received 5000 books from the royal library.

T. N. Hasselquist, a graduate of Lund University, had built a strong congregation in Galesburg, Illinois, and he began working for the establishment of a Swedish colony in Illinois. The Illinois Central railroad offered 1000 acres at $6 an acre and a commission to the seminary of $1 for additional acres sold to settlers. Against opposition from the synod, the convention accepted the offer. The school was moved to Paxton. Esbjörn wanted the school to stay in Chicago. The Paxton settlement, however, failed to grow, so the Norwegian segment separated and in 1870 founded Augustana College in Sioux Falls, South Dakota.

With the failure of the Paxton settlement, the Augustana board of directors purchased property between Moline and Rock Island for $10,000. The financial panic of 1873 caused some delay, but in September, 1875, the college moved to partially completed facilities in Rock Island. In the meantime, a new constitution made a clear distinction between the collegiate department, a preparatory program, and the theological course to prepare pastors for the new synod. The college followed the pattern of American colleges, while the theological department concentrated on the preparation of pastors for the new synod. Augustana effectively became the first institution of higher education in America to develop a graduate school of theology. The first step was the A.B. degree. The next step was two years in the seminary. The two-year course was extended to three years, and by 1879 the B.D. degree was awarded.

In the meantime, other segments of the Augustana Synod were active in their own educational efforts. The Minnesota Conference opened an academy in Red Wing, Minnesota, in 1862. In 1873 this became Gustavus Adolphus College in St. Peter, Minnesota. Then Bethany College in Lindsborg, Kansas was founded. Bethany offered its first baccaluareate degrees in 1891. Luther Academy was founded in Nebraska in 1893 and later on became a normal school and junior college in 1909. Upsala College joined the group in 1893.

Augustana College and Theological Seminary were inextricably tied together from the beginning. The institution was identified as Augustana College *and* Theological Seminary. Lars Paul Esbjörn was effectively the first president from 1860 to 1863. Indeed he was the institution, the president and faculty of the little school in Chicago. In the summer of 1862, just before the school moved to Paxton, Esbjörn went to Sweden to collect funds. While there he asked for a parish in his homeland and, in the spring of 1863, he resigned and returned to Sweden. He was never happy with the proposed move to Paxton.

T. N. Hasselquisst became the second president of the college and seminary. At Paxton the institution enrolled eight students. By 1867 the enrollment had grown to over 40. Instruction began in Rock Island in 1875. In 1877 the college graduated its first class in the new location. Twenty-five students were graduated in 1882. Seven non-matriculated female students appeared in the catalog for 1883-84. The first woman graduated from Augustana in 1885. By 1890 the enrollment reached 300.

In February 1891, with the death of Hasselquist, Olof Olsson became the third president. The curriculum continued to expand, and the supporting churches became concerned that the new departments took away from the original intent of the institution to provide training for advanced theological education. The church, in 1892, reaffirmed its resolution to keep college and seminary together as a common institution, but the debate about the combination of college and seminary continued into the twentieth century.

With the death of Olof Olsson in 1900, Gustav A. Andreen was called as the fourth president in 1901. In 1920 the church decided to proceed with new buildings for the seminary.

Again concern was expressed that the college and theological seminary were so closely tied. Some of the conferences presented requests that the seminary be severed from the college. The Synod replied in 1921 that the seminary and college would remain united and proceeded with the construction of the seminary buildings. Archbishop Nathan Söderblom was present at the dedication in November, 1923.

As a concession to those who wished a division of college and seminary, the faculty secured its own dean in 1920, and the seminary established its own chapel services. The debates over separation of college and seminary continued. A compromise was reached by having a subcommittee of the college board serve as the executive committee of the seminary. Conrad Bergendoff (M.A., University of Pennsylvania, Ph.D., University of Chicago) became head of systematic theology and dean in 1931. A. D. Mattson, Eric

Wahlstrom, and Carl Anderson joined the seminary faculty at about the same time. Dr. Hjalmar Johnson, later to join the seminary faculty, established philosophy courses in the college.

Dr. Andreen asked to retire in 1934 but was prevailed upon to remain as head, and a committee on arrangements to divide responsibilities of the presidency and the dean of the seminary was established. In 1933 the Augustana Synod passed a new resolution that candidates for ordination should spend a year in parish work under pastoral supervision. Dr. Conrad Bergendoff followed Andreen as president of the combined institution. Then in 1948, after college and seminary had been joined for 88 years, the Augustana Synod decreed the separation of college and seminary. The following year, after 89 years of union, college and seminary parted ways, and Dr. Karl E. Mattson, then President of the New England Conference, was elected new head of the seminary. There were 24 graduates in the class of 1949.

In 1962 Augustana combined with four other seminaries to form the Lutheran School of Theology at Chicago near the University of Chicago. In 1986, with the creation of the Evangelical Lutheran Church in America, the first bishop of the ELCA, Herbert Chilstrom, was a graduate of Augustana Seminary.

Augustana College continues to flourish in Rock Island, and the long educational tradition of the Augustana Church continues into the twenty-first century.

The Liturgical Core: Augustana at Worship

Harold R. Lohr

On Trinity Sunday, 1951, my wife and I—fairly recent arrivals in the Chicago area—continued our occasional church shopping by dropping in at Grace Lutheran Church, LaGrange. We sat down in a pew just before the Processional, and then shared the awesome experience with the congregation as the choir entered the nave, singing the opening hymn, "Holy, Holy, Holy!"

Then the pastor, O. V. Anderson, facing us from the altar, sang the same words (in the setting I later preferred above all the others): "Holy, Holy, Holy is the Lord of Hosts! The whole earth is full of His glory!"

And then, still facing us, he said, "The Lord is in His holy temple; His throne is in heaven. The Lord is nigh unto them that are of an humble and contrite spirit. He heareth the supplications of the penitent and inclineth to their prayers. Let us therefore draw near with boldness unto His throne of grace and confess our sins."

Let me tell you: I had never been a part of a worship service like that in my life. I had been a Methodist, a Baptist, a Swedish Mission Covenanter, an ELC Lutheran, and a member of the Lutheran Church-Missouri Synod—but this was different!

As G. Everett Arden, my seminary advisor, would say some years later, "to share in the Augustana Liturgy is to experience a little bit of heaven!"[1]

When the Peterson boys, Olav and Lars (better known by their Latinized names, Olaus and Laurentius Petri), returned from Wittenberg, where they had studied under Luther and Melanchthon, they really started something in Sweden.

As we all know, their enthusiasm about the Reformation in Germany—and their obviously charismatic and persuasive advocacy of Luther's posi-

---
[1] G. Everett Arden, Personal Conversation, September, 1954.

tions—with the support of the Swedish king, changed the entire Swedish Church.

The first Swedish liturgy was introduced in 1531, a mixture of Luther's two productions, the *Formula Missae* (Order of the Mass), mostly in Latin; and the *Deutsche Messe* (German Mass) in the German vernacular. Luther, in his adaptations of the Roman Mass, focusing on the evangelical principle (salvation by grace through faith), eliminated all actions and references to the mass as sacrifice. In other respects, however, he was conservative, writing:

> We assert, it is not now, nor has it ever been, in our mind to abolish entirely the whole formal cultus of God, but to cleanse that which is in use, which has been vitiated by most abominable additions, and to point out a pious use.[2]

Olaus Petri was the author of the Swedish liturgy, a version close to Luther's *Deutsche Messe*. Several revisions followed. Then in 1614 the king appointed a liturgical commission to develop a liturgy expressive of true church life. What emerged was close to the liturgy originally introduced by Petri.

By the middle of the nineteenth century the Swedish bishops had preserved a liturgy that was in use throughout the country, unlike that which occurred in Germany, where multiple forms were in use, with no overall unity at all. As periodic revisions were made—even as late as the 1940s—the bishops kept in sight the original emphasis of Olaus Petri, learned from Luther: the liturgy must speak the truth of the gospel; sin and grace must be the subject matter.[3]

The New Revised Standard Version of the Bible, in its politically correct language, translates Proverbs 22:6 in these words: "Train children in the right way, and when they are old they will not stray."

This is not poetry-of-the-year material, to be sure, and it loses some of the punch of the King James Version: "Train up a child in the way he should go, and when he is old, he will not depart from it."

But in whatever version, we subscribe to the idea. Some of us have seen our children and grandchildren grow to adulthood, faithful to the Word of God they learned in Sunday School, in regular worship, and in the community of faith. Others of us have experienced ourselves, or have seen our children experience, a drifting away from the church; and then, perhaps, a return to those values inculcated in childhood and in youth in the Christian community. Proverbs 22:6 has it right much of the time!

Those Swedish men, women, and children who emigrated to Midwestern America in the mid 1800s had been nurtured in the Church of Sweden. A universal liturgy, essentially unchanged since the sixteenth century, had

---

[2] Paul Zeller Strodach, "Luther's Liturgical Writings," *Works of Martin Luther*, 6 vols., Philadelphia Edition (Philadelphia: Muhlenberg Press, 1932) 6.70.

[3] G. Everett Arden, Lecture Notes, "Liturgics" (Rock Island: Augustana Theological Seminary) April 16, 1956.

shaped them by the truth embraced in the Lutheran Confessions, learned in the context of worship of the God revealed in Jesus Christ. Like the writer of Isaiah 6, they had experienced in the liturgy their entry into the presence of the awesome and fearsome God; had confessed their felt unworthiness before such a One; had experienced the release of forgiveness in Jesus; had heard the Word, "Who will go for us?" and had responded, "Here am I; send me!"[4]

Dr. Arden describes the profile of the "average" Swedish settler in the Midwest: a farmer; likely to be between 20 and 35 years old; a survivor of ordeals, both in Sweden and in America; adventurous, influenced by the new liberalism gaining strength in Sweden; in poverty; ambitious; and married.[5]

Arden also affirms that no nineteenth-century movement in Sweden was more influential in creating the climate from which Swedish settlers came than religious revivalism.[6] The chief characteristic of the movement was subjectivism, reacting against orthodox legalism and focusing upon an individual's personal experience of conversion. "Such a conversion experience, if genuine, would be motivated, not by obedience to some legalistic code, but by the individual's wholehearted acceptance of the forgiveness of sins. Forgiveness must be understood to rest entirely upon the atoning work of Christ."[7]

Arden identifies emerging branches of Swedish Pietism that were sharply critical of prevailing Lutheran beliefs and practices. Included among those attacked were the Lutheran clergy, many being regarded as incompetent, unspiritual, and the enemies of Christianity. This radical group, however, did not represent the main stream of Swedish Pietism, which was loyal to the established church, emphasizing justification through faith and the resulting sanctification of all of life. The question was not "being right in doctrine, but being right with God"—a personal experience of sin and grace.[8]

Alongside Pietism in Sweden was the Temperance movement, and it was exported to America with the immigrants too. Arden links revivalism and temperance as the two impulses that gave life to the religious faith of the people in America (not just the Swedish) and gave it a moral and ethical thrust.

He writes:

> It was a kind of religious commitment which sought to make the individual…person dynamically aware of himself as a responsible citizen of both the spiritual and social realms of life….For revivalism and temperance sought their goals by very nearly the

---

[4] Ibid., February 13, 1956.
[5] G. Everett Arden, *The School of the Prophets: The Background and History of Augustana Theological Seminary, 1800-1960* (Rock Island: Augustana Book Concern, 1960) 3-10.
[6] Ibid., part One, Chapter Five.
[7] Ibid., 35.
[8] Ibid., 41.

same means as did economic, political and cultural liberalism, that is, by an emphasis upon the centrality of the individual man, regardless of station or rank, with respect to his relationship to every dimension of life....The genius of the Lutheran faith, embodied for centuries in institutional forms was to be liberated from ecclesiasticism that it might become a more personal force in the every-day life of every man.[9]

Among the leaders who had considerable influence upon the growing number of Swedish settlements (and congregations) in Midwestern America were such pastors, also emigrating from Sweden, as Lars Paul Esbjörn, Eric Norelius (ordained in America), and Tufve Nilsson Hasselquist (1816-1891). These three, like many others of their contemporaries, were pietists. Hasselquist, elected the first president of the Scandinavian Evangelical Lutheran Augustana Synod of North America in 1860, can be considered representative of those who gathered like-minded people to form this new church.

Hasselquist and those other leaders in the Swedish communities were able to work with the people who became the recruits for the Augustana Synod in America. Those recruits were not the indifferent, the hostile, and those suspicious of the established church. As Arden describes them, they were the right-wing dissenters and the flock of faithful old Lutherans:

> It was this spirit they [the people] breathed, these ideals they professed, and this brand of religion they wished to transplant and preserve in their new homeland. Lars Paul Esbjörn, pioneer and founding father, and T. N. Hasselquist, patriarchal leader until his death in 1891, embodied this heritage and expressed it in their ministry....Let it also be said that, if there has been over the past century any single factor which has proven decisive in the creation and maintenance of what might be called an *Augustana ethos*, it is this tradition, this legacy that combines the steady faith of Old Lutheranism with the activism and spontaneity of right-wing Swedish dissent.[10]

The synod organized in 1860 included thirty-six Swedish and thirteen Norwegian congregations. Differences arose between the Norwegian and the Swedish congregations of Augustana, however, resulting in the peaceful withdrawal of the former in 1870. Those Norwegians, in turn, formed two new synods: the Norwegian-Danish Augustana Synod; and the Conference for the Norwegian Danish Evangelical Lutheran Church in America. This action in 1870 resulted in five Norwegian synods; as the two new groups added their presence to the Hauge Synod, the Eiselen Synod, and the Norwegian Synod.[11]

---

[9] Ibid., 57.

[10] G. Everett Arden, *Augustana Heritage A History of the Augustana Lutheran Church* (Rock Island: Augustana Book Concern, 1963) 15-16.

[11] E. Clifford Nelson, *The Lutherans in North America* (Philadelphia: Fortress Press, 1975) 192.

The exit of the Norwegians left the Augustana Synod primarily Swedish. Under Hasselquist's leadership the synod had melded a strong confessional identity with an evangelical piety, a church open to ministry on the American scene, and to partnership with other Christians of like mind and spirit.

The inference of Proverbs 22:6 is that a person becomes the individual who is shaped by all the values, influences, associations, movements, communities, and so on that make their impact upon his or her life.

Is it not to be expected that a church, open to the Holy Spirit, will also, like her Lord, "increase in wisdom and in years, and in favor with God and man" (Luke 2:52, NRSV)?

The Augustana Synod that entered the twentieth century and, in 1962, joined with others to form the Lutheran Church in America was shaped by a liturgy that never deviated from Reformation truths, and by a Pietism unafraid to proclaim the name of Jesus to individual sinners, forgiven for his sake within his church.

And especially in later decades of its life, this synod—always faithful to the Scriptures as interpreted by the Lutheran Confessions—grew increasingly wary of those Lutherans who required greater proof than this of Lutheran identity.

Like its founders—Esbjörn and Hasselquist and others of like mind—the synod remained open to the ecumenical scene, recognizing the fruits of the Spirit in churches beyond its own boundaries.

In addition, because Augustana was a church that gave Isaiah's response to the words, "Who will go for us?," the synod broadened its early moral and ethical thrust[12] to speak and act in ways "to promote justice, to relieve misery, and reconcile the estranged."[13]

Writing in 1947 Luther Reed said,

> A word should be said concerning the importance of the Swedish Church and the Swedish Liturgy in the general development of the Lutheran Church in America....
>
> Swedish solidarity expressed in the single state and the one established Church of Sweden finds its counterpart in America in the Augustana Synod, the single ecclesiastical organization which

---

[12] See Footnote 9.

[13] Cf. Constitution of the Lutheran Church in America, Article V, Section 1h. From 1974 until the beginning of the Evangelical Lutheran Church in America in 1988, Section 1h was included in the LCA Constitution as a charge to the church: "To lift its voice in concord and to work in concert with forces for good, cooperating with church and other groups participating in activities that promote justice, relieve misery, and reconcile the estranged." Although such specific wording does not appear in any Augustana documents known to this writer, the statement is descriptive of Augustana's commitment to social ministry. Certainly the people of the Augustana Synod, who became part of the new church formed in 1962, were full partners in sharpening the LCA's understanding of social ministry to amend the church's constitution to include this statement in 1974. The *understanding* continues into the ELCA, because Chapter 4.03. g. of this church's constitution reads exactly as Section 1h above, with the addition of the words, "to serve humanity," after "forces for good."

includes all Swedish Lutherans. Lutherans of German descent in the United States have established and still maintain many different synods and general bodies; they support different theological seminaries, and they use different service books and hymnals. The American Lutherans of Swedish descent give their fellow Lutherans an impressive demonstration of unity in having but one general body, one theological seminary (at Rock Island, Illinois), and one service book and hymnal....

With respect to the Liturgy proper, the Common Service provides English Lutherans in America, of all backgrounds and bodies, with a liturgy fuller and richer and in clear agreement with the type of service found in Germany and Sweden for half a century after the Reformation than is provided in any other Lutheran liturgy in Europe or America today. The essential content and order of almost the entire Swedish Liturgy is found in the Common Service.[14]

As Dr. Reed praised the Augustana Synod in the words printed above, he also expressed some regret for "what might have been." In the light of current discussions and disagreements about the actions approved by the 1999 ELCA Assembly to implement full communion with the Episcopal Church, Dr. Reed suggests the stand he might have taken, were he now among us:

It is greatly to be regretted that the growth of the free-church movement in Sweden and the failure of the established Church to hold many of its most spiritual and earnest members in the homeland should have led American Lutherans of Swedish descent to reject or ignore important features of their birthright. An important contribution which they could well make to American Lutheran liturgical development would be an heightened appreciation and use of institutions and practices preserved by the Church of Sweden and lightly esteemed by its descendants in this country—the historic episcopate, the use of historic vestments and pure ceremonial and the feeling for ordered and beautiful liturgical worship.[15]

The Augustana Heritage Gathering 2000 is more than an assembly of the old-timers of the family, coming together to talk about "the good old days" and "remember when?" To reflect upon the past—its glories and even its disappointments—is to remember who we are and to hold high our hope for a future that will embody what we and our predecessors have given and what those who come after us, we pray, will make even more rewarding and memorable.

---

[14] Luther D. Reed, *The Lutheran Liturgy* (Philadelphia: Muhlenberg Press, 1947) 124-25.
[15] Ibid., 125.

The Shepherds

Constant R. Johnson

The image of the Augustana pastor is shaped by my father and his contemporaries. He grew up on a farm in Nebraska, felt called to the ministry, left home at 21 with an eighth grade education, and spent ten years at Augustana: academy, college, and seminary. He preached in Swedish at his first parish, Evansville, Minnesota. We lived in Swedish heritage places—Chisago City, Minnesota (Wilhelm Moberg country), and Jamestown, New York. I heard him and his contemporaries talk about the Synod of '31 (or whatever year). They were, most of all, caring shepherds. The Augustana Church was a national family where everyone went to the national synod. With one seminary, every pastor knew seven years of graduates. Foreign Missions were important, and missionaries stayed at the parsonage on visits. I remember the bearded, retired India missionary who could do a great imitation of a crowing rooster as well as the eccentric bachelor from Africa who cared enough for me to give me a used tube of British toothpaste. We rolled bandages for the mission fields at the Junior Missionary Society. Social Missions were important too. We sold "Mai Bloomar" and other items for Bethphage and orphanages.

The image of the church and its pastors was not shattered by going to seminary. I don't know how much time professors had spent in parishes, but they had a shepherding outlook on the ministry. I recall very little of Paul Lindberg's classes. It may be that this was an era when creative educational materials were not available and maybe it wasn't of prime interest to me. But he was an unusually caring person, who had time to talk, and I spent more time talking to him in his retirement in St. Peter, Minnesota, than I did at the seminary. The most unique figure at the seminary was A. D. Mattson. It wasn't that he didn't fit the mold of the caring shepherd; in reality, he expanded the horizon for caring. If Augustana was big in foreign and social missions, it was not big in social action. His sayings stayed with me over the years. "If the pastor can belong to the Rotary Club, he can be with the labor movement." "The Farm Bureau doesn't speak for all farmers."

I bought and read the books of Walter Rauschenbusch and marveled at the insight and style. I have told over and over again A. D.'s story about a church where most of the members were dairy farmers and belonged to a cooperative. The church practiced discipline, and when one member was caught watering the milk, he was called before church officials. When he was confronted by the cooperative, he swore. The church disciplined him…for swearing. A Native-American lawyer, Vine Deloria, Jr., attended the seminary for a year. A reviewer of his book, *Custer Died for Your Sins*,[1] said he looked on Augustana as a citadel of Old Testament prophecy. A. D. had courage. He obviously enjoyed reading his hate mail. When Henry Wallace was running for president, there was a rally at Wharton Fieldhouse. Some of us students were interested enough to usher at it, especially since A. D. was giving the invocation. His prayer was one of the beautiful prayers of Raushenbusch. His participation drew some flak from Quad City Lutherans. Our loving housemother heard so much when she went out that she just stayed in. I have a very personal interest in A. D. His daughter, Ruth, wrote a book that detailed communication from him after his death, via a clairvoyant. One paragraph is entitled "Constant Johnson."[2] The clairvoyant conveyed his impression that Constant Johnson (my father) was near death. An obituary a few weeks later confirmed this. I know little about this kind of communication, but am intrigued by it and pleased that A. D. remembered his classmate from the 1919 class.

---

[1] Vine Deloria, Jr., *Custer Died for Your Sins: An Indian Manifesto* (New York: Macmillan, 1969).
[2] Ruth Taylor Mattson, *Witness from Beyond* (New York: Hawthorn Books, 1975) 143-44.

Eric H. Wahlstrom (1892-1980): An Augustana Paradigm and

G. Everett Arden (1905-1978): Passion and Perspective

LaVern K. Grosc

Our class graduated from Augustana Seminary in 1950. I believe we felt that we were in attendance when Augustana was at its zenith. The first half of the twentieth century was a time of change and accommodation, a time of readjustment and of new direction, and a time of anticipation and preparation for what proved to be even greater change ahead.

I. 1900-1950 SETTING A NEW COURSE

Our class began the year after World War II ended. The period between the two World Wars had a profound effect on both the Augustana Synod and the Seminary. It marked the beginning of the move toward Lutheran cooperation and subsequent mergers and drew certain boundaries that are still evident today. In one sense, it was government regulation that gave impetus to Lutherans working together. In their desire to provide pastoral and chaplaincy services to Lutherans in the armed forces, some process for screening and recommending chaplaincy candidates was mandatory. Patriotism and nationalism also played a role. In the public mind, Lutherans were viewed as being German and northern Europeans and hence not trustworthy as to their loyalty to this nation. The war thus hastened the "Americanization" of Lutheranism in this country and hastened the language transition to using English. Further, Lutheran cooperation was also driven by the needs of fellow Lutherans in war-ravaged Europe and the necessity of providing care and continuity for the orphaned mission fields around the world that had been virtually cut off by the war.

Impetus was given also to Lutheran unity as witnessed by the formation of the Norwegian Lutheran Church in America in 1917, made up of the three largest groups of Norwegian heritage. (The largest Norwegian group that did not join was the Lutheran Free Church.) The following year, the eastern Lutherans, who had been in North America more than a century longer than those from the Midwest, reunited to form the United Lutheran Church in America. This included the General Synod of the Muhlenberg tradition, the United Synod of the South, and the General Council. They had divided over issues rising prior to those the Midwest faced, i.e., the Revolutionary War, the birth of a nation, slavery, the Civil War, etc.

The disparity between eastern and Midwestern Lutherans remains even to this day. Among the reasons are the differing times of immigration, the cultural and theological context at the time of their departure from the old world, as well as the different circumstances they faced in the new world.

This was particularly true of those of German ancestry. Those who left Germany in the eighteenth century had faced and experienced orthodoxy and pietism, and many came as indentured servants. Those who came a century or more later had faced rationalism and the absolutist restoration tendencies following the Napoleonic defeat and marked by the Congress of Vienna in 1815. Emperor Friedrich Wilhelm III took this opportunity to issue the Edict of the Prussian Union in 1817 whereby one church was created out of the Calvinist and Lutheran traditions, or the Evangelicals and Reformed as they were called in Germany. Thus the Emperor, who was Reformed, and his wife who was Lutheran, could commune at the same table. We need to remind ourselves that at the beginning of the nineteenth century, approximately one-third of the population of Berlin was made up of French Huguenots, i.e., Calvinists who had fled persecution in their own country.

Staunch German Lutherans both resented and resisted this enforced "unionism" and were persecuted accordingly. This climate affected most of the Midwest German immigrants, but none as strongly as the group we know as the Missouri Synod. They, under newly elected Bishop Martin Stephan, assembled a group that filled four ships and sailed for the new land. They did not enter an east coast port but came via New Orleans and the Mississippi river as far as Perry County in Missouri. When Bishop Stephan was found guilty of adultery and theft, he was cast out. Thus a second characteristic in addition to the fear of unionism developed, namely mistrust of hierarchy and of clergy and a demand for a strong form of congregational polity. Those sensitivities continued to run deep in many Midwestern Lutheran groups.

Thus it is not surprising that the rapid Americanization following World War I reawakened old fears particularly in the light of the increasing cooperation marked by such alliances as the National Lutheran Council. In 1930 the American Lutheran Church was formed by four geographical synods all of German origin, and five Midwestern Lutheran churches formed the American Lutheran Conference, motivated in large part by fears and suspicions of the eastern Lutheran establishment, i.e., the ULCA. Although a member of the American Lutheran Conference, the Augustana Synod never felt comfortable with the "exclusive confessionalism" espoused by this group.

Augustana had inherited its ecclesiology from its mother church in Sweden. In addition, the 20th century ecumenical movement was beginning to take shape. One of its founders and shapers was Archbishop Nathan Söderblom of Sweden. Thus Augustana was one of the few Lutheran bodies in this country to participate in the Life and Work Conference in Stockholm in 1927, and again the Faith and Order and the Life and Work Conferences in 1937, held respectively at Oxford and Edinburgh.

Not directly related to these events, but nevertheless of great significance for the development and direction of Augustana Seminary and the Synod was the death of Dean and Professor Conrad Emil Lindberg. Dr. Lindberg, with great faithfulness and commitment, had headed the Augustana Theological Faculty since 1900. However, times had changed and the challenges were different. The noted historian George M. Stephenson observed that in that thirty year period, not a single seminary professor had a bona fide Ph.D. degree nor any published research of record. Many voices throughout the church and the seminary student body itself urged that the Seminary chart a new course. As a consequence, four professors were released from their duties at the end of the 1930-1931 school year. This opened the door for the seminary faculty that most of us remember and came to love and respect. In 1931 four new faculty members were installed: Conrad J. Bergendoff, Eric H. Wahstrom, A.D. Mattson, and Carl A. Anderson, all of whom had done extensive graduate work and were competent and qualified scholars. Among those added to the faculty in the next period were: C. G. Carlfeldt in 1938, Hjalmar Johnson in 1944, and G. Everett Arden in 1945.

II. ERIC H. WAHLSTROM (1892-1980) AND G. EVERETT ARDEN (1905-1978)

These two men profoundly influenced me at the seminary and throughout my ministry and further theological development.

Eric Wahlstrom, that tall, lanky, unassuming and humble Swede, was to me a paradigm of Augustana's essence. Born in Sweden in 1892, he emigrated with his parents when in his teens. With a warm evangelical heart and a penetrating and brilliant mind, he pursued his education at Augustana College with a B.A. in 1919. After a two-year stint of teaching at Luther College in Wahoo, Nebraska, he entered Augustana Seminary and earned his B.D. in 1924. He pursued graduate study at Yale while serving a parish at Meriden, Connecticut, and again in China when serving as a missionary there from 1925-1927. Additional graduate studies were pursued at the University of Chicago, Union Theological Seminary, and Uppsala University. As professor of New Testament Language and Literature, he taught at the seminary from 1931 until his retirement in 1961 at the age of 69. He then taught an additional four years as a guest professor at Pacific Lutheran Theological Seminary. He remained active and alert. His incisive mind kept him abreast of research and scholarship in his field almost until the end. He died on March 16, 1980—12 days short of his 88th birthday.

In addition to his work in the New Testament, he helped bring Lundensian theology to this country and to the English-speaking world with translations of works by Gustav Aulén, Ragnar Bring, Gustaf Wingren, and several others. His own publications mirror his life and his interests. He wrote *My Father Worketh Hitherto* (Rock Island: Augustana Book Concern, 1945), a brief outline of missionary expansion; *The New Life in Christ* (Philadelphia: Muhlenberg Press, 1950), a penetrating study of Pauline and New Testament theology; a little gem written for the Lutheran Student movement, entitled *The Church and the Means of Grace* (Chicago: Division of Student Services, National Lutheran Council, 1949), which remains today a penetrating and perceptive study of ecclesiology; and after his retirement from Augustana Seminary in 1961, he wrote a seasoned perspective on the Bible as a whole in his book, *God Who Redeems* (Philadelphia: Muhlenberg Press, 1962).

Eric Wahstrom was a gentle man with a wry sense of humor and a mischievous smile as he stroked his hair and mumbled "Val" in his Swedish accent. Students were drawn to him as a teacher and as a pastor to whom one could go with any problem. His warm piety and unassuming presence were never threatening and always welcome. When the time came for my own ordination in 1954, I was honored when he agreed to be my ordination sponsor and to lay his hands upon me in the conferral of the Office of Holy Ministry.

In many ways G. Everett Arden was a contrast to Eric Wahlstrom, yet in others they complemented each other. Both were firmly anchored in the historic Lutheran theological perspective. Dr. Arden was a favorite of the class of 1950. He had joined the faculty just the year before we entered the seminary and thus, we were joint newcomers. More significantly, we were the first class he was to sponsor at the Seminary and a very close relationship developed. For me personally there were yet other reasons. He was born as Gothard Everett Anderson on April 29, 1905, in Wausa, Nebraska—a Swedish community in northeast Nebraska, just a few miles from where I was born and raised. He, like many of Swedish descent, changed his name. Why he chose the name Arden, I have never discovered. In addition, he and I shared the same nickname, "Deke." I suppose it was a shortened form of deacon, but it should not be surprising that if parents insist on giving their sons names like Gothard or LaVern, they would sooner or later be given a shorter nickname like Deke.

Dr. Arden was small and wiry of stature, but blessed with a deep, sonorous bass voice that could range from a hoarse whisper to a full-throated roar. He had earned a Ph.D. in church history from the University of Chicago and enthusiastically shared his knowledge and insights. He not only taught church history, he frequently re-enacted it in the classroom. Had awards been given to the professor in whose classroom it was most difficult to fall asleep, Dr. Arden would have won year after year. History and worship were for him living vibrant realities that he infectiously shared with his students. Consumerist and pragmatic attitudes in worship were ours in that day as well. Dr. Arden's adamant insistence that worship had more to do with God's centrality and gracious magnanimity than with our petty wants and desires has carried through a lifetime.

His dramatic skills and articulateness went beyond the classroom to his preaching and proclamation of the gospel. I recall so clearly his doing a series of sermons on a preaching mission at Emanuel Lutheran Church in Hartford, Connecticut, during my internship there in 1948-49. That rather large church had a three step rise from the nave to the chancel platform. Dr. Arden preached without notes and used those steps as a stage to hold the congregation absolutely spellbound as he spoke. He was not only a gifted teacher and worship leader, but a powerful proclaimer of God's Word.

Dr. Arden moved to the Lutheran School of Theology in Chicago when the Augustana Seminary was incorporated there in 1967. He returned to finish his teaching career just a few blocks from where he had served as pastor when he was called to be Professor of Church History and Liturgics in Rock Island. He retired from LSTC in 1974 at 69 years of age.

In the late spring of 1978 Dr. Arden was a guest professor at the Lutheran Theological Seminary at Gettysburg, and one Sunday he and his wife Irene joined us in worship at Christ Lutheran Church in York, Pennsylvania, where I was the pastor. They came to our home after the service, and we spent a good bit of the afternoon reminiscing and catching up on common friends. They were very excited because they were about to leave for a pleasure trip and vacation in the British Isles. That was the last time that I saw Deke Arden alive. A few days later we received the devastating news that while riding on a tour bus they had been struck by a Spanish lorry carrying steel. Dr. Arden was killed instantly. Words from the old Augustana hymnal echoed in my mind: "We are again reminded that here we have no abiding city." But at the same time, I knew that the heavenly chorus had been enriched with a new basso profundo.

III. A LASTING LEGACY

In the last half of the twentieth century, that church body tributary we called Augustana merged with other streams to form the Lutheran Church in America, which in turn flowed into a larger course called the Evangelical Lutheran Church in America. It is still our hope and prayer that one day there will be only one Lutheran river flowing on the American landscape. In that light, is there any lasting legacy that Augustana can offer to facilitate that goal? I believe there is, and it comes in the area that has been a perennial problem for American Lutheranism, namely, ecclesiology. Most of the past and current difficulties are focused in that area.

It is my opinion that the consistent Lutheran, Pauline, and Nicene ecclesiology taught at Augustana Seminary, two of whose chief proponents were Wahlstom and Arden, can serve as a guide. I mean an ecclesiology that starts with a consistent Lutheran theocentricity that emphasizes that God is the subject and verb of each theological utterance. The church is a creation of a gracious God, who through Christ has overcome sin, death, and the devil and through the Holy Spirit applies that victory and unites us by calling us through the Gospel to unite us with Christ and one another. Here the Pauline analogy of the Body of Christ clarifies the organic interdependent relationship established in baptism and illustrates that unity is not to be confused with uniformity.

But we are already into the Nicene marks of the church as being one, holy, catholic, and apostolic. Unity is a gift given in baptism and the calling of the Holy Spirit. It is our task and responsibility to manifest and live that unity as a reality in this world. All the subterfuge of an "invisible church" cannot hide our divisions in a body called to be visibly united.

Paul's concept of the Body of Christ is helpful in another way since the very term has eucharistic overtones and, in fact, the fourfold action of the Eucharist corresponds accurately to the Nicene marks of the church. The taking, blessing, breaking, and giving of the elements is paralleled by the unity, holiness, catholicity, and apostolicity of the church.

Like the bread and wine, Christ takes into his hands the elements, i.e., sinful human beings, and unites them with himself and with one another in the church. It is Christ's church, in the world but not of the world, but meant to be a means of grace to the whole creation. That unity is to be manifested in holiness, which is not primarily moral purity or sanctimonious piety, but rather in our being set apart for God's use and purposes. The continual prayer of the church must echo its Lord's Prayer that "not my will but Thine be done" and that it be "done on earth as it is in heaven." Like the bread and wine of the Eucharist, in Christ's hands we are taken, blessed and transformed, i.e., made holy, so we might be a means of grace and the body of Christ for others. Note here that holiness is not very compatible with democracy, which by definition says we want our will done and we have the autonomy and power to do it. The church is not a democracy, not a laocracy, not a clerocracy, but a Christocracy. Hence, such radical and autonomous congregational polities tend to be more self-centered than Christ-centered. If, as Luther stated, original sin means *"incurvatus in se,"* i.e., being turned in upon oneself, does not that form of congregationalism come perilously close to being the corporate ecclesiological form of original sin?

If the movement so far has been centripetal or inward, the direction now changes to the centrifugal. The rhythm of life is like breathing: inhaling and exhaling. We need to do both to live. But we cannot be sent unless we have first been gathered; unity precedes mission. Here the parameter of the church is described as catholic, i.e., inclusive and extensive in both time and space. The church, as an eschatological entity, lives "in the world," but its origin and destiny are "not of the world." The church lives in history and has a history, it is fully human and has a past, present, and future and, like all created things, needs to be conscious of this continuity. Thus traditions and ritual, while not of the essence of the church, are still important. The church is extensive in space and transcends boundaries, languages, and cultures. It was the world that God loved, i.e., the whole created and inhabited earth. The church, while first unified and transformed, must be broken apart to be shared with the world.

God's action to unify answers the question, who? Holiness and transformation respond to what, and the catholicity indicates where. The final question is obvious—why? Apostolicity is the clear answer—we have been called to proclaim and live out the gospel in the whole inhabited earth, we have been broken apart to be sent into the world. The church as the body of Christ has been made "a chosen race, a royal priesthood, a holy nation, God's own people" so that we might "declare the wonderful deeds of him who called" us out of darkness into his marvelous light (1 Peter 2:9). We are called to make disciples of all nations. That is the reason why unity is so important. The last recorded wish of our Lord was that his people, the church, might be one so that the world might believe.

These were some of the insights our heritage has to offer. I thank God for professors like Eric Wahlstrom, whose life and teachings were a paradigmatic example of these beliefs, and G. Everett Arden, who taught us to live the Christian life and to worship with passion and intensity even as we sought to view the church and life itself from God's perspective.

Three Years for Which I am Thankful

Marbury E. Anderson

I went to Seminary. I got ordained. And I have been busy in some facet of parish ministry ever since. Now, 50 plus years after ordination, comes a call from Paul Cornell asking whether I'll participate in this part of the program of the Augustana Heritage Association Gathering 2000 where we remember Augustana Theological Seminary. It stopped me in my tracks and gave me reason to think of the seminary, its faculty, and what I remember.

To my surprise, my memories are not chock full of anecdotes, peculiarities, or theological trends. John Kindschuh suggested that each of us on the panel might take two faculty about whom to give personal remembrances, in my case, C. G. Carlfelt and Carl Anderson. I must confess that I am ill equipped. I regret that I did not take Hebrew and thus failed to benefit from Prof. Anderson's special contribution. I associate Dr. Carlfelt with the most Swedish of the faculty who steeped us in Lundensian Theology but who never gave us the impression that this was the final definitive thought concerning God. Both were men whose demeanor provoked respect and for whom the title "Professor" seemed natural.

What I have decided as I reflected on the seminary is that the faculty members complemented each other. They were different, but did not let that bother them. Each had his own discipline; each was free to share without one of the others nipping at his heels. As I look back, I realize I came to the seminary to be prepared for parish ministry. Through the cumulative experience of this faculty I gained much that has been relevant and helpful in seeking to be a servant of Christ as a parish pastor.

In my reflections I have asked myself what the factors for ministry were to which Augustana Seminary contributed. Seven emerged. Likely some were in infancy as I left seminary. Others were more developed. The fact is that all of them, in one way or another, were linked to the three years in seminary and significant to me in the years which followed. Thus, remembering Augustana Seminary and its faculty, I recall the following things:

(1) *I came out of seminary convinced of the importance of intellectual honesty*. In seminary I had to come to grips with the human factor in the Bible as well as the divine. I had to embrace faith as the one way of knowing God and no longer think I could find proofs. I had to temper my claims concerning God and what I know to be God's action. I had to learn that the walk with God is a walk in humility.

(2) *I came out of seminary skeptical of wrapping up Christian faith in neat packages*. No atonement theory explains the whole of the crucifixion. No Biblical inspiration theory wraps up the way in which the Holy Spirit works through the Bible as a means of grace. Perhaps we are best open to God when we understand Christianity to be something of a paradox. For example, one professor took issue with usage of the word "accept" as our human response to God's offer. That same professor preached in an African American Church in Rock Island the following Sunday. Some of us students followed him there. To our surprise he talked to the people of that congregation of *accepting* Christ as Lord and Savior.

(3) *I came out of seminary aware of that which is "adiaphora," also the import of "motive."* This tempered the pietistic tendencies which I harbored from my background and makes judgmentalism mere quackery. At the same time I have been left with a deep appreciation of the depth of commitment to Christ that was inherent in the Pietistic background of the people of the Augustana Lutheran Church. I look back at the professors of Augustana believing they did a good job of appreciating our Augustana Pietistism while, at the same time, broadening us to see its limitations. I don't recall them belittling or exalting Pietism. What I do recall is the list of books I was to read while on internship. It included writings by O. Hallesby of Norway and Carl Rosenius, *A Faithful Guide to Peace With God.* These were balanced by such writings as *Preface to Romans* and *Christian Liberty* by Martin Luther.

(4) *I came out of seminary with a conviction of inclusivity*. This inclusivity embraced the whole church. We were made aware of ecumenicity and encouraged to see how our church was involved in developments that took place during the century and remained at work in the post-World War II years. (This did not include the Roman Catholic Church. Suspicions at the time were still strong and had to wait, at least for me, until the post-Vatican Council years.) Largely through the impact of Dr. A. D. Mattson, inclusivity involved the labor movement. We were challenged to see ourselves as standing with the struggling and less fortunate in their plight. Inclusivity embraced our whole theological perspective. Grace did not stand alone. It was *sin and grace.* Gospel did not exist in isolation. It was *law and gospel.* Confession and absolution were not in isolation beyond worship, but comprised the essence out of which worship developed and was expressed. (Of all my seminary courses, the one I remember with most appreciation was the study of Romans with Dr. Eric Wahlstrom, in which an outline by Anders Nygren played

a prominent role. Salvation "by grace through faith" is amazing for all "are under the power of sin.")

(5) *I came out of seminary with a heightened experience of what it means to worship God*. G. Everett Arden gave us significant measurements for key elements in worship: an understanding of liturgy, an awareness of architecture, a theology within hymnody, an appreciation of appropriate art, and a sense of the historical continuity of the people of God involved in worship. Dr. Arden spoke of the Sacrament of Holy Communion as the highest act of worship. The fact that our seminary's sacramental services were linked with St. John Lutheran Church emphasized the sacrament as always being a congregation at worship.

(6) *I came out of seminary convinced that the sermon was the single most significant thing I would do each week*. Prof. Theodore Levander, in the speech class of the first seminary year, assailed mediocrity in preaching and challenged us to be diligent, and to excel. I suspect he was hoping that one day in the Augustana Lutheran Church there would be someone who would be named among the great preachers of America. I have always appreciated that challenge and deeply benefited from Dr. Paul Lindberg's emphasis in Homiletics. He provided a framework for sermon preparation by telling us to take the text for the day, write out its heart thoughts, then to choose a theme for the sermon. His framework created a discipline that makes the sermon a Scripture lesson for life in today's world.

(7) *I came out a churchman*. I see this expressed primarily in the way through which the benevolences of the church were viewed. Some might ask what the seminary had to do with this. The answer is twofold: First, the seminary made us aware of the educational institutions of the church (the colleges); social missions (homes for aged, childrens' homes, and seaman centers), world missions (especially China, Tanzania, and India), and American missions (graduates were often assigned to start new mission congregations). Second, through the seminary we became aware of the cohesion of the church throughout the U.S. and Canada. As students and faculty, we came from all parts of the church, and we shared a trust in this church and its leadership. We felt a responsibility to live and work together; and we depended upon the church to provide guidance as to where needs existed. We came to expect the church to channel benevolences to meet those needs. Above all, we felt a responsibility to this church.

As I reflect, these seven factors highlight the contribution I feel and identify as the contribution of the Seminary in my life and ministry.

Thomas Moore wrote: "Fond memory brings the light of other days around me."

Three years in seminary—such a short time! Yet what an impact they have had in what by now is more than five decades. Fond memories for which I am thankful. Fond memories also for which I am hopeful that what has enriched life for me will ever endure to enrich the lives of others!

PART SIX

Global Outreach

Augustana's First Ventures into Africa

Vernon G. Swenson

In his book, *Foundation for Tomorrow* (Rock Island: Augustana Book Concern, 1960), Dr. S. Hjalmar Swanson uses the great history of Augustana Missions to look forward to the future. In the same way, I am going to look toward the future. My presentation is divided into three parts: Getting into Africa, Getting into Tanganyika, and Foundation for Tomorrow. The presentation is based on both personal recollections and the work of Dr. Swanson.

GETTING INTO AFRICA

In order to trace the beginnings of our story, we must go back to April 14, 1907, at Luther College, Wahoo, Nebraska. On that particular day, Pastor Fred Wyman presented a challenge, "Sudan for Christ—The Cross or the Crescent." Wyman was Pastor of Edensburg Lutheran Church in Malmo, Nebraska, which is about fifteen miles from Wahoo and today has a population of 113. The congregation has an average worship attendance of about 80 or 90. So Augustana's first call to Africa did not start in a big city or in a big congregation with a famous pastor. An eighteen-year old student was in the audience, and that day he decided "then and there that if God opened the way, he would serve him as a missionary." That young man was Ralph D. Hult. The vision never left him. God used this local pastor to touch the heart of Ralph Hult and he said, "I will go." Ralph went on to Augustana Seminary.

On Thanksgiving Day afternoon, 1916, while a senior at the seminary, Ralph went to the home of Dr. Carl A. Blomgren and poured out the burden of his heart. Dr. Blomgren read a Scripture passage, and the professor and student knelt in prayer. Words of encouragement followed. Then Ralph went out to interview and challenge students and faculty for the Sudan.

On January 29, 1917, the Augustana Foreign Missionary Society sent a petition to the Augustana Board of Foreign Missions to investigate the possibility of beginning a mission in the Sudan, the largest untouched mission field in the world. Later that same year, on June 14, 1917, the Augustana Synod in assembly unanimously adopted this resolution, "Resolved, that the petition of the Augustana Foreign Missionary Society, that a mission be established in the Sudan, Africa, be granted, and that the Synodical Board of Missions be authorized to call theological student Ralph Hult as missionary to this new mission field *on the condition that the said missionary society continues to give this mission its strong support*." Later that same day, the Board of Foreign Missions met and called Ralph Hult, and near the close of the synod convention, on June 17, Ralph Hult was ordained. The very next day, June 18, 1917, he was commissioned to go to Africa.

But World War I war delayed his departure for two years. In the meantime, on July 9, 1919, Hult married Gertrude Jacobson, and on November 13, 1919, he sailed for Africa.

Pastor Hult traveled up the Niger and Benue rivers to Ibi, Nigeria, to a mission station of the Sudan United Mission, arriving there February 1, 1920. He arrived at the Danish Lutheran Mission, Numan, Nigeria. It was a journey of about 700 miles. He did not find a new mission field area. All doors were closed. Consequently, he went to Garua in Northern Cameroon. He then organized a little caravan and between December 11, 1920, and May 31, 1921, he visited about 20 tribes. A party consisting of one of the Sara chiefs, together with a large company of his people, came out to meet Hult as he was entering their country. Hult later wrote that the Sara chief "and his people had been waiting for years for a teacher, who would come to their land and teach them…The appeal of the Sara tribe was so compelling that any further search for a field seemed quite unnecessary." In this time frame J. N. Steimer was also called to serve in the Sudan.

Hult went back down the Niger River and returned to Garua. By letter, he learned that Gertrude was waiting for him at Ibi. Hult requested permission to open a new field. This would have been in Cameroon. At Ibi he waited for a reply from the Board authorizing him to begin work among the Sara. A cable finally came from the Board, and it said, "Go to Tanganyika." As an obedient servant of the church, he went to Tanganyika by way of South Africa. Steimer also went to Tanganyika. Hult did not know that he would never return to his first call. He served in Tanganyika until 1926 and then returned to the States for furlough. He waited for the church to send him back to the Sara People, but that never happened. The Augustana Synod actually supported Hult's view in two conventions as well as by a special commission that was appointed by the Board to study the situation. However, at the 1929 convention of the Augustana Synod, the Board reported that due to the growing needs in Iramba in Tanganyika and the difficulties in working in a French- ruled territory (actually Hult had nothing but good relations with the French), it was decided that Augustana should concentrate on the Iramba.

GETTING INTO TANGANYIKA (NOW TANZANIA)

I. The Northern Field

Prior to World War I, German Mission Societies had established work in Tanganyika, especially in northern Tanganyika in the Kilimanjaro area. The missions flourished, and large congregations were established. But the war sent the Germans packing out of Tanganyika as the British took over.

While Hult was trekking around Nigeria and the Cameroons the needs of the former German fields in Tanganyika came to the attention of the Augustana Synod. In 1921 Dr. Charles Brown and A. C. Zeilinger were sent to Tanganyika to investigate the needs there. They found large congregations at Moshi (1600) Marangu (1400) and Machame (825), but no resident missionaries. Zeilinger volunteered to stay as a missionary. In doing so, Dr. Swanson points out, he followed the example of Barnabas at Antioch. Barnabas went to Antioch to check things out and ended up staying there (Acts 11:19-30).

Dr. G. A. Brandelle, President of Augustana Synod, made trips both to England and Germany. Negotiations took place between the German mission societies and the Americans with the result that the major work in northern Tanganyika (Mamba, Marangu, Mwika, etc.) was tentatively allotted to the Board of Foreign Missions of the Augustana Synod, "to have and to hold in undisputed possession and perpetuity." The Iramba field was unassigned. The Hults, John Steimer and his wife Edla, N. L. Melander, Herbert Magney, George Anderson, others coming from Europe (including Estonia), and Richard Reuch coming from Russia were soon on the field. It was truly an international staff, and this brought special challenges. I note by the number of persons sent so quickly to Tanganyika that resources must not have been a major problem. The Augustana Synod was ready and eager for foreign missions.

The agreements worked out in Germany and London by Brandelle with the Germans and the British sounded so good, but in actual practice did not work out well. Frictions soon arose, especially after the return of German missionaries to Tanganyika. Brandelle returned to London a second time and was advised that a new field might be preferable for the Augustana Synod. So much for perpetuity! Swanson points out that during all of these negotiations no missionary was present.

II. The Iramba Field

The new Iramba field was some 200 plus miles south from the Moshi, Marangu areas. Some work had been done there by three German missionaries beginning in 1911, but that came to an end in 1917 when the government removed the final missionary who evidently was suffering a nervous breakdown. But there were converts to the Christian faith, and a few remained faithful until the arrival of the Augustana missionaries. Hult and

Reuch were the first Augustana missionaries to reach the field. Hult remained three weeks, visited Iramba chiefs, and found three former bush school teachers who wanted to continue the work. Soon after this, both the Hults and the Steimers returned to the States for furlough. Steimer never to go back to Africa, and Hult did not for many years. They returned to the U.S. with a great deal of uncertainty as to what would happen to their call to Sudan. During World War II Hult was called to go again to Tanganyika, and he died in Dar es Salaam of a heart attack after being ill with malaria. The touching story is found in *On Our Way Rejoicing* by his daughter Ingrid Hult Trobisch. Eventually the Augustana Synod dropped the idea of the Sudan being a mission and focused all of its Africa attention on Irambaland.

The question remains: Who was correctly interpreting the Lord's will? Ralph Hult and J. N. Steimer, or Brandelle and the Board? I personally feel it was Hult, because in 1917 the synod, by a unanimous vote, resolved "that a mission be established in the Sudan, Africa," and Hult was ordained on a call to proceed. Swanson summarizes, "The Synod supported Hult's view at two conventions."

In 1927 it was "resolved, that the Synod authorizes and instructs the Board of Foreign Missions prayerfully and thoroughly to study the possibility of establishing a Mission in the said field (Sudan) and take such preliminary steps in this direction it deems advisable." The following year a special "impartial commission of five members" was elected to investigate this matter and report to the Board. This commission supported Hult's position, and its report was placed before the 1929 convention. The board at the same time reported that due to difficulties associated with work in French-ruled territory, as well as the growing needs on the Iramba field, "our calling to Africa is to concentrate on the Iramba field." The position of the Board prevailed. This terminated the services of Pastors Hult and Steimer.

I feel that the Augustana Synod could have entered both fields, and Augustana with its vibrant mission spirit would have risen to the challenge of both. What might Africa look like today if Hult's vision of the Sudan would have been fulfilled?

FOUNDATION FOR TOMORROW

The work in Irambaland flourished. Mission stations were established, congregations were organized, and the church was established. Widespread educational and medical work was developed. The Lord's blessing was certainly on the work. It is a great history. Doris and I feel deeply honored that we could have a small part in it. Augustana had an honorable mission vision.

I remember one day sitting in the office of the Kinampanda Teacher Training Center reading some old files of mission minutes. I came across a most interesting bit of history. In the report of the missionary convention (I have forgotten the year, but it must have been the early thirties) there was talk about devolution. They did not use the word "devolution" at that time.

That came later. There in the early days they were actually talking about turning the church and mission over to the nationals. That did not happen quickly, but it was not forgotten.

The first missionary conference we attended was in 1955, and at that conference two memorable things happened: (1) copies of the newly published Iramba Hymnal were presented; and (2) Pastor Reuben Pedersen, president of the mission, in his opening address, spoke about "Winds of Change." He challenged us to realize that we were facing the time when the work and ministry would be transferred to the national church.

By 1960 that movement was steadily moving forward. We had the privilege to be a part of that process. It was not an easy time, but it was a great time as we planned and worked with our African brothers and sisters to turn the work of the mission over to the national church. The church has continued to build on the foundation that was laid—Jesus Christ. That is what mission is all about!

Augustana's African Presence in a Later Era

Allan J. Gottneid

Pastor Swenson has presented one historical perspective of the Augustana presence in East Africa. This paper will add to that perspective from another viewpoint. The Augustana layman writer of this paper has personally seen, heard, and participated in almost all of the following events from 1954 to 1984.

Dr. Paul C. Empie has written that; "An essential factor in the good stewardship of missions is the practice of co-operation and co-ordination. The Lutheran churches of the world knew very little of either of these two procedures prior to World War I."[1] This paper is about cooperation and coordination.

Kenya was a British Colony, Uganda a British Protectorate, and the rest of the former German East Africa became a United Nations Mandated Territory, Tanganyika, with Great Britain having the responsibility for administration. The British Colonial Government insisted irrevocably that title to the former German mission fields must be vested in an American, and only in an American, corporation. This corporation was the National Lutheran Council. The NLC had requested the Augustana Lutheran Church to be its agent in supervising the work of these fields through the war years and some years thereafter.

The magnitude of the responsibility inherent in this request has not, nor can it be, fully realized or appreciated by anyone not actually on one or another of these former German mission fields. During the war years it meant transferring about twenty-five experienced Augustana missionaries to replace about 170 Germans who were either deported or interned for the

---

[1] Paul C. Empie, "Lutheran Co-operation in Mission at Home and Abroad," *Augustana Missions 1959*, ed. Rudolph C. Burke and Theodore E. Mattson (Minneapolis: Boards of Home and World Mission, Augustana Lutheran Church, 1959) 12.

duration. As the years went by and the work expanded, more and more Augustana missionaries were assigned tasks in these orphaned fields.

Overnight, as it were, Augustana, known for its own Board of World Mission work in Iramba-Turuland, became intimately involved in an area stretching from Morogoro in east central Tanganyika to the Indian Ocean, Dar es Salaam, and along the coast northwards to the Kenya border. This was the former Berlin mission field with work among the Uzaramo and Uluguru people. Then the area extended northeast to embrace all of the Usambara mountain range where Bethel had its field rich in diakonia enterprises. Then the area continued westward encompassing the Pare Mountain range, on to Chaggaland and Mt. Kilimanjaro, continuing west along the Kenya border to Meru and Arusha and across the Serengeti Plains nearly to Lake Victoria. This was the former Leipzig mission field. Add the Augustana Iramba-Turu field, and the total area comprises about one-fifth of the entire nation. Augustana was spread thin, but the Augustana presence was there!

Just as in America and Europe, where there was a felt need for better cooperation and coordination, so it was in Tanganyika. The American and European churches were represented by the Lutheran Missions Council (LMC), and the emerging indigenous churches, still without constitutions, were represented by a loose federation without any legal or constitutional backing, the Federation of Lutheran Churches in Tanganyika (FLCT). It was a start and hurried the devolution process to some extent.

Both the LMC and the loosely organized FLCT felt the need for a legalized federation of the seven participating Lutheran churches in Tanganyika. This was accomplished in 1956. The Federation named four of the existing institutions as FLCT institutions. These were the Medical Assistants Training Center at Bumbuli, the Lutheran Publishing House at Vuga, the Theological Seminary at Makumira, and the Lutheran Secondary School at Ilboru just outside Arusha. A fifth entity could be added: *Bendera za Kikristo*, the FLCT official "Church Paper." And the Augustana presence was in each of them!

The former Leipzig mission was the largest of the three orphaned fields. There were about 100,000 Lutherans in this church. This was the first indigenous Tanganyika church to complete its constitution. It was also the first to apply for membership in the Lutheran World Federation. It was now officially the Lutheran Church of Northern Tanganyika (LCNT). The veteran Augustana missionary, Dr. Elmer Danielson, was the first Superintendent.

The "Winds of Change," a term in the minds of many people and many nations at this time, were not only in Africa, but also worldwide. They blew with tornado-like effect early in the 1960s. Three major events must be considered: First, the formation of the Evangelical Lutheran Church in Tanganyika, June 1963, with Rev. Stefano R. Moshi elected president and Mr. Joeli Maeda elected as full time Executive Secretary. Arusha was named the ELCT headquarters. There were then about 400,000 members in the new church; today there are more than 2.5 million members in the ELCT.

Second, the Independence movement in Tanganyika and the merger of Tanganyika with the islands of Zanzibar and Pemba creating the United Republic of Tanzania in 1964. Third, the merger of the Augustana Lutheran Church with other Lutheran churches in the USA to form the Lutheran Church in America in 1962. Augustana lost her identity as an organization; Augustana as an institution was dead! There has been no resurrection! I call the remains the "Augustana Diaspora." We are examples of it. With these three notable new beginnings it was time for the mission societies and agencies to make some new beginnings themselves. The Tanzania Assistance Committee was created in 1965. Now all agencies supporting the work of the ELCT cooperated and coordinated their support for the whole church paying special attention to personnel needs, scholarship needs, and financial needs, rather than each doing its own thing for its own historic fields of endeavor. The Augustana Diaspora was present in all these developments.

Before going into some of these changes and the results of them, it is necessary to go back to the mid-1950s when an equally monumental event took place at the Marangu Teacher Training Center of the Lutheran Church in Northern Tanganika, November 12-22, 1955.

The LWF Commission on World Mission raised the subject of a possible All-Africa Lutheran Conference and decided to pursue the matter. Lutheran churches in Africa were contacted. Two letters of invitation were received; one from the Church of Sweden Mission in Rhodesia and the other from the Rev. Stefano R. Moshi of the Lutheran Church of Northern Tanganyika. The latter was accepted with gratitude by the LWF. The Lutheran Church in Northern Tanganyika was the "host church," and all the Augustana missionaries working in the LCNT were very much a part of this conference, each one being given several areas of responsibilities and tasks to perform both during the preparatory phase and the conference itself.

The LWF stipulated from the beginning that delegates from the African churches that had Lutheran work must be in the proportion of two Africans to one non-African, and they must come from these African churches. Only delegates from the African Lutheran churches could vote. Forty-seven African and 23 non-African participants in the conference were elected delegates. In addition to the delegates there were 18 speakers and 76 visitors. The vast majority of the visitors, 71 of them, were representatives of the FLCT churches in Tanganyika, most of them being students at the FLCT Theological Seminary, Makumira. Five co-chairmen—three African, two non-African—were chosen. African co-chairmen presided 7½ days of the ten-day meeting.

The stated purposes of this conference were: (a) to try to bring all the Lutheran churches and mission fields in Africa out of isolation so as to have them begin to think as an African Lutheran Church, and to have them see the vision of the Christian church throughout the whole continent of Africa; and (b) it was hoped that simply coming together would encourage the African church leaders to see their greater responsibility in Christianizing their people.

There is far too much to tell about this conference to be included in this paper, but a few notes can be shared. This was the first Pan-African conference of any kind ever held on the continent of Africa. It did draw world wide attention. *Time* and *Life* magazines carried articles and photos of it; all LWF member churches were invited to unite in prayer for the conference at its commencement. For the first time in their lives, black and white South Africans knelt at the Lord's Table shoulder to shoulder to receive the Eucharistic gift of grace as fellow Lutherans and fellow Christians. The African delegates found the prepared papers too long and too verbose, and they asked for more time to talk among themselves. This request was granted. They presented the conference with a brief list of the "Burning Issues Facing the African Churches Today" (1955). They called for an institution for advanced theological education to be established in Africa as soon as possible. Until such an institution could be developed, they requested scholarship opportunities enabling deserving Africans to study in European and American universities. They requested that local institutions in the various countries be upgraded to provide better training for teachers, pastors, and evangelists to keep in line with the rising educational standards in Africa. It was strongly felt that if more responsible positions in the church were filled by Africans, it would strengthen the younger churches and help them realize more fully their responsibility for the work. Finally, it would greatly help the propagation of the Christian faith in Africa if missionaries in their relations with Africans showed a better example of fighting all kinds of discrimination.

To briefly summarize the conference, I quote parts of the Preface to *Marangu*, the official report of the conference, written by His Excellency, Emmanuel Abraham, Ambassador and Plenipotentiary to the Court of St. James, at the Imperial Ethiopian Embassy, London:

> The All-Africa Lutheran Conference. . . was a great experiment. It was also for all those who had the privilege of attending it, a great experience. . . . It was stated by many of the delegates and observers to be epoch making. I am inclined to agree with this view. . . . It was to my knowledge the first occasion when Africans from many parts of the vast continent were able to meet freely on a common problem, in this case, the crucial problem of how best to preach Christ to their fellow Africans and to co-ordinate the labors of all Lutheran churches in Africa. . . . It was remarkable how the difficulties and differences seemed to vanish when it was remembered that the Crucified and Risen Lord was the focus of the discussions. The African delegates were also given an opportunity of speaking their minds more freely and fully, as it were, *in camera*, and the result was submitted to the Conference. . . . It was the hope of many an African delegate that the Conference should not be the last. This in itself is an indication of the success and usefulness of the Conference.[2]

---

[2] Emmanuel Abraham, *Marangu: A Record of the All-Africa Lutheran Conference, Marangu, Tanganyika, East Africa, November 12-22, 1955*, ed Fridtjov Birkeli (Geneva: Department of World Mission, Lutheran World Federation, 1956) 7.

What have been the results? There were some immediate ones. The Radio Voice of the Gospel was created, broadcasting in many languages to Africa from Addis Ababa, Ethiopia. The Swahili language recording studio was built in Moshi to become another FLCT institution. A Post-Ordination course of advanced theological studies was conducted for two years, using the facilities of the Marangu Hotel a very short distance from the site of the All-Africa Lutheran Conference. Scholarship programs enabling African Lutherans to study abroad opened up. A study of the meaning of the "episcopacy" was undertaken by a number of churches with the help of the LWF/DWM. Other All-Africa Lutheran Conferences did follow: Antsirabi, Madagascar, in 1960; Addis Ababa in 1965; and a similar conference was held later in Botswana with only African church leaders present. At the time of the AALC there was a poster proclaiming, "Today there are One Million Lutherans in Africa." This year (2002), forty-seven years later, there are over 10½ million Lutherans in Africa!

More results of these changes after the All-Africa Lutheran Conference of 1955 and the beginning of a new church and a new nation can be listed. The new church needed to take a good look at itself and to see what it had going and what it needed to be doing. A survey of all seven synods and dioceses was conducted by the ELCT office of Christian Education Research. Personal on-site visits were made to many ELCT "bush" and primary schools, to all secondary schools, all nurses training schools, all hospitals, the Medical Assistants Training Center, all Bible schools, all farm schools, all handcraft and home craft schools, music schools, schools for the deaf and the blind, and to many appropriate technology projects. A second validating survey followed two years later. Volumes of data were presented to the Executive Council of the ELCT to serve as basis for future planning.

From the very beginning of the ELCT, a desperate plea for a common syllabus for confirmation instruction was voiced loud and often. The new Tanzania government, in writing its National Education Ordinance, mandated the teaching of religion in all the nation's schools. Confirmation was an ELCT concern; religious instruction in the public schools was an ecumenical concern. The ELCT developed a life-long—cradle to grave—program for instruction in the Christian Faith. The basic statement defining what the ELCT meant by Christian Education was adopted by member churches of the Christian Council of Tanzania. Work began ecumenically on developing seven teacher guides and seven pupil books for a commonly agreed upon syllabus of religious instruction in the public schools. The ELCT proceeded to develop confirmation and many other courses of instruction for children, youth, and adults.

As the ELCT grew in size and services, changes in polity and terminology took place. The AALC interest in studies of the episcopacy came to fruition. The terms "synod," "superintendent," and "president" were dropped, and there are now only dioceses and bishops. This was a severance of sometimes envious and touchy historical ties with founding agencies.

Nationalization of basic human services, such as schools, and the takeover of hospitals created new challenges for the ELCT and other churches. In keeping with the "Burning Issues" report of the Marangu AALC the need for the ELCT's own school for training church leaders was particularly felt. The ELCT Junior Seminary located just outside Morogoro was built. This is a multi-program school having a six-year secondary program, a seven-year primary school program, a teacher training course to equip teachers to use the new education materials being developed, a language school, a farm school with both animal and plant husbandry taught, independent projects and experiments with solar heating, and methane gas production for heat and light, etc., going on.

The Junior Seminary format of multi-programmed educational opportunities began to be copied by individual dioceses. While meeting very important needs, this format did not answer the need for higher educational opportunities. Again, very much in line with the AALC "Burning Issue" call for an institution of higher education, the Tumaini University came into being to provide training for future leaders. The university has three campuses: the Iringa University College with Faculties for the Arts and Sciences with degrees in Mathematics and Journalism, the Faculty of Business and Economics, the Faculty of Law, and the Faculty of Theology offering Diploma and B.D. programs. It also has a 70,000 volume library. The Makumira campus, the oldest of the three campuses with the Makumira University College offers B.D. and M.Th. degree programs. The Moshi campus of the Kilimanjaro Christian Medical College has a faculty for a five-year undergraduate M.D. program, a faculty for a three-year B.Sc. in Nursing program, and a faculty of Rehabilitation Services; it is affiliated with 16 other schools of health sciences, and it has published more than 500 research studies. In all of the foregoing, the Augustana Diaspora has been present and extremely active.

But let's return back to Augustana when it was the Augustana Lutheran Church, and this church was given the responsibility to care for not only its own field in Iramba-Turu, but also for three orphaned mission fields. As missionary families increased, so did the need for educating these children, and the Augustana School at Kiomboi was begun to serve the families of these four fields. Doors were opened to other Lutheran churches and agencies that likewise had needs for educational facilities for their children. This school has a marvelous history of love, care giving, and excellent educational experiences, both formal and informal, with a remarkable staff of loving temporary substitute parents for very many a family. But with the changing times, the Augustana School began to be seen by the government, the church, and other Tanzanians in general as a small American ghetto in the middle of the nation. The time had come for changes to be made. Augustana joined with a sister school begun by the Good Samaritan Foundation at the Kilimanjaro Christian Medical Center to care for KCMC staff families. Both the Lutheran Church in America (which had absorbed

Augustana) and the Good Samaritan Foundation passed their ownership shares to the ELCT, and this new merged school became an ELCT institution with ELCT holding the majority of seats on the Board of Directors. The school joined the International School Association and took the name International School Moshi. ISM starts with first grade and goes through six years of secondary school, culminating with the International Baccalaureate examination. Successfully passing this examination will qualify students to enter any university or college in Europe and to enter universities and colleges in the USA at a second year or sophomore level. It is truly international. It now has a branch located in Arusha as well as at Moshi.

There is much more that could be included with the Augustana Diaspora ever present, but time does not permit it. There are many ventures—such as fish farming and many other ventures—often personal interest projects, such as developing solar ovens, tool-making from scrap metal, producing effective and cheap brick-making equipment and other forms of construction materials and methods, making farming implements, and carrying on many other projects from growing cabbages to methane production. More than likely these individuals and small groups have not realized that they are part of the overall ELCT general plan for development. If the projects did not fit into the overall plan, the ELCT Executive Council could, and has said, "No. No way. We have better use for your time and money."

Again, in all of the above, the Augustana Diaspora was active. Nothing at all has been said or will be said about the ecumenical and international participation of the Diaspora in workshops, research, study programs, conferences, and so on engaged in under the auspices of the LWF, the WCC, and even the Holy See, the Vatican, the Christian Council of Tanzania, and the All-Africa Conference of Churches. So much for a very incomplete rundown on the Augustana presence in the later days.

We are the Diaspora. As long as our wobbly legs, shaky hands—as long as our dimming eyesight and fading hearing permit, we have the privilege and the obligation to continue, as the Diaspora, marching militantly forward every day of every year left to us under the very same banner that our Augustana predecessors did so characteristically. They proclaimed to all the world, and we must also, especially to the Church today: *Sola Fide*!

The Zamzam Story

Eleanor Danielson Anderson

There were nineteen from the Augustana Synod on the Zamzam in 1941. It's an Augustana story. Probably some of you have met and known the Augustana missionaries: Pastor Ralph Hult was traveling without his family. Because of the critical shortage of missionaries, he had agreed to go back to help in one of the fields that were formerly served by German Lutherans. Ralph's wife and their ten children were staying back in the States. Also on the Zamzam was Ralph Hult's sister, Ida, who was married to Dr. Carl Einar Norberg, and they had three childlren, Marie, Carl, and Ruth; they were all on the Zamzam. Some of you knew V. Eugene Johnson and his wife, Edythe; two of their four children, Victor and David, were with them on the Zamzam. Then there were two young women missionaries going to Africa for the first time: Esther Olson, who later married Lud Melander, and Velura Kinnan, who had quite a career as a missionary educator.

Then there was Mother and her six children. Mother's name was Lillian—Mrs. Elmer Danielson. My brother Laurence is the oldest of us children. He turned eleven the day before we got back to New York City in 1941. I am second oldest of the children, and I had my ninth birthday during the trip—on the prison ship, the Dresden. Evelyn is next; she was seven-and-a-half. Luella was four-and-a-half. Wilfred was a little past three. And Lois was the baby of the family; she was a year-and-a-half.

Like most of the Augustana missionaries, our family had been in Tanganyika previous to this. We had completed two terms there and had come back in 1939, three weeks before Lois was born here in Lindsborg. We had chosen Lindsborg as our furlough home.

In the spring of 1940 we were packed, ready to return to Tanganyika. But war was starting in Europe. Everything was so unsettled. Tanganyika had once been a German territory and then later came under the care of the British. In view of the growing restlessness, it was felt it was not wise for women and children to enter Tanganyika or even to travel toward Europe and Africa.

There was a critical shortage of missionaries in Tanganyika because the German Lutherans had been deported. Some reference was made to that last night—the "orphaned missions," the areas where German Lutherans had served and were now taken out of the country. The Africans were not quite ready to assume the leadership. They needed experienced missionaries. The question came to us: Would Dad go back by himself, since women and children could not travel at that time? Oh, that was a hard decision. We talked about it; we prayed about it. Laurence, Evelyn, and I were old enough to understand, but, of course, the little children did not know what was being considered. We had a little home here at 133 North Pine Street in Lindsborg. We'd sit at family devotions and talk about it, pray about it. Should Daddy go back and leave the family here? It was a hard decision. We were six children. Laurence had just turned ten, and baby Lois was not quite one year old. But sometimes God asks his followers to make some very difficult decisions, and this was one of them.

We felt led to answer "yes"; it seemed it was God's will that Dad go back by himself. But he had the agreement with the Board of Foreign Missions that, whenever it became possible for women and children to follow, then Mother and we children would go to Africa. Otherwise, Dad would come home ahead of time—he'd have a shortened term. For now he was needed, and he went.

I remember that hot afternoon in July, 1940, when we gathered in our living room for our farewell. After prayer, Dad went around the circle and hugged us and kissed us each good-bye. Little Wilfred, who was two-and-a-half, jumped up and grabbed Dad around the neck and would not let go. Dad, with tears streaming down his cheeks, had to put little Wilfred down and go on out the door. A friend was waiting in a car and took Dad to the train station at McPherson. It was a tearful, hard farewell, and yet, we felt it was in keeping with God's purpose. God needed our Dad in the work in Tanganyika.

Well, only a few months later—seven months later—we got a telephone call from Dr. S. Hjalmar Swanson of Augustana's Board of Foreign Missions saying he'd gotten a letter from Dad, asking whether Mother and we children could come with the other Augustana missionaries on the Zamzam. Dad had no idea the Zamzam was going to sail so soon, or he would not have made this request or inquiry. But Mother was one to tackle anything— anything humanly possible. So, when Dr. Swanson called, after we had talked about it and prayed about it, Mother answered, "Yes. We'll be glad to go on the Zamzam."

The big question was whether or not Dr. Swanson could get our visas in time. The Zamzam was to sail in less than two weeks. It happened that the sailing was delayed by three or four days. To make a long story short, we were on the Zamzam when it sailed March 20, 1941. Keep in mind that this was before Pearl Harbor. War was accelerating in Europe, but we were not, as a country, involved yet.

So, here we are, nineteen Augustana missionaries, including the children, heading for Tanganyika. We felt very, very special, really. The night before boarding the Zamzam, Dr. Emmy Evald, who had been our hostess at the Lutheran Home in New York City, and Pastor Gideon Olson of Bethlehem Church arranged a farewell service for all of us Augustana missionaries and families, sending us off. I had a special feeling that we were being sent by the whole Augustana Synod, and it was a very important and very sacred responsibility. Let me tell you now, lest I forget later, that three of the four older boys on the Zamzam were our Augustana boys: Laurence, Carl Norberg, Vic Johnson, along with Bob Buyse of the Africa Inland Mission. Later, whenever those boys would get into mischief, I was worried that somebody would tell Dr. Emmy Evald that we were not living up to the holy expectations of the Augustana Synod!

Out of the 201 passengers on the Zamzam, about 150 were missionaries, including children. We represented about twenty Protestant denominations, besides a group of seventeen Roman Catholic priests and teaching brothers. So three-fourths of the passengers were missionaries, going to many parts of Africa. This was an unusual experience—to be traveling not only with so many Augustana missionaries, but in such a big missionary group. The night the ship finally sailed, after sitting in the harbor an extra day, missionaries gathered out on deck and spontaneously began a beautiful hymn-sing. It just went on and on, singing one favorite hymn after another as the ship glided out of the harbor.

Besides the fact that this was a ship carrying so many missionaries, another unusual thing was that it was a ship owned by Egypt. Egypt was a neutral country. But, just to be safe, we were going to avoid the war zone. We were not going to go through the Mediterranean as we usually did. Instead, this ship was going to go from New York to Trinidad, to a port in Brazil, then diagonally across the South Atlantic to South Africa. Many passengers would get off in South Africa. The Zamzam would then continue up the east coast of Africa. We from Augustana would disembark in Mombasa, Kenya. The ship would continue on through the Red Sea and back to its home port in Alexandria, Egypt.

We left New York on March 20th. During the first part of the journey we settled into some routines. There were Bible study groups, language study groups, and just getting acquainted. Our two Augustana missionary teachers, Esther Olson and Velura Kinnan, were on their way to establish a school for missionary children in Tanganyika. They had a generous supply of paper and pencils and books with them. And so, what did they do but organize a school on board ship! We were about fifteen children of school age. Here we had thought: "This is March and we are getting out of school back home." But soon we were back in school, which we basically appreciated. The older boys, however, were a little ornery at times.

We stopped at Trinidad. During the next part of the trip, from Trinidad to Recife, Brazil, we were dismayed one day to see the ship's crew with buckets of black paint. And what were they doing? They were painting any glass surface on the outside of the ship. They painted it black. Also, they had little, round, black covers they were giving out to put on porthole windows. When there were not enough covers, porthole windows were painted black, too. We were told: "Be sure you turn off any light inside before you open any door to the outside of the ship." From now on, the Zamzam would be traveling in strictest blackout, without even any navigational lights.

Of course, many people protested. V. Eugene Johnson became a spokesman for the Protestant missionaries, and he went to the captain and objected to the blackout. But, the captain merely said, "I have orders; this is the way it will be." Nobody could figure out from whom he got the orders, or why. We were left in the dark, literally and figuratively.

We began to feel somewhat uneasy. People began to say more and more often: "We just have to trust God more completely. We're in his hands. Remember, God is with us." We kids in school talked too. What would we do if our ship were attacked? Well, the boys worked out a plan for how they would rescue all the chocolate candy bars. Ornery or not, those boys became our heroes! Seriously, it made us increasingly uneasy. Every night now, we were sneaking along in total darkness as if there were an enemy out there. If the Zamzam were truly a neutral ship, we should not have enemies. There was the feeling that we were hiding—that something was not right.

One night about midnight, we heard the ship's whistle blowing. Our family had two small cabins, each with three bunks, and baby Lois slept in her baby buggy. These two cabins shared a small corridor with a door that opened onto the port side deck. Hearing the ship's whistle blow, Mother said, "Something's wrong, kiddies. I better find out what's happening."

So she went those few steps through the corridor, opened the door, stepped out onto the deck. She stepped ankle deep in cool water, and all she could see was water everywhere. Naturally she thought the ship was going down. She hurried back in and said, "Kiddies, get your lifejackets on. We need to get ready to leave quickly."

Just then there was a knock at the door. It was Pastor Guilding. He said, "Mrs. Danielson, I'm shutting your door tight. A little light was streaming out."

"What's wrong? I hear the whistle and there's water."

"We've just had a heavy tropical downpour—a sudden downpour. And apparently the gutter system has gotten clogged."

This was a ship with open railings, but near the floor of the deck there was a little ledge. Because the gutter was clogged, the deck was flooded. "There's nothing to worry about," Pastor Guilding assured. "That whistle is the fog horn. We don't want to risk a collision."

After thanking Pastor Guilding, Mother said, "It's OK, kiddies. You may take off your lifejackets and go back to sleep." We thanked God and then snuggled back in bed to finish the night of sleep. That felt so good.

The next day at breakfast, passengers asked each other: "Did you hear that fog horn? Were you alarmed?" Some people admitted that they had been uneasy at first but soon figured it out. Others started talking, table-to-table: "Did you hear about Mrs. Danielson? She got the children out of bed and got lifejackets on." I was old enough to feel very embarrassed. But, Mother did what was right to do, of course.

In view of what happened later, we thank God for that experience. Sometimes God works in ways that we don't see at the time. After breakfast that morning, taking Lois in her arms and with me tagging along, Mother went to the ship's purser. You see, when we had taken out our lifejackets during the night, we discovered we had only six lifejackets—one per bunk. Since Lois slept in her baby buggy, no lifejacket had been provided for her.

Mother said to the purser, "I discovered last night that our family has only six lifejackets. We are myself and six children, so I should have one more. Would you please give me one more?" The purser looked at Lois, who was now about twenty months old, and said, "Well, if anything would happen, the baby would drown anyway." Mother was sweet but very firm, as she said, "But you must have another jacket someplace, and I would feel better if we each have one."

The purser saw Mother was determined, so he went into a back closet and dug around and finally came out with a very bedraggled, old, beaten-up lifejacket. "I'm sorry, but this is the best I can find, Mrs. Danielson." Mother took the jacket and thanked him.

She went back to the cabin, got out her needle and thread, and started mending holes. The jacket had lots of holes. Mother tightened straps, too. The jackets were made like a pillow in front and a pillow in back, pulled over the head, with shoulder straps and then straps to tie on the sides. Mother realized that all of the lifejackets were in poor condition. All of them were holey and missing straps. So she spent much of that morning mending them. This she probably—most likely—would not have done if we had not had that scare. God works in ways we don't always understand at the time.

We stopped at Recife, Brazil, and now we were going to head diagonally across the South Atlantic. I'll just mention that April 13th was Easter that year, and we had a beautiful worship service with Ralph Hult preaching. Esther Olson and Velura Kinnan organized the children with recitations and singing. The Augustana people gave a lot of leadership among all the missionaries.

We had a little scare on April 14th. At teatime in the afternoon, we started to make a U-turn and go back to South America. We couldn't see any reason for the turn, but we noticed that the ship's officers were watching a certain area of the horizon very, very carefully. We wondered: "What made us turn?"

The next day, we saw on the bulletin board a little notice from the captain saying that he had been alerted that there was a "suspicious vessel" in the area, so he had made the turn as a "precautionary measure." But, during the night he had turned again, and we were on the course to Africa again. He assured us there was "no further cause for alarm." There was no more explanation; we tried to believe everything was normal again. Nothing unusual happened on either the 15th or 16th. Whatever that "suspicious vessel" was, we assumed it was out of the way.

On April 17th Mother awakened unusually early and lay in her bunk thinking, "Only four or five more days until we stop at Capetown." We would not be getting off the ship—we'd go up the east coast as far as Mombasa—but at least the long part of the trip would be over. By April 17th it had been just about four weeks of travel from our departure from New York on March 20th with six lively children. I don't wonder but what Mother was maybe counting the minutes, much less the days, until the trip would be over. But even more than eagerness for getting to land again, I think Mother mostly wanted to get to Capetown to see if there would be a letter from Dad waiting at the ship's office.

Mother and Dad were always sweethearts. The last letter we had received from Dad, before leaving Lindsborg, had been dated in November. And this was April 17th. She was eager to get a letter from Dad. She could hardly wait to get to Capetown.

All of a sudden, as she lay there thinking, Mother heard a loud, explosive sound. She said her first thought was of a Kansas thunderstorm. But no, this was not exactly like a thunderstorm; she'd better figure out what it was. So she very quickly went down that little corridor, opened the door, and looked out. It was early morning. The sky was blue-gray; the water was blue-gray. Mother could see, sitting on the water about three to four miles distant, a black warship. As she was looking, she saw a red spurt of fire, and she knew this was enemy action.

Mother hurried back into our cabin. Really quite calmly she said, "Kiddies, we're being fired at by an enemy ship. Get dressed. Get your lifejackets on. Help one another. And remember, whatever happens, Jesus loves you. Jesus loves you more than Mommy or Daddy."

Laurence put on his Sunday suit and his new safari helmet. I put on my Sunday dress, but I left my pajama bottoms on. And so did Evelyn. The three youngest children could not understand why they were being pulled from their bunks, and these lifejackets were being put on. As soon as they were put on and tied, the children untied them and whined and wanted to crawl back into bed. Mother didn't bother trying to dress the little ones; she just tried to keep the jackets on.

Now the shells were coming, one about every ten seconds. We'd hear either a whining overhead or a splash in the ocean as shells missed their target. But some shells were hitting the Zamzam. Some people were injured. We could hear shrieks and cries and moans. There was the smell that comes from explosives. As we waited, we wondered: "Where will the next shell hit?"

The ship started to list. We were on the side the shelling was coming from, so it tilted our way. Our only exit was that door onto the port side deck, so, if the ship kept listing and rolled over, we'd be trapped. Mother said to Laurence, "Sonny, do you think we should get out now?" Very wisely Laurence answered, "I don't know, Mama. Maybe we're just as safe staying right here." And so we stayed. Mother realized the ship did not increase its tilting. Pumps had been started and damaged compartments closed, so the whole ship did not flood. We remained tilted but did not continue to list more.

But what should we do? The shells kept coming. About one every ten seconds. Mother huddled us together and kept reminding us, "Kiddies, whatever happens, remember that Jesus loves you." She didn't say we would get out alive. She did not promise everything would be better. But she did say again and again, "Remember Jesus loves you more than Mommy or Daddy."

The shelling kept on for about ten minutes. Suddenly a shell hit right above us. That jarred our cabin so badly that the lights went off, the mirrors broke, the lavatory cracked and hung on its pipes, and there was broken glass all over the floor. Laurence heard somebody say we should get down on the floor and brace ourselves for the next shell. "But look at all the glass. What shall we do, Mama?"

Just then the purser came in, the man we had gotten the lifejacket from. He said, "Mrs. Danielson, can you manage?"

"Yes, but we don't know what to do. We haven't heard any signal."

"The signal system was destroyed by the first shell. Just get to your lifeboat now as quickly as you can. The shelling has stopped." Then he left.

But before we left the cabin, Mother put her arms around us as best as she could with our lifejackets on and offered a prayer that, if we would not all be together in this world again, that we would be together in heaven. And she prayed that God would give our Daddy special strength for whatever he would have to go through.

After that prayer, holding Lois in her arm and grabbing Wilfred by his hand, with little Luella holding onto Mother's skirt and the rest of us following, Mother led the way to our lifeboat station. The boat had already been lowered from the upper level deck. Pastor Hult was in our lifeboat, so he helped us climb in. The ambulance drivers helped, too. They were passengers.

The crew members were in a panic. They were Egyptian, and they had considered the Zamzam to be a holy ship. They thought nothing bad would ever happen to it. Now that it had happened, they screamed and cried to Allah and did not show any consideration for the passengers. Just before Mother was going to get into the lifeboat, she said, "Oh, kiddies! I forgot my purse. I'll be right back." She didn't have much money in her purse, but the passports were there.

We just grabbed onto Mother. "Don't go, don't go, Mama." She said she took one look at us and decided that maybe the only passport we'd need was to heaven, and Jesus had already granted that. So she stayed with us.

I am so sure that, if she had gone back those twenty or thirty feet to get her purse, the crew would not have waited for her.

Our lifeboat was lowered and touched water. The crew immediately started rowing toward the stern of the Zamzam. Right away Mother felt some water around her feet. She had cut her toe, and the salt water was stinging her toe. She thought the water was from the splashdown. She looked again and noticed that the water was accumulating. Then somebody said, "We're leaking! Water is coming in. Look at all these holes!" Sure enough, there were hundreds of small holes. Our lifeboat had been hanging near where a shell had exploded, piercing the lifeboat with shrapnel.

We begged the crew to stay at the Zamzam. We could climb up a rope ladder and find a raft. It would be better than going to sea in a sieve, as it were. But the crew could not be reasoned with. They had control. They had the oars, and they just kept rowing farther and farther past the stern of the Zamzam and then out into the big open space, as the water was coming up our legs.

We looked for things with which to scoop the water out. Mother said, "Here! Take my son's helmet." So Laurence gave up his new safari helmet. Two empty tin cans were the only provisions in the lifeboat, and they were used for scooping. Evelyn and I cupped our hands and scooped, as did others. We thought that, if enough people kept scooping, we could keep the boat afloat. But the water gained on us. It was coming in faster than we could get it out. We were rowed farther and farther away from the Zamzam, as the lifeboat filled, just like a tub filling.

Mother knew the boat could not take much more. She held Lois more tightly and grabbed Wilfred's arm as she looked around at us, not knowing what the next minute would bring. Would she still have her children? Would her children still have a mother? She called out to us, "Kiddies, be brave in Jesus."

And then the lifeboat went down. We went under the surface of the water but soon bobbed up. The thrust of going down somehow pushed Lois' lifejacket off, leaving it blocking Lois' face. Mother could not put the jacket back on Lois, so she pushed it to the side. From that point on, baby Lois did not have a lifejacket on, but she was too young to care, as long as she was in her mother's arms.

Mother had lost her grip on Wilfred, but he came up quite close to her. However, his lifejacket tilted him back so his little face was straight up, and the water was sloshing over his face. The ocean is never smooth as glass; there are always billows. Mother would pull Wilfred upright, but, as soon as she let go, his jacket would pull his head back again, and he struggled to get air. She realized Wilfred needed someone to hold him up all the time.

But where was Luella? Mother could see Laurence, and Evelyn and I were close by. Luella, who was four-and-a-half, was of rather slight build. Could she have dropped out of her jacket? Was she gone? A terrible fear gripped Mother. Then she saw Laurence stir into action, pushing a crew member aside and reaching down. Laurence yanked Luella to the surface. She had been trapped under the crew member. Little Luella was sputtering, and it took a while to get her breath, but she was alive.

So now we were all above water. Mother realized we must not swallow this salt water or we could get deathly ill. She called out, "Keep your mouths closed, kiddies, and pray." I don't think we knew why we should shut our mouths, but we obeyed. Mother didn't say anything about sharks, but we were in water where there could be sharks. Mother thought about how old and rotten these lifejackets were. Would they soon start soaking up water? We'd be helpless. Again, she did not say the worrisome things she was thinking. Of course she thought about Daddy. How would Daddy find out and how would Daddy take all of this? Daddy was very tenderhearted. If it happened that he lost some or all of his family, how would he take it?

All Mother could do was pray. She said later that, in her heart, she was singing "Thou Blest Rock of Ages, I'm Hiding in Thee." She called out to us, again and again, "Kiddies, remember Jesus loves you. Whatever happens, remember that Jesus loves you." In fact, that made such an impression on others that later someone wrote in a magazine article that Mother had led us in singing "Jesus loves me, this I know." Can you imagine a choir of children singing as they bob in the ocean! We did not sing, but it is very true that Mother kept reminding us that Jesus loves us. Nobody told her, "Be quiet, woman." There were people who were not missionaries in the group, but nobody told her to be quiet. At later reunions, people have told us how much it meant to others that Mother shared her faith and reminded us of Jesus' love.

The lifeboat eventually came up because it was made of wood. Three of the younger children were put on its overturned bottom—Wilfred, Luella, and Evelyn. An oar floated by, and Pastor Hult pushed the oar under Mother's arm to help give support as Mother kept holding Lois.

We had been in the water about forty-five minutes when we realized that the raider—the warship—was coming toward the Zamzam and us survivors. It came in closer and closer. The raider's crew had machine guns out; and there was the Nazi flag. We thought this might be our end. But, lest I forget to tell you later, let me say that those machine guns were for shooting sharks. The Germans had no intention of shooting at us. But at the moment we did not know it—and it was frightening.

Here then is this warship coming, with machine guns and a Nazi flag, and there's the Zamzam tilted and slowly sinking, the passengers and crew are in lifeboats, sitting on the surface of the water, and some are bobbing in the water—a very, very dismal scene. Then across the sky came a perfect, glorious rainbow, just as if God had put it there right then, for us, to be reminded that he was with us. God knew what we were going through. He cared. He loved us. Even those who were not Christians seemed moved and touched by seeing that rainbow. We who were Christians were certainly strengthened and given hope by it.

The raider came in as close as they dared, shut off their motors, put down two motor launches, came over to us, pulled us out of the water, and chug-chugged back to the side of the raider. Rope ladders were lowered from high above. We climbed up that rope ladder. That was about the scariest thing I have done, as the ladder went straight up. But right behind me was a German sailor to help in case I stumbled. The two little children, Wilfred and Lois, were brought up in baskets.

When we got up on deck we were met by German sailors with tears in their eyes, full of kindness. One who could speak English said to Laurence, "We didn't want to do it, but it was orders." Those who met Mother were so apologetic. They realized this had been a mistake—a mistake of war, in which innocent people suffer. They had assumed that, because we were traveling blacked out, we were in some way involved with the war, maybe a troop ship, aiding their enemy. Instead, here we were—women and children, missionaries, innocent people.

Many things happened that day. Our family was taken into the officers' cabins and warmed up; our wet clothes were removed, and we were wrapped in towels. The Germans gave us chocolate cookies while we were getting warmed up in the officers' bunks. I've said that from that moment on, I forgave the Germans for what they had done. The cookies tasted so good!

After we were warmed up, we were taken to the bottom of the warship, three levels down, to a big room filled with bunk beds. This ship was accustomed to rescuing survivors when they could. The captain was a wonderful gentleman who had been in the Navy, a German Lutheran, Captain Rogge. He treated people decently. His staff treated people decently. They had doctors ready to help us. Mother had to have her toe attended to because she had cut it on the broken glass in our cabin.

While we were gathering in this big, bottom room, along with others from the Zamzam, the Germans were taking what supplies they wanted from the Zamzam. Then, in the early afternoon, we were taken up onto the deck of the raider. The Germans needed an accounting to know who had been killed, drowned, or was missing. They went through the list. From over three hundred thirty crew and passengers from the Zamzam, not one person was missing or killed. Three had been badly injured, and one man did die about ten days later, but not on that day. The captain said that, because no life had been lost on April 17th, he did not have to report this incident until he wanted to—and he was not planning to report it soon, if at all.

When Mother was asked to step forward for the roll call, the officer said, "Mrs. Danielson, you had six children. How many are still with you?" Mother was only about five feet, three inches. She looked up at the towering German officer and said, "I thank God he saved us all." That's how we all felt.

After the Germans had an accounting and knew that everybody was on the warship, they wanted to get rid of the Zamzam quickly, because this raider was a hunted ship. Though it used a fake name, it was actually the Atlantis. The British were looking for it. The raider did not want to leave any trace that it had been in that area and had sunk a ship. So, once they were sure everybody was off the Zamzam, and they had taken what they wanted, they put three time bombs on it. We were invited to watch.

Laurence got to go over to the railing on the side where the Zamzam was, so he could watch. Mother took me, the second oldest, and the rest of the children to the other side of the deck. I said, "But Mama, I want to see it!"

Mother said, "No, Eleanor. Sometimes you have bad dreams. I don't think you should see it."

"I promise I won't have bad dreams." I kept on and on, begging. "Laurence gets to watch. It isn't fair!"

Finally, Mother gave in, as mothers sometimes do, and I walked over to the side of the deck where Laurence was. I looked out on the ocean where I had seen the Zamzam a few minutes earlier. Now there was nothing there except white, bubbly, churning water and some debris. Laurence said the Zamzam blew up and turned on its side. In eight minutes it was gone. The Germans machine-gunned the debris, so there would not be any trace. Then we steamed away.

What was going to happen to us now? The captain apologized. He had had no idea the Zamzam was a ship with mostly missionaries. He did not want us on his hands. He said he was signaling another German ship to transfer us to.

Sure enough, that night the Dresden arrived. The Dresden was a freighter that had accommodations for about thirty people, and here we were over three hundred thirty from the Zamzam. The next day all of us, except the three badly-injured men, were transferred to the Dresden. The men were put in the two cargo holds. They had a rope ladder to go up and down. They slept on pads. Stuffy, stuffy cargo holds. When the weather was decent, they spent the day up on deck. They lined up with tin bowls for food. Calisthenics were organized. Guards were always watching.

The women and children were more fortunate. Mothers and children were crowded into the few cabin spaces. Single women slept in the lounge and along the edge of the hallways. Any spare inch was used at night for sleeping. Our lifejackets were given back and used for pillows. We had a thin pad to sleep on with no sheets or blankets. Bathroom facilities were very limited. It took a few days before we got clothes back. Whatever clothes had been taken from cabins on the Zamzam were given back. Some got a lot; some got nothing. We shared.

The hardest thing I remember was the food. For breakfast it was a wallpaper paste; at least, that's what we called it. It was just a starchy gruel, with no milk or sugar or anything to make it better. For lunch and supper it was a watery soup. There'd be maybe a string of beef or two little pieces of carrots or a macaroni piece. Mother was so unselfish. She would share whatever solids were in her soup. "If Wilfred got the pea yesterday, I get it today!" We kept track. Every bite of food was appreciated. At first, though, we would not eat it. Like most children, we turned up our noses. "We're not going to eat this stuff—especially the bread." We could see bugs that had been in the flour, now baked in the bread. But when you get hungry enough, you eat anything. And you are thankful for it.

We were so thankful, too, for a drink of water in the morning and a drink of water in the evening. That's all there was. They were rationing it out.

The sinking had happened about two-thirds of the way across the South Atlantic between Brazil and South Africa. For about nine days we went in circles. Apparently the Germans did not know what to do with us. Then we had a rendezvous with the raider. We must have gotten orders, because after that we started going north.

There were two big questions. One was: What does Daddy know, and how is he holding up? We had no way to communicate with him. As far as we knew, it had not been announced that we'd been sunk. All we could do was pray. Pray and pray. We prayed for Daddy. Everyone had loved ones. The Hult family, for example. The V. Eugene Johnsons had two teenagers they had left in United States. We prayed for churches back home. We prayed for churches in Africa. We prayed not only for our Augustana Lutherans, but we prayed for the other denominations. A wonderful feeling of being one big family developed, a wonderful bond of caring for each other, united in Christ.

I don't remember the experience of being on the prison ship as a terrible, terrible thing. I remember the hardships of not enough food and water and other shortages. But there was kindness, there was love, there was unity in Christ. There was a sense of dependency on Christ. Mother has written that sometimes, when she felt she just could not go on any longer, she gave her weakness to Christ and let him fill her, to give her his strength. She realized she could not do it on her own, but he gave her the strength she needed.

I think also that Mother's example taught me that children learn a lot from how their parents handle things. Because Mother did not complain a lot, things didn't seem as bad as they were. She did not say, "Oh, isn't this terrible that we don't have a good place to sleep?" We just lived with it and got along.

Also, I want to emphasize that, although we were always guarded, we were treatly kindly by the Germans. That made a big difference.

The other big question was: Where are we going? Eventually we realized we were heading toward Europe. Germany had conquered France by then. We were told we were being taken to German-occupied France. To get there, we went through the British Blockade. It was extremely dangerous. Every hour, night and day, we knew we could meet our death if a convoy or submarine or plane came along.

On May 19th, because the Zamzam had not been heard of since it left Brazil six weeks earlier, the Zamzam was declared lost, presumed sunk.

Nobody knew for sure, but most likely it was gone—with everybody on it. On May 19th it was headlined in newspapers and on the radio: "Zamzam feared lost. No news..." and so on. Dr. S. Hjalmar Swanson said that day was the "Hour of Gethsemane" in the Augustana Synod. The Board of Foreign Missions—those who lived in the Minneapolis area—gathered to pray and to comfort each other.

But how good God was that the very next day, May 20th, United States time, we had arrived in France. The news went out that all Americans were alive and in France. There was a period of only twenty-four hours of real grief. Many people had worried or wondered before that, but it was only twenty-four hours from the time of the news of probable loss until the time of announcing that we were alive. Dad, being in Africa, got the news too, and for him it was a day-and-a-half of grief. But how good that it was not weeks.

We were in German-occupied France now. Those who were not citizens of the United States were taken on to various German war camps. For us from the States, the American Embassy official came in and secured passports and visas. The Red Cross took care of travel arrangements. We went on a train through Spain and into Portugal. Various ships took us back to America.

Our family came back to New York on June 23rd, having left March 20th. Dr. S. Hjalmar Swanson met us at the pier, as he met all the other Augustana missionaries, except Pastor Hult, who came a week after we did. There was such a wonderful feeling of coming back to the United States, coming back to this wonderful country, coming back to the love of our church people, and being welcomed wherever we went. There were gatherings of Augustana people praising God and giving thanks.

Our family came home to Lindsborg, Kansas. We remained here. Dad came home near the end of the War. Mother and Dad and three of the children went back to Tanzania after that. Then only two of the children. And finally Mother and Dad served alone, until 1968. They had an active retirement here in Lindsborg and lived into their 90s.

Only God knows the results of the Zamzam experience. Dr. Swanson wrote that there was a new fervor for people becoming missionaries. Instead of being defeated by this event, there were young men saying, "I'm going to be a missionary. I'm going to go to Tanzania." There was a new interest in missions.

My Dad, in Tanzania, says that, at the same time, because the missionaries had not gotten there on the Zamzam, the Africans realized more clearly that they would become the leaders. That sped up the development of the indigenous church.

I don't know what God does through this story, but I know it is his story. My sister Luella says the Zamzam story helps us realize that there are little miracles every day. This is a big story, a big example, but God works in wondrous ways in little ways, every day. Luella challenges us to look for those little ways and to give thanks to God. Also, it is a story of trusting God. When I was a widow, I often thought of the Zamzam story and thought that, if God brought us through that tragedy, he can bring me through whatever else is happening in life.

Sometimes I get a letter from a young mother, saying, "You know, I thought about your mother. I have two kids and I don't know how I can manage. And then I think about your mother with six children on the Zamzam. And I know that if God helped your mother through all that, he can help me with my two."

Who knows? Who knows how God uses the Zamzam story? We leave it in his hands. To Him be the glory.

Elmer Danielson: Vision, Joys, and Tears of a Missionary Dad

Lois Danielson Carlson

As the youngest of Elmer Danielson's six children, I feel the least qualified to represent our family in sharing his story. I never even knew our dad until November, 1944, at the age of 5. And again, I never saw him from the time I graduated from high school until two days before my graduation from Bethany College. But that wasn't so bad. He missed out on much more than that. Among his six children, he missed four out of six high school graduations, four out of six college graduations, two out of six weddings and numerous athletic competitions, music concerts, special honors, major life events.

It is very difficult to talk about Dad without including Mother. I can say without any reservation, that theirs was one whale-of a love story, a romance that never waned. As long as they could write, they sent each other love notes and poems and gave each other romantic gifts. And when they moved to Bethany Home in 1993 at the ages of 90 and 94, they insisted on having their beds side by side.

In many ways, Dad made it easy for us to talk about him. He was the master of documentation. He faithfully kept journals and diaries and was a prolific letter-writer. He was extremely well organized, extremely disciplined, extremely neat. He didn't just talk about doing something; he always followed through. When he put together photograph albums and scrap books, each picture was accompanied by a detailed caption. He was a sentimentalist who hung on to many things, things that were well labeled and always had a place.

In 1989 Dad wrote his memoirs for his family. Titled *A Story of a Great Commission Family...as Dad Saw It*, it chronicles his "spiritual journey" from childhood to 1989. In this unedited baring of his soul, Dad shared with humor, candor, and deep emotion fascinating details of his youth, of his work in Tanganyika, and of his undying devotion to his family regardless of the separations of time and space. It is an absolute treasure, and some of what I present today comes from these memoirs.

Twelve years earlier, in 1977, Dad had written *Forty Years with Christ in Tanzania*, a magnificently thorough and accurate account of the growth of the church in Tanzania from 1928 through 1968, the years spanning his missionary service. Though punctuated with personal reflections and experiences, its painstakingly detailed content was possible because of the reports, minutes, letters, and journals Dad had kept. This book, originally published by the Department of Global Missions, was reproduced by my sister Eleanor Anderson in 1996 with some editing and the inclusion of a handy index.

In addition to these two books chronicling his life, work, family and faith, Dad loved to write letters. My siblings and I received volumes of letters from him, very personal letters addressing whatever was going on in our lives at the time. Each letter seemed to evolve at some point into a sermon, something for which Dad was forever apologizing, but of which we never tired. We saved these letters, and some of us still have them, as they are indeed treasures. Dad was the consummate letter writer, whether writing to the famous or to the lowly. Each communication had a distinct purpose—whether to encourage or comfort or admonish or inform.

My brother Wilfred and I lived in Tanzania with our parents well into our teen years and thus were able to see and experience Dad's ministry more clearly than our older siblings whose years in Tanzania were cut short by the *Zamzam* sinking in 1941. And then I had the great privilege of returning to Tanzania in 1963 as a missionary while our parents were still there. Even though Mother and Dad were upcountry in Arusha, and I was in Dar es Salaam on the coast, it was a special experience to be a missionary colleague of my revered parents and to view them from that perspective. I was still in Dar es Salaam in 1966 through 1968 when Dad served as the first Executive Secretary of the Tanzania Assistance Committee headquartered in Geneva, Switzerland. In that capacity he oversaw the distribution of personnel and funding sent to Tanzania from churches in Europe and America. This gave me another interesting relationship, another perspective.

So, how did Elmer Reinhold Danielson, born in Meriden, Connecticut on May 22, 1903, the oldest of four sons born to poor, hard-working Swedish immigrants, get to Tanganyika? First of all, he had a mother and a pastor who saw special promise in Elmer, encouraging him to finish high school and go on to college after he had already left high school to pursue training as a draftsman. Despite enormous financial hardship, he went off to Upsala Academy in East Orange, New Jersey, at the age of 16 to complete high school, and then entered Upsala College. He excelled in athletics and academics and, though he always considered himself a bit socially awkward and shy, he had a good time and was highly respected by classmates and faculty. Poverty made Elmer hardworking and resourceful. His family never owned a car and, although he was only 110 miles from home, their only visit on campus was for his college graduation after six years. Likewise Elmer rarely got home, but he always felt the warmth and support of his family and was eternally grateful for the sacrifices they made so that he could pursue his education. His family certainly could have used him as a breadwinner, to help support his younger brothers, but no one begrudged his pursuit of higher education. He was the only one to get a college education.

Elmer had been a good kid and was growing into a fine young man. His relationship with his church was fairly ordinary. But two events in 1924 made their mark on Elmer. First, he was chosen as a delegate from Upsala to a Student Movement gathering in Indianapolis where 6,000 young people from across the USA listened to "giants in world mission" from across the world. The theme was "The Evangelization of the World in This Generation." Elmer later wrote, "I was simply glued to my seat, and took copious notes. But most of all my heart was touched in a way it never had been before." Then a few months later, Elmer was one of two students selected to spend the summer at the Lake Independence Bible Camp in Minnesota to learn how to teach the Bible. It was the summer before his senior year at Upsala. At the close of the summer camp, Elmer had a most remarkable spiritual awakening which changed his life forever. It was in essence a conversion experience, a moment in which Jesus Christ became personal to him, a moment in which he committed his life to serving Christ from that day forward. Years later Dad often stated that he had no idea why he was given this Road-to-Damascus style experience, and he never believed for a moment that it made him better than anyone else. It was, however, an experience that remained vivid and fresh throughout his life. It was out of that experience that Dad followed God's leading into seminary and answered the call to go to Tanganyika as an Augustana Synod missionary in September of 1928.

Following his graduation from Augustana Seminary in Rock Island and his ordination on June 10, 1926, Elmer returned home to Meriden for the summer before leaving for Tanganyika. There were many people in his hometown who felt this promising young pastor would be wasting his life and talent in Africa. They believed he should serve people in America. Elmer had many opportunities to preach that summer, and one Sunday he pointed out that Meriden, with a population of 28,000, had forty Christian churches. The people to whom he was being sent in Tanganyika numbered 150,000 and didn't have even one church. They had never heard the gospel, nor would they hear it unless someone brought it to them. After that sermon he heard little or no resistance, except from family who were naturally worried about him and knew how much they would miss him.

Elmer was a 25 year-old, newly ordained single man when he left for Tanganyika in September, 1928. He had resigned himself to the possibility of remaining single indefinitely, at least for the next five years before his first furlough, and was mildly frustrated that he had not found that someone special with whom to share his life. But when he boarded his ship in New York harbor he discovered a lovely, dark-haired, dark-eyed girl from southeast Kansas. Her name was Lillian Larson, and he was immediately smitten. Lillian, however, was not so easily distracted. She, too, had answered the call to serve Christ in Tanganyika, and she wasn't about to let a handsome young pastor from Connecticut get in her way. Nevertheless, by the time they reached the Red Sea, Elmer had the audacity to suggest to Lillian that maybe they could serve Christ more effectively together than separately. After all, they were both assigned to work among the Iramba people in Central Tanganyika and certainly would be taking language study together. This may not have been a proposal, but it was close enough. Courting Lillian once they got to their destination was a challenge as missionaries were expected to be circumspect in all they did, and any kind of romantic behavior was considered inappropriate. But their young love could not be discouraged, and within a year they were married in what was the first Christian wedding in the area. Everyone rejoiced. When Elmer returned to America after their first five year term, he not only had a beautiful wife, but also two young children and a third due shortly. At the end of their second five-year term, they returned to the States just in time for the birth of their sixth child—me. This was the man who thought he might be destined for a life of celibacy?

 Dad had a remarkable capacity from the very beginning to feel at one with the Africans in Tanganyika. He had, in fact, a special ability to embrace a wide variety of racial and cultural groups very naturally and comfortably. He grew up in a New England neighborhood represented by several immigrant groups, where the Swedes were in a minority and often ridiculed. Even though his parents spoke Swedish at home, and he was confirmed in Swedish and preached his first sermon in Swedish, Elmer was a strong proponent of the "melting pot" concept and embraced diversity. As a college student, he spent one summer working in a landscaping business owned and operated by an African-American. He had great respect for this man, who had very little formal education. In elementary school, some of Elmer's friends bullied a Jewish boy. Although Elmer didn't participate in the harassment, neither did he intervene. So tormented was he by his inaction, that years later while on furlough after his first term in Tanganyika, Elmer looked up his former schoolmate and apologized to him. The man was quite astounded. Now a successful storeowner, he couldn't even remember the incident for which Elmer was apologizing some twenty years later. But this was the Elmer who demonstrated from the very beginning such a deep-seated respect for the Tanganyikan people, who always wondered what they were thinking, and how they felt about these well-intentioned, but often naive young missionaries. When one reads Elmer's journals, one marvels at his maturity of vision and purpose from the time he set foot in Africa—at age 25.

Elmer had an extraordinary sense of perspective from the very beginning. He was always cognizant of the fact that he was a foreigner in this land, and that the Tanganyikans must make the decisions and assume the responsibility for their own country, including the development of the church. The word "devolution" was coined to define this process by which foreign missionaries would, in essence, work themselves out of a job. For Elmer, devolution was not just a theory or concept; it was a sense of divine purpose which guided every aspect of his work. But it was his genuine respect for Tanganyikans and their capacity for God-given self-determination that was demonstrated in his work and life every day.

Those early years in Central Tanganyika were pretty tough, even for this poor immigrant son who was very used to hardship and hard work. He traveled on foot, by donkey, by bicycle, and occasionally had access to an old Model-T Ford. After only a few weeks in the country he went along on an eight-day walking safari with Tanganyikan evangelists preaching the gospel to remote villagers. Elmer was the only white person, and he was in awe of the evangelists' competence, faithfulness, and passion in sharing the gospel. It was on this safari that Elmer brought his first message in Kiswahili, and again he was awed by the Tanganyikans' kind appreciation of his stumbling effort.

After Elmer and Lillian married in August, 1929, they were assigned to a new mission area at Ushola. It was a remote area littered with huge, house-size boulders. The people in the area had tremendous medical needs, and the first order of business was the establishment of a simple medical facility, which became their home while medicines were dispensed from an open garage. When Lillian was pregnant with their first child, the missionary doctor insisted that she come to Ruruma a month in advance of her due date, since they had no car and no medical personnel at Ushola. During that month of separation, Elmer walked the twenty-three miles to Ruruma every weekend to visit Lillian in order to see whether their child had been born, and then walked the twenty-three miles back to Ushola. During his fourth weekend visit their first child, son Laurence, was born.

Elmer and Lillian's second child, Eleanor, was born at Ushola. When this baby girl was less than a year old, she developed a dangerously high fever. With no doctor, no car, and, of course, no telephone available to them, Elmer arose before daylight to ride his bicycle the twenty-three miles to Ruruma to call a doctor. As he pedaled his bicycle on the sandy track of a road through the dense bush, a large rhinoceros suddenly crashed through the thicket, stopping on the sandy track right in front of one very startled bicycle rider. Over the years, Elmer's children loved to hear this story about how their dad slammed on the brakes, the bike skidding sideways, while the rhino snorted and pawed the ground, not able to see well enough to fully detect this frightened white man, and not able to get a good scent with the breeze blowing away from him. After what seemed like an eternity, the frustrated rhino went on its way, and Elmer sped on to Ruruma. Returning to Ushola by car with the doctor, they found little Eleanor much improved. Even though Elmer often regaled his children with wild animal stories, he was ever so cautious not to sensationalize the adventure aspect of missionary life. When he spoke to churches and others, his emphasis was always on the miraculous work of the Holy Spirit in the lives of men, women, and children. He rarely mentioned wild animals.

In 1937 Elmer and Lillian, and their lively brood of five, moved from Ushola to the Wembere plains, a remote area accessible only by foot, up a steep escarpment, for much of the year. It was a very happy home, a home where Elmer constructed a small swimming pool for his children and helped them plant trees. But in their midst were people with great need. One day several lepers came to Elmer. One carried in his outstretched hands, which had been reduced to fingerless stubs by this terrible unchecked disease, a letter pleading for help. Elmer responded with compassion and action, the result being the establishment of a facility that provided shelter, medical care, and an opportunity for some semblance of dignity and hope. Wembere, like Ushola, presented endless opportunities for the gospel in action, including preliminary work on a permanent church building. The people were hungry for the gospel message. Then in 1939 Elmer's furlough came due. Lillian was pregnant with their sixth child and had to be carried up the escarpment as they started their journey to America. They left their little home ready for their return.

Elmer and Lillian determined that, with their growing family, they needed to establish a stateside home. With prayer and careful consideration, they chose Lindsborg, Kansas, where Lillian had attended academy and college. They knew it was a safe, healthy community where they could leave their children as they grew older, and that with the presence of Bethany College their children could get a higher education. So it was that they settled in Lindsborg just a few short weeks before the birth of their sixth child.

Elmer and the family were scheduled to return to Tanganyika in May of 1940, but war was already ravaging Europe and northern Africa. Elmer feared taking his family onto the high seas with the dark clouds of war looming. It was not a time for women and children to travel overseas. Elmer and Lillian and the older children spent much time in prayer and family discussion. Elmer knew that if ever he was needed in Tanganyika, it was now, as all the German missionaries would be interned, with the Augustana missionaries becoming responsible in some way for that work. But even the small Augustana group diminished in number with the threat of war discouraging travel. Ultimately Elmer agreed to return to Tanganyika alone with the stipulation that, if Lillian and the kids could not join him within a year, he would be allowed to come back to the States. Elmer's departure, rescheduled for July, was an agonizing experience. He had just seen me take my first steps a few days short of my first birthday. Oldest son Laurence at 10 was certainly reaching the age where he needed his dad around. And how could he bear to be apart from his precious sweetheart Lillian? But it was little Wilfred, 2½ years old and very much a daddy's boy, who clung to Elmer ferociously as goodbyes were being said. He would not be consoled. Finally Elmer had to literally peel Wilfred's little hands from his clothing, setting him down at arms' length on a table, out of reach. Elmer, tears streaming down his own face, turned away, and walked to the car without looking back. It hurt so much that, a few days later in the midst of great loneliness on his trip to Africa, he poured out his soul by writing a prayer in poetic form. He thanked God for the gift of Lillian and each child, beseeching God to watch over them, citing the specific personalities and needs of each. It was a beautiful, powerful prayer from an anguished father and husband. In true Elmer fashion, he kept a copy of this prayer, which has become yet another family treasure.

Elmer returned to Wembere in 1940 to that isolated home he had enjoyed so much with his lively family. But now it was so empty. The piano he and Lillian had bought in England on their return to Tangayika in 1934 often kept him company on those long evenings after the sun went down. He played hymns and sang, and was often accompanied by the sounds of wild animals roaming about in the African night.

Being alone for those few months was bearable because of the expectation that Lillian and the children would be joining him. All was ready for them. He knew his sweetheart well, and knew that she would jump at the first opportunity to return to Tanzania but, if not, he had the Board of World Mission's promise that he could re-join his family in America. When he learned that Lillian and the children had secured passage on a neutral ship, the *Zamzam*, in the company of a dozen other Augustana missionaries, he was thrilled. They would be sailing from New York on March 20, 1949, a little less than 8 months after he had told them goodbye. He knew Lillian and the children would have good companionship on the journey, and that the others would be of great help to them. Others were traveling without families also. There was Ralph Hult, who was leaving his wife and ten children behind in America, and Esther Olson and Velura Kinnaan, two single lady teachers. His joy was tempered with only mild apprehension, knowing that traveling the high seas with six children in tow would not be easy, but his faith was strong, and he believed so firmly that he and Lillian were doing God's will.

Elmer eagerly awaited a telegram from Lillian from Capetown after April 20, the anticipated arrival of the *Zamzam* to that first port on the continent of Africa before sailing up the eastern coast to Dar es Salaam in Tanganyika. In those days nothing happened right on schedule, so when he heard nothing after two or three days, he was not particularly concerned. Besides, if there were a problem, certainly he would be informed. But many days passed, and his gnawing worry grew into full-blown alarm. He contacted the American Consul, the shipping line, anyone who might know why the *Zamzam* had not yet arrived in Capetown. No one had any information. Alarm changed to fear. Then very early in the morning of May 21,

Dr. Stanley Morris came to Elmer at the Sekenke Gold Mine where he had been up all night with a young miner dying of Black Water Fever. Stan was in tears as he told Elmer that the BBC had reported that the *Zamzam* had been sunk, and that all on board were presumed lost. How could Elmer grasp the enormity of this information—his sweetheart and six precious "kiddies" killed in enemy action in the South Atlantic? It was too much, too horrible. Months later he would write about this experience, about sinking into the depths of anguish, yet somehow, inexplicably, holding on to a faint glimmer of hope, hope that a miracle had happened, that the BBC news report was not accurate.

The young gold miner died during the night of May 21, and it was Elmer's responsibility to attend to his burial and to conduct a funeral service. He believed Lillian would want him to do this for Mack, the very young Scotsman. The burial needed to be completed that day before sundown. It was May 22, Elmer's birthday. In the midst of this preparation, word was sent to Elmer that the BBC had just reported that the passengers of the *Zamzam* had arrived in German occupied France, and that all but two of the 144 aboard were accounted for. Did he dare to believe it? And how could he rejoice in the midst of burying a young man in his 20s? At the funeral, Elmer and Stanley sang a duet, "I Know that My Redeemer Liveth." Never had Elmer felt such a mixture of sheer joy and relief in the midst of such sorrow. (In 1994 the Handel version of this same song would be sung by Elmer's granddaughter at his funeral.) Later that evening, he gathered with other missionaries around the radio to get news first-hand. At the very end of the broadcast, mention was made of the *Zamzam*, once again with confirmation that its passengers had indeed landed safely. But even in the midst of such joy and relief, Elmer was plagued by questions as to what Lillian and the children had suffered and how they were doing. What was their condition, emotionally and physically? And he agonized over the fact that he, husband and father, was not there with them, to hold and comfort them, and especially to help his dear Lillian with the task of attending to the children.

Lillian and the children were fine, but they were not allowed to proceed to Tanganyika. They returned to Lindsborg to resume their life as well as possible. Lillian encouraged Elmer to continue Christ's work in Tanganyika, assuring him that they would be fine. Because of the critical shortage of missionaries, Elmer felt compelled to stay regardless of his longing to be with his family. But he also felt that this circumstance gave the Holy Spirit a chance to work in wondrous ways, raising up indigenous leadership, initiative, and responsibility. The paucity of foreign missionaries opened the way for the Tanganyikans to play a more active role in the development of Christ's church in their midst.

Elmer was asked to oversee the mission work orphaned by the interned German missionaries. He became immersed in these expanded responsibilities as he traveled throughout Tanganyika to supervise work in five former German Mission areas with their 80,000 young Christians stretching from the shores of the Indian Ocean to the western shores of Lake Victoria. This was a personal blessing in disguise, as he had less opportunity for loneliness and worry. During this time, he also buried two valuable, much needed Augustana missionaries, missionary giant Ralph Hult, and the young Marty Bystrom, both succumbing to the ravages of malaria. Throughout Elmer's days alone in Tanganyika, his faithful attendant was Immanuel, who made every effort to make sure that Elmer took care of himself while handling all the household responsibilities.

In mid 1944 Elmer was able to return to his family in America. World War II was still raging, dictating that he travel a far southern route. His 12,000 mile journey by train, boat, and plane from Iramba to Lindsborg via Argentina started in June and ended on November 4, 1944, when his family met him at the McPherson train station 15 miles from Lindsborg. What a reunion! It had been almost four and a half years since he had said goodbye. My brother Wilfred and I could not remember having ever seen our dad or heard his voice. I was now almost 5½ years old. Laurence, who had been an ordinary sized 10 year-old when Dad left, was now 14½ and towered over him at 6' 1." Being reunited with his sweetheart and six children overwhelmed him with emotion, and he could hardly drink it all in.

Elmer was also overwhelmed by how much he didn't know about us, by how many experiences he had not shared with us. In many ways he was on the outside, trying to make an entry into our world. But his time at home was scarce, as obligatory deputation work beckoned. As eager as he was to share with churches and church colleges Christ's work in Tanganyika, he was often torn by the scarcity of time with his family, especially after his long absence from them. But his furlough was only six months. Even so, when he returned to Tanganyika in October 1946, he was once again traveling alone as Lillian would stay an extra year before leaving the three oldest children in America for educational reasons. The "younger trio," as our parents called us, accompanied Lillian back to Tanganyika in September of 1947.

When Elmer returned to Tanganyika in 1946, it was to the slopes of Kilimanjaro rather than to his Iramba home. For the next ten years he served as Superintendent of the very progressive Lutheran Church of Northern Tanganyika. It was a time of growing political activity in the country and of tremendous growth and maturation of the church. When Mother and my sister, brother, and I arrived in October 1947, we were schooled at home by our mother so that we would have time with our dad. But spending time with our dad meant accompanying him on trips to oversee work in that large northern area, entertaining ourselves while he sat in meeting after meeting, camping in empty mission houses, traversing impossible roads, walking two, three, four hours to remote mountain-side churches, and listening to him preach in his impeccable Swahili. When at home at Machame, this disciplined man could be found in his map-lined office from sun-up to sun-down, meeting with one visitor after another, working to solve one problem after another. He invariably returned to his office at night after listening to the BBC news and having devotions with the family. I can still see him carrying an Aladdin kerosene lamp as he walked the short distance from our home to his office, sometimes not returning until midnight. That was his only uninterrupted time for sermon preparation, report and letter writing, and attending to the myriad of other details which were a part of his broad responsibility.

These were exciting years. In 1947 the African church sent its own missionaries to evangelize the Sonjo tribe across the Serengeti. This development was one of Dad's greatest joys as a missionary.

As stated, these were political times—within the country and within the church, and Dad was often on the edge of controversy. He was deeply convinced that foreign missionaries should not be making the decisions for the indigenous church, at least not without African representation. Likewise he believed Tanganyikans had a right to self-determination as a country. And when he expressed concern about the growing power of the European settlers, who wanted to consolidate their land holdings by taking over land from the Africans, squeezing them into an apartheid-like system, he really got the attention of European authorities. Ultimately a United Nations commission came to discuss the matter with the Meru people whose land was involved. Dad was called before the Executive Committee of the European Council and once was visited by the police. He firmly believed that individual Christians cannot remain silent in the face of injustice.

During the 1950s only my brother Wilfred and I were in Africa with our parents. We attended boarding school in Kenya, as we had for several years. In August of 1955 Wilfred graduated from high school, and it was determined that Mother, Wilfred, and I would return to the States immediately to be present for sister Eleanor's wedding. Dad's furlough was not due until March of 1956, and so he was to remain in Tanganyika, left alone again. I remember the night the decision was made. Dad and Mother clung to each other and sobbed. I had not seen that depth of emotion from them previously and, in hindsight, I now know that Dad had never needed Mother so much before. He was dealing with enormous tension and responsibility in a less than supportive atmosphere. By January of 1956 he felt ill, having contracted an illness which he interpreted as total mental exhaustion. It was necessary for him to return to the States immediately, about three months early. He had been given medication to help him manage the trip, but he threw it away and relied on the power of prayer instead. It took several weeks before Dad returned to normal and felt comfortable venturing out in public.

When Dad and Mother returned to Tanzania together in 1957, it was doctor's orders that he not take on administrative leadership responsibilities. In 1966 he left his beloved Tanganyika, now Tanzania, to become the Executive Secretary of the newly formed Tanzania Assistance Committee headquartered in Geneva, Switzerland. It was there, in 1968, that he finished out his *Forty Years with Christ in Tanzania*.

Dad and Mother retired in Lindsborg in early 1969, enjoying twenty-five beautiful years of total togetherness—no more separations—spending as much time as possible with their children and grandchildren and other family. As to be expected, Dad, the consummate pastor, held several interim pastorates, preached often, and served as co-chaplain at Bethany Home for several years. In 1993, two months after his ninetieth birthday, Dad lost his mobility due to bone cancer. He and Mother had to give up their independence and move to Bethany Home. During those few months before his death on May 9, 1994, his favorite nurse aide was a Bethany College student, the grandson of the very same Immanuel who had been his right-hand man during those years alone at Wembere. And when Dad was ready to go, Mother and all six of their children gathered around his bed, singing, laughing, crying, and finally sharing the Lord's Supper together. You could almost hear that heavenly voice saying, "Well done, thou good and faithful servant. Welcome home!"

PART SEVEN

Women of Augustana

The Women's Missionary Society

Jane Telleen

The story of the Augustana Women's Missionary Society is the story of women exploring leadership roles for the first time on a national scale. As in every national movement, much depends on having a leader who was in "the right place at the right time." Such a leader was Emmy Evald.

Emmy Carlsson Evald grew up in a traditional Swedish-American immigrant community in Chicago, but with a remarkable role model: her father Erland Carlsson, a revered Lutheran minister. In later years, Emmy told a friend she remembered seeing how people literally lined up in the church on weekdays to talk to him, because he had a reputation as a very wise man.

Emmy inherited her father's leadership abilities and his commitment to making a difference in the world. Her organizational and leadership capabilities were encouraged at Rockford Seminary for Women, where she attended college along with many other gifted reformers, including Jane Addams. Emmy was intensely interested in mission work, and after she married the Reverend Carl Evald, she started a missionary society in her own church. But she felt this small-scale approach was not effective, and thought that missions should be a higher synod priority. So at the synod convention in 1891 she broached the idea of a missionary society to four other ministers' wives. They agreed to go home and talk it up. The next year fifty wives at the synod convention in Lindsborg wrote a resolution to organize the Women's Missionary Society as an official part of the synod. They had to ask a man, Dr. L. G. Abrahamson, to present their petition for synod approval, and there was much debate. But eventually the Women's Missionary Society was born. Emmy Carlsson Evald was elected president, a post she would hold for the next 43 years.

At first she and her officers had some start-up problems. Membership didn't increase as expected until separate regional "conferences" were established, each with its own officers. This was a shrewd move. By giving women more leadership opportunities, more women wanted to join. They threw themselves into their work, determined to prove that they could do God's work as well as men. And Emmy Evald was an effective organizer and inspirational speaker. In the early years their fundraising was done for joint projects recommended by the men's Foreign Mission Board. But as they became more successful, they became more independent. By 1903 they sent out missionaries from among their own membership, and paid the salaries of women missionary doctors. If they couldn't find women doctors, they paid to send women to medical school. They supported a hospital in India and sent the first American woman missionary to China. They even made up a deficit in the men's mission society. The General Council of the Lutheran Church commended the women for their work.

Despite their success, every step they took had to be authorized by the men's Foreign Mission Board. In 1907, when the Society had raised $12,000 for a new hospital in India, they petitioned the General Council to become independent, arguing, "Women have proved they can do the work well, but before the women expend the money, they desire that the future management of the hospital be wholly under the control of the Woman's Missionary Society."

The hospital was needed badly, so the synod gave in. From then on, the WMS became a power in its own right. Emmy Evald was credited with having the foresight to get control of the fund disbursement. During the next 20 years the society did hundreds of thousands of dollars worth of business. Through the WMS, women learned to buy and sell property and run foreign missions—becoming, in effect, officers of an international non-profit corporation.

It's no accident that all this happened while women were seeking the right to vote. The time was ripe, and Emmy Evald had been a charter member of the International Women's Suffrage Association. The WMS took no official position on suffrage, but in the year of ratification, 1919, their *Mission Tidings* newsletter ran new slogans that spoke volumes:

"Woman's status determines to a very large extent the character of her nation."

"The thermometer of a man's character is his attitude to women."

Then the WMS, in some people's opinion, went too far. The year after women got the vote, in 1920, Augustana College and Seminary asked the WMS to raise funds for a new women's dormitory, which they jubilantly took on as a sort of "home mission." Within a year the women had raised $121,000 in pledges toward the goal of $150,000 and engaged an architect to draft plans. But the male seminary students and faculty objected to the prominent building site chosen by the WMS because it would cut off their imposing view. They recommended instead a site across the street in undeveloped, marshy land. It became a "battle of the sexes," and Evald wrote:

> The women who have entrusted us with their money have expressed their desire that we do not put the building into a 'back yard'....They...want a 'prominent and imposing site for the Woman's Building.'

Mission Tidings reported: "The daughters are waiting—waiting to see if mother wins out."

For some time, some ministers had resented the fact that the WMS solicited in their churches for money that would have gone to their local projects. And then the mothers themselves split ranks. A number of Rock Island women, upset because so many decisions were made from headquarters in Chicago by Emmy Evald, sided with the ministers, and presented a petition of 375 signatures to the synod siding with the seminarians. The synod deferred to the petitioners, and the WMS signed over the money to the college for a dormitory located in the marshy land. The Woman's Building was dedicated in 1927 and, ironically, named Carlsson Hall after Emmy Evald's father. No official WMS representative was present.

This confrontation made many women reconsider whether independence was worth the cost of being called unChristian. Undoubtedly the episode discouraged Evald, who spent most of her last years developing a home for girls in New York City and resigned as president in 1935. Both women and men sought a renewed spirit of cooperation rather than competition, and the WMS became a member of the new Board of Home Missions. By 1942 they had representatives on all major boards for missions, but since they were the minority in each, they no longer had a forum for independent decision-making.

So how will history treat Emmy Evald and the Women's Missionary Society? The WMS was neither radical nor unique; it came into being when so many other women's groups began, and disbanded when others did. But it played a crucial role in the history of the Augustana Lutheran Church. The Women's Missionary Society gave its women a forum for making a difference on a grand scale. It saved the lives of hundreds of people overseas. It gave women the chance to serve society as doctors and administrators overseas. And it gave mothers and homemakers the opportunities to succeed in areas of life outside the domestic. And Emmy Evald, as founder and leader of the Women's Missionary Society, provided younger generations of church women with a role model and a tradition, hopefully not forgotten, of accomplished church mothers as well as church fathers.

Two Augustana Women: Wife Anna Olsson, Daughter Anna Olsson

Alf Brorson

Anna Olsson is a fairly common Swedish name for women, but that doesn't mean that the woman behind the name is in any way common. The most well-known Swedish-American author of literature for children bears this name as well as her less renowned mother.

Anna Olsson's name is associated with a very particular book, originally entitled *En prärieunges funderingar* (*A Child of the Prairie*). Consequently, misunderstandings arise since both mother and daughter had the same name. It is, however, the eldest daughter of Dr. and Mrs. Olof Olsson who was the Prairie Child. Wife Anna was, with the dedication of her husband, the faithful spouse and mother.

The attention of scholars has focused on Anna's husband, Dr. Olof Olsson—the legendary young preacher from Värmland, Sweden, who became the spiritual founder of Lindsborg, Kansas, organising the Smoky Valley church-wise, law-wise and school-wise after his arrival in the summer of 1869, before becoming professor and third President of Augustana College and Theological Seminary in Rock Island, Illinois. In the light of history, he is one of the Augustana Synod's most influential theologians, especially in the field of music.

In looking for biographical facts about the wife of a pioneer pastor, remarkably few can be found. Usually we are only told her name, date of birth, and number of children. But what could have been accomplished without her? She shared the work of her husband for the congregation, not least because the parsonage, in addition to the church, in many ways was the focal point of the congregation. This meant that she always had to be prepared to receive guests.

The pastors or pastors-to-be who emigrated to America knew that without a wife by their side, their work would be hard and lonesome. So, if they weren't married at the time, they very wisely saw to it that they were before they embarked on their Atlantic journey.

Mrs. Anna Olsson, the first pastor's wife in Lindsborg, belonged to this important group of Swedish-American women. What they did, although their contributions may seem not very conspicuous or much written about, was nevertheless an inclusive life's work! There are many different kinds of workers needed in the vineyard of the Lord.

Wife Anna's life reflects deep personal experiences and a close walk with God. She did not take an active part in the official debate on important theological questions, but she had an unflinching belief in Christ as Savior and, consequently, knew in daily practice that wherever we live and whoever we are, the church represents values that enrich individuals and society. She didn't speak much for herself; her life speaks for her.

There are not many pictures of wife Anna, but there are some documents—her own letters, passages about her in books and articles on her husband and his time, and of course daughter Anna's widely-known book about childhood experiences in early Lindsborg—to make possible a modest, composite portrait. To my knowledge, however, there is only one written document to be found exclusively on Mrs. Olsson: a 20-page booklet—a eulogy entitled *To the Memory of Mrs. Anna L. Olsson* by the Rev. C. Otto Granere, who also published a 19-verse poem to her memory, including a beautiful picture portrait, in *Korsbaneret* (*The Banner of the Cross*).

Also, in memory of his beloved wife, Olof Olsson published a small, beautifully written volume of poetry and prose, entitled *Det kristna hoppet* (*The Christian Hope*). In the language of Ernst Skarstedt, it is "full of consolation for a broken heart." The loss of Anna affected Olof very deeply. He was never again to be the same man.

Wife Anna Olsson died from a heart failure in her Rock Island home on March 18, 1887. Only 46 years old, she was honored with a large funeral at the First Evangelical Lutheran Church in Moline, Illinois.

Anna Lisa Jonsdotter, which was her maiden name, was born on March 8, 1841, the daughter of a miner, Jonas Peter Nilsson of Bottesbol, Agen, in Degerfors, Värmland, and his wife Maria Lovisa Ersdotter.

Anna's father died at the time she was ten years old, the oldest of five siblings, and her mother later married Olof Olsson, the hired hand of the farm and bore another five children to him. As things would turn out, Anna was to know another two Olof Olssons—her husband and her father-in-law.

Anna was married to Pastor Olof Olsson on December 21, 1864. They had gotten to know each other at the *Mor i Vall Home* in Karlskoga. This was an orphanage, a school and a Sunday school, and also a center for the revivalist movement of that period of time. Olof had returned from a depressing stay at a Mission Institute in Leipzig, Germany, and it fell upon Anna to give this dismal young man his spirit back—and she did: "She pulled him out of his melancholy and his brooding mind."

After his ordination and a period of service out west, Olof returned to his home village and his wife-to-be. They first settled in Persberg, where he became a preacher for the miners and school teacher for their children at Skavnäset, and most Swedish stories about their charity go back to their stay in Persberg. Life in this poor mining town on Lake Yngen in eastern Värmland in many ways prepared a young, idealistic couple for what was later to happen in Kansas.

Then, after some years of hard testings in Persberg, Anna, Olof, and their firstborn, daughter Anna, moved to Sunnemo where Olof served as a parish minister for two unforgettable years until the time of their emigration to America in the spring of 1869.

While in Sunnemo, the Olsson family lived in the beautiful, and to this day standing, old red parsonage at Noretorp. Wife Anna couldn't forget this Swedish home, particularly during her first years of homesickness in Kansas—and a warming tile stove, like the one in Sunnemo, would be evasive to her for the rest of her life.

The Olsson family left their home, their friends, and their congregation in a beautiful valley in the heart of Värmland to travel to a place in the making, far out on the Great Plains in America—and their family formed a fairly large group of people!

Among the 276 people on the ship's passenger list were not only 28 year old Anna, her husband Olof, and their two-and-a-half year old daughter Anna, but also Olof's parents and his younger brother, Anna's mother and younger sister, and their four half-brothers and half-sisters, all between six and eleven and a half years of age. There were twelve family members leaving for America on that ship. Later Anna's younger brother also emigrated to America, and her stepfather came over too.

Included in the Olsson party, therefore, were not only his wife, daughter, parents, and brother. Three Olof Olssons in Anna's family alone came to live in *Framtidslandet* (The Land of the Future). They were an entire family unit; only Anna's one year younger sister remained in Sweden, and to my knowledge, only one descendant, a great grandson of hers, now lives in Sweden.

It wasn't until the end of June that these settlers from Värmland finally arrived in Lindsborg, and the last part of the journey across the unfamilar, wild, and open prairie was made by horse and carriage.

The final destination had neither a church nor a congregation, or even a proper home for them, although land had been broken for them prior to their arrival. What a difference it must have made to come from a comfortable parsonage in Värmland to a pioneer stone house in Kansas, where snakes crawled in—or dropped from the ceiling into the soup tureen. But we also have to bear in mind that the Olsson family was better off than many other Swedish-American pioneer families. Soon the Olssons even had an organ!

From the very outset of their life in the New Land, people gathered, sometimes in the Olsson home, to practice singing, and Anna, who also knew how to play the organ, was one of the members of the first choir. She was a soprano, her husband a bass singer. Both could read notes, but to help others sing in parts, Olof transcribed notes to numerals, a method used by him already as a schoolmaster in Värmland. Thus, a small choir was organized soon after the arrival of the Swedish pioneers in Lindsborg!

In the words of Dr. Emory Lindquist, "The great Messiah tradition in Lindsborg, which traces its origin to 1881, was based on this early interest in music, which was developed by Olsson."

Anna and Olof Olsson used the example of the Good Samaritan as their model for social involvement. At all their places of residence, from Värmland to Illinois, they were always looked upon as compassionate, generous, and hospitable. They never seemed to get tired of giving a helping hand to someone in need. Being born and raised as they were in the modest circumstances of nineteenth century rural Värmland, they were well trained for their vocation, coming to the hardships of pioneer America. As Anna noted in a letter of 1873, "for the sake of God, nothing is impossible."

Sharing her husband's life meant great sacrifices for her to start a new life on the Great Plains. Wife Anna's devotion to her family and to her husband's work constitutes an epic theme.

Still, even she, Olle's pious wife, was required to undergo examination before she was received as a member of the "pure congregation" that was first founded in Lindsborg! The communicant member was required to clearly understand the sacraments (which, according to the Swedish church records, she had long since demonstrated), and the pastor and his deacons examined each prospective member as to the faithfulness and reality of their Christian confession. Even wife Anna.

One explanation might be that this procedure, to require the pastor's devoted wife to undergo such an examination, could be due to a democratic overreaction. Once in the Land of the Free, no one should be given any kind of privilege reminiscent of the old country! Not even pastor Olsson's own wife. And, there wasn't much she could do about it.

After urgent requests from Augustana College and Theological Seminary, Olof was granted a leave of absence from his churches in Kansas, and in the first part of 1877, the family moved to their new American home in Illinois.

In Lindsborg, as eight years before in Sunnemo, Anna had much rather stayed where she now felt at home, but once again she followed her husband to another field, and once again she made herself feel at home, this time never to move again. Rock Island was to be her last dwelling-place on earth.

To Anna, now an Augustana professor's wife, the new situation meant that she still had to do a great deal of entertaining, and there were missions, children's homes, nursing institutions, and hospitals to pay attention to, apart from her being a member of the Women's Society in Moline.

Regardless of whether she was playing her role as the wife of a Pastor in a rural farm community or the spouse of a professor of divinity, her life was filled with daily duties. She didn't create any great events, she was not heard in the big debates on major issues, and she never did (as did her husband and children) return to see her homeland again.

She was a pastor's wife at a time when most things needed were produced in the home or on the farm. She knew the crafts that Swedish pioneer women brought with them to America. Like many parents back then, Anna and Olof Olsson also had to meet the tragic loss of their children in infancy. They had eight children, four of whom preceded their parents in death, and on wife Anna's death, her eldest daughter Anna was twenty, and Johannes, her youngest, only nine years old.

Thirty years later, in 1917, daughter Anna published *En prärieunges funderingar*, its very first word being mother: "Mamma is coming!" Just a few years ago *En prärieunges funderingar* (literally, *The Contemplations of a Prairie Child*) was published in a facsimile reprint of the Swedish 1926 edition by the Literary Society of Värmland. It is also for sale in the United States, where the second edition of *A Child of the Prairie*, translated by Martha Winblad and edited by Elizabeth Jaderborg, was published by the Folklife Institute of Kansas in 1978.

The book is not forgotten in major, contemporary books on the history of Swedish literature either, and readers, historians, and critics on both sides of the Atlantic Ocean have long been in agreement about their appreciation of it, so completely different from anything else from Swedish America.

The author's name is Anna Olsson, on whose third birthday on August 19, 1869, Lindsborg's original Lutheran church was founded under her father's leadership.

What researchers uncover as revelations was for Anna something she had herself experienced as a little girl on the Great Plains of Kansas. Anna was born in the mining town of Persberg, Värmland, in 1866.

In the English translation of *A Child of the Prairie* there are some comments by the publishers on what to little Anna were "funny" Swedish words—one of them being *skavnäset*, said to mean "snub-nosed" in the local dialect of Värmland. True, *näsa* means nose, but to my knowledge there is no such word as *"skavnäset"* for snub-nosed in Värmland, nor in all of Sweden. The fact is that *skavnäset* was the name of the place on the lake in Persberg (Färnebo) where her parents lived when she was born, before the family moved on to Sunnemo.

Swedish-American history is a matter of knowing history, biography, and geography, as well as language, and unknowingly we might make such factual errors at times. It is not unusual to come across them every now and then in books and historical documentaries about the Olsson family.

As a child not yet three years old, daughter Anna belonged to the one-fourth part of more than one million Swedes who left their homeland during the emigration years from 1850 through 1930, and her life as well was realized outside the borders of her native country. She died in 1946, at the age of 79, having lived in Rock Island, Illinois, for more than 70 years, and like her parents and her siblings she rests in the soil of America.

The Olsson family grave is located in Riverside Cemetery in Moline, Illinois. The First Lutheran Church in Moline was the spiritual home of the Olsson family during all their Rock Island years, and also the church where Olof Olsson preached his first sermon in America, enroute to Lindsborg in the month of June, 1869.

Anna Olsson received a good education, and in 1888 she became the second woman to graduate from Augustana College. The following year her father, who was by then widowed, began an educational trip of Europe with his four children, which for Anna's part meant that she studied German language and literature, and attended lectures on psychology, at the university in Zurich. From 1895 through 1900 she also served as headmistress for the Ladies' Hall at Augustana in Rock Island, Illinois, and for a time, prior to that, she also taught in the Education Department of what today is Bethany College in Lindsborg, Kansas.

As an author, Anna Olsson wrote mainly short stories—her pen name being Aina. Her first story was published in 1901, the year after her father's passing, and her last book, *Ängelns gåva* (*The Angel's Gift*) came in 1918, the year after *A Child of the Prairie*.

She was a prolific writer, who often wrote about people's everyday lives. Her stories were published in papers and calendars. She translated children's stories, and in addition to her five books she also published *Barnens tidning* (*The Children's Magazine*). But her reputation today, we might say, has to do exclusively with *A Child of the Prairie*, which in 1927 she also rendered into English, entitled *I'm Scairt: Childhood Days on the Prairie*.

A Child of the Prairie is more than just a "children's book." It is the story of an adult woman's experiences as an observant child, having the knowledge of conditions that prevailed in Lindsborg at the time it was founded by people from Värmland. It is written in such a way that a precocious little girl's nature comes through—and with a literary control of *rotvälska*, the mixed language used by the first generation Swedes in America. Daughter Anna knew exactly how to add the spices of Swedish brogue, that very special Swenglish vernacular, used by the pioneers from Sweden, in her stories.

En prärieunges funderingar was the first book I ever read where I could understand what it could be like to be an immigrant in America, and it still strikes me, when I reread it on a personal level, how similar life in the first Lindsborg parsonage in many ways could be to that of my parental home in Värmland—although much later and in far less dramatic circumstances. Our mothers, by the way, had the same name, too!

A perspective from the first parsonage in Lindsborg opens toward the great, wide world—from the world of fantasy to reality and to all appearances a would-be-wise child's thoughts and observations. We are told how she played, and we are told about the lives of immigrants from Värmland, their way of thinking and their *hemlängtan*, homesickness. This longing for home also affected the little girl, and her picture of Värmland is, as someone once said, about "a wonderful land of sagas that included all the splendor found in the world."

There is a noted chapter on Värmland in Anna Olsson's book. Even I, who was born and raised there, have to admit that Anna was overdoing it a bit, saying "Värmland is the best place that can be found on this earth," which to a large extent had to do with her mother's longing for home in the early days, but she was absolutely right about a lot of other things. "In Värmland grows so many beautiful flowers. Blue and white anemones, and lilacs, and lilies-of-the-valley. And daisies." Lilacs and lilies-of-the-valley were also her father's favorite flowers, and they were brought to his last sickbed by his children.

Our part of Sweden is often referred to as very scenic and generous. Geographic factors are constant. There are glittering lakes, there are rivers and creeks, there are green valleys between large forested tracts, and the mountains are distant blue, or, as Lindsborg's Carl Swensson once wrote in a travelogue, "The beauty of Värmland is a trinity. Her name is: lakes, mountains and forests."

Scenic beauty alone, though, won't do for a living. To many Swedes, this Garden of Eden called Värmland was no doubt a good place to be born, but in order to fullfill their mission in life they had to leave, and I can't help expressing a rather hazardous opinion here, although there are quite a few cases in point, that for quite some time now our beloved province out west has let go of too many talented people—and loads of our gene bank were transferred to America.

Although Anna, pushing three, first believed that Värmland was just a few Swedish miles away from the Smoky Valley, she no doubt had very good memories of her childhood days. She published her book 40 years after her family had come to Rock Island, and 30 years after the death of her mother.

Like her brother and sisters, Anna never married, never had children of her own. In Rock Island, so I have learned, it has been said that the reason why neither Anna, Mia, Lydia, or Hannes ever married was because they made a promise to their father that they would not—but I have also been told in Lindsborg that it was Mrs. Olsson who made her children promise the same thing. Whether any of the two asked their four surviving children not to marry, we do not really know. There could be various reasons, of course, but I won't speculate.

My favorite chapter in *A Child of the Prairie* is Chapter 25, "The Cucumber." It is about how daughter Anna played, and how she "sinned" when she baptized a cucumber. The opening line reads: "Jag gjorde Synd, när jag döpte gurkan (I sinned when I baptized the cucumber)."

Alma Lind Swensson
December 11, 1859—December 11, 1939

Doris L. Spong

When Alma Swensson, the twenty-year old bride of young, popular Pastor Carl Swensson, arrived in Lindsborg, Kansas, on a hot, September day in 1880, little did she dream of the exciting years that were in her future.

Bethany Lutheran Church had waited a year for their chosen pastor to be ordained after graduating from Augustana Seminary in Rock Island, Illinois. They had elected his bride to be their organist and choir director, having learned that she had been an organist at First Lutheran Church in Moline, Illinois, since she was 12 years old.

Pastor Swensson had big plans for this prosperous Swedish community. He quickly founded a Bethany Church Academy for the education of the pioneer families. Inspired by the Augustana College performance of Handel's Messiah, he wanted Bethany also to perform this most famous oratorio.

Alma Swensson said, "If Carl wants to have the Messiah sung here, I shall do all I can to help." That is exactly what she did by training the Bethany Church choirs and those of the four neighboring churches in the Smoky River Valley. Basic instruction was provided during rehearsals held two times each week. These untrained singers had notes, sometimes marked with numbers, so they could learn the difficult contrapuntal music. They traveled across fields and poor roads to practice.

By Holy Week in 1882 Alma had prepared them to sing several choruses. She sang the soprano solos. The organist, Pastor Olof Olsson, Professor and President of Augustana College and Seminary, who had performed in Rock Island, brought the Augustana orchestra to Bethany. Concerts were held at Bethany and three other area churches as well.

This marked the beginning of a great tradition of the annual holy week Messiah Festival. Lindsborg became a Mecca for this event. Visitors came from all over the USA. National recognition has become extensive in magazines, news media, and now on radio and TV.

Two buildings have been erected to accommodate concerts: Ling Auditorium and, in 1929, Presser Hall, the current auditorium. It houses music classrooms, studios, and offices. Presser Music Company of Philadelphia provided a large financial gift for this building.

Alma Swensson, the young pastor's wife, and mother of two daughters, contributed to the successful event by her musical and organizational leadership during the initial years. Her dignified and regal appearance inspired confidence and respect of the community.

As Bethany Academy, later named Bethany College, developed, the faculty assumed management and administrative leadership.

LEADER IN WOMEN'S MISSIONARY SOCIETY

On June 6, 1892, women from many congregations of the Augustana Synod gathered at the Bethany Lutheran parsonage with Alma Swensson as the hostess. They were expecting this to be a typical Swedish coffee party. They looked at pictures and chatted as a few women were busy moving in and out of the rooms. Finally the leader, Emmy Evald, explained the purpose of the meeting. It was to organize a women's missionary society in the Augustana Synod.

Emmy Evald of Chicago had already organized a missionary society in her own church, Immanuel Lutheran. The purpose was to promote the cause of missions. Mrs. Evald had been in contact with such outstanding leaders as Jane Addams, founder of Hull House, and Susan B. Anthony who worked to pass legislation needed for women's suffrage in 1920. She knew that many Protestant women's groups were also founding societies for missionary work around the world.

Mrs. Evald delivered forceful and convincing messages based on biblical challenges that Jesus gave his disciples (Matthew 28). She asked the ladies who agreed to sign a document requesting permission to organize a women's missionary society. Fifty women agreed and formed a procession to bring their request to the business meeting of the Augustana Synod that was in session at Bethany Church. They carried banners with red crosses and sang the Swedish song, "Till Verksamket" ("Go Forward").

The pastors and lay delegates, all male, had a heated debate for hours before the request finally passed. Certain restrictions would be included in the constitution.

The women returned to the Bethany parsonage, elected officers, and made plans for a future meeting to be held at the same time and place as the next synodical annual meeting. Emmy Evald was elected president with Alma Swensson as secretary.

In 1906, at the convention in Denver, the WMS decided to publish a quarterly magazine with the cost of a subscription at 25 cents. Alma Swensson was elected editor. The purpose of the publication was stated in the editor's own words in the *Lutheran Companion* magazine of May 28, 1922, on page 22:

> The need of a missionary periodical is to make known the work of the organization it represents. The Missionary Society is one of the great agencies of the Christian Church that strives to reach out to all parts of the church, at home and other lands. A woman's missionary paper was almost unheard of at that time. Can we be deeply interested and concerned about the work carried on by the WMS without reading MISSION TIDINGS? MISSION TIDINGS information gives interest, inspiration, love and devotion and sacrifice in time and money.

Great changes came to Mrs. Swensson when her illustrious husband suffered a severe heart attack while he was on a speaking tour in California. On February 16, 1904, at the age of only 46, he died. He had had a busy schedule as a parish pastor, the president of Bethany College traveling to raise money for the college, and as an active Kansas state legislator. He had traveled extensively speaking eloquently in the USA and Sweden. His frequent absences left Mrs. Swensson with the responsibility to give support and advice at the church and college. She also continued as organist at the church for 40 years.

A tribute to the WMS on its thirtieth anniversary was given by Gustav A. Brandelle, Augustana Synod President from 1918 to1935, and was printed in the *Lutheran Companion* of May 28, 1922 (page 625). This quotation commended the educational work of WMS:

> Large sums have annually been devoted to the maintenance and development of the activities of the church both at home and abroad. In this way it has been of great service to the Synod. Its great significance, however, has not been along financial lines. In our mind, its most potent influences for the good of the cause has been the work of educating the young girls and women in particular the lines of missions and charities. Many thousands of these are banded together for the purpose of receiving valuable information as to the need and importance of the spread of the Gospel and building the church.

AN IMPORTANT HERITAGE

Alma was awarded an honorary Master of Arts degree by Bethany College in recognition of her important role as music director for the first years of the now famous Bethany Messiah Festival.

The WMS gave a gift of $5000 toward the Alma Swensson Hall after her death, December 11, 1939.

Her memory lives on as we note that she changed the role of Augustana Women through the founding of the WMS. Now the women of the church are involved in support, active participation, and leadership in the total church.

Lastly, her gifted leadership came through her articulation of the fine arts—in the performances of Messiah and through the written word in the magazine, *Mission Tidings*.

Thanks be to God for the life of Alma Swensson!

Emmy Carlsson Evald: Passion, Power, and Persistence

Kathleen S. Hurty

Things don't always happen at once. Good ideas come into being over time, cultivated and watered by creative conversations and collaborations—and, I would add, by God's Holy Spirit. As Margaret Mead suggests, two or three people and a good idea can change the world. In fact, Mead continues, it's the only thing that ever has. The story of Emmy Carlsson Evald and the Women's Missionary Society illustrate this in a unique way. We can be sure, however, that it also takes passion, persistence, an adroit use of power, and. . . a lot of *chutzpah*!

The idea of women organizing was evident throughout the nineteenth century, and as waves of Northern European immigrants settled in America, Swedish Lutheran women were among organizing leaders in the ethnic enclaves they inhabited. In Chicago in 1860 (the same year the Augustana Synod was formed), a Senior Sewing Society was founded at Immanuel Church with responsibilities to decorate the church and to care for seminarians studying at Augustana, then located in Chicago. In 1877, the women formed a Junior Sewing Society, setting a new trend in the Church for young women and girls. But women would not long be content to limit their activities to sewing. More than likely, sewing was the backdrop against which lively conversations about the church and the world took place. By 1888 the context was ripe for the persuasive power of the Rockford College graduate and pastor's wife at Immanuel—Emmy Carlsson Evald—to enlarge these active women's perspective to include the broad mission of the church and the spread of the gospel around the world. She organized a local 200-member Women's Missionary Society at Immanuel Church, along with two large Junior Mission Societies. Pioneering the India box work and lace projects that were adopted by other societies, these local Chicago women took needlework into the realm of global education, service, and collaboration. The organizing of local women's and junior mission societies proliferated in the Augustana Synod throughout the latter half of the nineteenth century. [1]

Little did four women, who got together in 1891 at the Augustana Synod meeting in Center City, MN, realize what a massive effect their idea to extend this organizing work nation-wide with global partnerships would have. Let's say these locally involved missionary society activists met over coffee, while their husbands were conducting the business of the church. What we do know is that they started talking about what they would rather be doing (i.e., making decisions about the mission of the church—which was, in those days, not their prerogative as women). They began to share their creative ideas, their dreams and their strategies. Their ideas grew in the electricity of this interactive time together—today we'd call it synergy—and they passionately started plans for a church-wide national movement of women focused on mission efforts to share the 'good news' of the gospel globally. One of these women was Emmy Carlsson Evald.

Emmy, educated in the public schools of Chicago, in the Fryxell Girls Seminary in Kalmar, Sweden, and at Rockford College in Illinois, brought into the conversation an early vow she had made: "I, with God's help, promise to organize a Women's Missionary Society in the Augustana Synod."[2] She had been much impressed with the work of Swedish and German missionary organizations and knew of women engaged in exciting ways in the mission of the church. She had also been at Rockford College with Jane Addams who founded Hull House in Chicago, and Catherine Waugh McCulloch, a Chicago lawyer, both of whom had a strong passion for justice. These idealistic Rockford women graduates were steeped with the fiery passion to serve rather than sit back. Emmy Carlsson Evald put her focused energy to work organizing classes for youth and women's work, and helping to found the Augustana Hospital in Chicago in 1884, as well as participating with the broader community in preparation for the 1893 World's Fair which Chicago hosted. She therefore had years of locally grounded experience in the Chicago area.

The other three women, meeting that afternoon with Emmy Carlsson Evald (though their names are not recorded in the available material), must have been passionate about the capacity of women to be a force for mission. So they agreed to meet the following year at the Augustana Synod Convention to be held in Lindsborg, Kansas. Since it was the custom for wives of pastors and lay delegates to accompany their husbands to these synodical meetings, they agreed to spread, during the year ahead, their dream of organizing a women's missionary society, inviting the spouses to gather at the time of the next synod meeting. Emmy's dream was the catalyst.

---

[1] Lani L. Johnson, *Led by the Spirit: A History of Lutheran Church Women*, (Philadelphia: Lutheran Church Women, 1980); distributed by Fortress Press.

[2] Ibid., 8

Thus, in June of 1892, fifty women from all over the country came together in Lindsborg, and in three amazingly brief meetings crafted their plans. The first of these, at the Bethany Church parsonage, was dubbed "a coffee-less coffee party."[3] After meeting two more times to clarify their plans, these determined, stately women marched to the synodical convention and presented their resolution to found the Women's Home and Foreign Missionary Society (WHFMS) requesting "permission to organize a society to assist the missionary work of the church at home and abroad."[4]

The discussion of the men at the Synod convention was apparently heated, and there was much resistance to the ideas of the women. In their petition they pointed to traditional "women's activities" rather than radical departures from the conventions of the time, but they made it clear from the beginning that they were creating a *women's* organization, building on women's strengths and skills. First, they would create in every congregation of the Augustana Synod a Women's Home and Foreign Missionary Society. Second, they would be independent of the synod, yet related to the synod. Third, the newly crafted Central Board would direct and control the money raised, and determine the spending. These were powerful principles, and in no small way reflected Emmy Evald's strategic thinking. According to Professor Emeritus Esther Albrecht, Evald "is not truly understood in today's thinking."[5] How many men, she wonders, were really aware of the potential impact of the principles they had finally affirmed in their less than unanimous vote? The women, however, most likely understood the power of subversive ideas honed in the synergistic settings of sewing circles.

When the women heard that their petition had been granted, they offered a prayer of thanks and then elected officers. Emmy Evald was elected president and became a preeminent spokesperson for the fledgling organization, a position she was to hold for the next 35 years. Under her leadership "with ingenuity and imagination, the WHFMS recruited members, raised money and created multiple programs of service....Her influence was so great that one pastor said she was 'the most powerful person' in the whole Augustana Synod."[6]

The leadership saga of Emmy Carlsson Evald is a story of power, passion, and persistence. Graduating in 1883 from one of the pioneering women's colleges at a time when many did not value higher education for women, she cultivated life-long friendships with Jane Addams and other dedicated and gifted public figures. No doubt many of her leadership skills

---

[3] Reported by Augusta Stenholm Flodman, June 6, 1892, who was secretary of the group at the time; from the papers of Doris L. Hedeen Spong, former Executive Director of WMS.
[4] Evelyn Stark, "From Missionary Society to Auxiliary," *Lutheran Women* (April, 1978) 3.
[5] Letter from Emeritus Professor Esther Albrecht, Texas Lutheran College, to friends, April 27, 2001.
[6] Mary Pellauer, *A Cloud of Witnesses* (Chicago: ELCA Commission for Women and the Women of the ELCA, no date).

were honed in this environment. Rockford College[7]—then called Rockford Female Seminary, but with as demanding a curriculum as that of men's colleges—began granting Bachelors Degrees in 1882, so she was among the first classes to be awarded the degree. Married in 1883 to the Rev. Conrad Evald, the successor to her father at Immanuel Church in Chicago, she used her organizing skills in a variety of ways. Not only did she organize and run a successful household, which included the couple, eventually two children, and many guests, but she also founded a Bible class in 1883, which grew to over 300 members. The *Chicago Tribune* (March 6, 1938) noted the remarkable eminence of this class, which she had founded 55 years earlier "before the day of great Bible classes" which came into prominence in the Protestant milieu of the early twentieth century. In 1891 she was appointed President of the first World Congress of Lutheran Women, and, as we have noted, organized the Women's Home and Foreign Missionary Society in 1892 serving as its president from then until 1935. At the Chicago World's Fair in 1893 Emmy Evald chaired the Women's Division of the Religious Congress.

Emmy kept close contact with friends in Sweden, the native land of her father and mother and the place where she had studied as a young girl and was confirmed. She must have watched with interest the founding of the Fredrika Bremer Association in 1884—an association, named for the famous Swedish novelist with the express purpose "to carry into effect the equality of opportunity, rights and obligations between women and men in their homes, professional lives as well as society. The association is politically and religiously independent."[8] So impressed was Evald with the work of this organization that in 1905 she founded the Fredrika Bremer Society in Chicago. She represented Sweden's Fredrika Bremer Forbundet and Swedish American women at the National American women's Suffrage Association in Washington, D.C., in 1898. Long active in women's suffrage, Dr. Evald is given credit as the one "who nominated Susan B. Anthony to head the woman's suffrage drive which culminated in the constitutional amendment granting the ballot to women."[9] An undated picture from the Archives shows a young Emmy Evald, along with Susan B. Anthony, Anna Howard Shaw, a great Methodist leader, Carrie Chapman Catt representing the United States, Alice Stone Blackwell of the Women's Journal, and others. Emmy's signature includes Sweden under her name. Since others were representing various countries, perhaps this was a meeting of the International Women's Suffrage Association, of which she was a charter member.

---

[7] Rockford College History (http://www.rockford.edu). Rockford College was an educational pioneer from the very beginning. In the 1840s, when Americans still doubted the value of educating women, the decision to make the curriculum at Rockford Female Seminary as demanding as that of a men's college was a bold one, and the college continued to display its pioneering spirit in the decades that followed. In 1882, Rockford Female Seminary granted its first bachelor's degrees. In 1892, Rockford Female Seminary became Rockford College.

[8] From the Swedish organization's website (http://www.fredrika.org; English translation available).

[9] John Evans, *Chicago Tribune* (March 6, 1938).

As Jane Teleen points out, Dr. Evald seems to separate her churchly use of power and her use of public political power.[10] The WMS never took action to campaign for the vote. Instead, a decision was made "to keep questions of woman's responsibility and power within the church separate from larger questions of woman's power in the country as a whole." While this was a conservative choice, it was probably practical to put her energy into building a structure for "herself and her own people." Teleen conjectures that she might have lost her base of support, from both women and men in the church, had she at that time chosen to involve the WMS in politics. While we might hope for a different choice today—the organized voice of women of faith must surely be a public voice—still, Dr. Evald was a public figure in many ways. She involved herself personally in national and international organizations having goals she could actively affirm.

From the sometimes glowing, sometimes critical, remarks about Emmy Evald during her long and fruitful tenure as President of the WMS, one could gather that she did not share power. She is painted as an assertive woman, organizing societies, raising money, dogged in her commitment to supporting missionaries and building buildings, considered by some a pest (because she could raise more money than the pastors could!), taking on those who disagreed with her, basking in the hyperbole of praise that came her way, and persisting in service to the WMS through 43 arduous years! However, with a closer look, it becomes clear that her organizing strategies actually involved full participation of women locally and nationally. Professor Albrecht offers several illustrations:[11] Evald "saw to it that every woman could play an active part" by suggesting both afternoon and evening circles; she engaged Mrs. Alma Swenson as editor of the *Missiontidning* (later *Mission Tidings*), and while Emmy submitted write-ups for the magazine, Alma took full responsibility, gathering stories from the mission fields and keeping women in local congregations fully informed (they were required to subscribe as a part of belonging). She created a number of departments in the national organization and gave the leaders free reign to develop their programs. She believed that funds for the salaries of women missionaries and for buildings (schools, hospitals, women's homes, etc) could be raised by numerous small contributions. The "Missionary for a Day" program offered women a concrete way to pay the daily salary of a woman working overseas by contributing $2.50. And the dime books could be filled with 'egg money' or collaborative collections and sent in to support the creative ideas the women together were thinking up! She stimulated the organization of Junior Mission Bands, and Young Women's Missionary Societies (an idea taken up later by other denominations) so that all could participate.

Her leadership skills involved clarity of mission; empowerment of skilled staff to take the lead in various areas of work; full communication through

---

[10] Jane Teleen, *Swedish Pioneer Historical Quarterly* 30/3 (July, 1979) 190-91.
[11] Ibid., Albrecht letter.

Mission Tidings magazine, through letters, pamphlets, and gatherings; and engagement of women in meaningful activity, all assuring ways of broad participation. She used the power of storytelling to lift up the work of the women who served overseas, to describe the needs in the cities and in the countryside, to give people a reason to give. She was passionate about causes, and persistent in persuading women to complete the challenges they took on. She was a tireless fund-raiser. Together she and the women of the church built 74 buildings in the United States and overseas, supported the first woman doctor to serve in Africa, and provided funds for the support of women missionaries in India, China, Africa, and other countries. Hers was the power of passionate persuasion, mixed with a great deal of persistence and a goodly measure of collaboration and *chutzpah*!

Evald's successful fund raising strategies are a story in themselves. Considered by some pastors as intrusive to their local projects, or to the regular budget of the congregation, her efforts nevertheless were so successful that jealousy or chagrin may have stimulated some of the criticism. The fund-raising for the Women's Building on the Augustana Campus is an example of how she went about this work. Appealing to women's commitment to mission and to equality, she published emotionally titillating brochures in Swedish and in English, filled with illustrations and language to engage givers—an audience she well understood. In the brochure,[12] three young women standing outside closed gates, surrounded by suitcases, appear forlorn. The drawing was captioned, "Shall we close Augustana's gates and bid our daughters go elsewhere for lack of suitable living quarters?" She cajoled those who had not contributed, encouraged others to double their gifts, told of examples of generosity that could be replicated. The goal for this project was $150,000. The brochure was published after $78,425 had been raised. The text included references to scripture, rationale to support home missions, an urgent plea, veiled threats, blatant critique of those who were lax in giving, italicized stress points and a number of superlatives:

> The greatest need of the hour is the Woman's Home at Augustana College. Let us 'for love of Christ and in His name' have vision, zeal and heart to provide money to build a home for *our own girls*, the daughters of the Augustana Synod. The Lord tells us 'He that giveth shall not want, but he that hideth shall have many a curse.'… 'For the love of Christ and in His name' we plead that every Augustana woman be a giver. Surely this deserves your support!"
>
> We thank God for every woman that 'looketh well to the ways of her household' and had the wonderful vision and love to sacrifice to give towards this worthy Home Mission work….
>
> All the women in 153 churches have done their part—few of the women in 348 churches have contributed—all women in 744

---

[12] Brochure from the papers of Doris L. Hedeen Spong.

have not given a cent. If you have given what you could, go *'for love of Christ and in His name.'* [to get your friends and members of your church to give].

This passionate effort was successful. The women reached their goal. However, as Teleen points out, after they had raised the money, "the college and Synod then denied them the right to decide on the building site, layout, and cost."[13] Following a complicated series of events, in which local women, college board members and the Synod were pitted against women in the national office, the WMS Board finally had to capitulate, signing the money over to the college. Teleen quotes the reaction of Mary Andreen, the wife of the college president and a friend of Emmy's, following the dedication in 1927: "Those who had worked hard to push it through were made to feel like those of unsavory reputations who were not wanted and could scarcely be tolerated."[14] The deep contention over these matters dampened Evald's spirits for a time. But she moved on, beyond bitterness, to new energy consuming endeavors.

Emmy Evald's later years, after resigning from the presidency of WMS, were spent once more in raising money and managing another home for women, a 'tiding-over house' for young women coming to New York City which opened in 1930. Her enthusiasm was overt, and hardly modest. She "proudly asserted" at age 80 in the *Omaha Bee-News* (June 17, 1937) during the WMS Conference held there, that "During the past seven years I have become the mother of 6,000 homeless girls," referring to the number of women whose lives were touched by the Lutheran Home for Women on East 82nd Street in Manhattan. In the Tenth Anniversary Souvenir Booklet of the Home, high tribute was paid:

> God gave Dr. Evald at the age of seventy-three the faith and courage to fulfill Jesus' command, and care for the homeless and the stranger by buying, remodeling and equipping the first Lutheran Home for Women in New York City, assuming also the responsibility of Managerial Director. Sometimes under very trying days, but with prayer to God, the Home has been a great miracle. To her the zest of living is the joy of work, no matter how lowly the duties.[15]

While the history of the home is later complicated by its shifting mission and its measure of inter-generational conflict, its presence in the city stood for some time as a signal to lonely women who needed a place to be safe and secure. When the building was sold in 1960 it had tripled in value, and the money was put into Seafarers and International House with the stipulation that ministry with women be continued.

---

[13] Ibid., 184.
[14] Ibid., 193; quoted from the Gustav Andreen papers, carton 18, Denkmann Library.
[15] Booklet, signed by Emmy Evald and sent to the Rockford College Library, December 31, 1941. There was a section in the library set aside as the Emmy Evald Room. Papers researched by Phyllis Hult.

In December of 1946, Emmy Evald died at age 89. Hers was a full rich life. She had called herself (probably in jest) 'the oldest woman in the Augustana Synod.' She was proud of her accomplishments and relished in acclaim, but gave glory to God, nonetheless, and relied heavily on the often quoted principle of her life: "I am just a tool in my Master's hand."[16] Her honors were many. She was made a Knight of the Royal Order of Vasa by King Gustav of Sweden in 1922 in appreciation of her work on behalf of Swedish Americans, earned a Master's Degree from Augustana College, and received an honorary doctorate in the humanities (L.H.D.) from Upsala College in East Orange, New Jersey, in 1935. She was a mother, wife, student, activist in women's suffrage, organizational founder, leader, manager, public speaker, fund-raiser and supporter, a visionary woman used by God for great things. By any standards her accomplishments are remarkable!

Deeply imbedded in the work she did was the belief that women, by organizing for mission, would gain skills for leadership in the church. Margaret Mead would not have been surprised at the comments of Emmy Evald in a 1929 address, when she said,

> Let us praise Him and give Him thanks — for the hidden and unused forces that were set in motion, women's self-development and self-expression and self-realization that have made their impact felt the world over.

We could wish that the effects of her long struggle would have been different; that women today would have full participation in the total life and decision-making of the church, that the Women's Building at Augustana would have been built at the top of the hill instead of on swamp land and named after Emmy Evald instead of her father, that she might have relinquished the presidency of the Women's Missionary Society earlier to others. Yet for all the criticisms, she lived a beautiful life! She dreamed big dreams, and worked collaboratively with passion and persistence and power to put these ideas to work for the sake of the church and the world—and she made a difference!

It didn't happen overnight. It was a long struggle. The struggle to give women their rightful place in church and in society continues. But I for one am grateful, ever grateful, for women like Emmy Evald—the one baptized Emeli Christina Carlsson—whose ideas, shared with others, changed the world.

---

[16] Charlotte Odman, "A Great Leader Gone: Mrs. Emmy Evald, Lover of Missions, Dies," *Lutheran Companion* (January 1, 1947), quoting a tribute by Dr. C. O. Bengtson.

PART EIGHT

Two Notable Persons

Gustav Andreen: Up Close and Personal

Gretchen Revay Esping

INTRODUCTION

It is truly a heartfelt honor for me to be addressing members of the Augustana Heritage Association. I must publicly give thanks to the Rev. Dr. Vance Eckstrom for paving the way with other members of the Augustana Heritage Planning Committee for inviting me to share some personal insights taken from primary sources about Gustav Andreen. I would also like to thank Ms. Donna Hill of the Augustana College Library for her help in providing pieces of the puzzle as well.

This presentation is dedicated to two outstanding women in my family—my great-aunt Inez Esping who was the Head Librarian at Bethany College for many years, and our family historian—and to Esther Marie Andreen Albrecht, Gustav's daughter and premier biographer.

Gustav Andreen is probably not a well-known name in Lindsborg, Kansas, even though all his mother's family lived there, and they were the only family he had in the United States. Here in the Smoky Valley lived his grandparents, as well as two aunts, four uncles, and numerous cousins. It seems that little is known of Gustav's father's family, but when both his father and mother were dead, Gustav moved the remaining brothers and sisters to Lindsborg, Kansas, and a new home was created by him and his sister Lydia. But now I am getting ahead of myself.

When I was twelve, I was at the "Aunties' House," a large five-bedroom house complete with a water collection system in the attic that collected rainwater runoff and piped it to the kitchen. The house was pristine—white of course—two and a half stories, a house in Lindsborg where eight sisters, all well educated, professional women lived together or rather used this house as "home base" over a period of fifty years. They pooled their resources so each one would have an education, and although none of them ever married, they also pooled their hopes and dreams and made a life together. This was the Aunties' House, complete with a parlor, a library, an ever present white lace tablecloth on the dining room table with silver spoons, and cups with saucers waiting watchfully beside the African Violets in the south dining room window. It was Aunt Inez who began talking to me about Gustav Andreen.

"Who's that?" I asked.

You could see Inez, in good Swedish fashion, growing absolutely stone silent, setting her jaw for an unpleasant task, and becoming even more calm and resolute, asking: "Hasn't your father told you about Gustav Andreen? I gave him a book...."

"No," I said innocently.

So guess who got in trouble that Sunday afternoon? It was Malcolm. My father was a well-known blacksmith and silversmith in Lindsborg, and at the age of forty-eight, it was he who was brought up short and had to answer to his aunt for not having told me about our relative Gustav Andreen. My father had always reminded me that any story is only one generation away from being lost forever. You have to tell the stories to the younger ones, and you have to listen to the old folks, commit to memory their stories, poetry, and songs. And now my father had failed to do just that with me!

So who was "little Gust" in the family, and why was he important to the story of the Augustana Synod? This was in 1963, and the Augustana Synod was merging into the larger Lutheran Church in America. It was probably this closing of a chapter in immigrant history, this merger, that had triggered my great aunt's brooding over the past, and that set her to talking about a part of our family's history and Gustav Andreen. She told me the stories, and I listened, but now I've done the research, read the books, and tried to thread it all together.

Simply put, Gustav Andreen and I share a grandfather. Gustav's grandfather was Julius Esping who was my great-great grandfather. Julius Esping emigrated from the east coast of Sweden, the Västervik, Gunnebo, Oskarshamn coast in Småland, to Chicago, arriving only a few months after Pastor Erland Carlsson in the early fall of 1853. Carlsson advised the forty-four year old master blacksmith, Julius Esping, to move to Geneva, Illinois, where there was a foundry where he could work at his trade. There were thirteen persons in Julius Esping's party, one of whom was his daughter, Hilda Helena, who was to marry Pastor Andreas Andreen, and another daughter, Albertina Wihelmina (Aunt Minnie), who would marry Pastor A. W. Dahlsten. A brother to these two girls was also in the emigration party, Otto Wilhelm Esping, my great grandfather. These family ties would become absolutely essential to the survival of the Andreen family.

THE MAN-CHILD

In trying to piece together some history about his parents who were both dead by the time Gustav Andreen was sixteen years old, he wrote to Cousin Theodore Esping, a nephew to Julius Esping, and one of the young men in the Esping immigrant party in 1853. Theodore writes:

> I remember well when your Father was married to my Cousin Hilda in Geneva, Ills. She was one of the most attractive young ladies in that locality, and had many admirers. [At] The time of the wedding[,] The Young men of the town [Geneva, Illinois] rolled a big boiler from the sawmill up to the house. And as many as could get around with sticks hammered away. That is over 50 years ago. Otto and I are the only ones lift of the Esping Families.[1]

The father's name was Andreas (also known as Anders), who was ten years older than Hilda Helena Esping. They were married on May 6, 1857, in the Swedish Lutheran Church of Geneva, Illinois, to which Julius Esping, Hilda's father, had contributed $5.00 to the building fund in 1855 to build the church she was now to married be in. The Lutheran Church in Geneva had been sharing a building up until that time, but now they were to have their own church building.[2] Anders, who had attended school in Växjö, Sweden, had been the first Swede to enroll at Illinois State University, a seminary student of Lars Paul Esbjörn. In April of 1855 the Northern Illinois Synod issued him an *"ad interim license"* to preach and administer the sacraments, but Anders Andreen's ordination did not occur until September 12, 1856, along with Eric Norelius and P. A. Cederstam in Dixon, Illinois.[3] Since Anders had met Hilda while he was an assistant to Pastor Erland Carlsson, traveling to distant Swedish settlements from Chicago, Carlsson could also take some pride and part of the responsibility in bringing two young immigrant people together.

A little girl, Lydia, was born (May 9, 1858) while Andreas Andreen was pastor of First Lutheran Church of Rockford, Illinois. A period of six years followed in which Andreas and Hilda had three stillborn children. What an unimaginable blow to this young immigrant family to have to bury three babies in Illinois and Indiana. So was it any wonder that when Gustav Albert was born (March 13, 1864) he was considered, beyond any doubt, a gift from God in all fullness and magnitude?

Now the brothers and sisters came like the changing of the seasons: Hilda Innocentia in 1865, Philip Andreas in 1867, Otto Ebenezer in 1869, Victoria Elizabeth in 1871, Carl Oscar Emanuel in 1872, Emil Alexis in 1875, and Lillie Victoria in 1876.

---

[1] Letter from Theodore Esping dated March 28, 1911, Shaniko, Oregon, to Rev. Gustav Andreen, Rock Island, Ill. ("Esping Letters," Andreen Correspondence, Augustana College, Rock Island, Ill.)

[2] Church Archives, First Lutheran Church, Geneva, Ill.

[3] Daniel Nystrom, "Boyhood Years," *Andreen of Augustana* (Rock Island: Augustana Book Concern, 1942) 12.

In 1872 Gustav, then eight years old, wrote to his uncle Otto who was working on the Union Pacific Railroad:

> Swedona, November 9, Grace and peace! Now I want to write to you, my dear Uncle Otto. Greet your brothers and tell them that we are well. But Mrs. Lund has now died. She died on October 10, 1872, at 10 o'clock in the forenoon. The watchmaker is also dead, and he died some time earlier. I think more have died this year than any other year in this congregation. Now they have begun to vote some for Grant and some for Greeley. I think Grant will be president, but if he becomes president, they probably will do to him as they did to Lincoln. Now I don't know any more to write. Gustaf Andreen The End.

This was the relationship between a twenty-three year old uncle and his eight year old nephew. Gustav had been four and a half when he had last seen his uncle, and Otto had been a teenager of eighteen or nineteen who, along with his father Julius, had decided to follow Julius' other son-in-law, Pastor A. W. Dahlsten from Galesburg, Illinois, to homestead in the Smoky Valley of Kansas. Gustav's grandparents, Julius and his wife Sophia Louisa Berzelius Esping, were in their late fifties when they came to Kansas. It was very hard to begin a new life on the prairies, but it would have been harder still to be separated from their daughter, Albertina Wilhelmina, who had married Pastor Dahlsten in Geneva. Dahlsten, who led the Galesburg Agricultural Company, and Olaf Olsson, who led the First Agricultural Company of Chicago, had been fellow students of Pastor Peter Fjellstedt in Uppsala, Sweden, before either of them had emigrated to America. They had corresponded and had finally decided to move to the Smoky Valley with two groups of immigrants.[4] Olsson led the Värmlandingar immigrants directly from Sweden, and Dahlsten led the Smålandingar, a group of earlier immigrants to Illinois, who desired both cheaper land and the "pure congregation."

In reply to his nephew's letter, Uncle Otto answered:

> Hays City Ellis Co Kansas Dec. 22 of 72 [1872] My dear little Gustavus: Grace and peace! I have delayed longer then I had intended in answering your letter. But I know that you will forgive me for being so negligent. I shall be more punctual in the future. Little Gust itt is now some time since I saw you last. I suppose you have grown to be quite a little <u>man</u> now. Why, itt is more than three years and one half. You must have changed considerable in appearance during that <u>long–long</u> time. I know that I have—You would not know me more now—were we to meet anny where. I would verry mutch like to come out and see you now. Butt my cercomstanses will nott allow it. We aare practising Economy now. You see we wish to gitt settled down as soon as posible on our Farms. And God has blessed our efforts so far with success and he will hereafter if we only trust in him, confide all our trubles to

---

[4] Personal Correspondence in a private collection of relatives of Pastor A. W. Dahlsten.

him alone and he will never forsake us….Now my dear boy, I want you to ask your dear kind mother to write me a few lines. Your dear Pappa I don't suppose is of anny use to ask. He has I am afeard forgotten the faithful friend of his "old Otto." If they would know with what fearful anxiety I have been waiting for one cheerfull line from them they would gladly sacrifise a few moments in my behalf. Remember me kindly to all. Yours as ever affectionate Uncle, O. W. Esping.[5]

I have included these letters as examples of the relationships that were being established with young Gustav as nephew and grandchild.

Gustav Andreen was only eight years old, but what would his life be like in another eight years? He would become this man-child expressed earlier by his Uncle Otto. Certainly he would be "a kid" sometimes, but he was already being guided and groomed by his father for special work, whatever that might be. This was a boy who at three had been sitting on the knees of Dr. T. N. Hasselquist.

AUGUSTANA COLLEGE AND THEOLOGICAL SEMINARY, PAXTON, ILLINOIS

By the age of nine in 1873, Gustav was to accompany his father to the synodical meeting in Paxton, Illinois, and to see Augustana College for the first time. Earlier that same year the Board of Director's Meeting of the Augustana College and Seminary was held at the Andreen home, the home of the newly elected board member, Andreas Andreen. It was decided at that meeting to move the college to Rock Island, Illinois. Jonas Swensson, the president of the Augustana Synod at that time—and the father of Carl Aaron Swensson who was to become the founder of Bethany College in Lindsborg, Kansas, in 1881—preached his last synodical sermon at Paxton and was then overcome by emotion and lay on the floor unconscious.[6]

While excitement was growing in Rock Island and Augustana College and Seminary, within the family, Gustav's Uncle Axel Oskar Esping, a Civil War veteran, died in Freemount, Kansas, from illnesses and general weakness from his war experiences (May 3, 1874). Gustav and Uncle Axel had also exchanged letters over the years, but the ink of Axel's letters has not remained legible. There are no extant records of how the Andreen family reacted to the news of Axel's death. Perhaps it was expected, and it was only a matter of time before he was taken home.

The new home of Augustana College and Theological Seminary was only about twelve to fifteen miles north of Swedona, Illinois, where Andreas Andreen was pastor in the fall of 1875. His parents had agreed that Gustav,

---

[5] Letter from O. W. Esping dated Dec. 22, 1872, Hays City, Ellis County, Kansas, to Gustav Andreen. ("Esping Letters," Andreen Correspondence, Augustana College, Rock Island, Ill.)
[6] D. Nystrom, "Boyhood Years," 28.

at the age of eleven, should become a student at Augustana College.[7] In 1876 he resolved to keep a diary and recorded: "Soon it is Christmas. Then I may go home to Mother."[8]

These were still carefree years, but in June of 1878 Gustav's grandmother, Sophie Louisa Berzelius Esping, died at Freemount, Kansas, and was buried next to her son Axel. To date I know nothing of the circumstances surrounding her death or the reactions of the family. Grandma Esping would have been sixty-four years old, and Gustav and his grandmother had not seen each other in almost ten years. Gustav had been only four when his grandmother moved from Illinois to the plains of Kansas.

But the full impact of death upon his youthful adolescent years was not far off. Two months after his grandmother's death, on August 26, 1878, Gustav Andreen's mother, Hilda Helena Esping, died after an illness of only a few days, leaving her husband Andreas with nine children, the youngest of which was two years of age. The oldest sister Lydia was now twenty, but Gustav, the oldest brother, was only fourteen years old.

Lydia Sophia Andreen Carlson recalled her mother's funeral for her granddaughter.[9] Hilda Esping Andreen was forty-one when she passed away, and whatever the illness the coffin was not opened for the children to have one last glimpse of their mother. Lydia described her father's inconsolable grief. During the funeral Andreas Andreen had tried to open the coffin while it rested at the front of the church. Being unsuccessful and finally having to be restrained by members of the congregation, he took his seat. But during the homily once again Andreas Andreen attempted to mount the coffin and to lie upon it. This time men of the congregation lovingly but firmly restrained fifty-one year old Pastor Andreen, and the service was quickly over.

No family letters exist that I have found in regard to Hilda Esping Andreen's death. But try to imagine the world from the perspective of her father, Julius Esping. What a dreadful, devastating summer. Julius' wife Sophia had passed away in June and now his oldest daughter in August.

But life must go on for everyone. Gustav went back to school at Augustana College, and Mrs. L. P. Esbjörn, now widowed, had returned to America from Sweden. One of her sons, Constantine Esbjörn, had been Gustav Andreen's tutor in earlier days. In the practical God-given way of the immigrants, Andreas Andreen married the widow Esbjörn for all the goodly and practical reasons, to have a mother for his seven children still living at home. The townspeople of Swedona, Illinois, thought this was all much too much of a rush, especially since Hilda Andreen had been the Pastor's trusted

---

[7] Often there existed a "Model School" which was an elementary school setting with elementary age children used in practicum for students of teacher education. The "Academy" was a high school or gymnasium, a college preparation school. The "Normal School" was a two-year teacher education program. These were separate schools that were often under the auspices of a College.

[8] D. Nystrom, "Boyhood Years," 32.

[9] Interview between Lydia Sophia Andreen Carlson and her granddaughter, Marianne Glad.

helpmate, and "no one could take her place" in what seemed to be a blink of an eye.

But Pastor Andreen was irreconcilable to the loss of his wife. Less than eighteen months later, while he was visiting his son Gustav at Augustana College, on February 14, 1880, Pastor Andreen took his own life. At the time the inquiring physician determined that he suffered from a mastoid infection, severe headaches, and pain associated with a massive inner ear infection for which there was no cure. But the impact of "one of their own," one of the founders of the Augustana Synod and Augustana College and Theological Seminary, committing suicide, was just not acceptable. At that time, if a person committed suicide, he or she could not be buried on holy, consecrated ground around the churchyard, but rather was buried outside the church wall, or outside the churchyard. The fact that the suicide of his father was neither treated kindly nor understandingly did not help Gustav to see his own position clearly. He felt that he was disgraced in the eyes of many people. He felt a loyalty to this father. He concluded that the judgment of his father's last act rested in Higher Hands.[10] Andreas had left his dearly beloved son Gustav to be responsible for the younger brothers and sisters. A few days after his father's death Gustav wrote in his diary in Swedish:

> Måtte det nu skedda göra ett ratt intryck på mitt arma hjerta. (May this which has happened make the right impression upon me.) No home more on this earth. O! Dear God! Help us through this life and bring us poor children to Thy home.[11]

Brother and sister, Lydia and Gustav, had to become mother and father and breadwinners for the younger brothers and sisters. The widow Esbjörn had her own hands full trying to provide for her children, but the Andreen and Esbjörn families always remained on close intimate terms.

EARLY CAREER

Gustav persevered and graduated valedictorian of the 1881 graduating class of Augustana College. In the meantime, Lydia had met Nils Otto Carlson of both Salemsborg and Lindsborg, Kansas. No doubt her aunt and uncle, Minnie and A. W. Dahlsten, who were in the parsonage at Salemsborg Lutheran Church, had helped to introduce these two young people. In the meantime the younger brothers and sisters had moved to Salemsborg to be near their Grandfather Julius and their numerous aunts, uncles, and cousins in the Smoky Valley.

This is what families did and sometimes still do. Families united to form strong support groups for those remaining, and that is exactly what the Espings, Dahlstens, and Andreens did in the summer of 1881. Gustav

---

[10] Esther A. Albrecht, *Gustav Andreen and the Growth of Augustana College and Theological Seminary* (Diss., University of Illinois, 1950) 26–27.
[11] Ibid., 27; Letter from Gustav Andreen to Carl Esbjörn, Rock Island, Illinois, April 6, 1884.

secured a teaching position in the fall at Holtman School in Smolan, Kansas, a small farming community about four miles north of the Lutheran Church at Salemsborg. Here he was—seventeen, with a Bachelor of Arts degree, and his first teaching job in a country school in the middle of Kansas.

Bleak though this may sound, along with Gustav Andreen moving to Kansas, two other classmates—that is, three-fifths of the 1881 graduating class of Augustana College—came to the Smoky Valley that same fall to teach at the new Bethany Academy founded by Rev. Carl Aaron Swensson. In the fall of 1881 John A. Udden became the first professor of Latin, English language, civil government, and United States history at Bethany Academy, and Edward Nelander became the first President, as well as instructor in mathematics and natural sciences. Bethany Academy had been founded in October 1 in the sanctuary of Bethany Lutheran Church in Lindsborg, Kansas. Rev. Carl Aaron Swensson, a 1879 graduate of Augustana College and Theological Seminary, had a knack for recruiting the brightest and best for "his" Bethany. So why then did he not recruit Gustav Andreen to teach for his new school? Gustav's uncle, Pastor A. W. Dahlsten, was even on the first Board of Directors of Bethany Academy where he served on and off as secretary of the Board for the next twenty-five years.

The Board of Directors of Augustana College did recognize Gustav Andreen's talents and offered him a position on the faculty beginning in January, 1882, to teach Latin, English, and Swedish history. Gustav Andreen had never wanted to be a teacher but did so to provide materially for his sisters and brothers who lived now in Kansas. On November 12 of that same year, 1882, Gustav's older sister Lydia, who was by then almost an "old maid" at the age of 24, married Nils Otto Carlson who had just turned 22. They lived on a farm between Lindsborg and Salemsborg, and it was there that the Andreen brothers and sisters were to find their new home. Sister Hilda Andreen, who was a year younger than Gustav, entered Bethany Academy in the fall of 1882 along with her two first cousins, Luther and Anna Dahlsten.[12]

Gustav Andreen was called to Augustana College to be on the faculty and teach, but he had always felt his true calling was really in law. After he had been at Augustana College a little less than two years, he wrote to the Board of Directors of the college to ask when it might be convenient for him to leave and begin studying law. He was told that there would never be a convenient time.[13]

But in August 1884, Gustav Andreen began to study law with Oliver Olson of Rock Island, working for $20.00 a month as a clerk and errand boy. The salary at Augustana College had been irregular and slow in com-

---

[12] *Catalogue of Bethany Academy at Lindsborg, Kansas, for the Academic Year 1882-1883* (Lindsborg: News Book and Job Printing House, 1882).

[13] Letters exchanged between Carl Esbjörn and Gustav Andreen and between Gustav Andreen and the Board of Directors of Augustana College, November and December 1883. Augustana College Library, Rock Island, Illinois.

ing, and he had been forced often to borrow money from his dear friend and stepbrother, Carl Esbjörn. Not only were there salary problems, but Gustav found the faculty at Augustana College to be uncooperative and haphazard in their planning.[14]

Eighteen months later on the 21st of December 1885 Gustav Andreen received a telegram at the law firm of Oliver Olson, from Rev. Carl Aaron Swensson: "You are unanimously called as teacher for next term. Thirty-five dollars a month and everything free. C. A. Swensson." Since he had been living on cheese and crackers by his own account[15] while helping his brothers and sisters, he readily accepted the teaching position at what had now become Bethany College.

Gustav Andreen was contracted by Bethany College to teach English and Greek his first year back in the Smoky Valley in1886. His classmates John Udden and Edward Nelander were still there after five years, although the subjects they taught had changed. Udden, who was to return to Augustana College, taught natural sciences, and Nelander, who had now been relieved of his duties as president of the institution, now taught mental science and pedagogue. Carl Aaron Swensson who had founded the Academy now became the president of the newly established "College."

In the fall of 1886 Victoria, Carl, and Otto Ebenezer were all in the first class of the college preparatory studies at Bethany. Not only was Gustav to be a college professor, but now he was also able to provide a college education for his younger siblings.

From a letter dated August 2, 1886, from Marion Hill, Kansas, we see that being a professor was not his only task; he had another calling, new to him, and yet so familiar from his childhood. He writes:

Rev. C. A. Swensson Lindsborg, Kansas.

> Dear Carolus:…You warned me that fright and tremor would size me especially when ascending the pulpit the first times. This, though very, very true, is cast into the shadow and disappears beside another experience of last week, which consisted in being called to the bedside of a dying man. Oh, I felt as if I would rather be sick unto death myself, than, ill-fitted as I was, try to prepare a soul to meet God. I prayed with trembling that the responsibility should be shifted, that the man should be better etc.—but I found him groaning with pain and anguish, and his wife and children bathing in tears. "Han tror sjelf han skall dö; ack, bara han får sin själ frälst!" ["He believes he shall die, Oh only that his soul may be saved!"] The wife repeated to me with much emotion. What I said to the man I do not remember, it matters not. But I came away filled with the love of Christ—and what would we poor mortals have to offer a parched and dying soul, if it were not for the good tidings of a Jesus willing to save sinners? The

---

[14] E. Albrect, *Gustav Andreen*, 28.
[15] Ibid.

man afterwards recovered, which however makes this my experience none the less real and intense....Your humble servant, Gustav Andreen.[16]

Another person that Gutstav met at Bethany who would be a link to Yale in 1893 was William A. Granville from Vasa, Minnesota. At this time, 1886, Granville taught commercial arithmetic, bookkeeping, and typewriting at Bethany College. The following year, 1887, both Carl and Otto Andreen were in the second class of the college preparatory and normal studies along with their cousin Luther Dahlsten and a half sister, Hannah Dorothea Esbjörn, of Rock Island, Illinois, who was studying shorthand and piano at Bethany.

But there was also a new star on the horizon. A young woman of Swedish and Norwegian descent from Junction City came to Bethany College to be an assistant in the primary department of the Model School. Her name was Marie Augusta Strand. Maybe now, with all of his brothers and sisters accounted for and looked after, Gustav would have an opportunity to begin to ponder his own life and to begin to care for himself.

In 1888 brother Philip also joined the family in Kansas, coming from Minneapolis/St. Paul to study business at Bethany College. Also in 1888 Gustav's old friend and classmate John Udden left Bethany College during the summer, and his other classmate, Edward Nelander, would leave the following year, 1889.

By the summer of 1890 Marie and Gustav had become well enough acquainted to be married on August 7 at the home of Marie's parents in Junction City. By the fall of that year the last brother Alexis was finally in school at Bethany in the college preparatory courses, and Gustav had become the senior faculty member with only Carl Aaron Swensson having more seniority. Marie Strand Andreen was promoted to Lady Principle of the women's dormitory and Philip Andreen had become an instructor in gymnastics at Bethany.

For some people in the United States, the 1890s would become the decade known as the Gay '90s. For many others, especially for farmers in Midwestern and Southern agricultural states, the decade brought the establishment of the Farmer's Alliance, the Granger of the Patrons of Husbandry and the People's Party known generally as the Populists. Already in 1873 the Augustana Synod, under the leadership of Jonas Swensson, had taken a stand against the farmer's lodge known simply as "The Grange" because of its "ritualistic order of membership and its classification as a secret society."[17] Jonas Swensson stated in his report to the Synod in 1873:

> Another thing which not only prepares the way for unbelief and denial but is counted upon to give this adversary (the devil) such terrible power, even when it appears in a more open and outrageous battle against Christianity, is the presence of so many

---
[16] Bethany College Archives, Letter from Gustav Andreen to Carl Aaron Swensson, Aug. 6, 1886.
[17] Emory Lindquist, *Vision for a Valley* (Lindsborg: Bethany College Press, 1953) 58-59.

societies of unbelievers and secret societies, which rise up and seize everything around them with alarming rapidity....We have this year in particular, reason to be reminded of these principles when a comparatively new society under the name, "The Grangers of the Patrons of Husbandry," has attempted to force itself unto several of our congregations. In its inner workings ...this society with its horrible oath, its ceremonies, and its principles is just as much a enmity with Christianity as any other.[18]

It is not possible to go into all the historical details of the growth and development of a new third party. Third parties have become quite common again in the 1990s, so we have some frame of reference even today.

Let it suffice to say that Jonas Swensson as synodical president in 1873 introduced the potentially explosive language of the politically charged designation "a secret society" which was to be attached to lodges, gatherings, and even entire political parties. Nearly twenty years later Jonas Swensson's son, Carl Aaron Swensson, felt so threatened politically by the growth of the agrarian movement in Kansas and throughout the United States that he classified the Farmer's Alliance as a secret society and publicly excommunicated seven members[19] of Bethany Lutheran Church from the pulpit on August 12, 1891.[20]

How is this related to Gustav Andreen? One of the excommunicated members, the Secretary of the Smoky Valley Alliance, No. 2535, was Gustav's uncle, O. W. Esping. This was the "Old Uncle Otto" to whom Gustav had written as a child and with whom he and his brothers and sisters had stayed on numerous occasions when they moved to the Smoky Valley. Now his uncle had been excommunicated before God and the congregation. In Kansas alone there were over 120,000 members of the Farmers Alliance. More than likely not all of these members were Swedes, nor were they Lutherans, but in Lindsborg, a strong Swedish Lutheran Republican stronghold, they were being excommunicated from the pulpit for their politics by Pastor Carl Aaron Swensson. From the extensive research I've done in the Bethany College Archives in Carl Aaron Swensson's massive correspondence, I would dare to say, in hindsight, that this lashing out at some of the original pioneer families of the Smoky Valley was such a blatant politically motivated gesture that it marked the beginning of the end, personally, for Carl Aaron Swensson.

In 1892 Philip, Carl, and Alexis Andreen were still attending college classes, although they were all close to finishing their education. Gustav began to teach a class in commercial law at Bethany College in addition to

---

[18] *Protokoll, Hållet vid Scandinaviska Ev. Lutherska Augustana-Synodens 14 de Årsmöte, Paxton, Ford County, Illinois, den 24 Juni-1 Juli 1873* (Red Wing: H. C. de Remee, 1873). Swenson Center, Augustana College, Rock Island, Illinois. English trans. by Dr. Emory Lindquist as it appears in *Vision for a Valley*.

[19] O. W. Esping, Charles J. Johnson, John Wistrand, A. Peterson, J. A. Stone, Gustav Swensson, and Mr. Isrealson.

[20] Bethany Church Records: Dismissal of Members, p. 240, August 12, 1891. Bethany Evangelical Lutheran Church, Lindsborg, Kansas.

being professor of Greek and German. There seems to have been a rather dramatic rearrangement of faculty members at the college between the years 1891 and 1892. W. A. Granville, who was by now professor of mathematics at Bethany, had taken a leave of absence to study at Yale. A. W. Kjellstrand, professor of Latin language and literature at Bethany, had also moved to Yale. During the 1890s there was a relatively large group of graduate students of Swedish descent from Augustana, Bethany, and Gustavus Adolphus who were all pursuing graduate studies at Yale.[21] In 1893 Gustav and Marie Andreen were also able to join them.

AT YALE

Bethany College had promised the young couple, who by now had their first son Paul Harold, a loan to help with Gustav's studies, but there is no record of that loan being made. Maria Andreen noted that they arrived in New Haven, Connecticut, with $1.25 in Gustav's pocket![22]

In the midst of his new life at New Haven, Connecticut, Gustav received a letter from his Uncle Otto:

> Lindsborg, Aug. 10th, 1893 My dear Gustaf and Family. Grace & Peace Your very welcome letter at hand. Thanks. It done my heart a whole world of good to hear from you and your dear family. God bless you all is my daily prayer. What a comforting thought it is in all our troubles—that the good Lord is with us and that he gives us strength for each trial as we need it. We have missed you and your dear wife very much. You were both of great consolation to me. May heavens richest blessings flow over you for it first and last spiritually. But allso in a worldly sense of view may allways our first desire be to do the Lords will. And then we can rest assured that whatever happens is for our good. He will give us victory over all of our enemies praise his name for hearing and answering prayers.
>
> Let us give ourselfs to the Lord wholly. And he will keep us and nothing will come but what he sees is for our good, if we but walk in the light. How clear the christian path is when we are enjoying the sunshine of the gospel. And how dark it seems if we loose sight of Jesus. For he is the light. We never need get into a place where we have to do wrong unless we want to. Well praise the Lord it is getting lighter all the time for me as the end is drawing near our time is sutch spiritually that we need to crawl nearer Jesus God helps us to be faithful until [the end?]. [I] write to you about that my mind gits [befuddled?]. I am getting nervous of late. Now I don't ask you to excuse either the one thing or the other that I write to you about. I shall write my thoughts as they come. And as I conscientiouly see things in the light of the world

---

[21] Carl E. Seashore, "Student Days at Yale," *Andreen of Augustana*, 43.
[22] E. Albrecht, *Gustav Andreen*, 34.

of God. If I say anything about persons I do it with love. I have thank God not a particle of hard feelings towards anyone. But I do not believe in gulping down everything as laid down. And acted out by some of our modern lights. I don't have to do it thank God. The good shepperd says that his sheap hear his voice and know his word and they do. If some persons cant bear me for that I cant help it and I don't want to help it either. That is in the way they want to drag down God's world to suit their unclear ideas. We have been invited back to membership of the church here. But I have not got it clear to my mind yet what we was kicked out for. Or what the reason is that we now can join the church again. It's a mystery to me. I shall abide by the God who knows me. You can see how men can get astray just on small things. For [example?] the Bishops visit here in America. Not doubting he is a good man how his presence turned the heads on otherwise sharp enough men who are now [bent?] on erecting a Bishopship within the [synod?]—the glitter and pomp you know, that's the rubb. I want out and visited Otto and Lydia [Gustav's older sister] a few days ago. They are all doing will. Carl [Gustav's brother] started for Chicago yesterday. Erickson and Thora [Gustav's sister Victoria] are doing nicely. Thora looks the best I have ever seen her to. I think the world of them both. I believe Thora got a good husband. The times here are by far the worst I have seen in my life. The wheat crop was a failure. Now the corn crop is as good as ruined by the drought and in the fall of all this no price on anything. The Farmers have to sell. There is a universal calamity howl now all over this country. I tell you the old party cracks are hitting us right and left now. We are of course getting all the blame. Sometimes I am tempted to believe it is ignorance pure and simple. I have otherwise thought that the majority of them know better. And that it was pure and [un?]adulterated cussedness that prompted their motives. Please write when you can. Your letter done me good. My Family are doing very well. With love to you and Family. Your Uncle, O. W. Esping.[23]

That letter was written on the second year anniversary of his excommunication from Bethany Lutheran Church. There had been a note earlier in 1891 from Uncle Otto to Gustav, asking whether the clergy could do that in this country. That is, can the pastor excommunicate a person from a church if they had different political views from the pastor? Gustav reassured Uncle Otto that, no, the clergy and the church cannot do that in this country, and Gustav assured him that he would take the matter up at the next Augustana synodical meeting. I have not yet pursued that material, but I did find a reference to a reprimand by the synod of Carl Aaron Swensson in the mid to late 1890s.

Once again Otto writes to his nephew:

---

[23] "Esping Letters," Andreen Correspondence, Augustana College Library.

Lindsborg, Nov. 20th, 1893 Dear Gustavus: Grace and Peace—Forgive me for my long delay. I am very thankfull for your very kind and considerate letter. Your letters does me good....Our Convention was the most pleasant convention I ever attended. At the republican convention they quareled over the officer so that it all came very near ending in a genneral fight. The same exactly at the Democratic convention. [These are state conventions that he is referring to.] It was the most disgusting scene imaginable. Our candidates all have a clean record but in spite of all we were defeated not only in our county but all over the state. This we have in a great meassure Rev. Swenson to thank for especially in our county. He takes one step after the other further away from the People he seems to be owned body and soul by the Republican party, wall street and Lombard Street England. There is no one so blind as a person that has eyes and don't see that are so prejudiced that they don't want to see. I see he is now President of the general council that is a great deal to say. I have plainly noted that just as he has been honored with important position he has gown greater in his own eyes till today he felt above both God and man. God allmighty isnt any thing now any more in comparison to him. He goes futher than at least I have ever read of any pope to go. He condems 1,500,000 people with one sweep of his pen calling them for a godless party because they dare to differ with him in politics. He condems thousands upon thousands of our best citicins in this country that daily....[The letter is unfinished but is signed] O. W. Esping.[24]

CONCLUSION

I would like to conclude with just a couple of thoughts, thoughts that may lead to a sequel. What I have presented to you today is about one third of the research I have done on Gustav Andreen and his years preceding his election as President of Augustana College and Theological Seminary. For the decade 1894 to 1904 I have a very generous amount of primary sources already "percolating" but still too fresh to write about or from which to draw conclusions.

My conclusions, based on the personal correspondence between Gustav Andreen and his Uncle Otto W. Esping, are highly influenced by the additional research materials that are yet to be analysed and shared. The information to date shows a great joy and deep affection between a nephew and his uncle over a period of twenty years. As time went on, Gustav was profoundly impacted by a sense of duty, first to his brothers and sisters to give them a home and a good advanced education, and then to an uncle who was a desperate and disillusioned Kansas farmer during the recession of 1884 and the catastrophic climate changes and recession of the 1890s. From

---

[24] Ibid.

O. W. Esping's early diaries, kept for a period of four years while he worked on the Kansas Pacific and the Union Pacific railroads,[25] he exhibited a deep personal faith and spirituality, tried and tested under unimaginable conditions while he worked with other immigrant groups laying track through Kansas, Colorado, and Wyoming. O. W. Esping's faith was an inheritance from the "*Läsare*" movement in Sweden, the "Readers," the Swedish revivalists who were drawn to the United States for freedom of religious practices as well as cheap land.

Gustav Andreen held very different political views than his uncle, but the right of each person to have and to hold their own political views, even though contrary to those of the pastor and the church, was at the heart of why Pastor Andreas Andreen, Pastor A. W. Dahlsten, and the Esping Family, along with thousands of others, emigrated from Sweden to the United States between 1848 and the 1930s. Gustav Andreen's great knowledge of and love for Swedish history and his understanding of American ways placed him in the arms of the Augustana Synod and Augustana College and Theological Seminary.

---

[25] The handwritten diaries of O. W. Esping, written in Swedish, are still in the family.

Conrad Bergendoff as Ecumenist

Byron Swanson

Conrad Bergendoff, churchman, theologian, seminary and college professor, and president is also a committed and enthusiastic ecumenist—not an easy task, given the era into which he was born. For a deeper understanding of Bergendoff's great contributions as an ecumenical leader, it is helpful to begin in the year 1910. That was the date traditionally accepted as the beginning of the modern "Ecumenical Movement." At the Edinburgh World Missionary Conference that year, Charles Clayton Morrison, editor of the *Christian Century*, reported to his readers that "the theme of Christian unity is running throughout the whole conference like a subterranean stream. It breaks through the ground of any subject the conference may be considering, and bubbles on the surface for a time. It is almost the exception for a speaker to sit down without deploring our divisions. The missionaries are literally plaintive in their appeal that the church of Christ reestablish her long lost unity." The ecumenical movement had begun. It was "the great new fact of our era."

The year 1910 was also the fiftieth anniversary of the founding of the Augustana Lutheran Church. In two memorial volumes of essays published for that Jubilee year, Augustana was reminded again and again of its confessional beginnings and heritage. Typical of the essays was one written by Augustana's president, Eric Norelius, who repeatedly praised the church for its confessional convictions, warning against any compromise or distortion of the confessions by engaging in practices such as unionism (the fellowship of Lutherans with others not in complete doctrinal agreement).

A third significant event in 1910 was Conrad Bergendoff's confirmation, marking the beginning of his adult ecclesiastical membership in the Augustana Lutheran Church. Right from the beginning, then, whether he was aware of it or not, Bergendoff would be forced to deal with a basic question which would concern him for the rest of his life: Can Lutherans be true to their confessional heritage and at the same time participate in ecumenical endeavors?

The warnings from Norelius and other fiftieth anniversary essayists made it clear that Augustana, like all of American Lutheranism in 1910, was not receptive to ecumenism. The major reason, made evident in the quotation from Norelius, was the concern for confessional integrity. While Augustana's confessionalism was not as rigid as some, through its membership in the General Council it did insist that the articles of the Unaltered Augsburg Confession "were statements of truth . . . in perfect accordance with the Canonical Scriptures," and they were to be accepted "without equivocation or mental reservation." All of the other confessions of the Lutheran Church were also declared to be "pure and scriptural statements of doctrine." In addition, because of their fear of unionism, Augustana adopted the defensive Galesburg Rule which insisted on "Lutheran pulpits for Lutheran ministers only—Lutheran altars for Lutheran communicants only." Augustana's confessional position, like most of the rest of American Lutheranism at the time, has often been described as "scholastic confessionalism." Dogmatic, polemic, absolutistic, and defensive in its claim of pure doctrine or orthodoxy, it represented an overwhelming obstacle that stood in the way of ecumenical involvement. There were other factors, of course, that also kept Augustana and the rest of American Lutheranism from jumping on the ecumenical bandwagon. Language barriers, preoccupation with the assimilation of immigrants, and internal strife over ethnic, cultural, linguistic, personal, and doctrinal differences had splintered American Lutherans into 24 separate bodies by 1910. Bergendoff was now a member of one of those bodies. Two years earlier, in 1908, his Augustana Church had rejected an invitation to join the Federal Council of Churches of Christ in America. Then, in 1910, it had disregarded an invitation to participate in the Edinburgh Missionary Conference. And one year later, in 1911, Augustana repudiated the invitation to attend the first Conference on Faith and Order. For the young Bergendoff it must have seemed impossible to be Lutheran and ecumenical at the same time!

But there were latent forces in Augustana and American Lutheranism to which Bergendoff was exposed that had the potential of making the "impossible" possible. The language problem and the problem of assimilating immigrants would diminish in the next few decades. Even Augustana's position of "scholastic confessionalism," a deeper and much more persistent problem, was being challenged. One of the checks against this position was the warm and earnest "Augustana" pietism that characterized Bergendoff's father. Pietism, by seeking to be right with God—rather than right in doctrine—tended to minimize theology and thus weakened the dogmatic and uncompromising stance of orthodoxy.

An even greater challenge to "scholastic confessionalism" was Bergendoff's exposure to Luther whose emphasis on the gospel—that is, the good news of the forgiveness of sins, freely received from a gracious and loving God—was the core of his theology. This was Luther's "unitive principle," namely, that Jesus Christ and his grace gave the church its unity, and those who did not teach this doctrine were guilty of separating themselves from the church, thus creating sects and schisms. The desire for unity was also clearly evident in the irenic and conciliatory Augsburg Confession which stated quite simply that "for the unity of the church it is enough to agree concerning the teaching of the gospel." And even the more scholarly, defensive and polemic Lutheran confessions retained this emphasis on the gospel of God's grace, calling it their "material principle" and proclaiming it "the chief article of the entire Christian doctrine." This understanding of the confessions can rightly be called "evangelical confessionalism," and one who is committed to it can freely unite with others of any faith who accept this basic principle. "Scholastic confessionalists," from the seventeenth century on, had not abandoned the gospel's insistence on justification by grace. But they did obscure it, and the place it was given in their systems tended to make it simply one doctrine among many. Thus the church which had adopted the name of Martin Luther was in danger of losing the dynamic central emphasis of Luther on trust and faith in a merciful God, and substituting instead static knowledge and dogmatic, absolutistic, and polemic claims about that God.

But the "danger" for Bergendoff was nearly non-existent! Introduced to Luther through his father, the Small Catechism had been his standard textbook in Sunday school and confirmation, and in his early teens he had committed it to memory. In 1915, during his senior year at Augustana College, he bought and read the first volume of the *Works of Martin Luther*. And two years later, in 1917, during the Luther quadricentennial, he read more Luther, including three books about the reformer by Böhmer, Jacobs, and Köstlin. His doctoral dissertation in 1928 was on the Reformation in Sweden. In 1930, he wrote a book on the Augsburg Confession. In 1958, he edited and translated volume 40 of *Luther's Works*. Most revealing of all perhaps was what he did in 1930 when he was appointed Dean of Augustana Seminary and professor of systematic theology. For 40 years this position had been held by C. E. Lindberg whose position of "scholastic confessionalism" was clearly set forth in his text on *Christian Dogmatics*. Lindberg's attempt to uncompromisingly preserve the "pure doctrine" of seventeenth century orthodoxy had isolated him for the most part from both Luther and contemporary thought. And because his courses and text were in Swedish (and remained so until the year after Bergendoff had graduated from the seminary), the effect was to isolate and separate rather than unite and communicate with the rest of the Christian world. Under Bergendoff, however, the scholastic approach was discontinued. (As Bergendoff later mused: "How ludicrous to define God.") Instead, students were assigned lengthy readings in Luther (whose works became the focus of the course), and in the process they were introduced to "evangelical confessionalism." Bergendoff's students also read Gustaf Aulén's grace-centered and anti-scholastic *Faith of the Christian Church*, as well as many non-Lutheran authors, including Karl Barth.

There were other latent forces at work in the life of Bergendoff—especially in his younger and more formative years—that helped give him an "evangelical confessional" outlook and an openness to the ecumenical movement. Bergendoff was a serious student of the Bible and not surprisingly, the Bible as an inescapable witness to God's love and mercy for humankind, and of the expectation that having been loved, humans will express love and acceptance toward each other.

While working at New York's Gustavus Adolphus Lutheran Church in 1917-1918, he took seven New Testament courses at the interdenominational Bible Teachers Training School (today's New York Theological Seminary), and without any conscious effort to do so, memorized the Gospels of Matthew and John. Additional Bible courses at Lutheran Theological Seminary in Philadelphia (1918-1919) and at Augustana Seminary (1919-1921) certainly would have increased his awareness of the Bible's frequent ecumenical themes.

Still another factor that contributed to Bergendoff's appreciation of Christian unity was the missionary movement. The ecumenical movement grew out of the missionary movement as was overwhelmingly illustrated in Edinburgh in 1910. Bergendoff was elected president of the college and seminary "Foreign Missionary Society" and saw the membership swell from 12 to 2000 and the giving increase from $20.00 to $9,000.00 in three semesters. Bergendoff's leadership of the FMS and the sponsorship by the FMS of a "Young People's Christian Conference" which brought together over 500 youth from throughout the Augustana Synod has remained as "one of the great memories" of his seminary days. But even more significant for this essay was the understanding that Bergendoff articulated that the "hope of the world" was not an absolutistic, Swedish-Lutheran brand of scholastic orthodoxy, but simply "the bringing of the gospel of Jesus Christ to all the nations."

There were, of course, many other factors that helped open ecumenical doors and weaken the barriers established by "scholastic confessionalism." During his last two years in college, Bergendoff served as reporter and then as treasurer of the Augustana Prohibition League, delivered an oration supporting prohibition, and presented a paper on the subject. His concern was consistent with that of the Augustana Synod at that time but also allied him with groups such as the Federal Council of Churches. Thus (although perhaps unconsciously) another link was established with Christians outside the Lutheran Church.

Inevitably, links were also made by the very fact that during his formative years Bergendoff lived in three major metropolitan areas of the United States. After graduating from Augustana College, he enrolled for a year of graduate study at the University of Pennsylvania in Philadelphia (1915-1916). Then he went to New York for two years to work at Gustavus Adolphus Lutheran Church, do more graduate study at Columbia University, and take classes at the Bible Teachers Training School (1917-1918).

Then he returned to Philadelphia for a year of study at the Lutheran Theological Seminary at Philadelphia (1918-1919), and finally, after graduating from Augustana Seminary, he moved to Chicago to serve Salem Lutheran Church for nine years (1921-1930). These major population centers brought him into contact with many new cultures and new ideas, speeded up the Americanization process, and made exposure to and appreciation of other non-Lutheran Christians much more likely.

Only one more ecumenical influence in Bergendoff's life will be mentioned, but it is probably the most important of all. Until the second decade of the twentieth century, Augustana had, for the most part, embraced a "scholastic confessional" and non-ecumenical stance. There were, however, a few among the leaders in the church who were exceptions as they demonstrated some sympathy toward other denominations. Among them were Lars P. Esbjörn (especially in his early years), T. N. Hasselquist (an influence on Bergendoff's father), Olof Olsson (accused of heresy because he was the least scholastic and the most ecumenical of all the men in the Augustana Church in the nineteenth century, who befriended Bergendoff's father and according to Conrad, Olsson was the greatest influence in his father's life), and S. G. Youngert (one of Conrad Bergendoff's professors at Augustana Seminary).

But it was Nathan Söderblom, the archbishop of the Church of Sweden, who without a doubt made the greatest ecumenical impact on Conrad Bergendoff. Söderblom was already being called a "pioneer" and "prophet" of Christian unity, and after his death it was claimed that he would "stand out as the man who did more than any other . . . to unite . . . churches, nations and communions in a common fellowship." When Söderblom came to the United States in 1923, he was given a cold reception by American Lutherans who, for the most part, were still anchored in scholastic confessionalism and opposed to unionism. Söderblom's mission was to try to bring these Lutherans into the ecumenical movement, encouraging them, and (of course) the many ecumenists in this country to participate in his world ecumenical conference in Stockholm in 1925. His problem: the Lutherans were antagonistic because he was so ecumenical. (Thus to Lutherans he stressed his Lutheranism.) But this made the ecumenists antagonistic because he spent so much time with the anti-ecumenical Lutherans. One of those Lutherans that he met, who was not anti-ecumenical, was Conrad Bergendoff. Bergendoff knew enough about Söderblom to have positive feelings for the archbishop. He had read Söderblom's book on Luther, *Humor & Melancholy*, on his honeymoon (!), and he appreciated Söderblom's love of Luther, his evangelical outlook, his freedom from scholastic defensiveness, his concern for missions (Söderblom had also been president of the missionary society when he was a student at Uppsala University), his pietistic background, his scholarly achievements, and his almost irresistible personal charm which Bergendoff described as "overwhelming." But at this time in his life Bergendoff was not quite ready to call himself an ecumenist.

That happened three years later in 1926 when Bergendoff was finally able to take time to accept an invitation from Söderblom to come to Sweden and, among other things, serve as his secretary at a meeting of the Continuation Committee that had been formed to follow through on the Stockholm Conference of 1925. At the meeting, Bergendoff met some of the world's foremost ecumenical leaders, but even more important Bergendoff saw ecumenicity at work. Bitterness and hatred from World War I still divided the Germans from the English and the French. Although "unspeakably difficult," the parties were able to make "sacrifices on both sides," seek forgiveness of sin, and achieve reconciliation! For Bergendoff, this was a never-to-be-forgotten experience. Years later he confided that it was his "own introduction to the ecumenical movement." And "the inspiration of those days," he continued, "has never left me."

If there be such a thing as an ecumenical personality or nature, Bergendoff would certainly be the prototype. Even if there had been no influences (such as Söderblom) pulling him in this direction, Bergendoff's make-up alone would seem to make him a perfect candidate for ecumenical leadership. Being kind, generous, thoughtful, open-minded, even-tempered, tactful, accepting of others, optimistic, objective, honest, and irenic—all of these things so essential in ecumenical relationships—are simply a part of who Conrad Bergendoff is and has been. One of the best examples of this is found in an article he wrote for the student journal of the Missouri Synod's Concordia Seminary in 1961. The title, "A Letter to the Missouri Synod from One of Its Admirers," says much about Bergendoff's kind and generous ecumenical nature. He began by sincerely and honestly praising Missouri for its many strengths. Then, two pages later, he discussed tactfully, but with honesty again, some of the differences he had with Missouri:

> We differ, it is claimed, on a wider plane, in our recognition of each other as Christians. We are 'unionists,' and that is a cause for your keeping away from us. You don't like our membership in the World Council or the National Council of Churches. You hold yourself aloof from the Lutheran World Federation and the National Lutheran Council, implying there is something wrong in this kind of fellowship [Bergendoff, of course, was involved in all of these organizations.]....I can understand your thesis that we must not compromise our confession by worshipping with those who are not committed Christians. But for almost forty years I have had some connection with the ecumenical movement, and in all the commissions and conferences I have been involved in I have never had to compromise my faith....This has made me wonder and think....When I confess I believe in the one, holy, catholic, apostolic church I am speaking of a communion that embraces all believers, and the Lutheran churches have been slow, even reluctant, to draw the conclusions of this confession. When I refuse to have anything to do with other Christians I am not thereby defending more perfectly my faith—I am denying one of

the cardinal points of my faith....I cannot escape the thought that drawing a confessional curtain between ourselves and all other Christians is a sign of weakness....There is an art of Christian cooperation which we Lutherans yet practice poorly.

To correct the "poor practice" of Christian cooperation among Lutherans, Bergendoff devoted the rest of his life to ecumenical involvement. In addition to the organizations noted in the previous paragraph, Bergendoff was active and influential in comity talks between Augustana and the Episcopal Church, in Augustana's merger into the Lutheran Church in America, and in authoring several books (and chapters in books) that had unity as their theme. Honors from Roman Catholics and other varied sources have also acknowledged Bergendoff's ecumenical leadership. Six years after his "admiring" letter (quoted above) with its challenge to the Missouri Synod, Missouri's Concordia Seminary gave Bergendoff an honorary degree partly to recognize the fact that he was an "outstanding leader in inter-Lutheran and ecumenical approach."

So how does one describe the ecumenical contribution that Bergendoff has been able to make? Bergendoff—most often through the persuasively quiet channels of pen and speech (rather than through ecclesiastical office)—significantly helped liberate Augustana and elements of American Lutheranism from its scholastic bonds. And positively he has stressed the doctrine of justification by grace which has made it possible for many Lutherans in America to celebrate a oneness in Christ with all other Christians who share the same gospel of God's love.

A Personal Note from the Author

I cannot close without expressing my profound appreciation to "Dr. B" for all he added to my life. My years at Augustana College during Bergendoff's tenure as President were life changing for me—as was the opportunity later to get to know him as a person, an ecumenist, and a wonderful, grace-filled human being. Graciously he worked with me on my dissertation, which dealt with the on-going tension between confessionalism and ecumenism, and generously opened doors for me in Sweden. He introduced me to the life and works of Sweden's inspiring archbishop, Nathan Söderblom, and again my life was deeply and forever changed. I am grateful! I'm certain my experience has been replicated in thousands of other lives on a world-wide scale. Dr. B—what expansive gifts you have given to us all!

PART Nine

Two Sermons

Our Awful God

Dennis A. Anderson

Text: Mark 4:35-41

I.

Tossing about, I roll over on my right side, scrunch up the pillow into another shape and make one more futile attempt to sleep. My mind races ahead, creating ever more detailed images of some disastrous end to the problem with which I wrestle through the night. I feel like Jacob, chased from behind and with a potentially angry brother on the other side of the river Jabbok. On a sleepless night my frustration often increases when I notice my wife is sleeping soundly…snoring away in peaceful bliss to all my anxiety. My usual routine when I have a sleepless night is to get up and fill up the bathtub with hot water and read what I call my "bathtub book." It is usually a 900-1000 page book without a plot. Then back to bed. Sometimes sleep comes. Other time the anxiety storms on, waves and winds raging in my heart.

"Lord, do you not care? Lord, do you not care, if I perish?"

There is Jesus sleeping soundly while the world is being torn apart around us. When you are in crisis, and others around you seem calm and at peace, it can make you feel even more alone and abandoned. After all, misery does love company. At least we can commiserate together.

Sometime after adolescence we wake up to the reality that to live is also to face death. Innocent confidence in our own strength gives way to the reality that the ground under our feet is about as firm as water. It dawns on us that failure, pain, and death are real. Storms within and storms without.

An image from antiquity, shared by the Old Testament writers, is of God in a victorious act of creation doing battle with the forces of chaos and evil, identified with and located in the waters of the sea.

The storm the disciples experienced as their little boat crossed over to the other side, the Roman controlled side, the Gentile side, was real. The threat was sure. They were being swamped with water, beaten by the waves, tossed by the wind. Afraid. Scared to death. Scared of death. Filled with fear.

II.

The storms are real. What will happen to our kids in such a crazy mixed up world? Will I have a job after another corporate merger? The Pap smear or PSA test? I wonder. Homes breaking up, a scandalous number of children living in the midst of broken marriages. Prospective students now say to me, "My parents are still together," knowing that this is an unusual piece of family history. The moral storms rage inside and out. No one sees any landmarks, for we are in the dark.

There are storms inside this little boat called the church. We know them too well. At times we may fall prey to the winds of nostalgia and think the seas were all calm, back when…when we had Augustana as our church. No. We remember some of the storms over biblical exegetical methods. Re-reading the history of Augustana, I was reminded of the stormy weather beating at the Boat Augustana during its early years. There were the raging winds of disagreement between Esbjörn, Norelius, Hasselquist, and Carlsson over the Lutheran confessional identity of this fledgling new synod in America.

Augustana took, as its name, the very guiding document of the Reformation. Today, the 25th of June, we remember Philip Melancthon, the author of the words of the Augsburg Confession, which was presented before the Diet of Augsburg on this day in 1530. This Confession, by which this small Swedish immigrant church was named, has demonstrated its ability to call the church back to its true understanding of itself and its task of pointing to the everlasting foundation of the Christian faith and God's mission. Augustana, like Melancthon, was devoted to seeking unity as well as truth. It was in this confession of faith that Augustana found a strong rudder as it faced the winds of its day.

We know the storms, which threaten us in our day. The pounding waves of the historic episcopate, questions of sexual orientation, worship, music, and evangelism styles threaten to wash over the Boat called the Evangelical Lutheran Church in America and our colleague churches. The winds of isolationistic congregational parochialism threaten the mission of the whole church. The shortage of clergy and trained lay workers threaten us with a lack of hands to guide the boat. The moral storm rages both inside and out.

"Lord, do you care? Lord, do you not care if we perish?"

Just before getting into the boat, Jesus was teaching through the use of four parables on the impending rule of God. You can trust in the good seed! A harvest will come. He orders that the disciples get into the boat and go to the "other side." This is the first of several journeys to an area equated in Mark's gospel with everything east of the Jordan river. From Mark's Jewish perspective, this is Gentile territory, firmly under the control of Rome.

Mark's portrait of Jesus' miracles has him doing two miracles on the Jewish side, and then on the Gentile side. Then repeating the pattern. Jesus' mission is to share the gospel with those outside, with foreigners. The wall between Jews and Gentiles represents our need for sociological reconciliation, the breaking down of the walls of hatred and institutional separation among humankind. As Jesus faces this daunting mission to reach out across the borders, he sleeps soundly in the hands of the Father. Meanwhile, the disciples fret with fright. Not unlike Jonah, they are not confident in this mission to the "other" and are caught up in a great storm, desiring to escape ministering to their enemies.

The wind and waves are signs of everything that impedes Jesus' mission of boundary crossing. These forces of resistance to the mission must be stilled.

III.

In fear for their lives, the disciples cry out, "Lord, do you care?" Obviously, they, like the widow before the Judge, made enough of a racket with their pleas that Jesus woke up.

Jesus rebukes the wind. I can rebuke the wind and nothing happens. It blows on. I can spit into the wind. Then something happens! I get spit back in my face. Jesus rebukes the wind, challenges the wind, scolds the wind, rejects the wind. Then he says, "Peace, be still!" The wind ceases. Stops cold. There is a dead calm over the sea. From raging, threatening death to calm. Jesus looks at us, "Why are you afraid?" I know why I am afraid. I am afraid of chaos, disorder, that which is beyond my control messing up my life, messing up my plans. I am afraid that Greenspan's next speech may mess up the stock market and my pension. I become anxious about new challenges messing up the church and making the waters rough beyond endurance.

Jesus asks again, "Have you no faith?"

I am so much like the disciples in Mark. Jesus teaches. He explains it again. He does miracles. They don't get it. Later in chapter 6:45 the disciples have to be "made to" get into the boat to go to the other side. They didn't get it. I don't get it.

"Have you no faith?" "Yes, Lord I believe. Help my unbelief." I am like a critic of Christians, who thinks we are slow learners because we listen to sermons on the same subject again and again. Yes, I am a slow believer. I need to hear it again and again. Jesus stills the storm again, because it is raging again. My fear is here again.

But note, Jesus calms the storm, even without the disciples' faith. This is a critical point. It is not the faith that creates the calm. It is faith that appropriates it, opens the heart to it. "He [Jesus] said to them, 'Why are you afraid? Have you no faith?' And they were filled with great awe and said to one another, 'Who is this that even the wind and the sea obey him?'"

A more direct translation, "They were fearing a great fear." The disciples find themselves in the presence of one who can still the storm, shut in the chaos, and control the seas. This *is* one who is divine! The disciples are moved from fear of the storms to awe of God who stills the storms.

Think of this, the one who created order out of the raging chaos, the one who hung up the stars, the one who created the seas and the fish in it, the one who brought forth life from this earth and surrounds us with a wondrous cosmos, this one comes as the peasant figure Jesus to still the storm that threatens us. This God comes to tell you, "I know you, and love you. I forgive you! I will guide you and will calm the storm. All this even when you don't have perfect faith. I will not sleep through the storms even though it feels like the storm is capsizing your boat. I am the God who faced the storm of death on a cross and overcame even the ravages of death and greeted the still doubting disciples, 'Peace be with you.'"

It is in the face of this God, that we are in awe rightly "fearing a great fear." We are not done with God or Christ until, as Joe Sittler said, "until we can exclaim with the disciples in wonder and awe, 'What manner of man is this, that even the winds and the sea obey him!'" Amen

For Such a Time as This

Reuben T. Swanson

Texts: Matthew 10:38-39; Esther 4:8-15

I. THE TIME: ABOUT 500 YEARS BEFORE CHRIST

King Xerxes, also called Ahasuerus, lived the good life, a good royal life as he ruled a kingdom that stretched from India to Ethiopia. Befitting his station in life, he had sumptuous royal banquets and feasts. At one of them, he became overly merry and summoned his favorite queen to appear before the all-male banquet. She refused and for that, Queen Vashti was banished from the royal court forever. To replace her, the King conducted a beauty contest of which the winner was Esther (a cousin of a Jewish leader named Mordecai). That she was also a Jew was unknown to the King. At about the same time, King Xerxes made Haman, who came to hate the Jews, his Prime Minister. Shortly after coming to power, Haman (with the King's consent) issued an edict to hang Mordecai and to "destroy, kill, and annihilate all the Jews—young and old, women and little children on a single day...and to plunder their goods."

When that Holocaust-like proclamation became known throughout the empire, there was fear and loud mourning among the Jews. Their plight seemed hopeless. Mordecai, aware of the grief of his kinfolk and also in great anguish himself, sent a message to his cousin, the Queen, asking that she intercede on behalf of all the Jews with the King. She responded, saying it was the law that anyone who went before the King without being summoned was to face death unless the King held out the gold scepter. The Queen doubted that would happen, for she had not been with the King for thirty days. It was in such a setting, and amidst that crisis, that Mordecai wrote to his cousin, Queen Esther, "Don't imagine that you are safer than any other Jew just because you are in the royal palace; *who knows but what you have come to the kingdom for such a time as this?*" Esther got the message; she went to the King; she was received; she asked that the Jews be spared; the King granted her wish and the Jewish people were saved.

II. THE TIME: THE PRESENT, ABOUT 2000 YEARS AFTER CHRIST

No edicts comparable to that of King Xerxes and his Prime Minister have been issued, but nevertheless, many people in our land, and throughout the world today, have feelings of anxiety and hopelessness not unlike those of the Jewish people of King Xerxes' empire. Reminded daily of acts and threats of terror, of predictions of biochemical and nuclear warfare, of plans for the disruption and destruction of both public and private facilities, and being told by government officials that there will be another terrorist attack, there cannot but be fear and anxiety among American people.

The daily reports of business news too often today likewise result in feelings of anxiety and distress as they describe acts of greed and selfishness, deeds of deceit and betrayal. In Omaha, the initial home of three large corporations whose stock has been torpedoed by investors, there are many whose pensions have been significantly decreased, whose investment portfolios have been devastated, and even some who have been forced to sell their homes, all because of misplaced trust. Three weeks ago, the anchor on one of the morning TV shows held the front page of the *Wall Street Journal* before the camera and cited the headlines of articles reporting corporate and individual fraud and wrong-doing. It was a vivid reminder of the conflicts of interest, self-dealing, and corruption that seem to be running rampant. Reading and hearing such reports, it is to be expected that anger and distrust are going to develop toward those who were once held in esteem as leaders of our society.

It would be easy to conclude that the world's a hopeless mess; terror, deceit, and abuse are all too prevalent. There are predictions of gloom and doom everywhere. Peace, integrity, and concern appear to be irrelevant. We may be tempted to believe the impact we can make as faithful disciples will be minimal. But then the long-ago spoken words of Mordecai come to mind: *"But who knows but what you have come to the kingdom for such a time as this?"*

This is a time to remember—to remember the heroes of yesteryear, the world in which they lived, and the good that they accomplished. The Augustana Church was one hundred years old in 1960. At the centennial celebration on June 9th of that year, Dr. Oscar Benson addressed the convention on the topic, "Looking back to 1860." He was followed by Dr. Conrad Bergendoff who spoke to the delegates and visitors on the theme: "Looking ahead from 1960."

And that's what we're called to do: To look back in remembrance of people of faith and hope and for inspiration as we note Augustana's missionary zeal, its sensitivity to societal issues, its social service agencies, its educational institutions, and its commitment to be a united church.

And let us not believe they lived in less troublesome times than we or that theirs was a less stressful age than ours. The church from which comes our heritage spanned a 102-year period. It was a time when there were five wars: the Civil, the Spanish American, World War I, World War II, and the

Korean. It was also a time of two major depressions and the dust bowl. Yet in spite of these adversities, our forebears left a heritage of faith and hope.

We have a heritage to treasure! We have heroes to remember! This heritage and these heroes remind us that we can make a difference. We can make a witness—if we take up the cross and follow in the steps of the Master.

The next to the last verse of our Gospel was as a command and commission to our forebears. They knew that Jesus spoke to them when he said, "Whoever does not take up his cross and follow in my steps is not fit to be my disciple." These same words are also for us.

We know we must beware of terror and threats of terror, deceit, greed, fraud, destruction, and other acts of disaster and disruption. But we also know we are called to take up the cross and become disciples of peace, good will, mercy, and grace. We live in the midst of these two perspectives that are so opposite and contradictory. In that situation when tempted to give up, we hear the words spoken by Mordecai to Esther: *"Who knows but what you have come to the kingdom for such a time as this?"*

III. THE TIME: STILL, 2002, THE YEAR OF OUR LORD

At the time of the formation of this Augustana Heritage Association, there were those who voiced concern about it becoming an organization that was destined to focus only on looking back by means of a figurative rear view mirror. That concern is a legitimate and continuing one. As delightful and ego satisfying as it might be, we cannot let our reminiscing and nostalgic reflections be the sole purpose of our publishing a periodical, preparing a history, or gathering for biennial events. We recall and remember the past to inform the present and future. We gather to be inspired and strengthened in our faith and commitment to the Lord of the church so that we might effectively partner with other members of the church in fulfilling its mission.

In his report to synodical assemblies this year, Presiding Bishop Mark Hanson of the Evangelical Lutheran Church in America identified a number of tasks he foresees for the immediate future as the church responds to the call of God. Among them were the church's ecumenical partnerships and sexuality studies.

Our church is committed to fostering, and participating in, ecumenical relationships. We believe that the great commission to "Go and Tell" can be best heeded by joining together with church bodies of similar conviction. Support for the needy, relief for the oppressed, justice for the enslaved, and good news for sinners can all be more effectively provided as churches work together. Mission work is best done cooperatively by church bodies working together, not in isolation.

During the last few years, our church has taken action by carefully defined procedures to enter into full communion relationships with five other churches. Prior to these actions, members of the congregations of our church were encouraged to dialog about the proposed relationships. At the various church assemblies, the members of each church had opportunities to discuss, to question, to express opinions, and finally to vote. By those votes, decisions were made and subsequently appropriate actions taken.

It's to be expected that there will be people who love their church yet disagree and take issue with the decisions made by those elected to attend assemblies. However, disagreements should not be evidenced by mistrust and misinterpretation. But sometimes it seems that is what we have—in attitudes and actions totally foreign to those of the church body from which we have our heritage. As our forebears (who after making decisions on issues for which there were strong divergent opinions) affirmed the oneness and unity of the church, so we, their heirs, are today expected to do to the same. *Who knows but what we have come to the kingdom for such a time as this?*

At the assembly of our church in 2001, action was taken to authorize a multi-year study on sexuality. Reports by the task force charged with making the study will be made to the churchwide assemblies in 2003 and 2005 and a final report at the 2007 assembly.

Even the authorization of the study has evoked disagreement and heated discussion. Some have said that the outcome has been predetermined by the perceived bias of the task force members, while others affirm the intent of the 2001 Assembly's directive that the Scriptures be studied, that there be dialogue and discussion, and that all of us listen to one another. Our heritage, I believe, dictates that we not jump to conclusions.

The Augustana Lutheran Church was a church body that considered and discussed controversial issues that were current during its life. Through its seminary leaders, that church was in the forefront in the use of historical criticism to understand the Scriptures as well as in addressing and understanding the impact of social issues, such as racial justice and civil rights. No, we didn't agree with everything we heard at the seminary or from church leaders, but we listened and sought to be informed. We were one church and we kept it that way even as we considered issues that could have been divisive.

That is our heritage. As we confront different issues today in our church, as we become aware of concerns that are current in our society and the church addresses them from the perspective of the gospel, there will be disagreement, but we still must be one church. Our heritage should enable us to strive for that regardless of marked differences and strong feelings. *Who knows but what we have come to the kingdom for such a time as this?*

The last verse of our Gospel lesson reads: "Whoever tries to gain his own life will lose it; but whoever loses his life for my sake will gain it" (Matthew 10:39).

The Augustana Lutheran Church ended its corporate existence on January 1, 1963. Its life, however, continued, first in the Lutheran Church in America and now in the Evangelical Lutheran Church in America. As Augustana was our church, as the Lutheran Church in America was our church, so is the Evangelical Lutheran Church in America our church. Augustana sought not to gain or keep its own life but lost it for the sake of the greater church, and so it lives on.

In this security conscious age, the profiling of designated groups of people, it is argued, is inconsistent with the freedom promised by our nation's constitution to all its citizens. That may be, but profiling is not out of order in respect to the identification of Christians. People who associate with us should know without any hesitancy or question that *we are people of faith who have taken up the cross and followed the Master*. We are *faith people* grateful for a heritage; *faith people* who affirm our hope in the Lord; and *faith people* who support our church. We know that *we are those who have come to the kingdom for such a time as this*.

And now we are invited to the table, the Lord's Table—and in coming, called to give our lives for the sake of Christ by taking up his cross and following in his steps. Yes, we are those who have come to the kingdom for such a time as this.